On-the-Job Spirituality: Finding God in Work

Marianne E. Roche

ST. ANTHONY MESSENGER PRESS

Cincinnati, Ohio

Library of Congress Cataloging-in-Publication Data

Roche, Marianne E., 1954-
   On-the-job spirituality : finding God in work / Marianne E. Roche.
      p. cm.
Includes bibliographical references and index.
   ISBN 0-86716-456-5 (pbk.)
   1. Work—Religious aspects—Christianity. 2. Employees—Religious life. I. Title.
   BV4593 .R63 2002
   248.8'8—dc21
                                                 2001008281

Cover and book design by Mark Sullivan

ISBN 0-86716-456-5

*To my parents, Anne
and Bill, and my
family and friends
for teaching me
about love and work.
To my fellow author,
Dan Andriacco, for
leading the way and
pushing me on. To
my fellow spiritual
sojourner, Megan
Burt, for sharing and
celebrating the joys
and travails of the
inner journey. To my
contemplative guide,
Bob Walker, for
showing me the way
to true life.*

CONTENTS

. I n t r o d u c t i o n .

*By your endurance
you will gain your
souls.*

— Luke 21:19

*God works at the
heart of all activity.*

—Thomas Aquinas[1]

M y   P e r s o n a l   J o u r n e y

I have been a participant in the "working world" for about thirty years. During the last two decades, my primary vocation has been as a corporate, securities and regulatory lawyer for financial institutions. From the beginning of my legal career and while I was still at law school, my chosen career created inner strife and emptiness. I believe this void thrust me into my spiritual journey some fifteen years ago.

As part of that journey, I picked up roots and moved somewhere new. During the six months I took off from work at my new home, I began to reconnect as a member of the Catholic church. Then I returned to my legal vocation but reduced its primacy in my life. I engaged in many forms of parish ministry, obtained a master's degree in religion and considered formal religious life in the church. I continued to question the role of jobs in my life and in the lives of my coworkers. An inner call to more quiet prayer forms and some unique opportunities to establish a formal contemplative practice helped me deepen these reflections on jobs and work. When the opportunity to write this book was presented to me, this struggle, study, reflection and prayer about work had found a home.

The Call Before Us

The list is endless:

> *Carpenter for a contractor specializing in hotel renovation*
> *Clerk in a grocery store*
> *CEO of a Fortune 500 company*
> *Pediatric nurse in a cancer clinic*
> *Dishwasher at home after a family meal*
> *Lifeguard at an ocean beach*
> *Accountant in private practice*
> *Spiritual director at a retreat house*
> *Gardener in your own backyard*

The conclusion is clear. We all engage in work, each day of our lives.

For many of us, this work is a necessity or obligation to be endured so we can tend to things that are more pleasant or enjoy "real living." Such a dualistic view of work and life is a fundamental obstacle to a spiritual attitude toward work. This book attempts to evoke an understanding of just how each of us views our work. By reflecting on the very nature of work and on the internal and external forces that distort our attitude toward our work, I hope to challenge you to see the work of God in all our jobs and chores.

Our lifetime journey is the ever-deepening encounter with God in the time and space in which we live and breathe. Human work, whether for pay or not, is our call to creation, incarnation and redemption in this world.

Using This Book

This book on working spirituality is organized in four parts. Part One, "Work as Prayer," seeks a new understanding of work that encompasses our jobs, paid and unpaid. Work includes our household chores and, in many respects, much of what we do. Rather than being something we do to support our life, our work is our life itself. Work is a gift from God and is God acting in the world through us.

Part Two, "Overcoming Personal Barriers," explores the inner work or journey that will serve as a foundation for building a spirituality of work. Until we face our inner demons and foibles, we are not free and open to encounter God in our daily lives and work. Our ego, selfishness and sin get in the way of living out the understanding of work explored in Part One.

Part Three, "Confronting Cultural Opposition," explores some of the widely held beliefs and prevalent aspects of American society that conflict with a spiritual understanding and practice of work. We live and work in communities that influence our personal values and reactions. We must come to terms with these outside influences and understand that they impact how we view, value and approach work. These outside influences can block our journey to true freedom.

Part Four, "Creating a Personal Spirituality of Work," guides you in formulating a personal spirituality of work founded in Christian values. Understanding gained from reflection on the other parts of this book will be the foundation of personal principles and practices of a working spirituality for you in your work.

Each part consists of a number of short chapters containing reflections on work and your attitude toward it. Each chapter begins with a short quotation or Scripture verse that you can repeat to yourself to keep the topic in mind during the day, or that you can reword based on your own personal musings. Some chapters include an exploration of a Scripture passage, or real or hypothetical stories of work or tales of my own experiences. Spend as much time as you need with each chapter, using the Reflection Questions and Implementing Practices at the end of each chapter to deepen your understanding. These questions and practices ask you to explore the contents of the chapter in light of your own experiences. They also give you tasks, rituals or assignments to bring the contents of the chapter and your personal musings to your work in a concrete way. Making connections between each topic in the book and your personal circumstances will serve as a foundation for the development of your personal spirituality of work.

The Reflection Questions and Implementing Practices make this not just a book to read, but a book to work with. I recommend keeping a notebook or journal as you proceed through the book. Keep a record of your thoughts or comments on each chapter, your answers to the reflection questions and your experiences with the implementing practices. These notations will be helpful in formulating your personal spirituality of work in Part Four. Because spirituality and work are lifelong journeys, you may want to revisit portions of this book from time to time in order to address the issues raised here about your then-current work situation and spiritual stance. Comparing notes from this first reading of *On-the-Job Spirituality* to your reflections some years from now could elicit interesting insights to your growing understanding of God in your work and life.

---

[1] Saint Thomas Acquinas, quoted in Matthew Fox, *The Reinvention of Work: A New Vision of Livelihood for Our Time* (San Francisco: HarperSanFrancisco, 1994), p. 64.

xi

.Work as Prayer.

*Embracing an
Understanding of
Work as Our Daily
Living in God*

CHAPTER ONE

. *C h r i s t ' s   W o r k* .

God's work is God's nature, God's being, God's life, God's happiness.

—Meister Eckhart[1]

As we embark on this journey to develop a Christian attitude toward work, the logical place to begin is with Jesus Christ. The life of Jesus is the ultimate human life. In him, we see God and the perfection to which our human lives can aspire. Jesus' Incarnation is a sign to us that our contact with God occurs in the ordinariness of our human lives—lives that involve work.

Jesus etched out his relationship with God the Father in the daily events of his own life on earth. This life, as portrayed in the Gospels, includes work as a carpenter, preacher, teacher and healer. What do these Gospel stories of Jesus' work tell us about how to view or approach our own work?

We can only imagine Jesus' life as a carpenter, joining Joseph in his trade and possibly maintaining that business after Joseph's death. During those "silent years" prior to his baptism and public ministry, Jesus must have spent much of his time learning the art and science of carpentry from Joseph. In this manual labor, he worked closely with his materials and tools. He remained patient and attentive to the process so as not to damage his project by being too quick or rough.

Neighbors, friends and relatives in Nazareth came to the shop with requests for various wood pieces—chairs, tables, cabinets. Jesus likely watched Joseph's interaction with these customers and learned much about meeting the needs of others. Joseph would design the piece. Then he and Jesus began the careful process of choosing the right wood. The wood needed to be strong and malleable enough for the proposed use. It must have the proper grain and contain no defects or weaknesses that would jeopardize the stability of the finished product. Then the process of creating from the wood began—measuring, cutting, shaving and sanding. Jesus and Joseph took care when pounding sharp nails into the wood in order to avoid cracking the wood. They paid careful attention to the detail work for finishing the project. Finally, they delivered the completed piece to the customer.

After the formation process of his baptism and the forty days in the desert, Jesus left behind his work as a carpenter and initiated his public ministry. The attention, patience and care required in his carpentry were not left behind. He applied those traits in his new work as preacher, teacher and healer.

Jesus began his public ministry preaching the nearness of God (Matthew 4:17 and Mark 1:15). Jesus explained to the people of Nazareth what this meant when he addressed them in the synagogue by reading from Isaiah to describe his task (Luke 4:16–19). He was to bring freedom, healing and salvation to those most in need. This uplifting message became a reality as Jesus' healing ministry emerged. Rather than having a game plan that involved seeking out those he wanted to heal or healing everyone who needed it, Jesus traveled throughout the area and those in need sought him out or happened upon him.

When another person begins to tell us what to do or talk down to us, we often use the expression "stop preaching to me." The preaching and teaching of Jesus was anything but scolding, giving mandates or talking down to others. His approach was one of challenging dialogue. He prodded others to a new vision and way of living, but only to the extent they were ready or open to embrace it. By using parables, he allowed others to interpret his teaching within the context of their own experience and ability. Jesus rarely, if ever, wanted to hear or refute anyone's understanding of his message. He was content to move on with no certainty of his effectiveness or success. To the extent he did confront directly, it was only with the well-educated (like the Pharisees), the powerful (like Pilate) or those closest to him (the disciples).

Jesus was not one who needed the security of family, home and possessions. Throughout his public ministry, he was on the move, relying on the generosity of others for his basic necessities. He had no special possessions. He did not seek any material rewards for his good deeds or teaching. Despite his nomadic lifestyle, he always seemed at home wherever he was.

Jesus was quite flexible. He allowed the circumstances of life, and not his own plans, to dictate his agenda. While on the way to heal the synagogue leader's daughter, he paused to acknowledge the hemorrhaging woman, who anonymously sought his healing touch (Matthew 9:18–23). Without complaint, Jesus reached out to respond to the needs of others by teaching and feeding them. At the same time, Jesus recognized the continuing need for rest, prayer and time alone. After the interruption of the crowd, he found the time to be alone and sent the disciples off to rest (Matthew 14:22–23).

All this activity culminated in his final work, the work of his death on the cross. The surrender and freedom evidenced throughout his life was evident in the Passion. Despite his human desire to live and continue on an easier path, he accepted the reality of his life in the garden of Gethsemane. Strengthened by that surrender, he accepted and openly embraced the final act of every human life in his death.

Reflection Questions and Implementing Practices

- Read one of the four Gospels—Matthew, Mark, Luke, John—from beginning to end. Concentrate and take notes on what Jesus taught, on Jesus' spirituality and how Jesus lived his life. What does this review tell you about how Jesus perceived his own work?

- If Jesus were living his life on earth today, what do you think his work would be and how would he conduct that work?

- Each day for a week, review your attitude and action in your work, whether paid employment or domestic chores. How does your attitude and action at work compare to Jesus' attitude and action in his work?

---

[1] Meister Eckhart, quoted in Matthew Fox, *The Reinvention of Work: A New Vision of Livelihood for Our Time*, p. 95.

CHAPTER TWO

.Our Work as Spiritual Practice.

To be successful, the first thing to do is fall in love with your work.

—Attributed to
Sister Mary Lauretta

I used to consider my work to be what I did for pay. Even my volunteer work at parishes and nonprofit agencies was not included in my idea of work. To the extent there could be a religious dimension to work, I considered that dimension dependent on the content of the work. For example, parish or retreat ministry, social justice advocacy or healing professions are all forms of work that include a religious or spiritual dimension. I found it difficult to find the spiritual dimension of my own work as a corporate lawyer, except perhaps in being kind and fair to others at work. Therefore, I began to consider abandoning my profession to pursue work with a more obvious religious or spiritual content.

My inability to find the spiritual dimension in my work began to change when I began attending intensive contemplative retreats at a Catholic retreat center in Cincinnati. These retreats involved many hours of contemplative prayer each day. They also included designated work periods for which each participant was assigned a particular chore to do. These chores generally involved housekeeping or gardening at the retreat center. We were told to continue our contemplative practice or prayer during these work periods. As I attended more of these retreats, these work assignments became an integral part of my prayer while on retreat. Over time, I began to carry over that experience to my paid employment and domestic chores during the rest of the year. I began to view work differently and to see its central role in my relationship with God.

In our Christian tradition, God is fundamentally relationship, a Trinity of three in one. Our work has a trinitarian dimension that can deepen our own connection to the persons of the Trinity. God, the creator of the world, shares this creative power with each of us. In our work, each of us is given an opportunity to participate in the ongoing creation of our world. It is not necessary that we actually produce some new item. Rather, our very actions in concert with others impact our environment and contribute to its circumstances. No matter what kind of work we are engaged in, it is a part of God's ongoing creative force.

Jesus is the human incarnation of God returned to the Father. We, who are his Body, are his continuing incarnation. Our fiat as Christians and church is to be Christ in our piece of the world. As we work at our jobs, in our homes, at our parishes and in our communities, we are the very presence of Christ and are called to bring forth in our work the attributes of Jesus evidenced in his work.

The continuing work of God in our time is through the Holy Spirit, who challenges, inspires, strengthens and sanctifies each of us every day of our lives. Our responsibility is to open ourselves up to the Spirit in order to heed those messages and urges in making daily decisions. If we are open and bring that openness to our jobs and chores, all that we do is in collaboration with the Spirit.

In most Catholic parishes, there is an annual stewardship drive. Parishioners are asked to discern their call to service in their Christian community. The concept of stewardship is based on God's gift of all we have with the admonishment to be good caretakers of this bounty. This stewardship can consist of the giving of time and talent to the parish, as well as treasure, the donation of material goods and money. In prayer, we are to discern our call to stewardship and make a commitment for the coming year.

Our work is also a form of stewardship. We are to act as good stewards of the materials, persons and situations arising in our work. A worker in a dry-cleaning establishment should care for the clothes entrusted to the company, doing the best job of cleaning and charging fairly for the work done. In our employment, we owe care and attention to our employer's assets and should not put them to our personal or an inappropriate use. Similarly, in our domestic chores, we should seek not to be wasteful and to protect our environment from hazards.

Within our religious tradition, we speak of our call to service to God in our lives. Our work is imbued with this call to service. A father tending to the preparation of the family's evening meal is fulfilling the call to marriage and parenthood. The preparation and presentation of the meal is an act of service to the rest of the family. In a similar fashion, a social worker who assists a homeless woman with children to find housing and employment is responding to a call of service to others. These calls to a way of life are never separate from God.

An attitude toward work that acknowledges God's presence and our relating to God turns that work into prayer and praise. This transformation is brought about not so much by actively thinking about God during work, but rather by conducting our work with a dignity and care reflecting God's life in it. This attitude of stewardship and service will open us to God's action in us and make our jobs and chores unceasing prayer.

Reflection Questions and Implementing Practices

- What opportunities to contribute to God's creation does your work give you?

- Reflect on your conduct at work over the course of a week. How did you bring the presence of Christ to your work? In what ways were you open to the Spirit as you conducted your work?

- Considering the bounty of gifts you are presented with in your work, how are you a good steward of those gifts?

- Whom do you serve in your work? Have you missed opportunities for service? Begin trying to take advantage of these opportunities, one at a time, until that service becomes an integral part of your work.

CHAPTER THREE

. *W o r k   a s   G i f t   a n d   S e r v i c e* .

*If our jobs do not
contribute to the
common good,
we pray to God for
the grace to give
them up.*

—Dorothy Day[1]

A woman who forgoes paid employment to maintain the family home and tend to her children complains about dealing with her children and the endless list of domestic chores. Though glad to be earning a high salary, a securities broker begrudges every moment at work, which is more than sixty-five hours a week. He yearns for his "real life," which consists of those rare moments when he is neither asleep nor selling stocks. The circumstances of these two differ greatly, but their life outlook is very much the same. They each choose to be unhappy and unfulfilled in what they spend most of their time doing.

At first, you might consider that assertion of their choice absurd. Yet, many of us can identify with their plight from our own experience. If there is anything human beings enjoy complaining about, it is their work. A gathering of coworkers often becomes nothing but a gripe session. Parents at a school sporting event complain about all the household chores and errands they need to do. We live for weekends, vacations or retirement, bearing our work as some kind of sacrifice or punishment.

Of course, if asked, we would agree that all creation is the Lord's and is a gift for us to experience or enjoy. Yet, we have a hard time taking that ideal and making it concrete in terms of our jobs and chores. Our work relies on this gift of creation for its very existence. It is a divine gift itself, and each moment of our work is a moment to give thanks. This thanksgiving is not meant in the literal sense of saying thanks for each moment. Some regular giving of thanks can go a long way in reshaping our attitude. By imbuing our work with integrity, humility and attention, we engage it freely and completely. The very conduct of the work itself is the giving of thanks.

The Eucharist that Catholics celebrate is a ritual of thanksgiving. This regular gathering is not a respite from our usual toil. It is an opportunity to bring to the altar all the events of our lives as lived during the prior week and to raise them up in our hearts, as the bread and wine are raised, as gifts to God. In a way, we return a bit of God's creation to the Lord after we have invested ourselves in it.

This attitude of thanksgiving in and for our work requires a shift in attitude about our need for personal enjoyment. As we choose a career or job, we often seek some form of fulfillment, monetary or otherwise. That stance causes us to view the goodness of our work from the perspective of whether it makes us happy or whether it promotes some goal for personal growth. From this perspective, we can only be thankful for work that is pleasing to us.

Seeing work as an opportunity to serve other people and all God's creation moves the meter for judging work from meeting our own ego needs to serving the needs of others. Of course, seeing work as service seems simpler for persons involved in healing professions or in promoting social justice. One can look at the integrated life and work of Dorothy Day to see someone who viewed work as a means of serving God and others. Dorothy Day, through the Catholic Worker Movement, gave food, clothing and shelter to thousands in need and struggled for nonviolence and justice in our society.

But what about those of us whose work does not, on its face, appear to help others or to serve some noble purpose? Viewing service as dependent on some ranking of jobs according to how much they help others misses the point. God is in and works through all situations, even those where a divine presence seems impossible to find. This does not mean, in some trivial sense, that God is in our work because God is in all things. The dance of life and creation as given to us by God is not easily definable or knowable. Every moment of our lives is an opportunity to make God's love and justice incarnate in our specific circumstances. We may not know exactly how our work serves, but we can be assured that it does.

Our task then is to accept the difficulties, drudgeries and disasters of our work as part of the path we are on to serve God and God's creation. Whether it is advising a client on the recent drop in the Dow Jones average or the folding of the family laundry, our actions are opportunities to serve God's plan and to make our Christian values real and alive. We can move from seeing our work as a means to please ourselves and receive personal reward. In time, we can learn to embrace our work as a means to serve

God and to free ourselves to do God's work for the sake of the work itself, without regard to personal reward.

Reflection Questions and Implementing Practices

- Cultivate an attitude of thanks toward your work by periodically taking a moment to give thanks for both its joys and its difficulties.

- Think about your past jobs. No matter whether you enjoyed the job, list at least five gifts you received from that job. Consider whether difficulties experienced at those jobs were growth experiences that reaped a benefit later.

- How does your work, whether or not it is paid employment, contribute to the common good? How do you feel about that contribution or the lack of it?

CHAPTER FOUR

. W o r k   a n d
t h e   F a l l .

*God is at work in
and through man,
perfecting an
ongoing Creation.*
—Thomas Merton[1]

Many Christians have tended to view our work as a punishment for sinfulness, with the implication that if we had remained free of sin, we could be living a life of constant leisure with our feet up and not a care in the world. Could that really be the case? Some work seems necessary to maintain our existence because manna does not fall from heaven daily.

We must begin with the origin of this notion of work as punishment. A primary source is the story of Adam and Eve in the Garden of Eden. Though we all know the story, I want to repeat it in my own words in the hope of adjusting this negative interpretation.

After creating Adam from the ground and God's own breath, God created a luscious garden called Eden, which contained the infamous tree of the knowledge of good and evil (Genesis 2:7–9). God then placed Adam in this garden to till and keep it and commanded him not to eat of the fruit of the tree of knowledge

(Genesis 2:15–16). Seeing that Adam needed a helper and partner, God created Eve from one of Adam's ribs. After the serpent coaxed Eve to eat the forbidden fruit and Adam joined in, the two feared their nakedness and hid from each other and God. God recognized their fear as a result of eating from the tree and asked why his command had not been followed. In a fashion all parents must recognize, Adam pinned the blame on Eve and Eve on the serpent. God then spoke to them all and told Adam that the tilling of the land for food would be toil (suggesting that his previous tilling of the garden was not toil). God then clothed them and sent them from the Garden of Eden to the ground from which Adam was created (Genesis 3:23).

Human beings' image of God is always subject to change. In the past, although to a lesser extent since Vatican II, a predominant view has been of God as a judge who reviews our record and denies us paradise if our record is not clean. That view contributed to the interpretation of this Genesis story as God punishing Adam and Eve with pain and toil. I do not want to engage in theological ruminations on this story, but I do want to suggest some different ways of looking at it.

First, by its very terms, the story points out that Adam did work in the Garden of Eden even before Eve was created, for he was placed there to till the land. After the Fall and the mutual blaming session, God told Adam that his tilling of the land would be toil. Was this toil a punishment from God? I suggest that it was Adam's new attitude that created the toil. This new attitude came with the knowledge of good and evil, for with this knowledge came separation and distinction. By eating the fruit of the forbidden tree, Adam and Eve acquired the ability to judge differences. Suddenly their world fell into categories of good and bad or liked and disliked. This new sense of separateness was in evidence in their embarrassment about their nakedness and their hiding from God. Therefore, work was not a punishment for the Fall. If we, as Adam, choose to view and approach our work as toil we, in essence, punish ourselves.

Second, while the story can be viewed as one that seeks to explain why there is pain and difficulty in life, it can also be viewed as a story of maturation. The garden was a place set apart from the rest of creation. Adam and Eve lived in a state of naïve innocence, not completely in touch with all of life's reality. They are admonished not to eat of the tree of knowledge, for in doing so they would become open to all of life's harsh realities. In the ancient Hebrew world, knowledge was not an intellectual concept but, rather, was an embrace of the entirety of the thing known. In eating the fruit, Adam and Eve lost their innocence, as reflected in their fear of their own nakedness. Previously they had no problem with their nakedness because they believed no harm could come to them. Somehow they now felt vulnerable and self-conscious. With their return to the land from which Adam was created, they would encounter all aspects of human life, good and bad. God's statement to them could be viewed more as an acknowledgement of the realities of life than as a punishment.

Third, as Christians, we simply cannot think of work as a punishment for disobedience to God. To do so ignores the redemptive power of Christ in his Incarnation and Resurrection. We believe that in taking on human form, dying on the cross and rising from death, Jesus redeemed all aspects of our human life. In particular, as he dwelt among us, working at carpentry, healing, preaching and teaching, he sanctified and redeemed all human work. He challenged his disciples and us to continue this work.

Jesus' first admonition at the start of his public ministry was that the kingdom of God is now with us, not far off in some unknown paradise but present in even the tiniest events of our daily lives. Upon his death, Jesus was buried in a garden and is even mistaken for the gardener responsible for tilling that land when he is discovered by Mary Magdalene (John 20:15).

This new garden and gardener take us back to Adam, the first gardener tilling the first garden. With his Resurrection, Christ renders all things new in him. He restores the unity between God and God's people, who are all one in Christ. To continue to view work as punishment for Adam and Eve's fall fails to recognize the Incarnation, Passion and Resurrection of Christ. The church, as Christ's Body, is a continuation of the redemptive work of his Incarnation, Passion and Resurrection. We bring Christ to our work and can be Christ in our work.

Reflection Questions and Implementing Practices

- Review the second creation story in Genesis 2:4–3:24. What has been your understanding of this story in the past? Has anything in this chapter caused you to reconsider your perspective?

- We all attend school for years to gain knowledge. Our Christian moral code seeks to define good and bad conduct. Why then were Adam and Eve forbidden to eat the fruit of the tree of the knowledge of good and evil?

---

[1] Thomas Merton, *Contemplation in a World of Action* (Notre Dame, Ind.: University of Notre Dame Press, 1998), p. 157.

CHAPTER FIVE

. *T h e   V i n e y a r d* .

*The just person does
not seek anything
with his work, for
every single person
who seeks anything
or even something
with his or her works
is working for a why
and is a servant and
a mercenary.
Therefore, if you wish
to be conformed and
transformed into
justice, do not intend
anything in your
work and strive for
no why, either in
time or in eternity.*

—Meister Eckhart[1]

In the place and time in which Jesus lived, working in grape and olive vineyards was a dominant means of livelihood. This is reflected in the many references to vineyards and vines and related matters in the Old and New Testaments. Our modern unfamiliarity with vineyards makes it difficult to capture the meaning of these images in our lives. Three of the more dominant vineyard stories in the Scriptures, however, have something to say to us in our quest to spiritualize our work.

The first two are related stories found in the beginning of Isaiah 5 and in the three Synoptic Gospels (Isaiah 5:1–7; Matthew 21:33–41; Mark 12:1–9; Luke 20:9–16). In the Isaiah story, we hear of a beautiful vineyard carefully planted and tended. The owner guards his precious vines with a fence and a watchtower. He is filled with the expectation of an abundant harvest. However, at harvest time, he finds nothing but rotten grapes. In his disappointment, he commits to demolishing the vineyard and allows it to be overrun with wild growth. Later in Isaiah, a new fruitful vineyard is a sign of God's restoration of the world (Isaiah 65:21).

In the Gospel accounts, an owner leases to tenants a vineyard with similar protections as the one in Isaiah. The tenants reap a good harvest, but they fail to pay the owner his share of the harvest as rent. The owner sends servants to obtain payment, but they are injured or killed by the tenants. Then he sends his son, expecting the tenants to pay him more respect. Instead, the tenants kill the son in the hope of gaining his inheritance of the vineyard. In the three accounts, the owner either evicts or kills the tenants and gives the vineyard to others who will provide him with his share of the harvest.

These vineyard stories tell a familiar tale of preparation, effort, dashed expectations, destruction and renewal. The owner of the vineyard is disappointed with the harvest or the tenants. Despite the owner's effort and concern, the work initially produces no "fruit." Yet in both scenarios, there is some redemption and renewal, and God redeems the vineyard with new life.

Our work is our own vineyard. Whether it consists of the personal daily tasks of living or endeavors for our employer, we prepare for, make an effort in and bring expectations to our work. Our efforts do not always bear fruit, and our expectations are often dashed. People do not treat us as we hope they will. Projects and plans fail, or we are unable to complete the tasks assigned for the day. A new job, initially accepted with enthusiasm and optimism, soon reveals many of the difficulties of the previous job abandoned with great glee. Like the owner of the vineyard, we can bring about destruction in our poor treatment of others at work or in reduced effort and poor performance in conducting our work.

We do not have to proceed negatively when things do not go our way. Just as in these vineyard stories, we can redeem and renew these apparently dismal situations with a change in attitude or approach, an abandonment of unrealistic expectations or the implementation of changes in our work. A change in attitude or approach can be as simple as not reacting to disappointments, failures or problems as an excuse for sadness, anger or frustration. Instead, we can view these difficulties as a new opportunity for change in our work or for a more humble stance toward our own ideas and desires. Abandoning unrealistic expectations of perfection in our coworkers or family members can eliminate the perception of events or circumstances as disappointment or failure. This inability to achieve a goal may be a failure, but it is also an opportunity to review the goal to determine its validity. Strategic planning in any business involves some "stepping out" to take risks or try new approaches. If these attempts are unsuccessful, it is time to return to the strategic plan and redefine the goals and objectives. For example, a nonprofit agency may try out a new form of fundraising that does not bring in an adequate increase in donations. It is then time to return to the fundraising drawing board and not wallow in self-pity.

The second vineyard story for our reflection is the parable describing the kingdom of God as a vineyard owner hiring day laborers for his vineyard (Matthew 20:1–8). The workers hired first in the morning are promised the usual daily wage. The owner hires four other groups of workers during the day, and the last group is hired one hour before quitting time. At the end of the day, the owner pays each worker a full day's wages, no matter how long they worked. The workers who were hired first complain, claiming that they should be paid more than the others. The owner chastises them for their envy of the others and their criticism of his generosity.

This story is particularly difficult to accept with our American capitalist sensibilities. We have all often heard the motto of the women's movement demanding equal pay for equal work. This parable turns that motto on its head. It asks us to question our own tendency to compare the relative work and pay levels of others to our own. We tend to believe that we work the hardest and receive inadequate pay. We generally do see our pay as reward and not as gift. In this parable, Jesus asks us to rethink our attitudes toward work level and compensation, reminding us that the "last will be first and the first will be last" (Matthew 20:16).

The last story comes from Jesus' long prayerful discourse at the Last Supper (John 15:1–11). Jesus declares that he is the vine, God is the vine grower and that his followers are the branches that bear fruit. He points out that the branches are dependent on the vine for their life. The vine grower removes branches that bear no fruit and prunes the branches that do bear fruit, so that they will yield more.

In this story, Jesus reminds us that our work is never done in isolation. Our efforts are links to God and to others. It also reminds us that we are not rewarded for our efforts as we wish, for we need "pruning" to be even more fruitful.

R e f l e c t i o n   Q u e s t i o n s   a n d I m p l e m e n t i n g   P r a c t i c e s

- Review your day of work each evening for a week, noticing situations in which things did not transpire as planned. Consider how you reacted when your expectations were not met. Were your expectations realistic in light of all the circumstances? Reflect on what expectations you have for the next day and consider whether any of them need to be pared down.

- When you have accepted new employment, are you more concerned with whether your compensation is fair for the effort asked of you or with how your compensation compares to others? How has this approach influenced your attitude toward your work and your coworkers?

- Reexamine an employment or domestic work situation in which you believe you were treated unfairly. How did you react to that difficulty? Did you insist on immediate change to ease your discomfort? Did you bear the difficulty for a time? If you did bear it, did anything positive come from accepting this "pruning"?

[1] Meister Eckhart, quoted in Matthew Fox, *Breakthrough: Meister Eckhart's Creation Spirituality in New Translation* (New York: Image Doubleday Books, 1980), p. 464.

CHAPTER SIX

. W o r k a s L i f e —
I n t e g r a t i o n /
U n i t y .

*Diversity without
unity makes about as
much sense as
dishing up flour,
sugar, water, eggs,
shortening and
baking powder on a
plate and calling it a
cake.*

—Attributed to
C. William Pollard, author
of *The Soul of the Firm*

In the last vineyard story discussed in the previous chapter, Jesus left his disciples with a strong message of the unity of all in God. In his prayer at the Last Supper, Jesus petitioned God the Father that we may all be one, as he and the Father are one (John 17:23). Somehow, that sense of unity is not one we have tended to adopt in our personal lives. The separations and distinctions that Adam and Eve discovered after eating from the tree of knowledge are prevalent in widely held perspectives on work. These separations and distinctions chop up our lives into compartments in which we believe we function and live differently.

This dualism is at the root of the slogan, "TGIF" ("Thank God It's Friday"). How often do we hear "I can't wait for the weekend," or "I can't wait until I retire"? Someone I once worked with claimed she kept a job she did not enjoy, primarily because she received four weeks of annual vacation. Another coworker had returned to work for only forty minutes after a week's vacation at a resort town when she stated, "I cannot wait until my next vacation three months from now." The allure of weekends, vacations and retirement is a popular motivator in our culture. Yet living and working with this focus makes us tend to ignore or discard a significant portion of our lives, not only in terms of hours, but also in energy and attention.

At another job, I was explaining the new 401(k) program to a coworker, and our conversation turned to the "why" of retirement savings. Suddenly her eyes filled with tears and her voice cracked. She told me that her father and brother had dutifully saved for the great life and fun of retirement. In doing so, they both gave up many opportunities for life and fun in the present. They both died in their fifties, before enjoying the fruits of their retirement and savings. This woman's grief for her family members' lost opportunities in life was real and startling. I had to admit I shared her ambivalence about retirement savings.

As I reflected on this exchange, my understanding of her grief grew. Initially, my sense was that she was sorry that her father and brother had not had more fun during their lives, rather than saving for future fun. In fact, their loss far exceeded just having an insufficient amount of fun. All those hours and all that effort at their jobs were seen as a means to some future reward.

I wondered what joys and insights in that work each man had missed as he chose to focus on the future while remaining blind to the present.

Our tendency to separate our work is not limited to a work-versus-leisure distinction. Generally, when we use the word *work*, we mean jobs for which we receive monetary compensation. I know many women who choose to forego paid employment in order to spend more time at home with their families. They struggle because many people believe they are not working or contributing enough to society. Despite their keen sense of the correctness of this choice for them and their family, these women often second-guess themselves and feel it necessary to make excuses. Mothers with paid employment are often the worst critics of these unpaid mothers. The irony is that, from what I have seen, raising children well and maintaining a home with love are tougher tasks than most paying jobs I have had or seen.

Domestic chores are just as much work as repairing plumbing, selling clothes or preparing financial statements. The value and importance of work goes far beyond the compensation received, the item produced or the contribution to some business endeavor. The effort behind the loving preparation of a home and meal for a family Christmas gathering is priceless. The daily tending to children's homework and after-school activities can reap untold benefits in those children's future.

Even those who live for vacations or weekends, if asked, would admit that, during leisure times, they are often engaged in activities that require much physical or mental effort. These activities might be called "work for fun." I currently live by a surfing beach on Long Island. Throughout the year, people, including members of my family, head out to the ocean with surfboards in tow. As I watch them in their love affair with the ocean, I have no doubt that they expend great effort to get a mere handful of good rides during each surfing session. Whether shooting baskets, sewing a quilt or painting a picture, individuals expend much physical or mental effort in conducting leisure activities. This effort really does not differ from the effort expended in domestic chores or paid employment. It is only because these activities are perceived as fun that they are deemed different from work.

If we begin to see our work as conduct involving physical or mental effort and as activities that can be fun and relaxing, we can move from viewing our work merely as toil. Our definition of work can embrace all our efforts, whether voluntary or mandatory and whether for pay, need or relaxation. Work really encompasses any of our activities that involve effort. Our work is a fundamental part of our lives and is the incarnation of the life force of the Spirit in our midst.

Reflection Questions and Implementing Practices

- Over the next week, try to avoid limiting your plans for fun or relaxation to the weekend or your days off. First thing each morning, take a moment to plan some pleasant activity or time for relaxation during the day, even if for only five minutes. This may not involve coming up with some new activity. It may involve merely viewing current workday activities from a new perspective.

- Try to stop yourself before making comments such as "Ugh, it's Monday," "It's Wednesday and halfway to the weekend!," "TGIF" or similar comments that place positive energy on your days off and negative energy on your workdays. Keep a log of when you make these statements and see if your heightened awareness of this sort of talk reduces your tendency to use it. Reflect on whether your reduced use of these comments has any impact on your attitude toward your workdays and your days off.

- Formulating a retirement savings plan requires a balancing of responsibility, risk and reality. Look at your current retirement savings plan. How does it reflect your balancing of these three factors? If your retirement savings plan is a spiritual discipline, consider whether your balance of risk, responsibility and reality reflects your personal spirituality. If it does not, what changes might be in order?

CHAPTER SEVEN

.*Work   as   a   Reflection   of   Our* Imago Dei .

*...and it is no longer
I who live, but it is
Christ who lives in me.*

—Galatians 2:20

N o matter how we think we separate our work from the rest of our life, our life is intrinsically present in our work, whatever its nature. We put our values, beliefs, personalities and faults into action when we work, whether we are aware of it or not. Whether we are neat and organized, anxious and fearful, or merciful and compassionate, the traits we exhibit outside work will be evident in our work as well. No matter what our mental attitude toward our work, what we believe and value will show up in our jobs and chores.

Our Christian tradition teaches us that we are present in our work in an even more profound way. Genesis tells us that God created us in God's image. What exactly does it mean to be made in God's image? *Webster's Ninth New Collegiate Dictionary* defines the word *image* as "a reproduction or imitation of the form of a person," "an exact likeness," "a tangible or visible representation" and "incarnation." Applying these definitions to the verse in Genesis tells us that at our very core, we are God's presence in this world of time and place.

If we are God's presence in the world, are we somehow other than ourselves? Of course not, for our true self is in God. During our life, we embrace and adopt other "selves," including our name, gender, marital status, career and ethnic background. Though we carry these other selves, they are not who we really are. Our true self is in God and we are all the image of God in the events, circumstances and surroundings of our daily lives. To comprehend what this really means, we need to set aside our understanding of God as an entity separate from us. In much of our personal and liturgical prayer, we address God as a distinct being separate from us. In reality, we are not separate from God, for we are God's visible representation in the circumstances of our lives.

Does this mean we are God? Obviously not, for the totality of God is beyond and unknown to us. It does mean that we are not distinct from God. God is never absent or separated from us. God is the constitutive element of our true self, making up the very core of our being. Despite the endless differences between individuals, God's presence is a common thread in the core reality of all persons. God, therefore, is the unity that bonds all humanity, whether or not that humanity believes in God or articulates God's presence.

God sees with our eyes, listens with our ears and hearts, comforts with our touch and assists with our efforts. In seeing with our eyes, we gaze on God. In listening, our ears and hearts open to God's voice. In a caress, we touch God. With our efforts of assistance, we help and raise up God. Jesus declared that our salvation is in feeding, clothing, caring for and visiting him, which happens when we feed, clothe, care for or visit our neighbor (Matthew 25:31–40).

So, as we work, God is present in us, in all we encounter and in that work. This presence brings dignity to all human work. If we recognize that ever-present dignity, our work takes on meaning and can be a source of joy and peace, no matter what the nature of the work. All our actions in our jobs and chores are imbued with the Spirit. The continuing evolution of God's creation happens in our work, whether it is vacuuming a living-room carpet or selling popcorn in a movie theater.

Because all of our work is from and about God, it is all about love and compassion. No matter what the task, we can bring love of God, others and ourselves to it. Approaching our responsibilities from a peaceful, rather than a frenetic, anxious or angry stance, promotes nonviolence. Responding with kindness to those we serve, particularly when they least deserve it, promotes compassion. Seeking to be fair to and to forgive our coworkers, bosses and employees promotes justice. The work of the Lord is not limited to family, friends, charities and parishes. It is alive and flourishing in the marketplace as well.

Reflection Questions and Implementing Practices

- What has been your understanding of our being made in the image of God? Are there any ways in which you do not consider yourself to have been made in God's image?

- What "other selves" have you adopted during your life? Do you have a positive or a negative view of those selves? Are all those "selves" present in your work?

- Over the last three days, how have you fed, clothed, cared for or visited others in your work? Have you had opportunities to do so, and then chosen another path? When these opportunities arise in the future, make an effort to take advantage of them.

CHAPTER EIGHT

.Being Versus Doing.

There is no point in work unless it absorbs you like an absorbing game. If it doesn't absorb you, if it's never any fun, don't do it. When a man goes out into his work, he is alive like a tree in spring, he is living, not merely working.

—D. H. Lawrence[1]

In American culture, we tend to value jobs according to what the worker produces and is paid and whether the worker is professional, popular or powerful. As I am writing this book, after twenty years of practicing law, I am working in a bookstore, shelving books and assisting customers. Under the American work value system, I am receiving less pay, producing fewer important results, abandoning my professional status and dwelling on supposedly less important matters. I have been asked recently when I am going to get a real job and am chastised for being responsible about my attendance and effort at my present job. I have even been mocked for referring to it as a job. An acquaintance is incredulous that I am enjoying my current employment and that I do not find it boring. In the eyes of those following this American value system, I am currently a failure.

Looking back over the years of legal practice and looking ahead to reentering that field, the fallacies and falsehoods of the American value system have become clear to me. In the past, I have been paid high levels of income for my legal work, receiving more than most workers. So, if this value system is correct, I should have been more happy and at peace then than I am now. Producing corporate contracts, securities disclosure documents and regulatory legal opinions should have made me feel I was making a more important contribution to the world than I am in shelving books. As a lawyer fresh out of law school, I was an immediate member of the elite white-collar professionals club and should have felt better about myself than I do now. Because my legal work involved important business matters and my government work allowed me to exercise power in enforcement proceedings, I should have felt more important and powerful as a person than I do now. Nothing could be further from the truth.

This American value system for work has crumbled for me, for none of these "shoulds" materialized. My former higher level of salary did not make me happier. Employers exacted more of my time, claiming I owed it to them for my higher salary. Over the last ten years, even before taking the job at the bookstore, I have accepted reductions in pay in order to take new positions I believed held more promise. Despite our society's exaltation of persons with paper-pushing desk jobs, the masses of documents produced by me seldom felt like a major contribution to society.

It could be just as much drudgery as flipping burgers at a fast-food establishment. Although others often were impressed with my status as a lawyer, because of the practices of so many other lawyers, I have often apologized for being one and asked people not to hold it against me. I have not met a lawyer whose value to me as a person was predominantly due to his or her chosen career. Visions of power or importance have been dashed as I came to realize, no matter what the job, everyone (yes, even the president) is accountable to some other person or group. Limitations, stress and unwanted change are present in all jobs, and, if recognized, highlight the actual lack of power and importance in even the most critical jobs. My profession generally is not rated with much popularity. The personal failures of popular sports and entertainment figures, such as Darryl Strawberry and Robert Downey, Jr., give evidence of the vagaries of popularity.

So I have struggled with and ultimately abandoned this American value system. Being Christ at work is not a question of what I do or produce, what I am paid, what degrees I have or where I am on the ladder of power or popularity. I am not saying that high pay levels or important and powerful jobs are evil or should be avoided. However, as Christians, the value of our work cannot be based on the elements of this American system, which in the end demean the efforts of most workers. What then should the Christian value system for work be based on?

It is not as simple as saying that the job must involve social justice or the corporal works of mercy, for not everyone engages in employment that has those activities as their primary focus. I do believe that the true value of work does not lie in the work but in the worker. It is who we are and how we are when we are working that is the measure for the real value of our work, both to us and to others. How we bring God forth in our work, no matter what its nature, is the key. Doing our work well with careful attention, no matter what its content, recognizes and honors the inherent dignity in all human work. To shortchange our employers by slacking off based on the level of our pay dishonors our work and us. Our solace can be found in work well done, no matter what the product or reward or how others rank the importance of our effort. Being Christ in our work, without any particular emphasis on what we do or what we get paid for doing it, seems an appropriate basis for a Christian valuation of work.

Reflection Questions and Implementing Practices

- How do you value work? What is your view of women or men who refuse paid employment to have more time to be at home with their families?

- How do you treat persons you encounter who are in lower-paying jobs than you? As you visit a retail establishment that pays lower wages, be attentive to how you address the workers there.

- Looking at your own employment situation, what do you value in your work and career? How does that compare to what you value in the other dimensions of your life?

---

[1] D. H. Lawrence, from "Work," in *The Complete Poems*, edited by Vivian de Sola Pinto and Warren Roberts (New York: Penguin Books, 1964, 1971), p. 450.

CHAPTER NINE

.*A t t e n t i o n   t o*
W o r k   f o r   I t s
O w n   S a k e .

To get more done by doing less is a credo and a key operating style of Corporate Mystics. They put a great deal of attention on learning to be in the present because they have found that this is the only place from which time can be expanded. If you are in the present—not caught up in regret about the past or anxiety about the future—time essentially becomes malleable.

—Gay Hendricks and Kate Ludeman, *The Corporate Mystic*[1]

The practice of "living in the present moment" is becoming increasingly popular as a method of living a more spiritual life. Though not necessarily unknown in our American Christian tradition, the increasingly hectic, cluttered pace of our lives over the last forty years has made that way of living almost extinct here. With cell phones, faxes, computers, palm pilots and busy schedules, we are spread in so many different directions that the present moment has become elusive. More recent exploration of certain Eastern religions and philosophies, such as Buddhism and Taoism, has brought this perspective back to our culture.

What is the present moment? How do we find it and measure it? Why are we not usually living in it? Starting with the last question, of course we are always living in the present moment. The problem arises in our failure to be attentive to it. Instead of focusing our attention and awareness on what is right before us, we clutter ourselves with recollections, judgments and plans. No matter what we may be about at the moment, our mind wanders, taking our attention with it. Our mind relives or reconstructs past events or makes plans for the next project or some other future time, mentally living the moment before it ever begins. It incessantly rattles on, critiquing the whats, whys and wherefores of our current action. The ongoing critique strengthens our ego and tends to remove us from the present reality. When we dwell in past or future events, we dwell only in our minds, ignoring our present reality. Removal from or ignorance of our present reality separates us from God. The only reality is now, and the past and future are figments of our imagination. Though these ruminations are our present reality, the contents of them are like dreams. God breaks forth in the reality of now, whether the now is good or bad.

Our mental attempts to distort or discard that reality are a rejection of God.

Though it is the place of divine encounter, the present moment is difficult to grasp or identify. It has no beginning or end and is constantly elusive. Just as we say this is the present moment, that identified moment has faded into the next present moment. Not only is the moment itself impossible to grasp, there is nothing that can measure its start or finish. In essence, the present moment is unbounded by time, a piece of eternity open to us with each breath and at all times.

Our ego mind is an obstacle to finding the present moment. The ego prefers to be the master of ceremonies, dictating its own form of reality. I became aware of this devious power early in my contemplative practice. Once, as I sat in contemplative prayer on a silent retreat, I became aware of a bead of sweat slowly gliding down the side of my face. With so many typical distractions eliminated, the sensation from this one bead of sweat was almost painful. I desperately fought the impulse to wipe the sweat away. Then in an instant, my mind carried my awareness to a cramp in my knee. Despite its continuing presence, it was as if the bead of sweat had evaporated in an instant. My mind chose to experience only the cramp in my knee. This cramp in my knee also disappeared in an instant as a train passed by the retreat location, and my mind directed my attention to that noise. In that present moment, the bead of sweat, the cramped knee and the moving train were all very much in existence, yet my ego mind configured its own version of that reality, choosing only to accept the sound of the train.

So if the present moment cannot be measured and is blurred by the illusions of the ego mind, are we doomed in our attempt to grasp it? Can our attention be trained to focus instead on the present reality, which for our purposes is our work? A simple path to finding and resting in the present moment is what I like to call the "just" method. If our attention is held to the "just" of now, it is less inclined to wander to ego critique and categorizing and to mental constructs of the past and present. Over time, this focus on the present reality can become as natural as breathing.

The "just" method involves focusing your attention on what you are currently about. Initially this needs to be done artificially, but, over time, the discipline becomes a way of living. So what does it entail? When you walk, just walk. Rather than listening to a Walkman or worrying about the day's troubles, focus your attention on the movement of your legs or on feeling the soles of your feet on the ground. When you eat, just eat, without also reading, watching television or listening to the radio. As you make a salad, focus your attention on just the action of making the salad. Bring your mind back to the task if it wanders to your plans for preparing the rest of the meal or to other matters.

Applying this "just" method to our work in all its forms, we bring our mindful attention to each moment of our work. We deepen our encounter with the spiritual dimension of our efforts. Resting in just what we are about or just what is before us, without reflecting on our liking or disliking of that reality, allows us to be open to the work itself. As the work becomes the only reality, the ego self begins to "disappear." We lose our life and, thereby, find it. I have experienced this singular focus in my legal work, at the bookstore and in other situations. In my last legal job, as my in box filled up, I would focus my attention on just the task before me until it was completed. I did not waste energy with concern about the items that I needed to get to later. What a surprise to find that drafting a legal opinion could be a spiritual exercise! Similarly, as I have stocked and sorted books on the shelf or have planted a garden of flowers, both I and time have seemed to disappear as all there has been was the task at hand. Simple attention to our work for its own sake allows us more clearly to encounter God in our work.

Reflection Questions and Implementing Practices

- At a set time each day, record what your mind has been focused on during the previous fifteen minutes. Then reflect on what occurred or was before you during that time. Was your mind focused on what you were about? Did it exclude portions of your environment from its attention?

- Practice the "just" method for a set amount of time each day. Choose some time when you are usually at home and when you are engaged in work. How long were you able to remain focused on the task at hand? How often were you distracted? How did you react when you discovered you were distracted? Were you able to bring your attention back to the present task?

[1] Gay Hendricks, Ph.D., and Kate Ludeman, Ph.D., *The Corporate Mystic: A Guidebook for Visionaries With Their Feet on the Ground* (New York: Bantam Books, 1996), p. 11.

CHAPTER TEN

.Inner Work as a Foundation of Outer Work.

The greatest of man's spiritual needs is the need to be delivered from the evil and falsity that are in himself and in his society.

—Mohandas K. (Mahatma) Gandhi[1]

Jesus tells the Pharisees that the kingdom of God is within them and not in outer signs (Luke 17:20–21). In many of his debates with the Pharisees and in his internalization of the Jewish moral code, Jesus points out that the inner heart and attitude of a person say more about the character of the person than outer acts of piety or what that person interacts with. He makes it very clear that inner work and transformation are critical for proceeding along the spiritual path.

Some of our reflections so far have emphasized the importance of inner work as we seek to spiritualize our work. Our actions in our jobs and chores are an outer manifestation of our inner being and reality. If our ego self, with its illusions and dreams, reigns in our heart, then it will formulate the nature of our work, and who and how we are in it. In order for our true self in God to be manifested in our work, we need to be open to God's presence within us and diminish the reign of the ego self.

This journey inside to our true nature requires us to come to terms with the false ego self that promotes separation and self-aggrandizement. Without addressing and disarming our ego illusions, we can never take on our work as a spiritual practice. If God is not allowed to reign in our hearts, God's Spirit will not be manifest in our actions and efforts at our jobs, in our homes and elsewhere.

Scripture tells us little about Jesus' inner journey. We do know he spent an initial period of seclusion in the desert facing his demons in the form of wild beasts and the temptations of Satan. He often went to the mountaintop at night alone to pray, suggesting that he spent time in silent prayer. Jesus declared that those who pray in public seeking to bring attention to themselves are hypocrites. He praised silent prayer in solitude (Matthew 6:5–6).

Our inner journey to free up our true self must follow a path similar to that taken by Jesus. This may require a partial withdrawal or retreat from the current hustle and bustle of our daily lives. To go inside and face ourselves, we need time in silence and solitude, as did Jesus. To etch out a more spiritual perspective in our work, we cannot begin by responding to some outer circumstances or stimuli. We must cultivate our inner peace, for it is only the inner journey that can serve as a foundation for a spiritual, contemplative stance toward our work.

Our inner call and journey need to be cultivated with a discipline of spiritual practice such as contemplative or meditative prayer. Though there are many methods for such prayer, I want to suggest a method introduced to me some years ago that is the cornerstone of my own spiritual practice and inner work.

The simplest way to begin is to sit comfortably erect, breathe deeply and pay attention. Some time needs to be set aside each day for contemplative prayer, beginning with five minutes and working up to twenty-five minutes, if possible. I recommend following these instructions:

Find a quiet place free of disturbance with no music and no background noise.

Use a chair with minimal upholstery, preferably with no arms. Sit on the front two-thirds of the chair, not touching the back of the chair. Your knees should be about a fist apart and your feet flat on the floor. You may want to sit on a cushion or to place one under your feet. You should not move during the prayer time.

Your spine should be comfortably erect but not straight or excessively stretched out. Your spine should curve in at the waist, with your stomach protruding in front and your posterior protruding in back. Your head should be up and slightly forward with your chin comfortably tucked in. Your shoulders should be down and relaxed, not held up tight. Initially, in training your torso and back muscles to hold you up without leaning on the back of the chair you may experience some discomfort. Overall, you should feel comfortable.

Follow your breath. Work toward breathing "from" your abdomen by moving the diaphragm up and down to bring your breath in and out.

Use a mantra to follow your breath. It should be short and you should not think about its meaning. To avoid such reflection, it helps to count from one to ten with each exhalation and keep repeating that count. Suggestions for a mantra might include *shalom, Jesus, Yahweh* or *peace.* Remember not to reflect on the meaning of whatever word you choose.

Increase the time you spend in this new activity gradually, day by day, until you reach twenty-five minutes each day. Your prayer time should be about the same time each day, and the early morning is recommended.

When your mind wanders from following your breath with the mantra, take notice and calmly return to the breath and the mantra. Do not get into judging your "good" or "bad" performance.

For extended sitting, practice for individual twenty-five-minute periods, with five minutes of mindful walking around the room between sitting periods.

Reflection Questions and Implementing Practices

- At least once a week, spend fifteen minutes in silence. Afterward, reflect on this experience. Were you comfortable with the silence? Did you feel anxious or at peace during this quiet time? Why?

- Begin a daily discipline of contemplative prayer as articulated in this chapter or otherwise known to you. Keep a journal of some of your reactions or experiences during these prayer sessions. In particular, focus the wanderings of your mind and the reactions of your body. Periodically review these notes to see if your experience of this prayer form changes.

[1] Mohandas K. (Mahatma) Gandhi, quoted in Trudy S. Settel, *The Book of Gandhi Wisdom* (New York: Citadel Press, 1995), p. 41.

PART TWO

. O v e r c o m i n g
P e r s o n a l
B a r r i e r s .

*Taking the Inner
Journey to Freedom
and Openness*

CHAPTER ELEVEN

. C h r i s t ' s   H e a l i n g   P o w e r .

Woman, you are set
free from your
ailment.

—Luke 13:12

The Gospels contain over twenty incidents of healing in which Jesus expels demons, cures illnesses or raises the dead. At times, Jesus seeks or reaches out to the person to be healed. Sometimes, Jesus is sought out for assistance, either by the person who needs healing or by someone who loves that person. In most of these healing stories, Jesus has a direct encounter with the individual and through some action or statement heals that individual. This includes his curing the fever of Simon's mother-in-law (Mark 1:30–31), his releasing the demons from the man in Gerasenes (Luke 5:1–13) and his giving sight to the blind man who pleads for mercy (Matthew 8:22–26). In one instance, the hemorrhaging woman is healed by surreptitiously touching Jesus' garment (Matthew 9:18–25). At other times, Jesus heals someone who is at some distance from him. Jesus heals the royal official's son, the centurion's servant and the Canaanite woman's daughter in response to the pleas of the official, the centurion and the woman (John 4:46–53; Luke 7:1–10; Matthew 15:22–28). In the ultimate healing, Jesus raises the synagogue leader's daughter, the widow's son and Lazarus from the dead (Mark 5:35–42; Luke 7:11–17; John 11:1–44).

I have struggled with these healing tales, for they tend to present Jesus as some kind of magician. Some Gospel healing stories have a less magical nature. In Jesus' dialogues with the Samaritan woman and the adulterous woman, he accepts each, faults and all, and encourages her to renew her life (John 4:7–26, 8:3–11). Jesus heals these women of the burdens of their personal lives. In his post-resurrection encounter with Peter, Jesus asks Peter to affirm his love three times and frees Peter from the shame and guilt of his three denials (John 21:15–17). These healings are based on an intimate and compassionate encounter with Jesus.

This different perspective on healing is evident in the story of the raising of Lazarus. As they prepare to go to Bethany, Jesus tells his disciples that he is going to awaken Lazarus. Lazarus emerges from the tomb bound, and Jesus' first words are "unbind him, and let him go" (John 11:44). All the healing stories tell us about people who are unbound from various restrictions on their freedom and peace. Many of these healing stories deal with people being freed from demons or blind people being given vision and a new awareness. Such new freedom and awareness is something we all seek in our lives.

With our enhanced knowledge of psychology, we understand the impact of mental problems or mental illness on the body. The connection between the mind and the spirit is accepted by many today. We know that each of us carries our own demons from our family or cultural history or from the difficult experiences of our lives. In twelve-step programs and psychological therapy, the identification of the addiction, illness or other demon is a critical step in the healing path. This identification is difficult, for like Lazarus, we are bound and cannot see the power of our own demons. Once the demon is identified and named, its power is diminished. Underlying many of these healing stories in the Gospels is that the compassion, freedom and presence of Jesus released people of their demons.

The personal demons we carry have a direct impact on our work. To the extent we are not free and allow some demon to control our reaction to events, we impose these demons on others and deepen their impact on us. If we do not address how these demons distort our perception of reality, our approach toward our work will be tainted by these distortions. If we face and transcend these demons, we can bring freedom and peace to our work.

Reflection Questions and Implementing Practices

- Read one of the healing stories in the Gospels. Put yourself in the place of Jesus, then of the person being healed and then of others in the story. Imagine what they were thinking and feeling as the story unfolds.

- Think back to a time when you were physically ill or mentally down. How did your illness or depressed state influence you at your work and home? Once this infirmity passed, what changes occurred in your attitude?

CHAPTER TWELVE

. *F e a r   a n d*
A n x i e t y .

> *I desire to see you*
> *free of any servile*
> *fear, for I am aware*
> *that the fearful*
> *person does not*
> *persevere in the*
> *strength of holy*
> *resolution and good*
> *desire.*
>
> —Saint Catherine of Siena[1]

The Scriptures contain numerous admonitions for us not to be afraid. In his first inaugural address President Franklin D. Roosevelt told us the only thing we have to fear is fear itself. Why is being afraid such a problem? Why is fear not generally considered a sin, despite the many scriptural warnings against it? What does being afraid have to do with our work?

> *Ann's boss is about to initiate a new sales practice at the store. Ann is sure this program is problematic, but she is afraid to suggest that her boss is wrong. With the practice in place, sales drop for the very reasons Ann had been concerned about,*

and many personnel are laid off, including Ann.

Jeffrey misses his children's soccer practice every Saturday morning because he goes to his office. He has completed his work for the week and has no urgent matters requiring his attention. He goes to the office on Saturday only because he is afraid his boss or coworkers will think less of him if he is not there.

Karen and Jim, who both work full-time, have three children. Karen suffers from a lack of sleep. Consequently, she is often short with her children and is not performing well at her job. Karen also tends to most of the household chores. She is afraid to ask or allow Jim to help, because she is afraid he will think she is not a good wife.

Some people dwell in their fears regularly. They seek out reasons to be afraid and choose inaction if there is anything to fear in acting. This can become an obsessive concern about death or contamination from germs. They seek absolute security in their lives and act on their fears to give them a false sense of security. Life is uncertain and attempts to control it by living by our fears only give an illusory sense of security.

Another way of addressing fears is to pretend they do not exist. Just as those who live by their fears need to become aware of the impact of those fears on how they live, those who claim to have no fears need to become aware of suppressed fears that impact their conduct and speech in ways of which they are not conscious.

Stephen claims he is not afraid of anything. He works twelve hours a day and never refuses or questions any request from his boss. When his family takes one week of vacation a year, Stephen gives his boss and clients telephone numbers where he can be reached and calls the office at least twice a day. He spends over two hours each day on work-related telephone calls. No matter what his friends and wife tell him, Stephen refuses to see that this conduct is motivated by a fear of losing his job, or of not appearing to be indispensable.

Anxiety and worry feed fears. Some people generate significant energy worrying that something bad may happen. This anxiety may have bad physical effects, expressing itself in abdominal ailments or high blood pressure. Anxiety also can lead to depression or other psychological problems. Jesus recognized this tendency toward worry and anxiety in his disciples and suggested they be like birds or lilies.

"Therefore I tell you, do not worry about your life, what you will eat, or about your body, what you will wear. For life is more than food, and the body more than clothing.…And do not keep striving for what you are to eat and what you are to drink and do not keep worrying." (Luke 12:22–23, 29)

We generally find it difficult to hear this advice from Jesus. We tend to water down this message with excuses and reinterpretations, rather than face our own anxieties and fears.

Anxiety and worry over the unknown can wear some people down as they agonize over their actions and speech. People can become frozen, unable to take risks or initiate change, because they fear upsetting the apple cart. Rather than confronting untenable or unjust situations at work, they stagnate in worry. In this stagnation, they can become ashamed of their inaction, their work or their life situation, which they believe they cannot escape. Bound and oppressed by fear, anxiety and worry, they feel inferior, ignoring their dignity in God.

To face our fears, anxiety and worry, we need to cultivate courage. Cultivating courage requires recognition of our fears and their impact on us. Having patience with ourselves, we must strive to develop an attitude of facing what life does to us, without concern about potential risks or unknown events. If we face our fear of rejection or failure, we can act from our beliefs and values, rather than acting to please others.

Reflection Questions and Implementing Practices

- Consider a time when your conduct at work was motivated by fear of losing your job, or your conduct at home was motivated by fear of losing your spouse's or child's respect. Write down the details of the event and reflect on how you felt at the time. Were you aware that your fears were motivating you? How did you feel about yourself at the time? Looking back at the event, how do you feel about yourself now? Reflect on a time at work when your actions involved taking a risk and were motivated by your values and convictions.

- Make a list of things or events that frighten or worry you. How do your mind and body react when you experience this fear or concern? Looking at each fear and worry, imagine how your life would be different if that fear or worry did not restrict your action.

- Discuss with a close relative or friend one of your persistent fears or worries. Admit how you allow this fear or worry to restrict your actions. Discuss how you might act differently if you could lessen the power of this fear or worry. Think of some immediate actions you could take to reduce the restrictions this fear or worry imposes on you.

---

[1] Saint Catherine of Siena, quoted in Mary O'Driscoll, O.P., *Catherine of Siena: Passion for the Truth, Compassion for Humanity* (New Rochelle, N.Y.: New City Press, 1993), p. 37.

CHAPTER THIRTEEN

.Anger and Conflict.

> *...But I say to you that if you are angry with a brother or sister, you will be liable to judgment; and if you insult a brother or sister, you will be liable to the council; and if you say, "You fool," you will be liable to the hell of fire.*
>
> —Matthew 5:22

First thing in the morning when Peter arrives at the store, he notices that the night crew did not straighten up the store properly. When a coworker arrives, Peter cries out, "I hate people. If I could find out who is not doing their job, I would kill them." Later, a customer, who arrives at the store angry, starts barking orders at Peter, demanding immediate assistance and results. Peter, still fueled by his earlier rampage, becomes enraged and responds to the customer with a bad attitude. Next, Peter and the customer are screaming at each other. The increased noise attracts the manager, who asks Peter to go to the staff lounge. After assisting the customer, the manager returns to the lounge and reminds Peter that it is inappropriate to scream at a customer, no matter what the customer says. She also says that adopting the angry stance of a customer was only going to ruin Peter's day. Peter disagrees, claiming it is not fair to have to take abuse from obnoxious customers and then begins to rage about the failures of the night crew. The manager interrupts him, saying that the performance of the night crew is not relevant to the current discussion on dealing with customers. She reminds Peter that fighting with customers is grounds for dismissal. Peter, grumbling under his breath, mutters "OK," and leaves the room.

For the remainder of the day, Peter works with a black cloud of anger hanging over his head, taking it out on coworkers and customers. As he relives his rampages in his mind, he is distracted from his work and is chastised for not completing the tasks required of him. On the way home, he drives erratically and honks at everyone he believes is in his way or is not driving fast enough. He enters his home, and before his wife and children can say hello, he begins to yell about things in the house he does not approve of. Then he storms out and heads to the local tavern for drinks.

Is this story a silly exaggeration or does some of it ring true for you or someone you work with or know? In our society, we tend to have a negative attitude toward anger, unless it is our own anger responding to injustices done to us. Anger and conflict are a constant part of our life. Sometimes they can be a motivating force, encouraging people to act for the rights of others. Many people in the civil rights movement or in social justice work have been motivated by their anger at the injustices imposed on those they seek to help. This righteous anger energized Mahatma Gandhi, Martin Luther King, Jr., and Dorothy Day to seek significant social change. In Peter's case, however, his ego-based anger is an inhibitor, not a motivator. Things not going the way he believes they should trigger his anger. His anger is fueled as he adopts the anger of the customer and continues to dwell on the causes of his anger long after the events have passed. The situations in which Peter found himself are not uncommon, and becoming angry in them is not necessarily unwarranted. The critical choice is in reacting to anger. If we react to our anger from inner turmoil, the anger multiplies and explodes, like adding gasoline to a fire. If, instead, we react to our anger from inner peace and take a few deep breaths before forging ahead, the anger becomes more like dying embers.

Negative attitudes toward anger encourage the stifling of angry reactions, letting them simmer and fester for later, more intense release. Some situations call for an angry response. If that response is not made, it is time to let the anger go and move on. Storing it inside and ruminating over it will result in an inappropriate explosion later. This was Peter's reaction when he entered his home, screamed at his family and stormed out to get drunk.

Often, as with Peter's reaction to the work of the night crew, anger is fueled by a desire for perfection in others. This demand for perfection is fueled by our desire to mask our own imperfections. If we focus our attention on someone else's errors, maybe our own will be missed. How often do you say to yourself or hear someone say, if only "they" had done what they were supposed to, everything would be fine. Interestingly, we often seek to blame other's imperfections for circumstances created by our own errors. Rather than focus on others' imperfections in light of our expectations of perfection, we need to see them in the light of our own imperfections. Remember the admonition of Jesus to remove the log from our own eye before grabbing for the speck in another's eye (Matthew 7:3–5). Viewing others' imperfections in conjunction with our own, we gain a deeper understanding and acceptance of others' foibles. With this understanding and acceptance, the edge or coarseness of others' mistakes and weaknesses begins to soften and fade.

Anger is related to our attitude toward conflict. Those who enjoy brewing in anger will seek out conflict in order to have opportunities to engage in angry battle. Their outbursts seem to come out of left field, because the person is manufacturing the conflict. At the opposite end of the spectrum are those who believe anger is wrong and take great effort to avoid conflict. These individuals will lie about their own views or needs, if they believe expressing the truth will result in a conflict. Conflict is a reality of life but not one to engage in as a battle. Rather, we are called to bring together the sides of a conflict or to allow the competing tensions to coexist. This approach to conflict challenges us to let go of our own opinions and positions.

Jesus reminds us to love our enemies and to pray for those who persecute us (Matthew 5:44). He reminds us of how easy it is to love those who love us. Similarly, it is easy to love those who act as we believe they should, saving our anger for those who do not. Cultivating our inner peace can calm our own anger and conflict. Then we can receive others' anger and conflict more easily. If we begin to be more open to others' anger or mistakes, reacting with compassionate and constructive responses, we will assist in defusing others' and our own anger.

Reflection Questions and Implementing Practices

- Select an individual with whom you are angry. Sit quietly and pray for this individual, imaging the difficulties or pain he or she may be dealing with. Consider this person in your prayer for at least a week. Reflect on how this ritual impacts your anger. Do you find yourself treating this individual differently?

- Get in touch with how you react when you become angry. Notice how your breath becomes shallow, your muscles tighten and your heart rate quickens. As you experience anger, try to catch yourself before the anger catches you. Breathe deeply, saying "shalom" to yourself for at least one minute before reacting to your anger.

- When in discussions with others, if you disagree with what they say, delay voicing that disagreement. Consider whether your opinion really matters in this instance, or whether there is anything positive to be gained by voicing your opinion. If there is not, try keeping silent.

CHAPTER FOURTEEN

. S t r e s s   a n d   T i m e .

*For everything there
is a season, and a
time for every matter
under heaven...
I have seen the
business that God has
given to everyone to
be busy with. He has
made everything
suitable for its time;
moreover he has put
a sense of past and
future into their
minds, yet they
cannot find what
God has done from
the beginning to the
end.*

—Ecclesiastes 3:1, 10–11

One of my nieces has a cute hamster that sleeps all day and arises early in the evening for a night of running on her wheel. Sometimes we can feel like hamsters running on a wheel, particularly when we are under significant stress. Stress from our jobs can impair work performance, age us, create conflict and destroy families. The problem, however, is not the existence of stress, but our reaction to it. Stress is a fundamental element of our lives. I often tease people who complain about stress by reminding them that the first time they have no stress will be when they are dead. Just as with fear and anger, the key to addressing stress in our lives is learning how to accept and react to it.

For many, including me, not having enough time can be a primary source of stress. Though I have improved on this score, in the past I found myself greatly influenced by what I called the "crisis of the time limits." As I descended the stairs in my home to leave for work, I would have feelings of frustration and stress. I realized it was because I had overextended myself and had twenty-eight hours of things to do in twenty-four hours. In fact, if we did allot all the time to prayer, exercise, sleeping, relaxing, food preparation, household organization, quality family time and work recommended in self-improvement books and magazines, we would need thirty-six hours a day to get to it all.

If we go to the local bookstore for help in dealing with the multiple demands on our time, we will find books that I believe only exacerbate the problem. We would find a plethora of books on "managing" time or "attacking" our time requirements. These books contain dozens of new time-consuming requirements to help us "save" time, which just burn up more energy and increase stress.

Despite all the timesaving devices we have in this country, Americans seem to be more pressed for time than other people. Rather than something to be managed or controlled, time is something to live. The events of our lives evolve in the present and attention to the present can serve us best in dealing with time.

Before we can engage time as something to live, we must come to grips with a stark reality. There are only twenty-four hours in a day, and most of those hours are scheduled before the day begins. We all need sleep and cannot continually chip away at our hours of sleep to have more time to complete our list of things to do. There have been a number of reports in the press that adults in this country do not get enough sleep because they are so busy. Failure to obtain adequate sleep is a major contributor to our stress level. Whether on the to-do list for home, for work or for leisure, we need to reconsider whether these supposedly important items really require our attention. We may need to eliminate some items that are not necessary in order to make our time requirements more reasonable.

After allocating an appropriate amount of time each day for sleep, we need to become realistic about what we believe we need to do. I am one of those people who is great at making lists of things to do and then revising the lists, rather than accomplishing what is written there. I can schedule two days of items to do for one afternoon. Most of us cannot tend to everything because our plates are too full. Sometimes our plate is full because of failing to attend to what needs to be done. Procrastination can be a primary cause of stress. Rather than burning energy trying to get motivated, we need simply to do what needs to be done. If we accept and meet deadlines, tending to what needs to be done and moving on, the stress of time limits is diminished.

We need to pare down our lists and assign priorities to the remaining items. This involves merely asking what needs to be done next and proceeding with that matter without expending energy in concern about what remains on the list. Then we concentrate on the present need and proceed with that. Careful attention to how we use our time will reduce stress in our work.

Of course, stress is not caused solely by time limits. Stress is the result of our refusing to accept the reality of life. We fight change and seek to control others. We set unrealistic expectations and feel cheated when they are not met. We expect to have our desires met and to experience pleasure at all times. Our desire for the world contrived by our mind causes us to reject the world as it is. This propensity to create stress in our lives can have a depleting impact on our bodies. Just two years ago, when I was the legal and financial officer for a self-funded health plan, the plan administrator told me that the three most-used prescription drugs in the plan were for high blood pressure, depression and abdominal problems. I suggested if all these people began a meditation practice, the cost for these types of prescriptions likely would plummet.

A recent poll indicated that 25 percent of workers claimed the pressure and stress at their jobs was so high that they were often on the verge of losing their temper. On the other hand, almost half of the respondents believed they did not experience much stress at their jobs. What seemed to make the difference was whether or not the employees experienced a lack of control, minimal recognition and a stifling of their talents on the job. The level of work was not the problem. The level of stress on the job was lower if the individual was allowed to contribute meaningfully to the enterprise and was recognized for it.

A typical day is filled with transitions. We move from place to place and task to task. Each new situation involves a new environment and new demands. These differing demands create stress as we need to adjust to these changes. This stress is increased if we leap quickly to and from each of these places or tasks, not allowing moments of internal transition. A few years ago, I was in the habit of walking about a half mile between my office and home each evening. That quiet walk served as a perfect transition between job and home. As I crossed the park near my apartment building, the hassles of the office had faded.

Not all stress is bad. Some stress can enhance productivity and focus. Just before making a public presentation, I experience stress that serves to focus and energize my presentation. If you are driving and an accident occurs in front of you, stress will alert you to avoid becoming part of that accident. The problem is that our mind translates situations that our ego does not approve of in the same fashion as a public speech or a car accident. Some stress is lifesaving, some is motivating and some is wasteful. We need to learn to release wasteful stress.

We need to learn the three L's of stress: Listen to it. Lighten it. Live through it. Be aware of your stress and its source. Step back from your reaction and see if the reason for it justifies the reaction. Let go of unnecessary stress to lighten the wear and tear on your body and psyche. Then proceed with the remaining stress without letting it control you.

R e f l e c t i o n   Q u e s t i o n s   a n d I m p l e m e n t i n g   P r a c t i c e s

- Sit down on Sunday afternoon and think through your plans and schedule for the week. Lay out your plans for each day, assigning time for each task, for work, for rest and for adequate sleep. Are there enough hours in the day for you to accomplish everything? If not, begin to scale back, starting with the items that can be deleted, but do not reduce sleep or rest time to less than you need.

- What kind of transition rituals do you have to lessen the stress of a hectic day? Do you set aside some quiet time at the beginning of your day or after you arrive home from work? When you arrive at the office, do you take a few minutes to settle in before attacking the E-mail or in box? Take a few deep breaths between chores and tasks to acknowledge the transition.

- Begin to monitor yourself under stress, particularly your physical, mental or emotional reactions. Does your breathing change as you feel more stressed? What is causing the stress? Is it something that really matters? Is your stress the result of things not going your way? If it is caused by some outside matter, ask yourself whether your level of reaction is warranted. Keep a record of what causes your stress and your reactions to that stress. Notice if your stress reactions change with this heightened awareness.

CHAPTER FIFTEEN

. *Greed, Envy and Money* .

> *True, we've got all*
> *these things,*
> *industrial and*
> *financial systems,*
> *machines and soviets,*
> *working classes. But*
> *why go on having*
> *them, if they belittle*
> *us? Why should we*
> *be belittled any*
> *longer?*
>
> —D. H. Lawrence[1]

So many of us live by the bumper-sticker proclamation "the one with the most toys at the end wins," or by the old saying "the grass is always greener on the other side." The "most toys" syndrome is fed by our greed. Though we like to claim we need all the things we accumulate, *need* generally has little to do with what we gather and amass in our homes. Advertisements, particularly on television, bombard us with images telling us we need every new product produced. We accumulate to have more, in the hope that having more means to be more important or more happy.

Residing very close to our hoarding monster of greed is the green monster of envy. Looking around us, we want and even believe we are entitled to the money, possessions, prestige and success of our coworkers, friends and neighbors. Just the other day at work, two coworkers spent most of the day in a pity party comparing their work effort that day to one coworker who was not busy at the moment and another coworker who had stayed home that day. They heaped their pity party on the store manager, making her day more difficult. What had they gained by it? Nothing that I could fathom.

People in East Asia speak of the "hungry ghost," a creature with a huge belly and a minuscule mouth and throat. The creature constantly seeks to have its belly full, but its small mouth and throat prevent its ever being sated. It is said that the hungry ghost is never satisfied and always suffers. Greed and envy can make us into hungry ghosts with very large bellies.

Greed and envy are important in our attitude toward money. We must come to terms with our individual relationships or understanding of money in order to approach our work more spiritually. If money is the primary reason for staying in a job, we lose respect for ourselves. We become discouraged with our efforts and work environment. I once stayed with a job I did not enjoy or find rewarding because the money was good. Over time, I became increasingly dissatisfied with my position, and my dissatisfaction influenced others and spread throughout the whole workplace.

Some individuals can never amass enough money and possessions. Being a lawyer, I have worked with or for persons who make and have more than a substantial portion of the American populace. Yet, some of these people have been more preoccupied with keeping their riches and gathering more than people with much fewer resources. A major motivator for many well-off individuals who contributed and voted in the last presidential election was the prospect of electing an individual who would reduce taxes. I find that those with more money than they need are the ones who tend to complain most about taxes. Those taxes are often used to help those who are less fortunate. Persons who have visited Africa and other very poor areas tell of how the poorest of the poor are generous with their time and possessions. They give out of their need to be hospitable to a visiting stranger. On the other hand, people of affluence may be hesitant to give a dollar to a person on the street and too busy with a schedule to spend time with a troubled friend.

Though it is troublesome to hold money as the primary benefit from work, we should not go to the other extreme and view money as inherently evil. Money has a place in our world. In our economy, it serves both utilitarian and humanitarian purposes. Money enables us to support ourselves and others. However, if we allow our money to own us, we lose our human dignity.

Greed and envy also fuel unjust and abusive power structures in businesses and cause untold misery in our homes. If we lord it over others because of our higher pay or value our coworkers based on their compensation level, we ignore the human dignity and *imago dei* in all those with whom we work. If, in a family, each member strives to have more and do less, family discussions become battlefields for power and dominance.

When I was a child, my brother was always concerned about the size of his piece of cake compared to the portions of his three sisters. He would carefully scrutinize the four pieces of cake, and, if he was quick enough, grab the largest piece. Though this seems minor, how often does each of us act the same way in our jobs or chores?

This comparison of our own lot to that of others is at the core of the story of Martha and Mary in Luke's Gospel. Mary is at Jesus' feet, apparently absorbed in what he is saying or teaching. Martha is in the kitchen preparing the evening meal for all. Martha comes out and complains to Jesus that Mary is not assisting her. Jesus tells Martha not to be worried or distracted by many things but to focus on the one thing. He points out that Mary is where she is called to be. Jesus is not castigating Martha for working in the kitchen rather than sitting at his feet. He is criticizing her attitude. She is anxious about what her sister is up to and probably is envious that she cannot relax on the floor and listen to Jesus. He reminds her to tend to her tasks at hand, which include the preparation of a meal he likely was anticipating. Spouses, parents and bosses hear similar pleas based on some perceived unfairness in the divisions of labor between family members or employees.

Coming to terms with our endless desire for more or better by learning to be more content and thankful for what we have can change our attitude toward work. If our work is performed primarily to get something, envy and greed fuel it. If our work is an opportunity to give and serve, the monsters of greed and envy lose their power. Jesus reminded us, we cannot serve God and money, so the choice is ours.

Reflection Questions and Implementing Practices

- Take some cash from your wallet and look at it. How do you feel about money? Are you primarily a saver or spender? Are you generous with your money, or do you prefer to save for a rainy day or retirement? Do you fret if a major purchase is necessary? Do you control your money or does it control you?

- Make a list of your possessions. Go down the list and ask whether you really need all these items. Could someone else benefit from using any of these items if you donated them to charity? How often do you use or even touch these possessions? Make a list of items you don't have and desire. What do you really need on that list? Why do you want any item you do not need?

- Be aware of how and when you compare your plight or situation to that of others. As you make these mental comparisons, write notes to remind yourself. Reflect on them later. What motivated your envy?

---

[1] D. H. Lawrence, from "Why _____?," in *The Complete Poems*, p. 452.

CHAPTER SIXTEEN

. B o r e d o m ,
D i s c o u r a g e m e n t
a n d   F a i l u r e .

*Therefore, my
beloved, be steadfast,
immovable, always
excelling in the work
of the Lord, because
you know that in the
Lord your labor is
not in vain.*

—1 Corinthians 15:58

Our work is not always pleasant, exciting or successful. We often experience our work as dull, debilitating drudgery. The selfishness, stress and confusion we encounter in others, or feel in ourselves, as we conduct our jobs and chores can be discouraging to our ability to work. Sometimes this negative experience is based on reality and calls us to make a choice. Other times, it is illusory, hiding another problem. Finally, it can also be misguided, for it is based on false assumptions.

I am currently a shelver in a large bookstore. Under a newly implemented inventory system, all book shelvers spend a portion of their day doing maintenance, which includes making sure books are in the right department and are properly displayed on the shelf in accordance with specified guidelines. One day, two coworkers responsible for this function complained of how boring this maintenance process is compared to shelving newly delivered books. In reality, the two functions are similar, and the alleged boredom is really dissatisfaction with their job, their employer or the new maintenance system.

People often believe that the more complicated or sophisticated the work, the less bored the worker. I currently experience less boredom at work shelving books than I did some years ago drafting yet another annual securities disclosure report for a financial institution. The constant cooking and cleaning required in our homes can seem monotonous. The inability to obtain a promotion or a large raise can sap us of energy to do our work well, causing even more failure. Goals set in business by the worker or the company cannot always be met. In any economic environment, some business venture will fail. How can we be spiritual about something that is boring, discouraging or a failure?

The boredom and discouragement a mother of two young children experiences three years after deciding to forgo paid employment may be due to false expectations of nirvana. Upon the birth of her first child, Linda decided to quit her job, after eight years at a brokerage firm working sixty-five hours a week in retail securities sales. Linda was sure she would be content tending to family and home and expected her marriage to be happier with her added attention to it. She imagined she would have the time to keep her home immaculately clean and to prepare sumptuous family meals. Linda's mother was amused at her daughter's "happily ever after" picture of her role as wife, mother and homemaker, but kept her thoughts to herself. She knew only time and experience would open Linda's eyes and mind to reality. Later, with a three-year-old toddler and six-month-old infant, Linda moaned to her mother about how bored she was tending to housework and children day in and day out. She said she felt like a failure because the house never seemed clean, was never without some clutter, and as soon as a household task was finally tended to, it was time to do it again. Finally, Linda admitted regretfully that she often resorted to convenience foods or takeout for the evening meal. Linda's husband and mother sat down with her one night and helped her see how her problem was really her unrealistic idea of life as a homemaker. They were able to show her that the family was doing quite well, and that Linda needed to lower her expectations. They suggested that she ask them for help more often and that she take a little time each day for herself. Over the next three months, Linda heeded their advice and found new enthusiasm and energy in her work.

Our experience of boredom, discouragement or failure can be the result of our attitude toward our work and an inner call to change. No matter how good a position may look to others, if it is not right for us, we need to make a change. If we do not, we will experience negative feelings about our work and even cause our work to be less successful. If we cannot bring ourselves totally to our work at the appropriate time and do it well with careful attention, maybe it is time to seek a new job. Job-hunting is tiring and opens us up for rejection. We often stay in employment situations we find distasteful out of fear or avoidance of job-hunting. That stance toward our work quickly saps us of enthusiasm and energy. This translates into feeling bored or discouraged with our work. Without enthusiasm and energy, our performance is sure to suffer, almost ensuring some experience of failure. We need to explore our boredom and discouragement to determine if they are some inner call to seek out a different job situation.

Some work situations actually are boring, discouraging and a failure, and will to some extent always be so. We may even lose our jobs and suffer the added burden of involuntary unemployment. As Christians, we are called to live the Paschal Mystery, which includes Jesus' crucifixion. These kinds of real and unavoidable negative experiences in our work can feel like a form of crucifixion in our lives. As much as we would like it to be, life is not a "bowl of cherries," and we are often asked to embrace and bear difficult and even horrific situations. But just as in the Paschal Mystery, these negative experiences in our work can be resurrected by opening them to God's grace and spirit. Creatively approaching our work as art, as difficult as this is, can bring new life to these "down" times and experiences. The word *enthused* comes from a Greek word meaning "filled with God." Opening even the most negative work situations to God's compassion, mercy and healing can bring an enthusiasm not previously experienced.

Reflection Questions and Implementing Practices

- What about your job or chores do you find boring? How are these aspects of your work boring? Is there something else that is bothering you? Is it that things are not the way you want them to be? Is it another problem? Monitor your boredom to explore its roots.

- Reflect on a past failure in your work. How did you feel? Were you honest about your contribution to it or did you seek to blame others? Did anything positive come from it? If not, was it because you refused to be open to the positive lesson in the future?

CHAPTER SEVENTEEN

. *W o r k a h o l i s m* .

*Is not this the fast
that I choose: to loose
the bonds of injustice,
to undo the thongs of
the yoke, to let the
oppressed go free,and
to break every yoke?*
—Isaiah 58:6

Over the last seventy years, our society has learned much about addiction from developments in psychology and twelve-step programs such as Alcoholics Anonymous. An addiction is compulsive action that limits a person's freedom. Addicts engage in the compulsive action to lessen their guilt or shame about a real or perceived flaw or emptiness in themselves. The patterns and defenses of the addiction restrict the true self and increase the feelings of shame and guilt. Blinded to the power of the addiction, the addict only turns more deeply into the addiction to alleviate this deeper shame and guilt in a continuing spiral of deepening addiction.

We all carry addictions. Some are learned in our homes or from our friends. Some addictions are more outwardly damaging and less socially acceptable. Some are based in actions that of themselves are not bad or damaging and are socially acceptable. Though workaholism can destroy families and friendships, it generally is viewed as more acceptable than other addictions. Many workaholics are seen as hard workers and are often rewarded by their employers. Workaholism is not limited to paying jobs. One of my sisters knew a woman who rose at four o'clock in the morning every day to spend five hours cleaning her house from top to bottom. She would never go out until her meticulous house cleaning was complete.

Workaholism is as much a compulsion as drug or alcohol addiction. It restricts an individual's freedom by focusing his or her energy and attention on work above all else. In the name of company loyalty, potential advancement or financial support, workaholics become slaves to their jobs. Raises and promotions feed the addiction more, especially by serving as an outward sign of reward for the workaholic's efforts.

Often underlying this conduct there are feelings of shame or guilt. Fueled by a sense of insecurity arising from this guilt and shame, individuals may seek false assurance in work. They hope the compliments and rewards they receive for work done well will alleviate their guilt or shame in giving them some temporary false sense of being or doing better than they had before. This false sense of hope and meaning is quickly shattered. Constant overwork causes disconnection from family and friends, and these failures bring more shame or guilt. The individual drives back into work to alleviate those feelings, and the cycle begins again.

Sabbath does not exist for workaholics, because, unlike God, they take no rest. Their obsession makes leisure and relaxation uncomfortable, and they condemn coworkers who take time for leisure and rest. I spoke to a woman in her fifties who has served husband, children and grandchildren all her adult life and now has a management position in a store. I became tired just listening to her account of all the things she has to do. My suggestion that she go to a coffee shop alone and sit quietly with a cup of tea or coffee was met with doubt. She did not believe she could do that. She would say how much she wanted some quiet time at her cabin in the woods, but never went there. I wonder if she will ever find the time for this extended solitary reflection, if she could not find time for fifteen minutes at a coffee shop.

Workaholism continues to fuel itself until the workaholic can see differently and begin to pierce through the illusion. Sometimes it is a health crisis or the breakup of a marriage that jars someone to seek the truth about his or her relationship with work. While addicted to work, an individual cannot get in touch with the spiritual dimension of work. The work feeds an inner hunger, but the individual is blind to manifestations of grace in both work and play. Blind to their true selves, such people have lost touch with the *imago dei* that they are.

Reflection Questions and Implementing Practices

- Consider what addictions you carry. How do these addictions control your behavior and way of thinking?

- Consider what benefits or rewards you seek from your work. Why do you seek them? Do they fulfill your needs?

Chapter Eighteen

.Personal Interaction.

If one assumes a humble attitude, one's own good qualities will increase. Whereas if one is proud, one will become jealous of others, one will become angry with others, and one will look down on others. Due to that, there will be unhappiness in society.

—Dalai Lama[1]

When it comes down to it, our personal relationships and interactions in our work influence our attitude toward our work more than what we do or what we receive for what we do. I have mentioned this phenomenon to other people and most have agreed with me. Why is that?

Much of our work involves interaction with others, whether the others are employers and coworkers at jobs or family members at home. A number of the people I work with in the bookstore frequently say, "I hate people." This statement usually follows some altercation with a customer or failure by a coworker. I have suggested to them that a "people hater" probably should not be in the retail business. However, these individuals would likely run into difficult personal interactions no matter where they worked. They seek to blame others for their own discomfort and for failing to act as "they are supposed to." At times, they might allow the bad mood of a customer to ruin their day. They adopt the customer's bad mood in reaction or retaliation, rather than holding their own ground. I doubt they realize how they have empowered customers they "hate" by allowing them to dictate their own moods.

A whole book could be written on how healthy personal interaction can make the work experience more spiritual. I will only scratch the surface of this topic. Generally, we need to be realistic about our relationships. There will be good and bad times in any relationship. Up-front honesty is the best path to maintaining health in a relationship, particularly in times of strife. Harboring bad feelings for delayed, inappropriate retaliatory strikes is not only unfair but severely harms the health of the relationship. We must accept that no relationship is perfect and that some relationships will always be flawed.

Some years back, I worked for an individual who was an undiagnosed alcoholic. We had numerous clashes, and those interactions made the job miserable. As I came to understand the problem, I sought to change my reactions to his conduct. I did not give him carte blanche to mistreat me and others, but I did seek to approach our conflicts in a new way. Ultimately, because one half of our interactions were distorted by his addiction, I had to come to peace with the way things were and to lower my expectations of his conduct.

Another tool for improving interaction with others at work is to try and lower our judgment meters. We continually judge others and compare their effort and contribution to our own. Our minds can continually broadcast others' shortcomings, sometimes in an attempt to pump up our image of ourselves. This attitude of judgment becomes evident to those individuals in our interaction with them.

Negative feelings at work also can be spawned by idle chatter and gossip. Limiting personal interactions to business only can create distance and distrust among coworkers. We spend many hours at work, and it is important to cultivate healthy personal relationships with our coworkers. At the same time, hours spent gossiping about other coworkers or chatting about the foibles of the boss create negative energy in the workplace. We need to cultivate a healthy balance in our personal relationships at work so that they do not impede the work to be done or create more strife and discord.

Patterning our personal interactions on those of Jesus in the Gospels can benefit our work, our employees and our coworkers. Jesus' style of open presence to all those he met healed their bodies, minds and hearts. No matter who the individual was or what his or her attitude was toward Jesus, Jesus remained open and present to the person without losing his own equilibrium. Through communication and acceptance, we, like Jesus, can go a long way toward eliminating negative energy in our workplace and home. Nonjudgmental listening can aid us in receiving others in love. Our refusal to join the gossip, backstabbing or complaining can become an example to others. As we seek peace and joy in our relations with others, we bring peace and joy to our work.

Reflection Questions and Implementing Practices

- Think of a person you work with or for that you have negative feelings about or with whom you have a difficult relationship. What is the basis for that difficulty or negativity? Are you fair in your interactions and understanding of the person? Put yourself in this person's place, trying to see his or her point of view. How have you contributed to the difficulty or negativity in your relationship with this individual? Consider the addictions you carry. How do these addictions control your behavior and way of thinking?

- Keep a log of the number of times you engage in complaints or idle gossip at work. Who started these conversations? Who was engaged in them and about whom were you talking? If negative statements were made about someone who was not present, did you go along with the conversation or did you make positive statements about the person who was the subject of discussion? Did anything constructive come from the conversation?

- Is there someone you encounter frequently with whom you are in conflict? Consider the conflict both from your perspective and that of the other individual. Arrange a meeting with that individual and initiate a peaceful conversation about the strain between you. Listen attentively to the other individual before expressing your own views. Try to come to some more amicable understanding between the two of you and take actions each day to implement that understanding.

• Draft your own ten commandments for getting along better with others, particularly in your work.

---

[1] Dalai Lama, 1981, quoted in Matthew E. Bunson, *The Wisdom Teachings of the Dalai Lama* (New York: Penguin Putnam Inc., 1997), p. 61.

CHAPTER NINETEEN

. E g o ,   P r i d e
a n d   M i s t a k e s .

*The meaning of life
lies precisely in
realizing that we are
imprisoned in our
ego, in the limited
human self, and
within us, and
beyond us, are
infinite beauty and
truth and love.*

—Bede Griffiths[1]

W hen I was sworn in to the New York Bar along with a number of other law school graduates, the presiding judge read a short statement about entering the legal profession. This may surprise you, but one of her points was that we should recognize that we all make mistakes and must own up to and correct them when discovered. Does that seem a strange thing to say to new lawyers? I think not and only hope those new lawyers heard the message. The legal community prides itself on supposed perfection and fears malpractice suits for mistakes. Untold energy is spent to ensure no mistakes are made, but when one is made, the tendency is to hide it first and correct it second. In law firms, there is a tendency to keep mistakes secret from clients, if they can be fixed without detection. That mentality adds unnecessary stress to legal work. The words "I am sorry, I made a mistake" are rarely heard in law firms. Lawyers with their gift for words can rationalize any action, pinning blame anywhere but on themselves. Such striving and expectation for perfection is unhealthy and demoralizing.

The need to be perfect comes from our ego. We carry in our minds a keen, but illusory, sense of who we are, a "name, rank and serial number" of age, gender, family background, education, career, family status and accomplishments. This package supposedly comprises who each of us is. We claim to know we are more than all that; that we are images or children of God. However, our course of conduct and attention lie more in our ego selves. The fragile ego self requires constant building up; its protective fortress must be forever made stronger and larger.

In the traditional list of the seven deadly sins, pride is at the top. The evil in the outward actions of lust and gluttony pale in comparison to the evils of the inner state of pride. Pride tells us we are something special and unique as compared to all others. It deifies us, in a way, making us think that our greatness and goodness is derived from ourselves. Pride diminishes our true goodness in the core of our humanity, which is in its unity with God and God's creation. Such unity threatens the special ego, for it diminishes our unique importance.

As we identify ourselves with and act from this fragile fortress, we put ourselves in an "over against" position with others. We must remain special and on top. We adopt a stance of self-importance. No one may criticize us or question our actions. We work incessantly to maintain this façade and to live from it. Lawyers or doctors who think they are something special because of their professions are truly sad people. The sandy foundation of this fortress of importance continually fails them and compels them to promote their supposed importance all the more.

What do we do with our ego and our pride? We can follow the pattern of Jesus, memorialized in the early Christian prayer included in Paul's letter to the Philippians, and empty ourselves (Philippians 2:7). Psychology teaches us not to attack or suppress the ego, for that only strengthens its hold and weakens our awareness of it. Careful attention to our motivations and conduct can make us more aware of the power of the ego on our actions. With this awareness, the chokehold of the ego begins to ease up. Taking time to sit alone in silence and to reflect quietly on our day can aid in enhancing this awareness.

By seeking to loosen the hold of our ego and pride, we heed Jesus' admonition to lose our life in order to save it (Luke 9:24). The ego distorts our views and makes us self-centered in our work. We strive for constant rewards and compliments for ourselves, even to the detriment of others. We ignore the needs of others and never experience fulfillment. The ego's need for stroking is endless. Unless the rewards and compliments are neverending, we are thrown into the insecurity of our ego self.

If we open our minds and hearts to the fallacies of our false self, our true self can emerge. It has no concerns about its image or others' views of it. Its dignity lies in our God-centeredness, which can never be diminished. The words human and humility are both derived from the Latin word *humus*, which means "earth" or "dirt." We open to our true humanity if we adopt a cloak of humility, no longer seeking self-assurance from others. In humility, we embrace ourselves, including our mistakes and limits. We can accept unjust, and even unfair, criticism, for nothing can impinge on our true dignity in God. Our true self does not rely on perfection, omnipotence and power. Jesus' most powerful human moment came at the moment of his greatest powerlessness, as he was nailed to a cross and embraced death.

Reflection Questions and Implementing Practices

- Begin an entry in your journal entitled "Who Am I?" by sketching an answer to that question. Day by day reflect on each day's experience and enter in the journal what it has taught you about who you are. Consider whether your initial description of who you are needs reworking. Record those changes in the journal.

- As days pass, try to catch the number of times each day you are acting from a damaged or threatened ego. What were you feeling at the time? What triggered your ego defense system? Each evening reconsider these events. How would you have reacted or acted differently if your injured ego had not been in the driver's seat?

- In conversation, try to be aware of how much your attention is focused on your opinion of the topic at hand. Notice how you are more attentive to formulating your next comment than hearing what is being said. Attempt to enhance your listening skills and give your opinion less. Consider whether the exchange was really diminished because your opinion was withheld.

---

[1] Bede Griffiths, quoted in John Swindells, *A Human Search: Bede Griffiths Reflects on His Life* (Liguori, Mo.: Triumph Books, Liguori Publications, 1997), p. 119.

CHAPTER TWENTY

. *C o n t r o l*
a n d   C h a n g e .

*The thing that is
blind is not love but
attachment. An
attachment is a state
of clinging that
comes from the false
belief that something
or someone is
necessary for your
happiness.*

—Anthony de Mello[1]

Our desire to have control and to fight change is connected to the insecurities and illusions that foster our ego self. One of the great teachings of Buddhism is the impermanence of all things. Every moment is brief and then passes, never to return. The flow of ocean tides and the pattern of our breath teach us life consists of coming and going. What we eat or drink is used and then passes out of us. We enter this world in birth and exit in death. We all nod our heads in agreement with these statements, but then proceed to live our lives seeking to effect control and to stop change.

> *Keith arrives at his sister's house for Christmas dinner, anxious to savor the traditional family feast of roast beef and all the fixings. He is greatly taken aback when he finds that the holiday meal is an Italian buffet. He sulks all day because of the change in tradition.*

> *Molly has worked at the same office for ten years. As plans are made to relocate the office and simultaneously install a new computer system, Molly becomes anxious about what her new office will be like. She complains about having to learn a new computer system and in training continually mentions that the old system was better.*

All spiritual disciplines, including the Christian tradition, teach the constancy of change and the fallacy of control. Though we can seek to head our lives in a particular direction, our lives' events unfold without our effort or orchestration, despite the differing configuration by our ego mind. Accepting this state of constant change and no control requires adopting the "letting go" stance of nonattachment. It is human nature to create attachments to people, objects and routines. These attachments can cement our attitudes and actions, so that we miss new opportunities and experiences. A fundamental challenge of the spiritual path is to let go of these attachments and, instead, to accept life as it presents itself. I prefer to see this as a process of nonattachment rather than detachment, because the latter concept connotes a separation or aversion. I see nonattachment as an open and free experience of what is, without personal judgment, and a letting go of that experience to be open to the next.

By practicing nonattachment, we can become like sand on the beach, which accepts the ocean as each wave comes in. The sand openly accepts the wetness of the wave and the remnants of shells and creatures left behind. Yet, as quickly as the wave arrives, the ocean calls the wave back. The sand does nothing to hold on to the wave. In fact, some of the sand itself is carried into the ocean by the receding wave. If we follow the "just" method in Chapter Nine and the contemplative sitting in Chapter Ten, we can become more like the sand. We are open awareness in our lives, taking what comes in its fullness, allowing it to be without judgment or clinging. Rather than aching for what was or what might have been, we can remain open to the next wave or moment. This freedom toward the unfolding of our lives enables us to live more deeply and honestly. We no longer need the false security of control and permanence.

In our work, freedom opens us up to new surprises and graces. Just being about our work as it arises can become the fruit of the work we are doing. Our roles and plans no longer dictate the work, and we can freely encounter our work environment and experiences. This newfound freedom may not be well received by others. Our release of the need to control and our acceptance of change can highlight others' continuing addiction to control and permanence. We may find our way of engaging in work has so changed that our friends and loved ones do not recognize us. As we accept change as constant, we are constantly changed, to the consternation of those who think they have us figured out.

Applying this to our work in all its forms, if we bring our mindful attention to each moment of our work, we deepen our encounter with the spiritual dimension of that work. Resting in just what we are about or just what is before us, without determining our liking or disliking of it, allows us to be open to the work itself. As the work before us becomes the only focus, we begin to "disappear," losing our life to save it.

I have applied this single-minded focus to tasks at home and on the job:

> *As I prepare a meal,* I focus my attention on peeling the potatoes and other food preparation, the washing of the cookware and the setting of the table.
>
> *When gardening,* I keep my mind on the digging, planting, trimming and watering.
>
> *While working at the bookstore,* I draw my attention to the alphabetical shelving and organizing of the books.
>
> *During my work in a legal office,* I keep my attention on the research and the writing of the item before me. I bring my mind back when it wanders to the pile of items in my in box.

Simple attention to our work for its own sake allows us more clearly to encounter God in our work. By resting in the rhythm of our work, we can disappear and find God.

Reflection Questions and Implementing Practices

- Consider situations in your work, at home or away from home, in which you have minimal control. How do you react to your limited choices in that situation? Are you critical or envious of the person who does have control? Would you be willing to take the responsibility that comes with having that control? When you begin to feel negative about your lack of control in that situation, try to set those feelings aside and accept the situation as it is.

- Pick one day a week in which you will make a conscious

effort to be more open to events as they occur. Whether at home or at your place of employment, pay attention to what comes up and catch yourself before you judge or fight these events. Take some notes on what motivated you to judge or fight these events and how successful you were in not acting from that negative stance. Compare how you feel on the day you choose to turn off your critique meter to how you feel the rest of the days of the week.

- Choose a recurring task or job you tend to regularly. It can be a simple domestic chore or a repeating action at work, such as filing or answering E-mail. When you engage in this task, try to slow your thinking and focus only on the task at hand. If your mind wanders, bring it back to where you are in the task. After following this practice for some time, reflect on how you feel about the task and what you are experiencing as you conduct it.

---

[1] Anthony de Mello, *The Way to Love: The Last Meditations of Anthony de Mello* (New York: Image Books, Doubleday, 1991), p. 43.

CHAPTER TWENTY-ONE

. *M o r a l i t y* .

*Then [Jesus] called
the crowd to him and
said to them, "Listen
and understand: it is
not what goes into
the mouth that
defiles a person, but
it is what comes out
of the mouth that
defiles.... what
comes out of the
mouth proceeds from
the heart, and this is
what defiles."*
—Matthew 15:10–11, 18

Each of us has a personal moral system influenced by our parents, society and religious affiliation. Our personal moral code underlies our behavior, action and words. As Jesus taught, it is what comes out of a person that really matters (Matthew 15:18–20). Our outward conduct is a reflection of our inner character.

Our Christian moral system is centered in God as the source of all life, love and goodness and is based in our understanding of creation and human dignity. It is derived from natural law (an objective fundamental knowledge of goodness present in all people), the life and teachings of Jesus, Scripture, church teaching and the lives of members of the Christian community. Our Christian morality is linked intrinsically to our faith and incorporates our understanding of sin, forgiveness and mercy.

We manifest our personal morality in the world, particularly in our relationships with others. Our ability to act from a good moral base can be distorted if we are not truly free and aware. For example, if we still operate from the *do*s, *don't*s and *should*s imposed on us in childhood by our parents and other authority figures, we have not developed a mature adult morality. A mature adult morality withstands attack and responds appropriately in new situations.

Therefore, the path to a mature adult morality calls us to become more free and aware, leaving behind childish support systems and ego illusions. Again, careful attention will serve us in our journey to moral living. As our freedom and awareness are enhanced, we can develop a mature moral conscience that can see what ought to be done, not to serve the ego or respond to guilt, but to serve love and respond to true need. To form a mature moral conscience, we transcend the morality of our childhood. This personal mature morality comes from an enhanced knowledge and understanding of goodness. This new knowledge and understanding comes from our lived experiences, our adult faith, the life and teaching of Jesus, Scripture, church teaching, the Christian community and sources outside Christianity, including moral codes of other faiths. By taking the spiritual path of emptiness, nonattachment and contemplation, we become more free and aware to allow this goodness to be manifest in us.

The underlying values of our personal morality are reflected in our work. Often, we employ one moral standard in our homes and personal life and a different moral standard at our jobs. Would you ever, while visiting a friend, take a bar of soap from the bathroom because you need one at your home? At your child's sporting event, would you pick up another parent's cell phone and make a long distance call without asking permission? I believe just about all of us would answer no to both questions. If the questions are changed to whether or not you would grab a few pens at work for your children to use for homework or make long distance personal phone calls on the company phone, I believe many more of us would answer yes. Taking the bar of soap or using a cell phone without permission we would call stealing. However, the prevalent sense is that we are owed something by our employers, so the same kind of conduct with the company pens and the company phone may be deemed acceptable.

Of course, our morality at work goes to broader issues than taking paper clips home or using the company Xerox machine to copy your tax return. It incorporates how we treat others we interact with in our work, whether we give our employer a fair day's work and whether we treat those we encounter at work fairly.

A moral evaluation of our actions and attitudes at work directs our attention to the deeper meaning of our work and its foundation in God. In seeking to be morally good in the conduct of our work, we can come to discover a spiritual dimension that previously may have escaped us. This task, however, is never achieved in a vacuum. As we explore our personal morality, we need to come to terms with the values and mores of the society and culture we live in.

Reflection Questions and Implementing Practices

- Our Christian tradition has many outward signs of its moral teachings, such as the Ten Commandments and the Beatitudes. What are the core elements of your moral code? Do you consider that code daily as you make decisions or choices in your work?

- How moral is your treatment of your employer? What changes in your behavior seem necessary after this review? How can you put these changes into effect? How moral is your employer's treatment of you? Can you bear immoral treatment by your employer without retaliating with immoral conduct?

PART THREE

. Confronting
Cultural
Opposition .

*Understanding How
Widely Held Beliefs
and Prevalent
Aspects of American
Society Influence
How We View, Value
and Approach Work*

CHAPTER TWENTY-TWO

. *Jesus' Confrontation in the Temple*.

The Christian cannot separate his life of faith from the real world of work and struggle in which he lives.

—Thomas Merton[1]

Throughout the Gospels, Jesus confronts and openly challenges those in the know, those in power and those closest to him. He rebukes the disciples for their lack of understanding on numerous occasions, even referring to Peter as "Satan" when he suggests that Jesus should act out of fear and seek safety (Matthew 16:21–23). In a list of woes, Jesus castigates the rich and well-off (Luke 6:24–26). However, it is the leaders of the Jewish people, the priests, Pharisees and Sadducees, for whom he saves his most severe criticism. Due to their position of knowledge, leadership and power, he holds them to a higher standard and chastises them for burdening the community they are called to aid and lead (Luke 11:46). He criticizes their hypocrisy in seeking glory in their positions as religious leaders (Luke 11:42–53).

Jesus shows greater deference to the Romans and greater kindness toward Gentiles than toward these supposed holy men of Judaism. In doing so, he is pointing out the evils of any system that is more interested in its self-preservation than in what it stands for. It is more important to the Pharisees that they punish and chastise others who fail to abide meticulously by the volumes of Jewish prescripts than to lift up their fellow Jews with love and forgiveness. We, however, cannot be too hard on or critical of these Jewish leaders. We are parts of many systems of power and authority that can mistakenly serve their own preservation rather than the preservation of their own members.

Our nation, our economic system, our culture and even our church can stake out positions or take actions that are founded in maintaining control or perpetuating their existence. They may promulgate dogmas and rules, some of which, contrary to their greater purpose, are insecure grabs for self-preservation or obedience. We are bombarded with ways of believing and acting that are the product of this groupthink. Without always being conscious of our dependence on groupthink, we operate under these rules, thereby restricting our freedom and awareness. We are blinded to the truth and accept without question axioms that are agreed to by most people.

Jesus' confrontation of the system comes to its apex in his ejection of the merchants from the Temple. Jesus enters the Temple and begins to drive out those who sell animals and exchange money for Temple sacrifices. He forbids the carrying of possessions into the Temple and decries making God's house a marketplace and a den of robbers (Matthew 21:12–13; Mark 11:15–17; Luke 19:45–46; John 2:14–16). This public confrontation challenges the Temple leadership, which exercised its power and financed the Temple with this sacrifice business. In addition, Jesus was challenging the predominant economic system of Jerusalem, which was this marketing of goods for sacrifice. This was the equivalent of challenging the Vatican and the New York Stock Exchange at the same time. When Meister Eckhart (ca. 1260-ca. 1328), a Dominican priest and mystic, preached on this Gospel story, he claimed that Jesus was rejecting the market economic system, particularly applying its barter system to our relationship with God. By cleaning the Temple, he said Jesus was freeing us from attachment to self and ignorance and reclaiming the world for God alone.[2]

I am sure many of the bystanders in the Temple that day looked on Jesus with disbelief. They had been taught that this sacrifice system was critical to reconciliation with God. Who was this nomadic carpenter to challenge the system, which, supported by everyone, must be correct? Jesus remained in the Temple after this incident and began to teach. Many were inspired and moved by what Jesus had to say, likely causing further consternation in the Temple leadership. After listening to Jesus for some time, I wonder how many of these initially perplexed bystanders began to see the wisdom of his action. Maybe they began to recall the lines from Isaiah, in which God declared that the multitude of animal sacrifices made him sick and wished instead that his people would "learn to do good; seek justice, rescue the oppressed, defend the orphan, plead for the widow" (Isaiah 1:11–17). Those who knew Jesus may have recalled that this plea of God's was being lived out in Jesus' life. It was not merely in this action in the Temple that Jesus challenged the groupthink and power structures of his time. Jesus' very life was a challenge to the status quo and a call to renewal for individuals, society and culture.

We are no different from those bystanders in the Temple. We are surrounded by and function in power structures, cultural groups and groupthink every day. From our families to our ethnic group, to local political subdivisions, to countries of origin, to economic systems, to group worldview, to religious affiliation, we are formed and restricted by the status quo of each of these groups. Surprisingly, sometimes the desires of these groups are in conflict, throwing us into confusion or absurd rationalizations. For example, the church tells me to care for the poor, but our American capitalist system requires everyone to earn a living. When confronted with a beggar on the street, one could be confused by these conflicting ethics. Many resort to the excuse that the individual will likely buy alcohol or drugs with the money, so that giving him or her a dollar is not the kind of help that the church calls us to.

We must become aware of the various groupthink systems that form our opinions and actions. In particular, these perspectives or opinions impact our view of work and how we conduct our work. We cannot embrace a God-centered spirituality toward our work if these outside influences distort our view. If these restraints still bind us, we cannot be free. As we free ourselves, we may be called to confront, challenge and chastise these restrictive bindings of our society and government just as Jesus did.

Reflection Questions and Implementing Practices

- Read the four Gospel accounts of Jesus' confrontation in the Temple. Imagine yourself as Jesus, then as one of the disciples, then as a dove merchant, a moneychanger, a bystander and a Temple priest. What are you thinking and feeling in each persona as the events unfold? Are you troubled by Jesus' bold, confrontational style? Does my reflection on this story change your understanding of it?

• What are some of the societal, governmental, cultural and religious groups to which you belong? Write how you believe each of these groups influences you. Consider whether you are troubled about any of the teachings or way of thinking of each of these groups. Can you challenge these widely held views and remain in this group?

---

[1] Thomas Merton, *Life and Holiness* (New York: Image Books, Doubleday, 1963), p. 97.

[2] Meister Eckhart, "Sermon 12 (DW1, W6)," *Meister Eckhart: Selected Writings*, translated by Oliver Davies (New York: Penguin Books, 1994), pp. 152-158.

CHAPTER TWENTY-THREE

. *Western / Modern*
Worldview .

*Every single thing
you perceive is the
radiance of Spirit
itself, so much so,
that Spirit is not seen
apart from that
thing: the robin
sings, and just that is
it, nothing else.*

—Ken Wilber[1]

America and Christianity developed primarily within the critical, rational Western mind, formed by Greco-Roman philosophy, the Enlightenment and a scientific and technological worldview. Though Christianity's earliest roots are in the Middle East, its movement and growth northwest into Europe, and later into North and South America, resulted in its embrace by and expression in the Western mind-set.

The first Christians held the philosophy and worldview of Judaism and the mystical tradition of the church has always taken a less rational or logical approach to God. However, the church, particularly in formal pronouncements and teachings, adopted the rational philosophy of the Greeks and Romans. The adoption of this rational philosophy resulted in a heavy slant toward theology, the study or knowledge of God, and a lesser emphasis on mysticism and matters of the Spirit. The early councils of the church agonized over defining Jesus. The result was an emphasis on statements about Jesus rather than on reflection on the message of Jesus' statements, teachings and actions.

The early United States and the Enlightenment developed practically hand in hand. Descartes, the patron saint of the Enlightenment, declared, "I think, therefore I am." With the development of the printing press, the expansion of education and the initial development of the sciences, the knowledge of humankind was increased. Universities began to develop in the Middle Ages and, in each century since, the number of people attending them has expanded. Book knowledge came to be considered more important than heart knowledge. The church itself was a major contributor to this development, because it placed significant emphasis on the education of children. This glorification of intellectual knowledge conflicted with previous religious articulations, which had relied on pre-rational images and stories. These changed perspectives and ways of articulating and practicing religious faith contributed to the development of the various Protestant religious groups. In attempting to intellectualize bad events, many persons diminished God's role in current events. Many of the Founding Fathers of this country were deists, who believed God created the world and then became a detached observer, having no input or impact on events.

The increased knowledge of the Enlightenment exploded with scientific advancements and, in the last fifty years, with technological developments. Science's apparent ability to explain things caused us to consider it the preferred or only legitimate worldview. This further diminished much of society's view of the role of God, religion and spirituality in our world. The questions of whether God was dead or whether God existed at all were asked more frequently. Anything that could not be explained with scientific knowledge was myth, magic or silliness. All aspects of life were reduced to a commodity of quantitative value. Unless something could be experienced with the five senses, it was not real. The deluge of information available to us with technological advances accelerated this process. Anything of the soul or spirit was irrelevant or, at best, an entertaining sideline.

We carry this rational, scientific worldview into our work. Generally, this way of thinking values our work based on content, sophistication and compensation. It focuses on the product and not the producers. The individuals in the workplace and their various overlapping and conflicting relationships are deemed unimportant. This worldview teaches us to see our work as something separate from our soul and spirituality. As I have told people that I have been writing a book on work and spirituality, many have responded that the two have nothing to do with one another.

The challenge today, being met in many locales, is to gather this rational worldview and its predecessor non-rational worldview to a level that includes but transcends them both. This transrational worldview recognizes as supreme or all-encompassing something beyond scientific knowledge, which is Spirit. With this new worldview we can:

> *Allow experience and awareness,* in addition to knowledge, to teach us about ourselves, others and the world.

> *Recognize ways of knowing* or being outside the five senses.

Recognize that there is no place or time in which Spirit is not and that we are one with that Spirit.

Honor the qualitative, rather than the quantitative, value of ourselves, the world and others.

This very process of formulating a spirituality of work is part of embracing this all-encompassing worldview.

R e f l e c t i o n   Q u e s t i o n s   a n d   I m p l e m e n t i n g   P r a c t i c e s

- What is your view of science and technology? Do you prefer their logical, rational theories and conclusions to the theories or conclusions of religion, emotions or intuition? Do you need to see it to believe it? How do you reconcile scientific knowledge with your religious beliefs?

- How do you determine the worth of your work and the work of others? Does your response contain more qualitative or quantitative elements? Did you include the spiritual dimension of work in your response?

[1] Ken Wilber, *The Essential Ken Wilber: An Introductory Reader* (Boston: Shambhala, 1998), p. 12.

CHAPTER TWENTY-FOUR

. *Capitalism* .

So it is with those who store up treasures for themselves but are not rich toward God.

—Luke 12:21

Capitalism is founded in free enterprise, private property and self-interest. It upholds the reason or intellect of a human being as supreme and envisions a limited role for government. The rights of the individual are paramount. The individual property owner generally is free to use his or her property and efforts in any way needed to earn a profit. The production and distribution of goods at a profit is of primary importance. The property owner receives this profit often through a division of labor that places the owners above the laborers. The value of the worker is diminished as compared to the value of the goods produced and the profit earned. A capitalist society seeks to forge ahead with progress in increased production and profit. Production and profit making are sacrosanct and are not to be limited by religion, government or ethics.

The American economic system is based in capitalism. Capitalism promotes individual economic advancement and property ownership without government interference. However, in its early history, America's laissez-faire system of capitalism also allowed many abuses, including the utilization of slaves, the exploitation of workers and the oppression of women, minorities and the poor. A glaring divide between the "haves" and the "have-nots" became an integral part of our society and, unfortunately, continues today.

In the Declaration of Independence, Thomas Jefferson, a slave owner, spoke of the inalienable rights of life, liberty and the pursuit of happiness. These rights, in practice at the time, were afforded only to white male landowners. As industrialism and the market economy increased, the abuses of largely unrestrained capitalism increased. The union and women's movements began in reaction to these abuses. Over time, particularly during and since the Great Depression, the federal and state government passed laws and established systems to eliminate or reduce these abuses. Capitalism still exists in America today, but is more restricted than it was in the eighteenth and nineteenth centuries.

Though capitalism does allow for individual initiative and success, with today's stock market focus, capitalism necessarily focuses on the bottom line and shareholder return. This approach ignores the multidimensional impact of businesses on their employees, customers and communities. Because capitalism emphasizes profit and economic contribution, it tends to discount or ignore the value of work for no pay or the benefits of work other than for production and monetary return. Interestingly, this focus on profit and shareholder return oppresses even corporate leaders. A chief executive officer of a multi-bank holding company told me that, as his company had grown and sold more stock in the market, he did not enjoy his work as much as he did when the company was smaller and more privately held. Previously, he could make decisions taking into account all relevant factors, tangible and intangible, and consider what was best for the organization over time. Now at the end of each quarter he is hounded by investment analysts seeking a certain rate of return for their customers who have invested in the holding company stock. Our daily addiction to the Dow Jones level and the value of our retirement portfolio is similar to the dogged questions of these investment analysts. The relentless questions from these analysts have forced this executive to change the way he runs the business. His decision-making now has to take into account short-term return to the shareholders over the long-term benefits to the banks, the communities they serve and their employees, management and shareholders.

Some corporations have attempted to address the harshness of capitalism in the allocation of corporate money and effort. The original owners of Ben and Jerry's Ice Cream maintained an ethic of social responsibility in the conduct of their business. They imposed some of those requirements on the companies they did business with and supported socially responsible causes with corporate time and money. These requirements and activities involved social issues and causes important to the two owners. They required that the corporation that recently purchased their company maintain this social focus.

The church has spoken on the problems of capitalism for over one hundred years. In 1891, Pope Leo XIII issued *Rerum Novarum*, which questioned the primacy of economics, condemned treating human labor as a commodity and affirmed a role for the church in speaking to the morality and justice of economic systems, especially in the treatment of the poor and workers.

Since then, five popes and the Second Vatican Council have issued documents addressing economic systems. Overall, these statements have supported private property and free enterprise, but at the same time supported restraints on them to address poverty and injustice. These statements have warned against excessive individualism and significant inequality in the distribution of wealth amongst peoples and nations. The document of the Second Vatican Council, the *Pastoral Constitution on the Church in the Modern World*, stated that true human progress lies more in "greater justice, wider brotherhood and a more human social environment," than in technological advances (*Gaudium et Spes* 35). In an encyclical on human work, Pope John Paul II speaks of the subservience of capital to the human person (*Laborem Exercens* 12). On the one-hundredth anniversary of *Rerum Novarum*, he strongly affirmed the dignity of workers and human work and the right of workers to proper working conditions and a just wage (*Centesimus Annus* 6–8). The United States Conference of Catholic Bishops issued a joint pastoral letter in 1986 entitled *Economic Justice for All: Pastoral Letter on Catholic Social Teaching and the U.S. Economy*, which criticized the specific abuses or problems in American capitalism.

In formulating our own spirituality of work, we need to understand the implications of living in a capitalist society. It is a system that emphasizes self-reliance over community assistance and competition over cooperation. Understanding our participation in the abuses of that system or the exploitation of us by that system is critical to opening our hearts to the deeper rewards in our work beyond just profit, compensation and production. This economic system should not be hated or ignored, but through us it can be sustained and transformed in Christ.

Reflection Questions and Implementing Practices

- Consider how free enterprise has functioned at places you have been employed. What systems or laws limited that exercise of capitalism? What relationship did you have to the ownership of the property and earning of profit in that business? Did you feel that you benefited from the free enterprise system in place at that business? Did you feel that you were subject to unfair treatment or abuse in that system?

- What are your views on the balance between individual rights and group rights? How do you practice this balance in your family, in your community and in the workplace? Under what circumstances do you believe the rights of the individual must be set aside for the common good?

- Read slowly a copy of one of the papal or bishops' documents addressing economic issues. Write notes on your reactions and pray with the text. Do you believe that the document's criticism of wealthier nations, such as the United States, is justified? To the extent it supports elements of the capitalist system, do you believe that support comports with biblical justice and morality?

CHAPTER TWENTY-FIVE

. Success Is Having Money and Things .

Many people think, especially in the West, that having money makes you happy. I think it must be harder to be happy if you are wealthy because you may find it difficult to see God: you'll have too many other things to think about.

—Mother Teresa[1]

Our American culture has embraced two important elements of the system of capitalism—the acquisition of wealth and the primacy of the individual. Our addiction to wealth and individualism has increased geometrically in the last fifty years. In America, success tends to mean the individual acquisition of money and possessions. Many of us ascribe too much value to what can be acquired or consumed and deride the worth of intangibles. This is not a new notion, for it is present even in the Declaration of Independence, which uniquely imbues Americans with the inalienable right to pursue happiness. In practice, the pursuit of happiness has sometimes meant getting whatever makes us feel good with little concern for others. What some have called the obsessive self-focus of the baby boomers may be viewed as the culmination of two hundred years of this "me first" mentality.

When money and possessions are the primary focus of our desires, success and even self-worth are defined in terms of what we have' and not who we are or how we live. This was brought sharply to my attention recently in two contemporaneous exchanges. In the first, a young man who had just moved into my apartment building had a heated exchange with another tenant, claiming she had refused to listen to him because he was so young. He turned to me and said, "If she knew how much money I had, she would have listened to me." In the second incident, a manager at the store where I worked said that the customers would treat her with more respect if they knew how much money and property she had. It struck me that although these two people were many years apart in age and had very different life experience, they defined their self-worth in terms of their bank accounts and stock portfolios. Many of us cannot condemn these two, as we obsessively check the value of our 401(k) investments and purchase with credit cards what we do not need and cannot afford. Somehow, we believe that we are better the more we have.

Fed by these obsessions, some of us tend to value only work for which we receive monetary consideration, and continually require more compensation. Many of us cling to our money and possessions, worrying about losing them and anxious about getting more. With all this energy expended in obtaining and maintaining our money and possessions, we block our ability to receive, with open hearts and minds, the graces of life.

As Jesus reminded us, money has its place ("Give to the emperor the things that are the emperor's, and to God the things that are God's" [Mark 12:17]), but money cannot be primary ("You cannot serve God and wealth" [Luke 16:13c]). In the Lord's Prayer, Jesus taught us to pray for our daily bread. This simple appeal to have our immediate needs met contrasts sharply with an obsessive accumulation of money and possessions. In embracing a spiritual approach to life, and specifically to our work, we need to measure our success in terms other than money and possessions.

This is difficult in our consumer society, which values what can be produced, acquired and consumed over what is intangible and without monetary value. We clamor for the newest computer, DVD or fashion and have no time for matters of the spirit and soul. Such matters are considered frivolous or minor, despite some lip service to the contrary. This directly influences our work, for it requires us to be concerned with speed, efficiency and personal profit. We are not concerned about others or the nonmonetary benefits of our work. We posture with management or backstab coworkers to improve our reputation and position.

In order to measure success in our work beyond money and possessions, we need to seek out meaning, wholeness and connection in our jobs and chores. Meaning may be found in work well done or in service to others. Wholeness and connection are a matter of community and compassion in our work environments. None of these relate to what we produce or how much we earn. A shift in attitude from possessions to meaning, wholeness and connection does not occur overnight or happen as a result of reading the plethora of books with "soul" in the title. It requires the adoption of a consistent spiritual practice in our daily lives. Living more simply, embracing extended times of silence and regularly engaging in prayerful meditation can open our eyes, minds and hearts to our need for acquisition and allow us to become more free of that need.

Reflection Questions and Implementing Practices

- Do you consider yourself successful? How do you measure that success? How do you measure others' success? Is there any difference between how you measure your success and the success of others?

- What would make you completely happy? Is your definition of happiness based on our culture's definition of what should make you happy? Do you regularly do things in pursuit of happiness? Does that pursuit of happiness seek to fulfill your desires or does it encompass the desires of your loved ones, friends or community?

- Monitor your buying habits for a month. Track purchases to meet a need, an impulse or a desire. Note what motivated your impulse buying. Delay acquiring something you desire but do not need for a week or two. How many times does your desire for the item fade during that time? After waiting, do you decide not to purchase the item?

---

[1] Mother Teresa, *A Simple Path* (New York: Ballantine Books, 1995), p. 179.

CHAPTER TWENTY-SIX

. O v e r l o a d   o f
I n p u t , A c t i o n
a n d   M e d i a .

> *The core of difficulty
> at the heart of
> modern work life is
> its abstraction from
> many of the ancient
> cycles of life that
> allow the silence and
> time in which true
> appreciation and
> experience can take
> place.*
>
> —David Whyte[1]

Our consumer mentality has hit an all-time high in input over-load. We are bombarded with media images and messages (probably even rehashing them in our dreams). Most of these images and messages are received in quick and lively "info-bites." Individuals walk around with pagers, cell phones and Palm Pilots to be ever in touch with an endless stream of input. These technological advances keep us available to others, including our employers, at all times. Some employers expect their employees to maintain these lines of communication with the office during their supposed free time away from the job. This bombardment of information can be numbing.

A strong perception is that we all must have immediate access to the various forms of communication. Over the last year, I have not had easy access to a fax machine. I was surprised at the stunned reaction of others when I told them they could not fax me the information they wanted to send me. It seemed that, to some people, there was something wrong with me for not being connected. Many people feel the need to be available at all times for others to reach out and touch them. The flipping of calls by people with call waiting can destroy a conversation. The multiple, simultaneous dialogues teenagers have on computer instant message services are so fast and cryptic as to be meaningless, at least to the uninitiated. An acquaintance of mine told of returning from a silent retreat, which he had taken to have time in quiet and solitude for reflection and prayer, to find his new answering machine jammed with messages concerning the very busyness that he had consciously sought to separate himself from on his retreat. He said he felt as if he had not gotten away.

When I began to practice law, I noticed that the insecurity and fear of many attorneys I worked with was directly proportional to the level of contact he or she felt compelled to maintain with the office when away, even on vacation. Some people made long calls to the office twice a day. Others left the telephone numbers of the hotels where they could be reached, discouraging calls by saying they did not expect to be in the room much during the day. While the constant callers always carried a cell phone, the other group made clear that their cell phones were to be left at home.

Constant callers seemed afraid that others might discover they were not indispensable when the work of the office went smoothly without them. Advances in communications systems over the last twenty years have increased the ability and means by which constant contact can be maintained.

Input overload is not limited to contact with the office. It includes the visual and sound images of media, whether print media, television, radio, movies or the Internet. I have not owned a television for over four years, so my television viewing is well below the national average. Recently, while watching television at my mother's house, during a long commercial break, I experienced the rapid-fire visual images and loud sound bites almost as slaps in the face. I was not able to comprehend or reflect upon the non-stop assault of input. We need to ask ourselves if media is forming us in ways unknown. The short attention span and hectic pace of so many Americans follows the pattern of that rapid-fire commercial break.

Our culture glorifies the information superhighway of the Internet and believes that more information and access is better. In *The Age of Missing Information,* written in 1992, Bill McKibben compared the information he received spending a quiet twenty-four hours in the woods to the broadcasts of the 104 stations on his cable network during that same time frame.[2] The value and meaning of his experience in the woods far exceeded the vapid barrage of the programs in the television broadcasts. It is difficult for us to see the impact this barrage of information has on us for it is so much a part of our lives. In *Screen Saved: Peril and Promise of Media in Ministry,* Dan Andriacco recommends periodic media fasts to make us more aware of the effects on us of the input of media. These fasts, he suggests, will open our hearts more to God by creating silent, contemplative space in our lives and improving our mental and physical health.[3]

My ultimate decision not to own a television began with Lenten fasting from television viewing, which opened my eyes to the reasons I watched television and the lack of value in so much television programming. As I have practiced contemplative prayer and attempted to live from a contemplative or mindful stance, I have acquired an increasing aversion to excess input and stimulation, which was something I used to crave. I am less inclined to run off to see the next movie or attend a special event and find myself to be more selective in chores and content with simple walks on the beach.

Overall, however, Americans show signs of believing that faster and busier are better. American culture tends to frown on quiet, reflective times. We cannot even relax when we are supposedly at leisure. This tendency toward crammed rest is exemplified in large theme parks. I recently visited Disney World, which had expanded significantly since my last visit. I was on a business trip, but had some time to visit the attractions. As I reviewed the extensive list of places to visit, I became less enthusiastic about visiting them at all. I selected only a handful of exhibits or rides to visit and otherwise rested at the hotel during breaks. When I did go into the park, I noticed that many visitors, particularly small children, appeared drained. The hectic pace of a visit to Disney is the pace many families maintain on the weekend. The traffic on the weekends is often worse than the traffic during the week, as everyone runs to children's sports events, shopping malls and movies. Returning to a job or school on Monday can be a welcome rest from a jam-packed weekend.

We have no Sabbath from busyness, media or information

input. The biblical concept of Sabbath, still practiced by many Jewish people today, envisions a time of quieting down for rest, prayer, reflection and family. Senator Joseph Lieberman's observation of Sabbath during the 2000 presidential campaign brought this practice into the spotlight. This Sabbath practice includes a stepping away from much technology and media. Years ago, Sunday was more nearly a Sabbath day for Christians. I recall from my childhood that it was often a time for extended family gatherings. Now it is probably the heaviest shopping day of the week and many Christians have no time for Sunday worship, let alone Sabbath rest.

This constant hectic pace, whether at our jobs, chores or leisure, can cause us to resent our work. We think that if we did not to go to work or do our chores, we would have more time for rest. Our addiction to action and input would more likely ensure that we would find other busyness to fill our time if our jobs and chores were less demanding. If we do not take the time to rest and reflect, we can feel like hamsters on a wheel, running and getting nowhere. The resulting fatigue shortens our tempers and lowers our patience, causing strife in our families and at our jobs.

In doing our work, we need to find a way to lessen the information and action overload we experience. Through one of the prophets, God reminded us that we are saved in returning and rest (Isaiah 30:15). Using the mindfulness practice discussed in Chapter Nine, we can take our tasks one at a time with mindful attention. This attention can slow and calm us down so that the barrage of input and activity around us does not make us anxious or unsettled.

Reflection Questions and Implementing Practices

- Write a list of all the technological means you use or

carry that connect you to others. How many times do you use each item during a week and how many outside contacts reach you through these devices each week? Estimate the percentage of those contacts that were necessary or meaningful. Consider whether you could reduce your use of or reliance on these devices.

- Keep a journal for a month recording your use of or contact with media. Note the form of media and the length of your use. How would you rank the value of the information received? Based on this record, consider whether you need to make changes in your use of or contact with media.

- Establish some Sabbath time for yourself and, if possible, those you live with each week. It does not have to be a full day, but it should be the same block of time each week. Establish guidelines for your Sabbath time. Consider eliminating contact with most media and communication devices during this period. Include some time for quiet reflection or prayer during each Sabbath period. At the end of each Sabbath period, write a brief reflection on the experience. Review these reflections to see how this Sabbath rest influences you.

[1] David Whyte, *The Heart Aroused: Poetry and the Preservation of the Soul in Corporate America* (New York: Currency, Doubleday, 1994), p. 23.

[2] Bill McKibbon, *The Age of Missing Information* (New York: Random House, 1992).

[3] Dan Andriacco, *Screen Saved: Peril and Promise of Media in Ministry* (Cincinnati: St. Anthony Messenger Press, 2000), pp. 50-53.

CHAPTER TWENTY-SEVEN

.*Power and Injustice*.

*There comes a time
when a moral man
can't obey a law
which his conscience
tells him is unjust.
And the important
thing is that when he
does that, he
willingly accepts the
penalty.*

—Martin Luther King, Jr.[1]

Abuse of power and acts of injustice can create division and dissolution in the workplace. Even within a home, there can be "power over" relationships or unequal treatment that demoralizes family members. In addressing societal allocations of power and justice, we need to ask ourselves honestly which side of the equation we are on. Am I the person with power and do I exercise it fairly? Do I engage in or allow unjust or discriminatory treatment of others? We generally prefer to see ourselves on the victim side of abuse, injustice and discrimination. Even if we are victims, how do we react to this treatment? When should we protest and when should we bear it?

Most of us believe that superiors in relationships, whether bosses or parents, are always in the power positions and are freer than subordinates, particularly if we are subordinate. If we look closer, we may see that those with power over us are those without power with respect to someone else. I used to point this out to recent law school graduates who were joining the law firm. These new attorneys, as I had some years before, believed all they had to do was work very hard, kowtowing to partners, until they, too, became partners. Then everything would magically change. As partners, they would be in charge, exercise power and would not have to answer to others. I pointed out to these new lawyers that I had observed something different in the partners at the firm. These partners were answerable to other partners, particularly those in charge of managing the firm, and their clients. Senior partners and clients could be just as abusive to junior partners as junior partners were to associates.

Every organization requires some structure and management system in order to function. Others outside the organization can significantly impose power on the organization. I saw this when I was an enforcement attorney in a government agency that regulated financial institutions. The agency's decision to bring an enforcement action would materially influence an institution. If we are in a business organization, we need to be aware of and learn to deal with the bureaucracy of the organization and the outside influences on the organization. In any organization, internal and external constituencies have differing and sometimes conflicting interests in the operation of the organization. We need to get in touch with our role in this matrix. This includes recognizing those situations in which we are exercising power and those in which we are subject to it. If we are in a position of leadership and management, we are called to treat workers with dignity.

Many American companies and even nonprofit organizations (including Catholic parishes) exploit workers or volunteers with excessive demands. The leaders of the organization feed on workers' or volunteers' fear, insecurity or guilt to coerce more effort out of them. Some managers take a "drill sergeant" approach by abusing, oppressing, punishing and degrading those who report to them. Sometimes the motivation for this conduct is abusive treatment by that managers' manager. Other times, it is a lack of knowledge about true leadership. All workers and volunteers should be treated with the respect warranted by their human dignity in God. A business should be able to get what it needs from an individual worker, while still promoting that person's growth and benefit.

In many business organizations, there are different standards applied for management officials and subordinates. I have experienced this in many places I have worked. For example, the professionals and managers in an organization are held to a standard less strict regarding office attendance than are the support staff. Many workers at all levels of an organization are unable to confront this unfairness and misuse of authority. In fact, the leaders of the organization usually encourage that fear or inaction. If you act contrary to the norm and point out these inequities, you upset the apple cart and may jeopardize your position in the organization. There are times when we must speak out against abuses in our workplaces, even if we are harmed in the process. The higher up the organization we are, the greater our obligation to speak out against injustice. We may even need to initiate corrective action to eliminate this unfairness. If we are at the lower end of the organization and are on the receiving end of abusive power, we may not be in a position to effect any change. We can consider whether remaining in the organization is an untenable affront to our human dignity. If we find it to be so, we may leave. On the other hand we can set an example by how we react to the abuse we receive. Do we whine and complain about mistreatment? Much can be said for accepting the mistreatment with endurance, voluntary acceptance and compassion for the abusers. Is that not what Jesus called us to do in the Sermon on the Mount, when he told us to love our persecutors and enemies? (Matthew 5:44).

In the culture at large, discrimination, unfair treatment and injustice are prevalent. Therefore, they are no strangers in the workplace and in our homes. Those of us in the majority or among the "haves" must conduct a careful examination of conscience to come to terms with our own actions or words of discrimination, unfair treatment and injustice. That can be very difficult, because we are not the recipients of such treatment and do not know how it feels. This issue was discussed during a class in religion. The white female teacher stated that the heightened awareness of the mistreatment of African Americans in this country had reduced inappropriate comments and actions toward African Americans to a lower level than that imposed on women in general. An African American woman in the class respectfully disagreed, indicating that the level of inappropriate comments and actions was still quite high.

Sometimes it is difficult to see mistreatment even when you are the victim of it. In the movie *Malcolm X*, one of Malcolm's coprisoners, who was seeking to convert Malcolm to the Muslim faith, walked him through the dictionary pointing out the numerous instances in which "black" or "dark" connoted evil, while "white" or "light" connoted goodness. Malcolm's eyes, as well as mine, were opened in that exercise. I believe that, as we have attempted to clean up our act on the surface, the misconduct is more underhanded. This use of the words "black" and "dark" to mean "bad" sends a message, however unconsciously sent and unconsciously received, to and about darker-skinned people. Even innocuous comments such as "the situation is black or white" can have underlying racial overtones. I recently returned to live on Long Island. Based on the 2000 census, the number of Hispanic and Asian immigrants to this area has increased greatly. I have noticed, however, that many white residents' anger or impatience with these immigrants' accents is an accepted form of discrimination, which they pass on to their children.

In our work situations and homes, we need to speak out against discrimination and injustice. At times, such protest could damage our relationship with a family member or jeopardize our continued employment. We have a responsibility to raise others' consciousness about inappropriate treatment of others. Bringing justice to our families and workplaces is heeding the call of the prophets of the Old Testament. To avoid doing so is contrary to our baptismal call and is a direct rejection of the very mission carried out by Jesus during his lifetime.

Reflection Questions and Implementing Practices

- Consider whether there is injustice or unfairness in your home or workplace. If your inclination is to say no, put yourself in the place of someone else in your home or at your job and think about how they might answer that question. Are you the victim of that injustice or unfairness? Are you in a position to reduce or eliminate that injustice or unfairness? If yes, list actions you could take in that regard and begin to implement them.

- Many of us unconsciously carry prejudices or biases. Others are more blatant about their discriminatory views. Reflect on your views about persons who are different from you. Do you make general or negative statements about certain ethnic or racial groups? Do you react differently when you meet persons from various ethnic or racial groups? Are those statements or reactions based on prejudicial preconceived notions?

[1] Martin Luther King, Jr., *The Words of Martin Luther King, Jr.* (New York: New Market Press, 1983), p. 27.

CHAPTER TWENTY-EIGHT

. *E t h i c s* .

> *Examine yourselves*
> *to see whether you*
> *are living in the*
> *faith. Test yourselves.*
> *Do you not realize*
> *that Jesus Christ is in*
> *you?... But we pray*
> *to God that you may*
> *not do anything*
> *wrong...but that you*
> *may do what is right.*
> —2 Corinthians 13:5, 7

In Chapter Twenty-one, we explored personal morality and its impact on our work. The combined morality and values of the members of a group, society or culture are reflected in the ethics of that group, society or culture. This system of ethics is derived from religious traditions, parental lessons, cultural or societal mores and lived experience. Ethics are the principles of conduct governing the conduct of the group. They define what is good and bad and what each individual's moral obligation is according to the group's values. As a group becomes larger and more diverse, its ethics are often reduced to the least common denominator of what all can accept. In seeking to embrace all in the group, the ethics system cuts corners so as not to offend anyone. Ethics are based less in religious tradition as the religious traditions within the group become numerous and varied.

Fundamental to a group's ethical system is a belief that the individual rights of members sometimes must be subservient to the needs of the group. This suppression of individual rights is particularly prevalent in Japan. In order to maintain order and decorum, people in Japan are encouraged to act under the rules of the system and not to step out with personal effort or for individual glory. The approach is not to challenge the system to the limit but to overdo compliance with the system. In America, individual rights are more primary and rules are to be challenged to the limit. During the twentieth century, the primacy of individual rights increased, as we became more isolated and less reliant on one another. Our addiction to filing lawsuits for financial redress for any harm we encounter exemplifies our "me first" mentality.

In some respects, the different generations living in the United States today are living from different ethical principles. From today's senior citizens, to baby boomers, to Generations X and Y, the fast-paced changes in our culture have produced differences in ethics among various age groups. This is evident in the differences in work ethic among these different groups. At the time this country was created, the society adopted the Protestant work ethic, which mandates strong loyalty and hard work. As the waves of immigrants arrived, they, too, adopted this ethic of hard work. Recent studies show the significant differences between the work ethic of today's immigrants and the more affluent American teens and young adults. Many young adults today have a "me first" attitude toward work. At the same time, companies are less loyal to their employees, treating them more like disposable equipment. As the relationship between companies and their employees becomes more divisive and disconnected, the morale and dignity of workers are diminished.

A work ethic establishes guiding principles for conduct in the workplace and attitudes toward jobs and chores. The general work ethic of our culture and the specific work ethic within any individual organization can either uplift or diminish human dignity. They set the tone for loyalty, diligence, dedication, honesty and fairness in the conduct of our work. The group and individual work ethic directly influence the relationship between coworkers. If disregard for company property and inattention to the task at hand is fundamental to the work ethic of employees in a company, the coworkers will have less regard and concern for each other. If a company promotes unfair practices against competitors, that unfair competition will grow rapidly within the company as well.

As we seek to embrace a more spiritual attitude in our work, we must consider the ethical principles that guide us in our work. This can be difficult, for our ego tends to view our conduct as acceptable, when it is really rooted in the ego's selfish nature. One interesting way to get in touch with our conduct is to pay attention to what we criticize in those we work with. It is human nature to criticize others' behavior that parallels our own behavior. Just think of the coworker who visits others saying how "so-and-so" does not work hard enough and spends too much time talking to other coworkers. Yet, in this myriad of conversations, that person is engaging in the same activity she is criticizing.

Ethical reflection on our own conduct requires brutal honesty and humility. Coming face to face with our own hypocrisy can be a painful experience. It is only in such a tough review that we can really understand the various ethical tenets that guide our conduct.

At this juncture in the book, we have expended effort in reconsidering the role of work in our life and our role in work. For this effort to bear any fruit in our work, our reflections need to be translated into a new work ethic and system of ethical principles to guide our conduct.

Reflection   Questions   and Implementing   Practices

- What contributed to the formation of your personal morality? How does your personal morality compare with the ethics of your family, community, church or culture? If confronted with a situation that draws a different response from your personal morality than from one of these group's ethics, which path do you take?

- What is your personal work ethic? Does it take into account the interests of your employer and coworkers? Consider whether you need to amend that work ethic to implement your reflections on this book. Articulate your work ethic in a few simple statements. Review it each day to see if you have acted in accordance with that ethic in your work that day.

PART FOUR

. Creating a Personal Spirituality of Work .

Formulating Guiding Principles or Practices for Your Personal Working Spirituality

CHAPTER TWENTY-NINE

. F o l l o w e r s
o f   J e s u s .

*Since the Word of
God became
Incarnate, the
common task of the
human race to build
a just and truly
productive society
can be endowed with
a more than human
character. It takes on
something of the
nature of a
supernatural mission,
a prolongation of the
work begun by Christ
in his historical
existence.*

—Thomas Merton[1]

The stories in the Gospels and the Acts of the Apostles tell of the passing of Jesus' new worldview to his followers. Some of the most dynamic exchanges involve the named twelve apostles.

Jesus initially gathers them merely by suggesting they follow him. At times, his exchanges with other individuals seem to be more of a lesson for the twelve disciples than for the person with whom Jesus is conversing. At times, Jesus is very harsh with the apostles and, at other times, he sets aside time to explain his parables to them. He intrigues them with questions such as "Who do you say I am?" or by violating societal norms in front of them, such as talking to women in public. He sends them out with minimal support to continue his mission on their own. In his last gathering with them, he humbles himself before them by washing their feet. Finally, in their opening to the Spirit at the first Pentecost, these twelve are inspired and strengthened to live new lives in Christ.

Jesus' encounter with the Samaritan woman at the well is an energized and dynamic conversion of an unlikely candidate (John 4:7–30). A simple request for a drink of water leads to an opening of the woman's heart and mind to a renewed spiritual understanding. Freed of her burdens, she becomes a charismatic preacher, bringing the people of her town to Jesus. Clearly, her life was changed permanently after that encounter.

When we first meet Paul, he is Saul, a Pharisee encouraging the stoning of the early followers of Jesus (Acts 7:55–8:1). As he pursues this mission against Christianity, Jesus confronts him with the error of his ways. Declaring unity with his followers, he tells Paul, "I am Jesus, whom you are persecuting" (Acts 9:5b). Given new sight and a new name, Paul becomes the greatest and most outspoken evangelist of the early church, even challenging the original apostles regarding the conditions for accepting Gentiles as Christians.

The history of the church is filled with stories of persons whose hearts and minds are transformed by the love, peace and compassion of Jesus. One of my favorites is the story of Saint Francis of Assisi. A rich young man who becomes ill while fighting in a battle, he is called to reject the wealth of his family. He hears the call of Christ to rebuild his church. Initially, Francis takes this message literally and begins to rebuild a demolished church building outside the city walls. In time, he comes to understand the true meaning of that call. He formulates a spirituality and path in response. This spirituality and path is evident in the simple lives of Francis and his original followers. In his simplicity and poverty, we are challenged to follow Christ. When I visited Francis' hermitage and the site of his death, I was humbled by his holiness and his dedication to Jesus' message.

We are no different from the twelve apostles, the woman at the well, Saint Paul or Saint Francis. In every moment, Jesus calls us to a conversion of heart and mind. We are called, prodded, intrigued, enlightened and even dragged to new ways of being in Christ. Jesus asks us to incarnate that new way of being in our daily lives.

This reflection on our work is a means to hearing Jesus call for us in our jobs and chores. Adopting our own spirituality of work, we can seek to bring Christ's presence to our work and to those it touches. Though I have referred to the spirituality of work throughout this book, I have not directly indicated what spirituality is. Attempts to define it generally fall short, because they seek to define logically something that is beyond logic. *Webster's Ninth New Collegiate Dictionary* defines the word *spirituality* as having to do with matters relating to church, religion or spirit. Others define spirituality in terms of an individual's relationship with God or an individual's path of conversion, vocation and transformation in life. Sometimes spirituality is described as integration of all creation into a balanced whole. Spirituality also may be described as free and true humanity. My preferred understanding of spirituality is living the gift of life, free and open to its joys, tribulations and sorrows.

In developing a personal spirituality of work, we are responding to the continuing call of God in our lives. Getting in touch with that call takes time in prayer, reflection and experimentation.

Reflection Questions and Implementing Practices

- Read one of the four Gospels and reflect on the various ways Jesus calls others to his way and view of life.

- Read a biography of a Catholic saint or hero that intrigues you. How did God call this individual throughout his or her life?

- Looking back, consider how God has called you throughout your life. Have you always responded to that call? How has that call changed during your life? What is that call now?

- Draft your own definition of spirituality.

[1] Thomas Merton, *Life and Holiness*, p. 97.

CHAPTER THIRTY

. A New Understanding of Work, Open to Our True Self and Free within Community.

No one sews a piece of unshrunk cloth on an old cloak; otherwise, the patch pulls away from it, the new from the old, and a worse tear is made. And no one puts new wine into old wineskins; otherwise, the wine will burst the skins, and the wine is lost, and so are the skins; but one puts new wine into fresh wineskins.

—Mark 2:21

In Part One, we reflected on how to make our work Christ's work, so that we are his continuing incarnation in the world. We considered our work as cocreation and collaboration with God. In our work we are invited to service and stewardship. This enables us to transcend our limited self-interest. Rather then viewing work as an unpleasant necessity, we sought to see it as a gift and an opportunity for thanks. As we engage in our work, we receive endless chances to hear God's call to greater love and service. This new approach to work shifts our focus from what we produce or earn to who and how we are when we are about our work. Careful attention to the present moment of our work turns our work into prayer ritual. Our work is no longer distinct from the rest of our lives and is experienced as our very life imbued with the dignity of our centeredness in God.

I hope that as you read Part One, you took the time to connect and compare the contents to your own experience and understanding. The Reflection Questions and Implementing Practices provided opportunities for this connection and comparison. If you kept notes on your reflections, you may want to go back and review them. Consider what aspects of our exploration of work challenged, troubled or confused you. Have you experienced any changes in your attitude or actions at work as you applied any new understanding about your jobs and chores?

In Part Two, I turned your attention to the inner work required to transcend the demons, ego limits and personal foibles that restrict our work. We observed our personal foibles and demons, not with the goal of eliminating or suppressing them, but of becoming aware of their influence. It is only with such awareness that these foibles and demons can be disarmed. Part Two included a reflection on how our fear and worry lock us into inaction and stagnation. We considered how anger and conflict can distort our relationships with others. We noted how our reaction to stress and time limits can make us self-centered. Our relationship toward money and desire for more things was recognized as fundamental to our attitude toward our work. The addiction of workaholism was exposed for the harm it causes in families and workplaces. Our ego and pride and our need to control were identified as causes of inflexibility and self-protection. We noted how our interaction with others or aversion to change is fundamental to how happy we are in our work. We recognized that the values we live by are evidenced in our actions, not in our stated beliefs. We learned that if we are honest with ourselves about what motivates us, the emotional baggage, ego limits and addictions are weakened, and we can act and live from freedom and love.

Each chapter of Part Two included reflections and tasks to encourage you to explore these personal limits more deeply, offering an opportunity to determine which of these limits have the strongest hold on you. Many of these tasks asked you to monitor your actions and speech when at work to observe whether they are influenced by your personal demons. Has this reflection on your personal demons weakened their hold on you? Has your conduct in or attitude toward your work changed with this better understanding of yourself? Are you more aware of the restrictions imposed on others by their own demons and ego illusions? Have you become more patient with others in recognition of this?

In Part Three, we sought a deeper understanding of the outside influences and cultural mores that can dictate our actions and form our attitudes. The groupthink of cultural, company and family biases, rules and preconceived notions triggers automatic, nonreflective responses to events and clouds our free and open perception of reality. We considered how Jesus confronted "business as usual" and groupthink and considered whether we are called to similar action. Our review of outer influences began with an overview of capitalism and our Western worldview. We considered how our American culture embraces production, money and things as signs of success and diminishes the importance of people and true living. We took note of the speed and overload of information received by us and how that affects our conduct. Power and injustice, whether imposed by or on us, can destroy human dignity. We then considered what ethics or principles we really live by, rather than give lip service to, and how the ethics of our culture may conflict with our personal morality.

Just as you were encouraged to explore your inner demons in Part Two, you were encouraged in Part Three to explore the outside forces that influence you most. Were you surprised to discover some groupthink that, unbeknownst to you, strongly influences your actions and attitudes? Are you troubled by any of the cultural perspectives or attitudes that you have adopted as your own? Have you considered speaking out against any of these group perspectives to help others be aware of these limits on their freedom?

Reflection Questions and Implementing Practices

Based on your reflections and notes on Part One, write your own spirituality of work. Consider the inner work you want to pursue in order to support taking a more spiritual approach to your work by using your reflections and notes on Part Two. Consider what elements of groupthink most restrict your openness to God and your work based on your reflections and notes on Part

Three. You can do this in a number of ways. Here are some possible formats:

- *A personal ten commandments for conducting your job and chores.*

- *A personal definition of work, including how your work reflects your relationship with God. Set three goals for the coming year to incarnate that spirituality in your work.*

- *A mission statement for meeting God in your work. List three goals to implement that mission in your work during the coming year, which should tie into all three parts of the book. Under each goal, list no more than three more specific objectives that work toward achieving each goal. Review your progress on these goals and objectives every three or four months.*

CHAPTER THIRTY-ONE

. M e d i t a t i o n   a n d   M i n d f u l n e s s .

Be still, and know that I am God!

—Psalm 46:10

In Chapter Ten, I suggested a particular form of contemplative or meditative prayer that involves sitting erect and breathing deeply, repeatedly counting exhalations up to ten. As thoughts arise, you note and then release them. I also suggested a ritual of being in the present moment by following the "just" method in Chapter Nine. Under this practice, you reduce the number of things you do at once as much as possible and focus your attention or awareness on "just" what is going on now. Though these practices may seem new or unusual to you, they are a simple introduction to Christian contemplative prayer and living.

This contemplative practice is rooted in our tradition, beginning with the life and prayer of Jesus. It became popular as many detached from the growing power of the church as it was embraced by the Roman Empire and fled to the desert to lives of prayer and solitude. The tales of these desert monks involve very few references to religious practice and piety and, instead, reflect a spirituality intertwined with the ordinary events of their lives.

For example, when one of the old monks was asked how one could be saved, he responded by continuing to braid rope. From these unusual men and women of the desert, the contemplative tradition has continued to today. It has included Saint Francis of Assisi, Saint Thomas Aquinas, Meister Eckhart, Saint Catherine of Sienna, Saint John of the Cross, Saint Teresa of Avila, Thomas Merton, Anthony de Mello, Mother Teresa and many others. Despite this longstanding tradition of contemplative prayer and living in the church, most Christians believe the contemplative life is for religious who live behind convent or monastic walls. More recently, interest in Eastern or Asian prayer forms has reopened the tradition for some Catholic laity.

The contemplative monastic tradition recognizes a connection between life inside and outside the monastery walls. A primary foundation of Christian monastic traditions is the Rule of Saint Benedict. This Rule includes an important place for work as part of the life and prayer of the community. The monks' life of prayer includes the designated prayer of the Liturgy of the Hours and their assigned tasks in the work of the community. Much of this work financially supports the community.

The Christian contemplative tradition offers a practice of prayer and living that gives increased clarity and compassion. Contemplative prayer or meditation quiets the busy mind, allowing God's vision to emerge. Carrying this careful attention to the events and circumstances of our day opens our eyes, minds and hearts to a new vision of what life is. Finding some time for solitude and silence each day can reap untold benefits in our work. We react less to inner and outer distractions and can allow the gift of life to unfold before us.

The practice of mindfulness or careful attention is fundamental to Christian and other monastic traditions. The monk's lifestyle and reduced stimuli afford him the quiet and solitude to cultivate this practice. The challenge for those of us outside monastic walls is to cultivate an inner quiet and solitude in the midst of more action and noise. The contemplative sitting practice suggested in Chapter Ten is one method to connect with this inner peace and to quiet the racing of the mind. By slowing the mind, we can bring our attention to the present moment, whatever it is, and accept it openly and freely, without judgment or critique.

In addition to the "just" method described in Chapter Nine, the use of repetitive rituals and disciplines can help us focus our attention on the "now." We can create rituals and disciplines to our work to help bring us to the present moment of our activity. Here are some examples:

As you prepare a meal, bring your attention to the actions you are taking to convert the food into a meal.

Bowing is used in many contemplative traditions as individuals enter a place of prayer or meditation. This ritual can be translated into some action you do as you begin a task or enter a place of work. You could bow, take a moment to bring your attention to what you are about to do or recite a short mantra before beginning your work.

When a chore or task is completed, bring your attention to your breath, even if for just ten seconds, before going on to the next chore or task.

To manage a full in box, set priorities for the contents. Then tend to one item at a time. If your attention goes to the pile of things still to be done, bring your mind back to the task at hand.

> *Take periodic short timeouts between each task or chore or at*
> *specific intervals during the day.*

Daily or regular rituals or disciplines around our work engender a
more grounded sense to our actions. These rituals and disciplines
can help you to approach your work, whether at home or at the
office, as one thing at a time with careful attention to the detail of
the work alone. Not only does this prevent your mind from scur-
rying to stress, anxiety, discomfort or unrelated matters, but you
will experience a kind of disappearance of self. There is just the
task or chore, and no energy in self-reflection, consideration or
critique. Our open presence to what is, the very gift of life from
God, becomes the unceasing prayer urged by Saint Paul
(Thessalonians 5:17).

Karl Rahner, a renowned theologian of the twentieth century, said in a number of different ways in several of his writings,
that the Christian of the future must be a mystic or contemplative.
This does not mean we all must sign up as a Benedictine,
Carmelite or Trappist. It is a call to rest in the depths of our soul
enveloped in and by God. Though such a state is a gift of grace,
prayer rituals, such as meditation, and spiritual disciplines, such
as mindfulness, can open us more to receive that grace freely.

Reflection Questions and Implementing Practices

- To the extent you have practiced the contemplative
  prayer form suggested in Chapter Ten, reflect on your
  experiences. If that form of quiet prayer is not appropriate for you, find out about other forms, including center-
  ing prayer and the exercises of Saint Ignatius.
  Determine, with prayer and the help of a spiritual guide,

if you have one, what form of contemplative or meditative prayer is best for you. Set up a place for this prayer in your home, with a chair or cushion for sitting and a small altar. Commit to a certain amount of this quiet prayer each day. Establish rituals for the prayer, including the use of a candle or incense.

• As you bring your attention to the present moment of your work at home or in your job, how does your attitude change? Are you as concerned about yourself? Do you find that time passes by differently?

• Establish regular rituals or disciplines that help bring you to mindful attention as you begin, conduct and complete your work.

CHAPTER THIRTY-TWO

.The Value of Our Work.

> *Do not aim at reward*
> *or blessedness,*
> *neither this nor that.*
> *For such works are*
> *truly fully dead.*
> *Indeed, I say that*
> *even if you take God*
> *as your goal, all*
> *such works which you*
> *do with this intention*
> *are dead and you*
> *will spoil good works.*
> —Meister Eckhart[1]

We can train our minds to view and approach work from more than a linear, analytical or practical perspective. Such a change in view can lead to a new appreciation of the true value of our work. When the benefit of our work is no longer limited to what we produce or earn, we get in touch with a multitude of qualitative gifts that come from our efforts. Whether paid employment or domestic chores, all our work is an opportunity to engage in relationship and to recognize our interdependence as members of the human family. As we engage in work, we impact our society and our environment. Our careful attention at our work can bring peace to those around us. No matter what we do, we contribute to the condition of our society as we engage in our jobs and chores. Even if the activity we engage in seems meaningless, our work is an opportunity to touch our family, coworkers and community. As our consciousness expands to recognize the many dimensions to our effort, our work takes on a spiritual value.

Many years ago, the pastor of my parish asked us during his sermon how our eulogy would sound if it were based entirely on a review of our calendar and checkbook. This would create a eulogy that spoke to our use of time and money, both precious commodities in our culture. I recall being challenged by that suggestion and have frequently reflected on how I would feel about a eulogy based on my calendar and checkbook. Our paid employment provides most of our financial wherewithal. Obviously, some of those funds are used to meet our needs. To the extent we have liquidity and capital in excess of our needs, we are challenged to do God's work with those excess funds. The ability to assist others who do not earn enough to meet their needs is an indirect benefit of the efforts of our work.

In Chapter Six, we saw how our work could include more than paid employment and even domestic chores. Seeking a balanced approach to how we spend our time, we can expend efforts in volunteer activities or assisting family, neighborhood and friends. Such assistance can even be done in a coordinated effort with coworkers or immediate family members. In employment that does not outwardly involve service, we can provide service in our treatment of coworkers, bosses and others encountered on the job. As we noted earlier in the story of Mary and Martha, the issue was not that Mary's conduct was better or more holy than Martha's. Each woman was called, in that moment, to a different task, one to the preparation of the meal and the other to receiving spiritual guidance from Jesus. In each moment, we are called to different tasks, whether at home, work or play. One activity is not preferable or better than the other activity.

Our skills and expertise at our jobs can benefit others if we take them to organizations that provide social services to those in need. I have served on a number of boards of nonprofit organizations. In each instance, other board members and I were able to bring the expertise gained in our paid employment to these groups and charities. Such acquired ability is an indirect value of our efforts in our jobs.

By getting more in touch with the rhythm and circumstances of our actions at work and broadening our view of the impact of those actions, we may redefine what is or should be the "true fruit of our toil." Rather than be burdened by dashed expectations or restricted by quantitative measures, we can seek an inner satisfaction from the qualitative impact of our efforts. The daily bread we pray for in the Lord's Prayer can include this positive progress or reaction to our daily work.

A new valuation of our work needs to include a review of the types of work we do and the time and effort expended for each. Open to change and choice, we need to consider whether the work we engage in should or can continue in the same fashion. All change and choice involves some letting go. We may find that our meticulous housecleaning inappropriately reduces our time for God, family and friends. We may need to choose between bearing a difficult job with grace or seeking other employment, despite the financial risk. As we consider changes in our work, we need to take into account both quantitative and qualitative elements in that work and the broadened spiritual stance on work we have acquired.

I often have suggested to others that they should not leave a job they claim to hate until they come to terms with those feelings. Otherwise, they will carry those negative feelings to their next employment situation. I recommend that they learn to deal more positively with the difficulties on the current job and determine how they are responsible for some of those difficulties. This opportunity to reflect on our contribution to our suffering is a value of a seemingly bad job.

Sometimes small changes in our attitude toward our current work situation can bear great fruit. My friend Teresa told me about an encounter with a coworker who complained of a situation that could not be changed. She said that if this individual used all the energy expended on complaining to change her attitude toward the situation, then the task they were discussing could have been completed.

An expanded recognition of the value of our work can bring satisfaction to us in situations previously deemed meaningless. It also helps to recognize the ways we benefit from the efforts we make in our work.

Reflection Questions and Implementing Practices

- What is the value of your domestic chores and tasks?

- What do you value about your job? When seeking employment, what do you value in potential new jobs?

- How have you used your talents or gifts from your employment in other situations?

[1] Meister Eckhart, quoted in Matthew Fox, *Breakthrough*, p. 464.

CHAPTER THIRTY-THREE

Work as Sacrament, Liturgy and Mystery.

*Think of us in this
way, as servants of
Christ and stewards
of God's mysteries.*

—1 Corinthians 4:1

We all have a tendency to view religious practice as something related to church and directly involving God. When most Catholics consider sacrament, liturgy and mystery, they think of the seven sacraments, the Mass and religious matters that cannot be readily explained.

Before the Second Vatican Council, *sacrament* generally meant the seven specific church rituals, which were seen as a means to receive special graces. In Vatican II, the concept of sacrament was expanded beyond the seven designated sacraments. Jesus was described as the sacrament of God, for he was a visible manifestation of the hidden presence of God in the world. The church, as his body, is, similarly, the sacrament of Christ, for it is the incarnation of Christ's presence in the world with the aid of the Holy Spirit. In the new *Catechism*, sacraments are defined as "efficacious signs of grace, instituted by Christ and entrusted to the Church, by which divine life is dispensed to us" (*Catechism of the Catholic Church*, 1131). In essence, anything that is a visible sign of God's reality in our midst is a form of sacrament.

Our work can be a sacrament. We are created in God's image and are called to continue the work of Christ in our world. Therefore, our work is a means to communicate or effect the love and presence of God in our midst. As Saint Paul said, "it is no longer I who live, but it is Christ who lives in me" (Galatians 2:20). When we are at work, it is Christ who folds the laundry, builds the cabinet, medicates the patient or sells the mutual fund shares. Christ's compassion, mercy and peace are spread to others by our words and actions.

The Mass consists of two liturgies (with shorter rites to open and close the celebration). The Liturgy of the Word consists primarily of the reading of passages from the Old Testament (particularly the Psalms), the Epistles (particularly the Letters of Paul) and the Gospels. This is followed by the homily, which serves to break open these Scriptures in order to give them meaning and transforming power in our lives. It concludes with the recitation of the Creed and of petitions to God, which remind us of our dependence on God. In this reflection, we are given an opportunity to review the events of our lives in the context of these stories and basic dogmas of our faith. Such a review serves as an examination of conscience. We have the chance to reevaluate the events of our life in light of God's plan, and not our own. That review can open us to a personal transformation and challenge to respond to the call of our faith and our God. Our attitudes, actions and relationships of work are necessarily part of the dialogue between God's

Word and our lived experience.

In the Liturgy of the Eucharist and its recelebration of the Lord's Supper, bread and wine are offered up in the Eucharistic Prayer and consecrated into the Body and Blood of Christ. Members of the assembly bring up the bread and wine in the Presentation of the Gifts, often with the collection of contributions from the assembly. This ritual tells us that the bread and wine offered to God symbolize the combined experiences, efforts and existence of those assembled. The words of the Eucharistic Prayer are the words of the assembly, who authorize the priest to speak these words of thanksgiving on their behalf when they say, "It is right to give him thanks and praise." So in the Liturgy of the Eucharist, we bring the success, failures, efforts and difficulties of our work to the altar with those of all assembled and all in the world. As the bread and wine are lifted up to God in the consecration, so in a sense, is our work. God accepts and blesses these gifts, recognizing them as holy.

Our work is liturgy itself. Liturgy originally meant the public work of the people. The prayer of our life is as much a worship of God as the prayers of the Mass. Our efforts, conduct and attitude in our work can be just as much a giving of thanks to God as the Eucharistic Prayer. With this understanding, the rituals of the Mass and the rituals of our work become a seamless manifestation of our being in God. There is no separation between them, for our work and praise are one.

Among many Catholics, the response, "It's a mystery," is a comical explanation for any matter, religious or not, that makes no sense or cannot be explained. One of the readily designated mysteries in our faith is that of the Trinity. In our inability to comprehend three as one and one as three, we chalk it up to mystery. The concept of mystery in our faith comes from the Greek word *mysterion*, which did not mean that something was unknown. It indicated an indirect path to understanding. This understanding came less from reason and intellect and more from intuition and spirit. Therefore, the recognition of mystery in our faith is not meant to provide a pat answer for when no direct answer exists. The recognition of mystery provides a new way of thinking in order to come to some understanding.

We can bring this concept of mystery to our work. How often is the meaning of our work not apparent to us? Certain types of work are not valued by our society. These negative forms of groupthink can cause an individual in work that is not valued to have a demeaned view of his or her efforts. By seeing the meaning of such work as mystery, in prayer and reflection, that individual may be able to find the deeper meaning and value of those efforts. The small role our efforts play in the grand scheme of all human work also is a mystery. Though we may never come to grips with what that connection is, we can imagine some of it and allow the rest to be.

Reflection Questions and Implementing Practices

- How is your work liturgy? How does your work relate to the celebration of the Eucharist?

- How is your work a sacrament of God? How do you make God visible in the actions and speech of your work?

- How do you understand mystery? How is your work a mystery?

CHAPTER THIRTY-FOUR

. *R e t u r n   t o   t h e*
M a r k e t p l a c e .

*I sort of am myself
for a living.*

—James Taylor, musician[1]

In the last chapter, our consideration of work took a more religious tone as our work was woven into our Catholic notions of sacrament, liturgy and mystery. The ruminations of the previous chapters attempted to imbue work with a new spirituality and explored the personal and cultural barriers to our embracing that spirituality. Our understanding of work was broadened and linked to our entire lives. We have sought to become more attentive in our work, seeking a deeper awareness of the contact and impact of our attitude and actions. Through the Reflection Questions and Implementing Practices, we have pondered new perspectives, regimented new rituals and assembled a new approach to our work. So now what?

A short tale told by Meister Eckhart comes to mind. Meister Eckhart, a popular preacher among the common folk, was once asked what a person who has had a major spiritual insight or awakening while working in a stable should do next. Our inclination may be to respond with advice to run to a priest or spiritual director, to pray or to join a religious order. Meister Eckhart's response was that the individual should return to the work at hand in the stable. Jack Kornfield, a Buddhist teacher, promotes this thinking in the title of his recent book, *After the Ecstasy, the Laundry*.[2] For a spiritual path to have any true meaning and impact, it must be incarnated in our ordinary lived experience. Otherwise, our spirituality becomes a pious pacifier that anesthetizes or distances us from the joys and struggles of human existence.

So now it is time for you and for me to return to our work in the stable or to do the laundry. As I complete this book, I am preparing to reenter the legal profession. I realize I have set a challenging task for myself. I must practice what I have preached in this book. My ruminations here are meaningless if I cannot incarnate them in my future work experiences.

This is also true for you. After spending time and effort reading this book, answering the questions and performing the practices at the end of each chapter, it is time to embody these reflections and disciplines in the matter at hand—your jobs, chores and play. I hope for each of you that you return to your work with a new view, new value and new purpose.

Reflection Questions and Implementing Practices

- What aspects of your work have you seen in new ways in the course of reading this book?

- Draft a personal prayer for your work and recite it each day. Turn to it during difficult times in your work.

---

[1] James Taylor, from "James Taylor: Through Fire and Rain," *CBS News: 60 Minutes II*, CBS Worldwide, Inc., www.cbsnews.com/now/story/0,1597,256349-412,00.shtml.

[2] Jack Kornfield, *After the Ecstasy, the Laundry: How the Heart Grows Wise on the Spiritual Path* (New York: Bantam Books, 2000).

Input-Output and Regional Economic

Input-Output and Regional Economics

Harry W. Richardson

A HALSTED PRESS BOOK

JOHN WILEY & SONS
New York

Published in the U.S.A. by Halsted Press,
a Division of John Wiley & Sons Inc. New York.

ISBN 0 470–71954–0

Library of Congress Catalog Card No: 72 - 6873

Printed in Great Britain

Contents

Abbreviations

BLS	Bureau of Labor Statistics
CBD	Central Business District
CIQ	Cross-Industry Quotient
fob	free on board
GNP	Gross National Product
GRP	Gross Regional Product
HERP	Harvard Economic Research Project
ICC	Interstate Commerce Commission
I-O	Input-Output
LP	Linear Programming
LQ	Location Quotient
NASA	National Aeronautics and Space Administration
OBE	Office of Business Economics
RIOT	Regional Input-Output Table
SDP	Supply-Demand Pool
SEG	Social, Environmental and Governmental
SIC	Standard Industrial Classification
TAP	Technique for Area Planning

Preface

The objective in writing this book was to describe regional input-output techniques and to show the usefulness and limitations of input-output as a practical tool for regional economic analysis. It was a considerable advantage during the period over which the book was written to be engaged on empirical research projects in the regional input-output field financed by the Social Science Research Council. I am very grateful to Dr Geoffrey Hewings for many discussions about regional input-output analysis in the early stages and to Ian R. Gordon for reading the whole manuscript. I also wish to thank Dr Peter Victor for allowing me to look at his Ph.D thesis prior to its submission. As on many other occasions I am greatly indebted to Mrs Sandy Sharples for all the typing.

Harry W. Richardson

1972

1 Introduction

Input-output economics is a well-established, almost an old-fashioned, branch of economics – after all, it has now been with us for forty years. It is true that its regional applications have been more recent – less than twenty years old with a rapid acceleration in the quantity of work in the past few years – but even so they can scarcely be treated as a novelty. Despite its simplistic assumptions, input-output analysis has shown a remarkable degree of persistence. Perhaps at the national level there has been some slackening of interest, particularly in countries where short-term econometric forecasting has taken predominance over sectoral planning, but at the regional level interest is stronger than ever. An important reason for this is that input-output techniques can be implemented empirically in a field where data shortages and underdeveloped theoretical constructs restrict the scope for hard empirical research.

A strange feature about regional input-output analysis is that attitudes towards its usefulness and validity tend to be very extreme. Every regional economist seems to be either its dauntless champion or its fierce detractor. The aim of this book is to present a more balanced judgement. Whatever the limitations of the input-output approach, the regional economist must give it serious consideration. It provides virtually the sole avenue of escape from partial equilibrium analysis. The other general equilibrium theories available, Walrasian neo-classical price analysis and neo-Keynesian interregional macroeconomics, may be a little more satisfying theoretically but they are much more difficult to apply empirically. In particular, interregional trade flows are much easier to measure and make consistent with theory within an input-output framework. Moreover, some versions of interregional input-output models (of which the Leontief-Strout [149, 1963] gravity technique is typical) have the added advantage for analysis of the space economy that they take distance, in the form of transport costs, explicitly into account as a relevant variable. Another feature of the input-output model is that it is 'neutral' from a policy point of view – a fact that partly explains its appeal to western and communist, industrial and underdeveloped economies alike. At the same time, however, it has become possible in more recent years to extend an input-output model into an optimisation technique by converting it into a linear programming model.

These advantages go a long way to offset the well-known drawbacks – the restrictive assumptions, the high costs involved in obtaining the data required, the practical obstacles in the way of operationalising the dynamic models needed for long-run regional planning.

Because of its unique qualities, regional economists have had to stand up and be counted on their attitude to input-output analysis. Most regional economists have dabbled with the technique at one time or another. Their involvement can usually be traced to pragmatic grounds – that, given the objectives of their research, input-output was the most useful technique currently available. Perhaps the most striking case of this conversion is the work of the late Professor Charles M. Tiebout. Tiebout was responsible in 1957 for the most trenchant general criticisms of regional input-output models (248). Needleman's comment (191, 1968, p. 17) that 'His warnings of the difficulties involved in constructing and interpreting regional input-output tables have not been challenged, but neither have they prevented a proliferation of such studies since he wrote' neglects the fact that input-output analysts such as Miernyk and Shellhammer (171, 1970, pp. xix-xx) have answered these criticisms directly. Even more important, it ignores the subsequent change of heart by Tiebout himself. He spent the last five years of his life before his tragic early death in 1968 predominantly engaged in regional input-output research. His final paper was an attempt to project long-term regional growth of income and employment in Washington State up to 1980 from the 1963 Washington input-output table (251, 1969). In view of the fact that long-run projections are perhaps one of the more dubious uses of the regional input-output model, the gap between the writings of 1957 and 1967 is very wide indeed. I do not wish to start an argument as to whether the later Tiebout was more correct than the early Tiebout; perhaps the reader should make his own judgement at the end of the book. However, I would suggest that the regional economist who closes his eyes to the input-output approach throughout his working life has unnecessarily restricted his field of vision.

Finally, it should be pointed out that this book is not concerned with the intricate technicalities of input-output analysis or the higher reaches of input-output mathematics. Rather it is written for the regional economist with the specific intention of examining, in relatively non-technical terms, the scope for and limitations of the input-output approach in his particular branch of economic science. As such, it is as much a book about regional economics as about input-output techniques. This point became more and more clear to me, even as the book was being written. It proved necessary to give a fair amount of attention to several central themes of regional economics in order to do justice to the regional applications of input-output analysis. Such themes include comparison of national with regional economic structures and production functions, regional income and economic base multiplier analysis, the measurement of economic impacts on local communities, the measurement and stability of interregional trade, the uses of certain well-known regional techniques of analysis from location quotients to linear programming and gravity models, some principles of urban economics, regional economic forecasting, and the determinants of regional investment. All this explains why I deliberately chose the title *Input-Output and Regional Economics* in preference to the less clumsy *Regional Input-Output Analysis* that I had originally intended.

PART ONE: Theory

2 Input-Output Analysis

The development and nature of input-output

The first empirical application of the input-output model in the Anglo-American world dates from 1936 when Leontief published an input-output system of the United States economy (Leontief, **138**, 1936). However, Leontief's work on this development at Harvard dates back to 1931, while the first table of interindustry relations (of the Soviet economy) had been published in 1925. As has been frequently pointed out, the origins of input-output analysis go back much further in time. The circular flow and general equilibrium concepts and the emphasis on interindustry relations may be traced back to François Quesnay's *Tableau Economique* of 1758, while the interdependence between the production sectors of the economy stressed in Walras's general equilibrium model of the 1870s also has a notable place in the family tree. Indeed, as Dorfman pointed out (**57**, 1954, p. 121), what Leontief did was to simplify Walras's generalised model drastically to the point where the model's equations could be estimated empirically. This involved two radical assumptions. First, the large number of commodities in the Walrasian model was aggregated into a relatively few outputs, one for each industrial sector of the economy. Second, the supply equations for labour and the demand equations for final consumption were abandoned and the remaining production equations expressed in their simplest, linear, form.

The aggregation process is adopted to reduce artificially

the number of equations and unknowns. For theoretical purposes it was reasonable to assume that an input-output sector consisted of plants producing a single homogeneous product with similar techniques. But the translation into an empirical tool involved lumping together many separate activities into one sector. The prevalence of multiproduct plants makes it impossible to group together only those plants with similar output and input structures. The practical solution is to group processes and products which differ in some respects but which behave sufficiently uniformly to be used as a basis for aggregation. The emphasis on linear production relationships also creates its problems. The essence of the Leontief model is the technological relationship that the purchases of any sector (except final demand) from any other sector depend, via a linear production function, on the level of output of the purchasing sector. The constant and linear production function assumption solves all kinds of difficulties: for instance it gets rid of factor substitution and economies of scale, but it creates others. Time is missing, yet the purchase of inputs by one industry to make goods to sell to other industries implies a period analysis. Assuming away substitution may simplify matters, but it leads to a sharp difference between input-output and most other conventional economic models. Moreover, the notion of a linear production function is not very meaningful in many non-industrial sectors such as agriculture, trade, service industries and the government sector. The model is starkly simple. Its key variables are the outputs of sectors into which the economy is divided. Each sector's output consists of summing its sales to all other sectors and to final demand (consumption, investment, exports and non-local government). The amount of each product which each sector consumes depends *only* on the level of output in the consuming sector. Equilibrium in the economy is attained when the output of each sector equals total purchases from that sector, these purchases being determined by the outputs of all other sectors. None of the usual economic assumptions (profit maximisation, optimal resource allocation, consumer utility maximisation, etc.) crop up in this model. Everything is governed by 'the dictates of productive necessity: each output requires its inputs and that is all there is to it' (Dorfman, 57, 1954, p. 125).

The apparent naivety of the model's assumptions is misleading, and is in any event offset by many compensating advantages. The departure from reality of the assumptions was intended to reduce the variables in the model to sizeable proportions. The gain has been that input-output models are empirically implementable, and do not have to be put on ice to wait for the utopia of perfect data and no computer capacity constraints. Moreover, the implausible assumptions of the production function straitjacket do not appear to have turned out too badly. It is possible for money values to be used as a measure of physical purchases in real terms, since relative price changes do not distort too much the input purchase pattern per unit of output. The pace of technological change is slow enough for the input coefficient matrix of one year to be assumed to hold in the years before and after, and the major year-to-year changes take the form of variations in sales to final demand. Even if there is a bias due to technical change this almost invariably shows itself as too large a total of inputs required when the old co-efficients are used. Thus, even an out-of-date table will show something of value, i.e. the maximum input requirements. Perhaps most important of all, input-output models pass the critical test that for many purposes they predict reasonably well.

Progress in the development of national input-output models proceeded in the 1940s and 1950s. A more complete version of the 1936 study was made available in 1941 with the publication of *The Structure of the United States Economy, 1919-39*. The work was continued in the period 1942-4 at the Bureau of Labor Statistics. A ninety-six (later reduced to forty-six) sector table for the United States in 1939 was developed, and in 1944 the first practical application was made with an exercise aimed at estimating the effects of the ending of the war on employment. Two years later the BLS forecasts *Full Employment Patterns: 1950* were published. In 1949 the preparation of a two hundred sector input-output table for 1947 was put in hand based on data made available for about five hundred sectors. The next United States table was constructed only after a considerable time gap; the eighty-one sector table for 1958 was not published until November 1964. This table was probably too highly aggregated for an economy as complex as that of the

United States, and the 1963 United States table published in 1969 contained 370 sectors. Meanwhile in the United Kingdom early input-output work on 1948 data led to the construction of a full table for 1954; a seventy sector table for 1963 has recently been published and the development of the 1968 table is under way. This work was undertaken within the government, but simultaneously important research was being carried out at Cambridge on the Social Accounting Matrix. In several other countries, most notably Holland, Japan and some of the communist bloc countries, work on the construction of input-output tables has been even more impressive.

The chronology is running ahead of events. Turning back to the beginning of the 1950s there were one or two key theoretical developments which generalised the input-output model and made it more satisfying as a theoretical structure. In 1951 Samuelson, Koopmans and Arrow showed how the possibility of substitution could be introduced into the input-output model, thereby giving it much wider generality. The Samuelson theorem, as it is called (Samuelson, **215**, 1951), assumes that each industry produces only one commodity and that each industry uses only one scarce primary factor which is homogeneous for all industries. If it is further assumed that there are constant returns to scale, Samuelson found that even if each industry had a wide choice of alternative production processes it is compatible with overall efficiency for each industry to use only one of the processes available to it. Moreover, and this is the crucial point, this same process can be used regardless of the commodity composition of the net output of all industries taken together and regardless of the quantity of labour available. In the long run, a more important development was the work on linear programming and activity analysis by Dantzig and Koopmans (Dantzig, **53**, 1949, and Koopmans, **132**, 1951). Linear programming and input-output analysis are closely related, and the former can convert the latter into an optimisation procedure. This affinity has considerable potential in regional analysis, as will be explained later (see Chapter 10).

The development of regional input-output analysis also dates from the early 1950s. First, there was a spate of studies constructing regional input-output tables. These were rather crude operations by today's standards, since unadjusted national input coefficients were used. From these, combined with regional control totals of gross output, it was possible to derive an interindustry transactions flow table. However, there was no reason to expect national and regional input structures to be identical, and even the format of the tables produced was merely a miniature version of the national table with highly aggregated import and export flows. In a complete regional model the aim would be to disaggregate output by sector and by regions of origin and destination so that the model describes interregional trade as well as regional production. The second category of regional input-output research in the early 1950s was more on these lines, but was more theoretical and conceptual. The practical importance of this work has become apparent only in recent years. Isard outlined the structure of his 'ideal' interregional model in 1951 (Isard, **107**, 1951), an ideal yet to be implemented since it requires treating a regional industry as if it were an entirely different industry from the same industry in another region. Thus, a forty-region, eighty-industry model becomes equivalent to an input-output table containing 3,200 sectors. Nevertheless, the Isard model has become a yardstick against which the recent empirical interregional input-output studies can be measured. Of more direct relevance was the first attempt by Moses in 1955 (Moses, **185**, 1955) to implement empirically, albeit at a crude level and with very imperfect data, an interregional model for the United States. About the same time, Chenery developed a two-region model for Italy (Chenery, **40**, 1953). There is a direct link between these pioneering studies and the recent ambitious Harvard Multiregional Input-Output model (Polenske, **205**, 1970). Another important piece of work of the same period was the Isard-Kuenne analysis of how to measure the economic impact of expansion of a major industry on a region (Isard and Kuenne, **110**, 1953). At the same time, Leontief (**140**, 1953) developed his intranational model which showed how regional interaction could be traced through a hierarchy of regions, and thereby presented a framework for evaluating the impact of national-market industries on local economies; in essence, the intranational model was a half-way house between an interregional model and an economic impact study. These were the forerunners of the economic impact studies that have become commonplace in recent years. In addition, the Isard-Kuenne study showed how it might be feasible to take some account of agglomeration effects by treating the local direct input requirements of expanded output in the major industry as new additions to final demand.

These latter developments have had more impact on the pattern of regional input-output research in the last few years than they had at the time. More immediate results were obtained from regional rather than interregional models, and in particular from work which tackled the problem that regional production functions might differ from the national. If this were so, the use of unadjusted national input coefficients could not be justified. Moore and Petersen (181, 1955) were the first regional analysts to adjust national coefficients for a regional table to take account of 'differences in regional production processes, marketing practices, or product-mix'. A few years later Hirsch (96, 1959) published his St Louis MA study in which the input and output data were obtained, at least for large and medium firms, by survey. This set the pattern for regional input-output studies in the 1960s. In order to receive the regional analyst's stamp of approval, it became necessary to produce technical coefficients for any sub-national study area via the sales and purchase flows derived from a field survey of establishments. However, despite improvements in survey methods and in efficient sample design, this procedure was costly when the study area was large or the area's industrial structure complex. Accordingly, in recent years renewed efforts have been made to devise adjustment techniques to operate on the national input-output coefficients that are sufficiently precise to yield reasonable predictions. Although the survey-based regional input-output table is still the most common type of study, secondary data-based tables are becoming more frequent especially in cases where time and cost constraints are severe. A more satisfactory alternative, as yet little tested, would be for an adjusted coefficients table to be reinforced with survey-based rows and columns for key sectors.

The pace of progress in regional input-output research has accelerated in the last decade. A few of the important landmarks are: the detailed economic impact analysis of the effects of the space programme on the Boulder economy; the highly disaggregated (496 sectors plus 86 final demand sectors) Philadelphia input-output table; the very professional and careful study of input-output relations in 1963 in Washington State; the Harvard multiregional model; the attempt to implement a dynamic regional input-output model for the West Virginia economy; Moses's pioneering empirical implementation of an interregional input-output linear programming model for the United States (Moses, **186**, 1960); the Leontief-Strout gravity technique which opened up new possibilities for interregional analysis (Leontief and Strout, **149**, 1963); Tiebout's application of the Washington model for long-run forecasting (Tiebout, **251**, 1969); the work on secondary data technical coefficients associated with Shen, Czamanski and Malizia, Schaffer and Chu, and others. The significance of these and other major developments will be assessed later in the book.

Considered together, the regional input-output research of the last twenty years makes an impressive case for the value of input-output as a tool of regional analysis. At its minimum, it offers a form of regional social accounts with built-in consistency checks. These checks on data can be very useful at the regional level because of the imperfections in regional statistics. However, when the interindustry flows table is expressed in constant coefficient form and converted into a direct and indirect coefficients table (the Leontief inverse matrix; see below, pp. 26-30, 37-42) it becomes an operational analytical tool with a wide variety of uses: measuring the economic interdependence of the region's industrial structure; providing a set of disaggregated multipliers that are more precise and sensitive than the Keynesian income multiplier; calculating the effects on economic activity in individual regions of changes in the level and pattern of national demand; evaluating other economic impacts, i.e. any change in final demand; and as a technique for long-run projections and forecasts. This flexibility as an operational technique is partially offset by the theoretical weaknesses (or rather incompleteness) of input-output analysis. For instance, it cannot handle very well the effects of interregional competitive forces, such as the impact of technological change or lower factor prices in one region on output, prices and incomes in other regions. Trade patterns can be explained only by integrating a trade submodel with an input-output model, and the fact of regional trade also creates empirical difficulties, since import coefficients may be less stable than input coefficients. Finally, input-output models are ill-equipped to explain or predict the dynamics of structural change, such as entry of new industries or the obsolescence and disappearance of old ones. These deficiencies should not lead the analyst to lose faith in regional input-output models. However, they serve as a reminder that there are regional problems for which input-output analysis can offer no solutions, and there are others where input-output is only useful as a supplemental tool.

Input-output accounts

An input-output table fulfils two separate functions. First, it is a descriptive framework for showing the relationship between industries and sectors and between inputs and outputs. Second, given certain economic assumptions about the nature of production functions, it is an analytical tool for measuring the impact of autonomous disturbances on an economy's output and income. A set of input-output accounts is, first and foremost, a mode of description. If data are available or collected to set down the economic interrelationships of an area in input-output form, then the resulting accounts will be useful and valid for demonstration and consistency-checking purposes even if we reject input-output theory. The distinction between an input-output account and an operational input-output model is an important one. The former does not necessarily imply the latter, though it is fair to say that those who prefer input-output accounts to more traditional macroeconomic income accounts usually do so because of their faith in the scope for practical applications and in the utility of input-output *models.*

The major difference between input-output and income accounts is that input-output accounts break down the business sector into a large number of individual industries or sectors and record the transactions that flow between each sector; these intersectoral flows are shown as an interindustry transactions matrix in the account. Apart from this, an input-output account contains more or less the same kind of information found in national (or regional) income accounts, though occasionally in a slightly different form. For instance, the major components of GNP (GRP) as estimated by the expenditure and income methods are usually both obtainable from an input-output table. The final demand segment of an input-output table frequently divides final goods and services into the same expenditure categories (consumption, investment, government and exports) as are found in national accounts. Similarly, the value-added rows of an input-output table may consist of entries (wages and salaries, profit, interest and rent) similar to those used in the factor incomes approach to the measurement of GNP (GRP). Since most of the information found in basic income accounts is also required in input-output accounts, the latter provides a much more comprehensive accounting framework. Income accounts, on the other hand, are unable to show all the changes observable in an input-output table. For instance, shifts in demand from one commodity to another would go unnoticed in an income accounting scheme if total consumption remained constant, but such shifts would be revealed in an appropriately disaggregated input-output account. This is not merely a question of factual detail since relative demand shifts within a constant expenditure total can have extensive repercussions on total output via changes in interindustry transactions, and these can only be observed in an input-output framework. Although input-output accounts can be made consistent with income accounts, their emphasis is different. The dominant concern of income accounts is the composition of final demand, while input-output accounts focus more on the interindustry transactions that lie behind changes in final demand.

This difference in emphasis not only reflects a difference in appearance and layout between the two forms of account but, even more, is explained by the use made of input-output models. At this point, the distinction between the descriptive accounting framework and the operational tool of analysis becomes very blurred. The design of input-output accounts divides the economic structure of the economy into endogenous and exogenous sectors, somewhat analogous to the distinction between 'autonomous' and 'induced' elements in income theory. However, the latter is not shown in a set of income accounts, whereas the endogenous (the intersectoral matrix) and the exogenous portions of the input-output table are clearly demarcated. Although this sharp statistical division masks a certain degree of arbitrariness and ambiguity in the theory behind the table, it is on balance another advantage of input-output over income accounts. The endogenous-exogenous distinction is revealed in the division of outputs into two categories intermediate and final demand and of inputs into 'produced' and 'primary' (e.g. labour, capital). These divisions enable the analyst, when the table is used as a tool rather than merely an account, to work out the effects of an exogenous disturbance, i.e. a change in final demand, on interindustry transactions and hence on total production in each sector of the economy.

In a regional context, two other comments on the difference between input-output and income accounts are appropriate. First, though regional input-output accounts may be based on data provided periodically, they are most unlikely to be constructed on the annual or quarterly basis characteristic of income accounts. This is partly due to the fact that regional problems and policies are primarily of a long-term nature and hence annual accounts would be something of a luxury, but the primary reason is the cost of collecting data. Since much of the information needed for a set of regional input-output accounts would probably have to be collected via sample surveys of industrial and commercial firms, the costs of an annual table could be prohibitive. Second, the case for an input-output accounting scheme is strengthened at the regional level because of the importance of location factors and industrial structure in regional economies. Regional income is clearly affected by industrial structure, but the industrial structures of regions vary a great deal as a result of differences in locational requirements. A main component of regional income change will be locational shifts in industry, and consequently an industry breakdown of accounts may be critical for regional analysis and projection. In other words, although the input-output table itself does not contain explicit spatial variables, many of the changes that feature in such a table reflect spatial shifts in economic activity between regions. The advantages of an input-output approach are further reinforced by the importance of interregional trade in regional analysis. As any student of international trade knows, structural changes in trade are most easily understood when we have commodity or industry distributions. Since changes in interregional trade and in regional production are interdependent, the sectoral disaggregation offered by an input-output accounting scheme may be essential to analysis of regional economies. For instance, the multiplier effects of shifts in location or changes in regional trade may be accurately estimated with the aid of an interindustry model, whereas adoption of an aggregate income approach might yield only very crude results.

As the above remarks suggest, the utility of regional input-output accounts extends from the more banal descriptive purposes of any accounting system to the practical concrete applications of an input-output model. Since an input-output table is in itself an accounting system, and the prior existence of a table is obviously necessary for input-output analysis, it is evident that the input-output analyst cannot bypass the preliminaries of input-output accounting. This contrasts with regional income theory, for instance, where although a set of income accounts would be desirable its absence does not prevent analysis. As Hoover and Chinitz (**102**, 1961) pointed out, regional accounts have two main uses: consistency-checking and impact evaluation. The latter merges with the analytical objectives of economic models, and in fact this is what this book is about. Discussion of the consistency-checking function of regional input-output accounts, however, will be confined to a few brief remarks.

Consistency checks take many forms: checks on both sides of a single interindustry transaction flow, i.e. that the sales of industry *i* to industry *j* are consistent with industry *j*'s estimate of purchases from *i*; summing the sales (or purchases) of industry *i* to (or from) all other sectors and to final demand (or from primary inputs) and checking these against industry *i*'s total sales (or purchases), especially if independent estimates of industrial output are available; balancing the inputs and outputs of each sector, i.e. checking their column and row sums; the overall balance of the input-output account, i.e. the identity of value added (gross regional income) and local final demand plus net exports (gross regional product). Internal and external consistency are aided by comprehensiveness and by comparability with the accounts for other regions and by national-regional comparisons. Input-output accounts are probably more comprehensive than any alternative form of accounts, especially if the core account is supplemented by subsidiary accounts for capital stock, labour supply, land use, etc. The comparability of regional input-output accounts is a much more troublesome question, since regional size, industry definitions, the degree of aggregation adopted both in the matrix and in the exogenous parts of the input-output table, and accounting conventions differ widely from one regional input-output table to another. This reflects the fact that in most countries centrally collected data are not available for individual regional input-output tables. The failure to standardise regional input-output tables has provided the major impetus to the design and development of multiregional projects.

Fig. 1 represents an input-output transactions (or gross flows) table. It is not a regional table *per se,* since national tables are usually drawn up in this way. However, although there is a great variety of forms that regional models might take, particularly variations in methods of dealing with external trade, this is the standard layout for regional models. Although the table is in simplified form with certain entries highly aggregated and certain minor transactions omitted, it is useful for demonstrating key accounting identities. These are obtained by summing across the rows and down the columns. For instance, row *i* in the table shows the sales of industry *i* to all other industries (intermediate demand) and to consumption, private investment, government spending and exports (which are the components of final demand); intermediate demand plus final demand measures total gross output (or sales) of industry *i*. Thus in a *n* sector model:

$$X_i = \sum_j^n X_{ij} + (C_i + I_i + G_i + E_i). \qquad (2.1)$$

Gross	Intermediate	Final
output	demand	demand

Fig. 1   Simplified, input-output transactions table

To / From	Purchasing sectors $1 \ldots j \ldots n$	Local final demand Households	Private investment	Government	Exports	Total gross output
1	$X_{11} \ldots X_{1j} \ldots X_{1n}$	C_1	I_1	G_1	E_1	X_1
.	.	.	.	.	.	.
.	.	.	.	.	.	.
i (Producing sectors)	$X_{i1} \ldots X_{ij} \ldots X_{in}$	C_i	I_i	G_i	E_i	X_i
.	.	.	.	.	.	.
.	.	.	.	.	.	.
n	$X_{n1} \ldots X_{nj} \ldots X_{nn}$	C_n	I_n	G_n	E_n	X_n
Labour	$L_1 \ldots L_j \ldots L_n$	L_C	L_I	L_G	L_E	L
Other value added	$V_1 \ldots V_j \ldots V_n$	V_C	V_I	V_G	V_E	V
Imports	$M_1 \ldots M_j \ldots M_n$	M_C	M_I	M_G	–	M
Total gross outlay	$X_1 \ldots X_j \ldots X_n$	C	I	G	E	X

Conversely, column *j* shows the purchases of industry *j* from all other industries (intermediate inputs), from primary inputs (labour, capital, etc.) which are value added entries taking the form of wages, profit, rent, interest and taxes, and from imports. In the table value added is disaggregated into two components only: payments to labour and all other payments. Summing down column j yields

$$X_j = \sum_i X_{ij} + L_j + V_j + M_j . \qquad (2.2)$$

We may also sum across the totals row and down the totals column to yield the economy's total gross output:

$$X = \sum_j X_j + C + I + G + E \qquad (2.3)$$

and

$$X = \sum_i X_i + L + V + M . \qquad (2.4)$$

However, since

$$\sum_j X_j = \sum_i X_i$$

all the intermediate flows can be cancelled out. In this way we obtain

$$L + V + M = C + I + G + E . \qquad (2.5)$$

$$\underbrace{\text{Value added} + \text{Imports}}_{} \qquad \underbrace{\text{Final demand}}_{}$$

Transferring imports to the right hand side of the equation gives the traditional social accounting identity of gross regional income and gross regional product (expenditures), i.e.

$$L + V = C + I + G + (E - M). \qquad (2.6)$$

$$\underbrace{\text{Gross regional income}}_{} \qquad \underbrace{\text{Gross regional product}}_{}$$

The sum total of income payments by the productive system to the final sectors is equal to the total value of finished goods and services purchased by the final sectors for consumption, investment, government and net exports.

There are several qualifications and refinements to be introduced into the set of accounts described in Fig. 1, but these do not alter it in substance. A frequent convention, certainly when the model is used for analytical purposes, is to aggregate the final demand components into a single vector, Y. Thus,

$$Y_i = C_i + I_i + G_i + E_i . \tag{2.7}$$

Although the input-output table measures the flows of current transactions, there is also the problem of changes in inventories. The standard convention here is to treat production for inventories as sales to final demand and to regard the absorption of stocks for production as if they were primary inputs. The value added rows will, therefore, include a row that measures gross inventory depletions while a column vector in the final demand segment will be needed for gross inventory accumulations.

In Fig. 1 value added is highly aggregated. It is often desirable to subdivide it into several rows to cover not only wages and salaries but also interest, net rent and before tax profits, depreciation allowances and tax payments to governments. In particular, it may be useful especially in the context of 'closed' models, i.e. when we expand the inter-industry matrix to include final demand elements, to have value added rows that correspond precisely to final demand columns. For example, there would be a tax receipts row to match the government spending column and depreciation payments (or business savings) row to correspond to the private investment column. Closed models are often appropriate at the small area level when it is clear that the major exogenous disturbances come from outside the borders of the area in question. Various degrees of model closure may be adopted depending on how many components of final demand are shifted from the exogenous portion of the input-output table into the endogenous matrix. The most common change is to include households in the matrix, thereby making consumption a function of autonomous changes in income. Another possibility is to treat investment as induced, and to include investment among the endogenous sectors. At the other extreme, it is even permissible to transfer all items of final demand except exports into the matrix. In this case the input-output model becomes merely a highly disaggregated export base model (for an analysis of the export base model and its relationship to other types of regional income model see Richardson, **210**, 1969, pp. 19-36). The implications of these changes will be considered later (see Chapter 3, pp. 31-52). The only observation needed here is to point out that the structure of the model will affect the accounting identities. There is, as we shall see in this book, a great variety of input-output models, and to argue as if there was a single, uniform model would be grossly misleading.

Even with final demand subdivided as in Fig. 1, the individual elements may still be too aggregated for the analytical purposes of the inquiry. For instance, these may require the government spending category to be split up into separate components, such as central government and local government. Investment or exports may also be disaggregated as required. In particular, the treatment of exports as a column vector and imports as a row is difficult to justify conceptually at the sub-national level, though the procedure may be forced upon us by data limitations.

The 'openness' of regional economies as measured by the high proportion of flows to and from other regions relative to total flows suggests the desirability of disaggregating exports and imports by sectors of destination and origin and, if an interregional model is to be used, by region. The export column and import row could then be disaggregated in the following way:

$$M_j = \sum_i^n M_{ij} \text{ and } M_j^r = \sum_i^n \sum_s^z M_{ij}^{sr} . \qquad (2.8)$$

Similarly,

$$E_i = \sum_j^n E_{ij} \text{ and } E_i^r = \sum_j^n \sum_s^z E_{ij}^{rs} . \qquad (2.9)$$

The degree of disaggregation adopted would depend on whether a single-region model or an interregional model was required. In either case, a fuller treatment of external trade makes a great deal of difference to the structure and appearance of the input-output table. In the 'dog-leg' table of Fig. 2, for instance, the single regional model of Fig. 1 is expanded to include a full interindustry export matrix to the right of the transactions table and an import matrix below it on the left (hence the name 'dog-leg'). From the point of view of the accounting identities given in equations (2.1) and (2.2) above, all this means is that

$$\sum_{j}^{n} E_{ij}$$

and

$$\sum_{i}^{n} M_{ij}$$

are substituted for E_i and M_j.

The requirements of an interregional model are more onerous, however, since such a model needs two separate interindustry trade matrices for each pair of regions in the system (to represent flows in both directions) in addition to each region's internal flow matrix. A model for three regions

Fig. 2. 'Dog-leg' input-output table

Inter-industry matrix	Final demand	Export matrix	Total sales
Value added			
Import matrix			
Total purchases			

is shown in Fig. 3. As in Fig. 1, summing across the rows yields sales by each regional industry while adding up the columns yields each regional industry's purchases. Thus, gross output (i.e. without deductions for import content) of industry i in region r will be

$$X_i^r = X_i^{rr} + X_i^{rs} + X_i^{rt}$$ (2.10)

or, more generally, in a z region model

$$X_i^r = X_i^{rr} + \sum_s^{z-1} X_i^{rs} .$$ (2.11)

Furthermore, although for any given region external trade in any given commodity does not have to be in balance, in a closed interregional system total interregional exports must

Fig. 3. Interregional input-output model (three regions)

To \ From	Region r 1 . . . . . n	Region s 1 . . . . . n	Region t 1 . . . . . n
r 1 . . . n	X^{rr}	X^{rs}	X^{rt}
s 1 . . . n	X^{sr}	X^{ss}	X^{st}
t 1 . . . n	X^{tr}	X^{ts}	X^{tt}

equal total interregional imports for each commodity, i.e.

$$\sum_r^z \sum_s^z X_i^{rs} = \sum_s^z \sum_r^z X_i^{sr} . \tag{2.12}$$

This trade balance identity is valuable for the purposes of analysis and computation. From a theoretical viewpoint, interregional models are perhaps the most satisfying of all regional input-output models though their data requirements are very heavy and this has delayed implementation (the theory, applications and uses of interregional models are discussed more fully in Chapter 4).

Another desirable refinement to input-output accounts when we descend below the national level is to introduce stock data, particularly for the supply of land (especially called for in a metropolitan model; see Chapter 12) but also for the supply of capital and labour. In fact, stock variables (labour and capital) are implicit even in the standard input-output table, but they are treated as flows and their stock characteristics are not examined. The case for incorporation of stock data (in the form of 'human resources' and 'non-human resources')[1] in input-output accounting frameworks has been urged most strongly by Perloff (**196**, 1961) and by Perloff and Leven (**197**, 1964). They argue that the current production and income account is best regarded as the *core* account whilst stock-flow relationships for labour supply, land requirements and the capital stock are most easily handled as supplementary or *associated* accounts. Apart from the influence of capital stock on new investment in dynamic models (see Chapter 9, pp. 183-92) and estimation of land use requirements of forecast changes in final demand (see Chapter 12, pp. 245-7), there have been very few regional input-output applications that have paid full recognition to the importance of stock variables in regional and urban analysis.

Finally, a general convention in input-output accounts is

---

[1] In his most recent book (Leven, Legler and Shapiro, **152**, 1970) Leven has abandoned the term 'non-human resources' as being too clumsy, and instead uses the terms 'physical capital' to mean both nonreproducible and reproducible agents of production other than labour, and 'capital' to mean simply the reproducible agents of production.

that all entries in the table are in producers' prices rather than in purchasers' prices. Such items as transport charges, wholesale and retail trade margins and other distribution costs are treated as the outputs of the transportation and trade sectors, and are entered as explicit purchases (inputs) by the purchasing industry from these sectors. Sales of finished goods by the processing sectors are not traced through wholesale and retail outlets even in cases when they are not sold directly to final consumers. The treatment of margin sectors in this way allows the outputs of individual sectors to retain their identity so that purchasers by final demand can be directly related to the producing sector.

The simple input-output model

If we make certain assumptions about the economic system and in particular about the nature of sectoral production functions, the input-output accounts of Fig. 1 can be transformed into an analytical model. For simplicity of exposition let us abstract from the tricky empirical questions of separation of exogenous and endogenous items, disaggregation of final demand and value-added and the treatment of exports and imports by refining the accounting system of Fig. 1 into a skeletal framework of three sectors as in Fig. 4, where Y equals final demand and V equals value added. If we sum across each row and rearrange we find, taking the first row as an example, that

$$X_1 - X_{11} - X_{12} - X_{13} = Y_1. \qquad (2.13)$$

If the amount of industry 1's output purchased by each of the purchasing industries (1, 2 and 3) is a stable function of the latter's output we may rewrite (2.13) as

$$X_1 - a_{11} X_1 - a_{12} X_2 - a_{13} X_3 = Y_1, \qquad (2.14)$$

where

$$a_{11} = \frac{X_{11}}{X_1} ; \ a_{12} = \frac{X_{12}}{X_2} ; \ a_{13} = \frac{X_{13}}{X_3}.$$

The as are called *direct input coefficients,* and in an n sector model they represent the direct requirements of the output of any sector i per unit of output of any other purchasing sector j ($i, j = 1 \ldots n$). The crucial assumption for Equation (2.14) to hold is that the money value[2] of goods and services delivered by an industry i to other producing sectors is a linear and homogenous function of the output level of the purchasing sectors j[3]. More precisely, the specific assumptions are as follows: no joint products, since each commodity is supplied by a single industry and via one method of production; the linear input functions assumption means constant returns to scale and no substitution between inputs; addivity, i.e. the total effect of production is the sum of the separate effects, which rules out external economies and diseconomies; the system is in equilibrium at given prices; and in static versions of the input-output model, no capacity constraints so that the supply of each good is perfectly elastic, thereby

Fig. 4. Skeletal input-output table

From \ To	1	2	3	Final demand	Gross output
1	X_{11}	X_{12}	X_{13}	Y_1	X_1
2	X_{21}	X_{22}	X_{23}	Y_2	X_2
3	X_{31}	X_{32}	X_{33}	Y_3	X_3
V	V_1	V_2	V_3	–	V
Gross outlay	X_1	X_2	X_3	Y	X

[2] The input-output table may be expressed in either physical or money value terms. If we wish to sum the totals for individual industries, clearly money values have to be used.

[3] It is, of course, possible to employ a linear non-homogeneous function if changes in output only are being considered, i.e.

$$\Delta X_1 - a_{11} \Delta X_1 - a_{12}\Delta X_2 - a_{13}\Delta X_3 = \Delta Y_1, \text{ where } a_{11} = \frac{\Delta X_{11}}{\Delta X_1}, \text{ etc.}$$

ignoring problems of capital.

If the linear input coefficients remain constant over time, they provide a nexus for linking final demand to gross output. Input-output analysis describes the interaction of three elements of an economic system: final demands, the input requirements of each industry, and their gross outputs. The main analytical purpose of input-output is to determine the effects of specified changes in final demand upon gross output, given the input coefficients matrix. Such effects include not merely the direct impact, i.e. the first round of input requirements, but also the indirect effects of additional deliveries of these inputs on all industries in the economy. To capture all the first, second, third and higher order effects in a single set of equations we can express the input-output system in matrix form,[4] where the matrix equation represents a set of equations, with one equation like (2.14) above for each sector:

$$\mathbf{X} - A\mathbf{X} = \mathbf{Y} \qquad (2.15)$$

where $\mathbf{X}$ and $\mathbf{Y}$ are column vectors of gross output and final demand respectively, and A is an $n \times n$ matrix of direct input coefficients, a_{ij}. By resorting to the identity matrix I, defined as

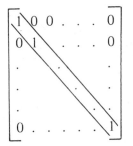

one may rewrite (2.15) as

$$(I - A)\ \mathbf{X} = \mathbf{Y}, \qquad (2.16)$$

[4]Henceforth there will be a modest use of matrix algebra in the book. Simple introductions to the use of matrix algebra in input-output analysis can be found in W.H. Miernyk (165, 1965), Chapter 7, pp. 128-51 and in M. Peston (276, 1969). For a more advanced treatment see Almon (277, 1967).

which can be written as

$$\begin{bmatrix} 1-a_{11} & -a_{12} & \cdots & -a_{1n} \\ -a_{21} & 1-a_{22} & \cdots & -a_{2n} \\ \cdot & \cdot & \cdots & \cdot \\ \cdot & \cdot & & \cdot \\ \cdot & \cdot & & \cdot \\ -a_{n1} & -a_{n2} & \cdots & 1-a_{nn} \end{bmatrix} \begin{bmatrix} X_1 \\ X_2 \\ \cdot \\ \cdot \\ \cdot \\ X_n \end{bmatrix} = \begin{bmatrix} Y_1 \\ Y_2 \\ \cdot \\ \cdot \\ \cdot \\ Y_n \end{bmatrix} \quad (2.17)$$

Under the condition that $(I\text{-}A)$ has an inverse (in practical circumstances this condition will be met if the **Y** vector contains at least one non-zero element) we may use the inverse matrix to express gross output as a function of (exogenous) final demand:

$$\mathbf{X} = (I - A)^{-1} \mathbf{Y}. \quad (2.18)$$

$(I\text{--}A)^{-1}$ is the Leontief inverse matrix. Let $B = (I\text{--}A)^{-1}$. Then

$$B = \begin{bmatrix} b_{11} & \cdot & \cdot & \cdot & b_{1j} & \cdot & \cdot & \cdot & b_{1n} \\ \cdot & \cdot & \cdot & \cdot & \cdot & \cdot & \cdot & \cdot & \cdot \\ \cdot & \cdot & \cdot & \cdot & \cdot & \cdot & \cdot & \cdot & \cdot \\ \cdot & \cdot & \cdot & \cdot & \cdot & \cdot & \cdot & \cdot & \cdot \\ b_{i1} & \cdot & \cdot & \cdot & b_{ij} & \cdot & \cdot & \cdot & b_{in} \\ \cdot & \cdot & \cdot & \cdot & \cdot & \cdot & \cdot & \cdot & \cdot \\ \cdot & \cdot & \cdot & \cdot & \cdot & \cdot & \cdot & \cdot & \cdot \\ \cdot & \cdot & \cdot & \cdot & \cdot & \cdot & \cdot & \cdot & \cdot \\ b_{n1} & \cdot & \cdot & \cdot & b_{nj} & \cdot & \cdot & \cdot & b_{nn} \end{bmatrix} \quad (2.19)$$

and we may write $\mathbf{X} = B\mathbf{Y}$.

Each entry in this inverse matrix is called an inter-dependency coefficient. The coefficient b_{ij} represents the direct and indirect requirements of sector i per unit of final demand for the output of sector j. Thus

$$X_i = b_{i1}\, Y_1 + b_{i2}\, Y_2 + \ldots + b_{ii}\, Y_i + b_{ij}\, Y_j + \ldots + b_{in}\, Y_n.$$

$$(2.20)$$

We can multiply the inverse matrix B by any size and composition of final demand in order to obtain the level of gross output for each industry. This provides us with a powerful tool of analysis since it enables us to measure the total impact on the economy of exogenous disturbances (i.e. changes in final demand).

3 Multiplier Analysis

Repercussions of changes in the level of expenditures on total income can be estimated via the concept of the multiplier. The original Keynesian income multiplier developed in macroeconomic theory has direct analogies at the regional level in the form of regional income and economic base multipliers. The basic difference between the latter and the national multiplier is the existence of additional leakages, particularly into interregional imports. All are essentially similar in that they are aggregate multipliers which fail to distinguish between the sectors in which the initial expenditure changes originate. Input-output models, on the other hand, enable us to derive sets of multipliers the main feature of which is that they are disaggregated, recognising that the total impact .on income (output, employment) will vary according to which sector experiences the initial expenditure change. Manipulation of the input-output table allows the analyst to estimate different types of multiplier depending on whether he is interested in output, income or employment effects. Also, the values attached to the income and employment multipliers are not uniquely determined but are governed by the degree of model closure (i.e. the allocation of sectors between the endogenous matrix and final demand). The objectives of this chapter are to show how alternative multipliers may be derived and to illustrate the links between input-output and aggregate multipliers.

Output, income and employment multipliers

Input-output multipliers are probably the most important tool used in local and regional economic impact analysis. A useful starting point is to distinguish between some of the more common types of multiplier.

1   *Output (or column) multiplier*
The output multiplier for industry i simply measures the sum of direct and indirect requirements from all sectors needed to deliver one additional £ of output of i to final demand. It is derived by summing the entries in the column under industry i in the Leontief inverse matrix table (see Figs. 7 and 9, pp. 38 and 40 which shows, of course, the direct and indirect requirements per unit (£1) of final demand for each sector. Although the output multiplier represents total requirements per unit of final output, it is not a particularly useful concept except as an indicator of the degree of structural inter-dependence between each sector and the rest of the economy. In economic impact studies we are more usually concerned with income or employment generating effects, and these require income or employment multipliers.

2   *Income multiplier (Type I)*
This is expressed as the ratio of the direct plus the indirect income change to the direct income change resulting from a unit increase in final demand for any given sector. The direct income change for each sector is given by the household row entry of the regional I-O table when expressed in input coefficient form (i.e. the direct coefficients table). The direct and indirect income change is obtained by multiplying each column entry in the standard inverse matrix (i.e. households excluded) by the supplying industry's corresponding household row coefficient from the direct coefficients table, and summing the row multiplications. Thus, the direct and indirect income change for sector j is given by

$$\sum_{i=1}^{n} b_{ij} h_{R_i} \quad (i = 1, \ldots, n),$$

where b_{ij} = inverse matrix coefficients and h_{R_i} = an entry in the row vector of household coefficients.

3 Income multiplier (Type II)

This is the ratio of the direct, indirect and induced income change to the direct income change due to a unit increase in final demand. The Type II multiplier takes into account the repercussionary effects of secondary rounds of consumer spending in addition to the direct and indirect interindustry effects. Income expansion due to successive 'rounds' of consumer spending is derived by expanding the interindustry matrix (A) by inclusion of the household row and column thereby making the household sector endogenous. The direct, indirect and induced income change per unit of final demand is shown by the household coefficient in the table of direct and indirect requirements derived from the expanded matrix with households endogenous; the household row in this inverted matrix lists the direct, indirect and induced coefficients for each sector. The direct income change is exactly the same as in the preceding case.

4 Other income multipliers

Although the Type II multiplier takes some account of induced income effects, this is on the basis of restrictive assumptions, in particular that consumption functions are linear and homogeneous. Miernyk's attempt to get round this problem is discussed separately (see pp. 47-9). His modifications involved two separate elements:

(1) deriving a non-linear consumption function by linking together a series of aggregate linear consumption functions for different income groups obtained from cross-section data;
(2) distinguishing between income increments to established households and increased income as a result of new employees (households) in the region.

From this information he was able to derive a new income multiplier (dubbed the Type III multiplier) which calculates the induced income effects more precisely and avoids the overestimation built into the Type II multiplier.

It is clear that other variants of income multipliers may be constructed. One obvious step is to 'close' the I-O model even further by transferring more sectors from the exogenous portion of the table (final demand) to the endogenous portion (the interindustry matrix). Bourque (26, 1969), for example, suggested one form of income multiplier that takes account of the induced effects of state and local government spending, while Hansen and Tiebout (79, 1963) elaborated a long-run multiplier which transferred all final demands (including consumption, investment and government spending) into the matrix with the exception of exports.[1] The more the models are closed, the higher the multipliers; on the other hand, another consequence is a narrowing of the base through which exogenous injections are pumped into the regional economy. Moreover, if induced investment effects are to be accommodated in an I-O model there is a much better way of achieving this from the theoretical viewpoint than by making investment endogenous in the matrix. The superior method is the development of a dynamic model (see Chapter 9).

5   *Employment multipliers*

Regional impact analyses are frequently preoccupied with the employment-creating effects of industrial expansion, because regional policymakers may be primarily and legitimately concerned with forecasting jobs in a particular area. For this reason, it is often useful to be able to derive employment multipliers as well as income multipliers from the I-O model.

The most satisfactory technique available for this purpose is the employment-production function approach using linear regression methods, first adopted by Moore and Petersen (181, 1955). In the Boulder study (168, 1967), for instance, employment-production relationships were estimated for each local industry with the aid of data obtained from the industrial surveys. In certain sectors, particularly the distributive trades, trade margins were used as an output equivalent while annual budgets served the same functions for

---

[1] Because Hansen and Tiebout used a simplified I-O table based on employment data, their long-run multiplier was, in effect, an employment multiplier, but the upshot of their suggestion could be adopted even more easily in income terms with a standard I-O model provided that the final demand sectors are disaggregated.

government agencies. The functions took the simple form

$$E_i = a + b X_i, \tag{3.1}$$

where E = employment and X = output. In virtually all cases, the results were reasonably satisfactory. The correlation coefficients were in excess of 0.65, and standard errors were low. Also, the employment-production functions were homogeneous, as shown by the fact that the constant terms were small.[2]

Given the slopes of the employment-production functions ($\pi=b$), the calculation of employment multipliers is relatively straightforward. The direct employment change for sector j is the slope of its employment-production regression line, π_j. The direct plus indirect employment change for j consists of the E/X coefficient for each i (π_i) multiplied by the total direct and indirect requirements from each i for one unit of final demand to j, and summed

$$\sum_{i=1}^{n} b_{ij} \pi_i \quad (i = 1, \ldots, n).$$

The employment multiplier analogous to the Type I income multiplier is the ratio of this direct plus indirect employment change to the direct employment change. Similarly, there is an employment multiplier parallel to the Type II income multiplier which measures the ratio of the direct, indirect and induced employment change to the direct employment change. The former is given for sector j by

$$\sum_{i=1}^{n} b_{ij}^{*} \pi_i \quad (i = 1, \ldots, n).$$

where b_{ij}^{*} represents an entry in the expanded inverse matrix with households endogenous. Provided that we have estimates for the E/X coefficients, it is possible to convert any particular formulation of income or output multipliers into employment terms.[3]

[2] There were three exceptions to this conclusion: utilities, local government and the University of Colorado.

[3] An alternative method of deriving employment multipliers is the Hansen-Tiebout approach mentioned above, and described more fully in Chapter 7, pp. 131-3. When employment forecasts are the primary objective and where researchers are starting from scratch rather than with an extant I-O table, the simpler and inexpensive Hansen-Tiebout model may be adequate.

It is difficult to offer firm generalisations about the size of regional I-O multipliers and their components because these can differ widely according to circumstances such as a region's industrial structure, the extent of interdependence among its sectors, its size and a host of other factors. However, there are a few very general comments that can be made. For instance, the direct income change will tend to be higher in labour-intensive sectors, whereas capital-intensive industries with strong links with other sectors in the regional economy may experience greater indirect effects. Service industries tend to have high direct income effects because a substantial proportion of their costs consists of direct payments to factors of production (wages, rent, etc.) rather than purchase of materials. Moreover, the immediate leakage into imports tends to be much lower for service industries than for manufacturing. However, the tendency for indirect effects to be greater in manufacturing than service sectors while the converse holds for direct effects implies a narrowing in the range of values for the Type I multiplier. There is thus no clearly marked relationship between large direct income changes and large multipliers. It is very important to take account of induced income changes if we wish to attempt to capture the total income effect of changes in final demand. Type II multipliers tend to be considerably larger than Type I multipliers, and in most cases the induced income change is greater than the indirect income change. As shown elsewhere (see pp. 42-3), the ratio of the Type II to Type I multipliers remains constant from sector to sector, though this does not imply that the ratio of the induced to the *indirect* income change is also constant.

As for the size of income multipliers, there are two safe generalisations. First, multiplier values vary widely from sector to sector, and the wider range highlights very clearly the importance of the sectoral composition of regional growth in raising regional incomes. For instance, the upper and lower limits for Type II multipliers in the Boulder study were 2·22 and 1·40 respectively [4] (Miernyk, **168**, 1967, p. 98), while in Washington State the range was 5·18 to 1·90 (Bourque, **26**,

[4]This excludes the dummy sector real property rentals which had a very high, though not meaningful, income multiplier.

1969, pp. 8-9). Second, income multiplier values tend to vary directly with size of area; *ceteris paribus,* national multipliers are higher than regional, regional than sub-regional, sub-regional than urban, and so on. The primary reason for this is that of the main leakages which reduce the generation of income (taxation – central and local, savings and imports), imports tend to be the most important and certainly are the most variable with size of area. The propensity to import varies inversely with the scale of area; thus, large regions[5] have high multipliers because they import less.[6] A subsidiary factor may be that the indirect income changes are greater in more complex regional economies, and we may reasonably expect the larger regions to have more interdependent economic structures.

A numerical example

It may help to clarify the preceding analysis to illustrate it with a very simple numerical example. Fig. 5 shows a hypothetical transactions table for a two-industry economy. The

Fig. 5. Hypothetical transactions table (£ m)

From \ To	1	2	House-holds	Other final demand	Gross output
1	20	45	30	5	100
2	40	15	30	65	150
Households	20	60	10	10	100
Other value added plus imports	20	30	30	–	80
Gross outlay	100	150	100	80	430

[5]The description 'large region' is an ambiguous term. It could imply either a large geographical area or a substantial population. Probably both area and population size have some impact on self-sufficiency and on the propensity to import, but population is almost certainly the more important variable.
[6]This is offset only to a very limited extent by the tendency for tax and savings leakages to be greater in the high income, which *may* be the larger, regions.

final demand and value added segments of the table are highly aggregated, merely being divided into households and other items. For the purposes of analysis, we concentrate on the interindustry quadrant of the table. Given the Leontief assumptions outlined earlier, the interindustry flows may be expressed in input coefficient matrix form as in Fig. 6. This shows the direct purchases from industry at the left per £ of output produced by industry at the top. To measure the total impact, however, we need to take account of indirect as well as direct requirements. This requires us to subtract the input coefficient matrix from the identity matrix and to invert the result, thereby yielding the Leontief inverse matrix, $(I-A)^{-1}$ or B, of Fig. 7. Each entry in this matrix shows the direct and indirect requirements from industry at the left per £ of deliveries to final demand by industry at the top. The Leontief inverse matrix is the key instrument of input-output analysis because it permits an immediate evaluation of the effects of changes in final demand on industry gross outputs[7] and also allows us, with a little manipulation, to calculate the values for income multipliers. This example shows that an increase in final demand for the products of industry 1 of £10 million will lead to an increase in industry 1's output of £15 million (including the original £10 million change) and to an increase of £6.7 million in the output of industry 2; similarly, an increase in final demand for industry 2 of £10 million will bring about an increase of £13·3 million in industry 2's output and of £5 million in the output of industry 1.

Fig. 6. Direct input coefficient   Fig. 7. Leontief inverse matrix,
         matrix, A $(I-A)^{-1}$ or B

$$\begin{bmatrix} 0·2 & 0·3 \\ 0·4 & 0·1 \end{bmatrix} \qquad \begin{bmatrix} 1·50 & 0·50 \\ 0·67 & 1·33 \end{bmatrix}$$

[7]In estimating the effects on output of changes in final demand from the matrix equation $X = BY$, it is often convenient to transpose the B matrix so that we can work out the impacts horizontally along the row. See, for example, Miernyk (**165**, 1965) and Hirsch (**96**, 1959).

Some of the multiplier results are shown in Table 1. The column multipliers are obtained simply by adding up the column entries of the Leontief inverse matrix. They measure the total value of industry requirements per unit of final demand for the industry in question. The higher the multiplier the greater the interdependence of the sector with the rest of the economy. However, these column (or sector) multipliers are of much less value than income multipliers. To estimate the latter we begin with the direct income change as measured by the household row coefficient obtained from the original transactions table; thus, from Fig. 5 it can be seen that the household row coefficient for industry 1 is 20/100 or 0·2 and for industry 2 is 60/150 or 0·4. The Type I multiplier is defined as the ratio of the direct and indirect income change to the direct income change. The direct and indirect income change for industry 1 is calculated by summing the products of the column entries in the Leontief inverse matrix and the supplying industry's household coefficient, i.e. (1·50 × 0·2) + (0·67 × 0·4) = 0·568; similarly, the direct and indirect income change for industry 2 is (0·50 × 0·2) + (1·33 × 0·4) = 0·632. The resulting Type I multipliers are shown in Table 1. However, as pointed out above, there is also a Type II multiplier which takes into account the induced consumption effects of expansion in final demand as well as the direct and indirect income effects. To calculate the Type II multiplier we need to return to the original transactions table of Fig. 5. The interindustry matrix is expanded by one row and one column to make the household sector endogenous. We draw

Table 1   Hypothetical model: some numerical results

Open model	Industry 1	Industry 2
Column multiplier	2·17	1·83
Household row coefficient	0·2	0·4
Direct and indirect income change	0·568	0·632
Type I multiplier	2·84	1·58

Closed model (households endogenous)		
Direct, indirect and induced income changes	1·03	1·15
Type II multiplier	5·15	2·875

up a new direct coefficient matrix, A^*, as shown in Fig. 8, and invert this to yield a new Leontief inverse, $(I-A^*)^{-1}$ or B^*, as in Fig. 9. (It should be noted that the expanded inverse matrix with households endogenous differs from the standard inverse matrix in that elements greater than unity are not necessarily confined to the on-diagonal entries. It is unusual, however, to have so many entries in excess of unity as in Fig. 9; this is a freak result which is a consequence of the high values of the input coefficients in this hypothetical and highly aggregated example. In a typical fifty-sector model most individual coefficients will have very small values.) The direct, indirect and induced income changes are merely the entries in the household row of the B^* matrix, i.e. 1·03 for industry 1 and 1·15 for industry 2. The Type II multipliers are the ratios of these values to the original direct income changes, and are given in Table 1. It can also be observed that the ratios of the Type II to the Type I multipliers are approximately the same, confirming the theorem described below (see pp. 42-3).

Given the Leontief inverse matrix, the effects on the economy of any combination of final demand impacts may be worked out. For instance, in the closed model (with households endogenous) we could hypothesise a situation in which final demand increased by £13 million for industry 1 and by £18 million in the household sector (industry 3), partly offset by a fall in industry 2's final demand of £23 million; total final demand therefore increases by £8 million. With the aid of the inverse matrix we can work out the impact of these final demand changes on industry gross

Fig. 8. Direct input coefficient matrix with households endogenous, A^*

Fig. 9. Leontief inverse matrix with households endogenous, $(I-A^*)^{-1}$ or B^*

$$\begin{bmatrix} 0·2 & 0·3 & 0·3 \\ 0·4 & 0·1 & 0·3 \\ 0·2 & 0·4 & 0·1 \end{bmatrix} \qquad \begin{bmatrix} 2·09 & 1·18 & 1·09 \\ 1·27 & 2·00 & 1·09 \\ 1·03 & 1·15 & 1·82 \end{bmatrix}$$

outputs (see Table 2). The increase in final demand of £8 million induces a net expansion in gross output of £30 million (a rise in industries 1 and 3 of £20 million each and a decline of £10 million in industry 2).[8] These individual gross output changes are themselves the net result of variations in the direct and indirect requirements of each sector experiencing a change in final demand. The overall effect on the economy's output is determined not merely by the size of the net final demand change but by its distribution among the various sectors of the economy. The entries in Table 2 describe the situation when the final demand impacts have worked themselves out. Since the predicted output effects are dependent on the assumption of constant input coefficients we can derive the new equilibrium gross flows transactions table from knowledge of the new gross output and final demand levels and the original direct coefficients matrix of Fig. 8. This new transactions table is shown in Fig. 10. The fact that the row and column entries balance supports the view that the economy is once again in equilibrium. The economy's total output has risen by £38 million, £30 million due to changes in industry gross outputs and £8 million due to the given changes in final

Table 2   Impact of final demand changes (closed model) (£m)

		Industry 1	*Industry 2*	*Industry 3 (house-holds)*	*Total*
Change in final demand		+13	−23	+18	+ 8
Change in industry gross outputs	Industry 1	+27	−27	+20	+ 20
	Industry 2	+15	−45	+20	− 10
	Industry 3 (households)	+13	−26	+33	+ 20
Total change in output					+ 38

[8]There are a few slight rounding errors in Table 2 to simplify the derivation of the new transactions table of Fig. 10.

Fig. 10 Transactions table after final demand changes (£m)

From \ To	1	2	3 (households)	Final demand	Gross output
1	24	42	36	18	120
2	48	14	36	42	140
3 (households)	24	56	12	28	120
Value added plus imports	24	28	36	–	88
Gross outlay	120	140	120	88	468

demand. Although the data are hypothetical, they illustrate the general proposition that quite large increases in the level of output may be induced by relatively small increases in final demand.

The relationship between Type I and Type II multipliers

There are, as described above, two common categories of income multiplier in input-output models. The Type I multiplier measures the ratio of the direct and indirect income change to the direct income change resulting from a monetary unit increase in final demand for any given industry, while Type II measures the direct, indirect and induced income effects obtained by making the household sector endogenous by expanding the A matrix by a row and a column. Although there is both a Type I and Type II multiplier for each of n industries in the model, it is unnecessary to carry out $2n$ separate calculations. Provided that it is assumed that the consumption function is linear and homogeneous, the relationship between the two types of multiplier is a constant one for a given I-O matrix regardless of the sector in question. Thus once the Type I income multipliers are known, there is a short-cut method of calculating the Type II multipliers without developing the augmented interindustry matrix that includes households. This important finding was first pointed out by Hirsch (96, 1959), and more recently proofs have been demonstrated by Sandoval (217, 1967) and Bradley and Gander (27, 1969).

All that the calculation requires is the scalar product of two vectors — that of direct plus indirect income effects and that of household consumption coefficients. The ratio of the two multipliers can be expressed as

$$\frac{\mu_{II}}{\mu_I} = \frac{(I - A^*)^{-1}}{H_R (I - A)^{-1}}, \qquad (3.2)$$

where A is the interindustry matrix, A^* is the expanded matrix with households endogenous and H_R is the row vector of household coefficients. It can be shown that this ratio is a constant and can be estimated without having to invert the augmented matrix since this constant is equal to

$$\frac{1}{1 - (h + H_R [I - A]^{-1} H_C)},$$

where h is the intrahousehold consumption coefficient and H_C is the column vector of household consumption expenditure coefficients.[9]

Disaggregated consumption functions and income multipliers

The assumption of an aggregate linear homogeneous consumption function is somewhat restrictive particularly at the theoretical level, and in recent years there have been attempts to relax this assumption. It was pointed out many years ago by Moore and Petersen (181, 1955, p. 376) and by Hirsch (96, 1959, p. 364) that using this simplified consumption function tends to overstate the income effects of changes in final demand. Moore and Petersen relaxed the homogeneity assumption by developing linear non-homogeneous functions from national time series data, but this did not enable them to take account of *regional* leakages via imports by consumers. The appropriate solution is to obtain local consumption functions for each sector, but this task is not an easy one.

---

[9] For the proof see Bradley and Gander, (27, 1969), pp. 310-12. Examples of the size of the ratio are 1·29 for St Louis (1955), 1·4 for New Mexico (1965) and 1·55 for Utah (1965).

Two attacks on this problem will be discussed here. The first, and most ambitious, is Miyazawa's theoretical solution (**179**, 1966, and **178**, 1968) for an interregional I-O model which, because of the almost unique existence of interregional I-O tables in Japan, he was able to test empirically. The second is the less general *ad hoc* method of disaggregating consumption in a single region model employed by Miernyk in the Boulder Area study (**168**, 1967, pp. 104-16). While Miyazawa's approach places great emphasis on disaggregation *per se,* Miernyk tries to find ways of relaxing the assumptions of linearity and homogeneity though his methods inevitably involve disaggregation.

Miyazawa's rationale for disaggregating the income multiplier effect is soundly expressed as follows (**178**, 1968, p. 40):

> The omission of the income formation process in I-O analysis is especially not justified in the interregional interindustry case, because the location of production depends on the location of consumption, and the latter cannot be determined separately from the calculation of income generated in each region.

In I-O analysis industry outputs have different values depending on the composition of changes in final demand, but, as we have seen, the induced income effect is the same regardless of the distribution of final demand. To ensure that induced income effects are responsive to the origin of the final demand change it is necessary to consider the distribution of income by disaggregating by income groups as well as by type of industrial value added. The concept used to show this is what Miyazawa calls 'the interrelational income multiplier as a matrix'. This demonstrates how much income in one group is generated by the expenditure from one unit of additional income in another group as a result of changes in output. It also traces intersectoral income repercussions in the income generation process which are normally excluded in I-O analysis, even in the closed (households endogenous) model.

Consider an interregional I-O framework of z regions divided into n sectors. Let

$A = nz \times nz$ matrix of interregional I-O coefficients.

$V = z \times nz$ matrix of value-added ratios of household sectors in each region (where each element $V_j^{rs} =$ income of a household in region r earned from 1 unit of production of industry j in region s).

$C =$ $nz \times z$ matrix of coefficients of regional consumption expenditure (where each element $C_i^{rs} =$ consumer expenditure on commodity i produced in region r from 1 unit of income earned in the household sector of region s).

$B =$ the usual Leontief inverse matrix $(I-A)^{-1}$.

Income receipts by household sectors in each region are determined by

$$VB,$$

which forms a $z \times nz$ matrix of coefficients showing induced income earned from production activities among industries and regions. On the other hand, induced production due to *endogenous* consumption per unit of income in each region's household sector is given by the following $nz \times z$ matrix

$$BC.$$

Combining these two expressions we get the following matrix

$$VBC = L. \tag{3.3}$$

This is a new z^2 square matrix obtained from the multiplication of the rectangular and square matrices V, B and C. This square matrix L is a set of coefficients showing the interrelationships among incomes in all regions through the propagation process of consumption in each region, i.e. its elements 1^{rs} shows how much income in region r is generated by expenditure of one unit of additional income in region s. However, since the process does not stop at the first round, it is necessary to trace subsequent rounds of income generation. This is obtained by inverting the L matrix, so we may write

$$K = (I - L)^{-1}. \tag{3.4}$$

The K matrix is the 'interrelational income multiplier as a matrix' and shows the direct and indirect income generation per unit of income change.[10]

To show how this affects the Leontief I-O model we divide final demand into two components, Y_c (consumption) and Y (final demand other than consumption). Thus, the output determination equation is

$$\mathbf{X} = A\mathbf{X} + \mathbf{Y}_c + \mathbf{Y}. \qquad (3.5)$$

If we wish to trace the income generation process it is necessary to make consumption endogenous, and this requirement means that $\mathbf{Y}_c$ must be expressed in terms of $\mathbf{X}$. Accordingly, we define the consumption function

$$\mathbf{Y}_c = CV\mathbf{X}, \qquad (3.6)$$

where C and V have already been defined. Substituting (3.6) into (3.5), we obtain

$$\mathbf{X} = A\mathbf{X} + CV\mathbf{X} + \mathbf{Y}. \qquad (3.7)$$

Solving, for X, we derive

$$\begin{aligned}
\mathbf{X} &= (I - A - CV)^{-1} \, \mathbf{Y} \\
&= (I - A)^{-1} \, (I - CV \, [(I - A]^{-1})^{-1} \, \mathbf{Y} \\
&= B \, (I - CVB)^{-1} \, \mathbf{Y} \\
&= B \, (I - L)^{-1} \, \mathbf{Y} \\
\therefore \ \mathbf{X} &= KB\mathbf{Y}. \qquad (3.8)
\end{aligned}$$

Thus, the disaggregated closed I-O model multiplier is the product of the Leontief inverse and a multi-sector (interregional) Keynesian income multiplier. In most countries it would be impossible to attempt even an approximate test of this model, partly because of the lack of proper interregional

---

[10]The standard Keynesian income multiplier is a special case of the K matrix multiplier. If no distinction is made between groups or regions in the distribution of income, i.e. assume $z=1$, the matrix V becomes a row vector of n order and the matrix C becomes a column vector of n order. If these are written as v' and c respectively and it is assumed that all value added consists of income to the household sector, then

$L = VBC = v'Bc = i' \, (I-A) \, Bc = i' \, c = \bar{c}$ (the Keynesian propensity to consume)

where i' is a row vector whose elements all equal unity.

So $\qquad\qquad K = (I - L)^{-1} = 1/(1 - \bar{c}).$

I-O tables, partly because of the sparsity of information on regional consumption expenditures.[11] Miernyk's method of dealing with aggregation, linearity and homogeneity in the consumption function is much more economical in its data requirements. One reason for this is that his concern is with a single small region rather than a complete interregional system. Two alternative, though not mutually exclusive, approaches were suggested. The first possibility was to estimate linear but non-homogeneous household expenditure functions for each individual sector of the type $E = a + bY$ from survey data, but the results obtained failed to pass statistical significance tests. The second approach involved estimation of a series of aggregate consumption functions for different income groups from cross-section data which could then be linked together into a single *non-linear* consumption function for the community as a whole. The advantage of this is that marginal rather than average propensities can be used. The aggregate function obtained by this method assumes a form rather like that in Fig. 11, where non-linearity is roughly achieved by joining together a series of linear functions estimated for separate income groups. The slopes of the regression lines decline in moving up the income class hierarchy, a result which is of course consistent with the *a priori* Keynesian hypothesis of declining marginal propensity to consume with rising income. A related finding is that low income households tend to spend a larger fraction of an increase in consumption *locally* than high income households.

An additional refinement was to make a distinction between the spending patterns of new households (typically immigrants into the Boulder Area) and additions to spending of established residents. The latter (called the per capita effect) is based on the aggregate consumption function of Fig. 11, while new households were assumed to have a propensity to consume equal to the community's average propensity to consume (the increase in consumption due to new households is called the population effect). Within a given income class the population effect is always greater than the per capita effect.

Fig. 11.

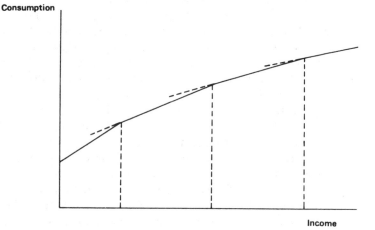

In order to separate out the two income effects, the following procedure was adopted. The first step required sectoral output-employment conversion ratios. Increases in final demand were then converted into increases in employment by sector which were then multiplied by the average wage in each sector. This part of the total increase in payments to households was assumed to represent the total income of new households. The residual was assumed to represent additions to the income of existing households and was divided among four income groups with the aid of census data. The change in community income as a result of new employees was multiplied by the column of consumption coefficients to obtain sectoral changes in consumption. The apportioned income changes to established residents were multiplied by the slopes of the appropriate cross-section aggregate consumption functions (as in Fig. 11), and the sum of these consumption changes was distributed among the processing sectors by multiplying it by each entry in the column of consumption coefficients expressed as a percentage of their sum. The overall changes in consumption in each sector resulting from the two kinds of income change induced further local production which in turn raised income payments to households, and so on. The full effects were calculated by an iterative process, and it was found that expansion converged towards zero after four rounds. In almost all cases, and not surprisingly in a rapidly growing community such as Boulder was at the time of the study, the induced income effects due to new residents exceeded those resulting from local increases in per capita income.

This method yields a new kind of income multiplier, described by Miernyk as pointed out above as the Type III multiplier. This measures the ratio of direct, indirect and induced income change to the direct income change where the former is computed by iteration after dividing total income changes into the income of new employees and marginal increments to the income of established residents. The Type III multiplier is smaller than the Type II multiplier (in Boulder it varied between 83·6 per cent and 91·0 per cent of the latter). This is because a smaller fraction of marginal income increases is spent on consumption, and because high income groups have higher propensities to import.

Input-output and economic base multipliers compared

It is clear from the previous section that there are analogies between I-O and other types of income multiplier. Particularly in cases where impact analysis is concerned with working out aggregate impacts, it is reasonable to inquire whether more simplified income multipliers might not be used in place of the I-O model. The justification for this is pragmatic – the high costs involved in constructing an I-O transactions table by direct survey methods or, if adjusted national coefficients are used, the limitations on disaggregation due to disclosure rules and the time lag in publication of national tables. In regional economic analysis the simplest of all multipliers is derived from the economic base model. Despite its primitive theoretical framework, practical problems arising from its application and the heavy barrage of criticisms that the model has had to face over the past two decades, there has been quite recently a resurgence of interest in it. Isard and Czamanski (114, 1965) and Garnick (67, 1969, and 68, 1970), in particular, have argued that for certain purposes economic base multipliers can be substituted for the I-O approach. Garnick (68, p. 36) has argued that:

Basic-service multipliers are . . . presented as cost-effective alternatives to I-O multipliers for small regional impact studies. Indeed there are inexpensive means for augmenting the former such that differential multipliers are derived approximating most of the differential multipliers derived from I-O matrices.

Isard and Czamanski (114, p. 32) conclude that: 'The size of the multiplier effect derived and the justification for the use of one model as against another depends primarily upon the problem at hand, data available and the time and the resources which the analyst can command'.

The argument rests on two props: the consolidated closed model I-O multiplier and the economic base multiplier are mathematically identical; empirical estimates of the Type II I-O multiplier and the economic base multiplier are, when defined in a comparable manner, approximately the same. The mathematical identity between the two multipliers has been demonstrated by Billings (20, 1969) and by Garnick (68, pp. 36-8). The gross output multipliers of equation (3.8), i.e.

$$X = B (I - CVB)^{-1} Y,$$

need to be converted into income terms to compare with the economic base multipliers. This conversion is carried out via pre-multiplying by the household value added coefficients. Thus

$$Y^* = VX = VB (I - CVB)^{-1} Y , \qquad (3.9)$$

where $Y^* =$ total income.

The economic base model divides the regional economy into exogenous basic sectors and endogenous local industries that are functionally related to total income.

$$Y^* = \sum_{i=1}^{d} Y_{L_i} + \sum_{i=d+1}^{n} Y_{E_i} , \qquad (3.10)$$

where $\sum_{i=1}^{d} Y_{L_i} =$ income earned in local-service industries $(i = 1, 2, \ldots, d)$.

$\sum_{i=d+1}^{n} Y_{E_i} =$ income earned in the basic or exogenous sectors $(i = d + 1, d + 2, \ldots, n)$.

We may also write as a definition

$$\sum_{i=d+1}^{n} Y_{E_i} = E,$$ (3.11)

while local endogenous income can be expressed in terms of total income:

$$\sum_{i=1}^{d} Y_{L_i} = \sum_{i=1}^{d} c_i Y^*,$$ (3.12)

where $c_i = Y_{L_i}/Y^*$ = the propensity of residents to consume locally produced goods and services in the local industries.

Substituting (3.11) and (3.12) into (3.10) we obtain

$$Y^* = \sum_{i=1}^{d} c_i Y^* + E$$

$$\therefore Y^* = (1 - \sum_{i=1}^{d} c_i)^{-1} E$$ (3.13)

Since Y^* is common to both, and if E equals the sum of elements in vector Y, then it follows that the consolidated I-O multiplier of equation (3.9), i.e. the average industry multiplier in which each inverse column sum is weighted by its industry share of total deliveries to final demand, must equal the aggregate economic base multiplier of equation (3.13). Thus

$$VB (I - CVB)^{-1} = (1 - \sum_{i=1}^{d} c_i)^{-1}.$$ (3.14)

At the empirical level results are not identical, since it is not possible to make a perfect match between the final demand vector of the I-O model and exogenous basic sectors. But the I-O and basic-service multipliers are essentially similar: both reflect the direct, indirect and induced income effects of exogenous changes in output and both are average rather than marginal multipliers. In a comparison of five areas[12] Isard and Czamanski showed that the economic base multiplier (after adjustments to treat investment and government expenditure as basic activities) was 'generally of the same order of magnitude' as the Type II I-O multiplier.

[12] California, Los Angeles, San Francisco, St Louis and Kalamazoo.

Garnick went even further. He argued that, with certain exceptions,[13] sector multipliers in the closed I-O model tend to cluster around the value of the consolidated matrix or the adjusted base multiplier. In addition, he estimated differential multipliers for broad industrial groups by combining the base multiplier approach with estimation of direct impacts on basic industries obtained by using adjusted national I-O coefficients.[14] These represented a sensible compromise between the aggregate base multiplier on the one hand and individual sector multipliers from a regional I-O model on the other.

[13]The main exceptions in his analysis of 1963 data for Washington State and Nebraska were resource-oriented industries such as food products, lumber and paper industries.

[14]Estimation of reasonable multipliers for the resource-oriented industries necessitated measurement of indirect effects among basic vectors via inversion of the regionally adjusted national I-O table.

4 Interregional Models

Introduction

As we have seen (Chapter 1, pp. 1-2), the intellectual case for I-O analysis rests very largely on the fact that it is a great rarity in economics – an operational general equilibrium system. It enables us not only to identify but, at the cost of certain rigid assumptions, to *measure* the interdependence of the economic structure. Since it may be argued that its general equilibrium character is the main virtue of the I-O approach, then this character should not be sacrificed lightly. When we introduce space and distance into the economy, however, as in regional I-O analysis, it is very difficult to retain the general equilibrium features of I-O theory. The most widespread regional I-O model in common use is the single region model. This is a *partial* model in its preoccupation with economic impacts affecting the study region alone and in its aggregation of the rest of the world into one other region. The interdependence of the local industrial structure is retained, but the model throws no light on the interdependence of economic regions. The single region model is an 'open' model which enables us to trace the effects of exogenous changes in final demand on economic activities in the individual region. But the model does not constitute an interregional system, for the origins of these final demand changes are not traced and the 'spill-over' repercussions of consequent changes in regional economic activity are not followed through. In short, the single region model allows us to take account of local interindustry feedbacks but neglects interregional feedbacks. The implication of this point is clear. If regional I-O studies are to qualify as general equilibrium analysis, then interregional rather than single-region I-O models must be developed.[1] The theoretical structure of interregional I-O models was first discussed two decades ago by Isard (107, 1951), but apart from impressive pioneering work by Moses (185, 1955) little progress was made in applying interregional models until recent years, primarily because of data limitations and computer capacity constraints.[2] Very recently, interest in interregional models has revived, particularly with the ambitious forty-four-region–seventy-eight-industry model which has been developed at Harvard under the direction of Dr Karen R. Polenske (HERP, Harvard Economic Research Project). Generally, there is growing recognition of the value and utility of interregional models. As one US government economist has put it: 'The contribution of I-O to regional analysis will not reach anywhere near its full potential until a comprehensive system of interregional I-O tables can be developed' (M. R. Goldman, Comments on Czamanski and Malizia, 51, 1969, p. 79). Polenske has expressed this rather more strongly, when commenting on a regional I-O study of the standard type: 'The refinement of the horse and buggy should be discouraged when the need is for an entirely new vehicle. The emphasis should now be shifted to constructing multiregional I-O tables' (203, 1970, p. 40).

Interregional models have advantages and uses that are not common to other regional models. In the first place, an operational interregional model provides via its accounting framework consistency checks on its data; for instance, total interregional imports must equal total interregional exports,

[1] The terms 'interregional model' and 'multiregional model' may be used interchangeably. On the other hand, a distinction is sometimes made. The former may refer to the case where the regions in the model exhaust the system (e.g. the components of the national economy), and the latter to any group of interdependent regions often forming only a part of the national economy.

[2] Even ten years ago the computations needed for implementing an interregional model would have been unthinkable. Polenske points out (202, 1969) that in 1951 it took fifty-six hours to invert the matrix of the 1939 US forty-two-sector table; by 1969 it took ten to thirty-six seconds to invert a hundred-order matrix according to the size of the computer used.

and identities of this kind enable the analyst to check the estimates of trade flows into and out of individual regions. In this way, use of the interregional I-O accounting framework throws light on weaknesses in the available statistical information. The existence of an interregional model would greatly enhance the usefulness of subsequent small region I-O studies, since the more aggregate data would act as a control and prevent a regional or subregional analysis from producing absurd results (usually wildly overoptimistic forecasts). Second, the data requirements of an interregional model are, with the aid of acceptable short-cuts discovered by recent research, not disproportionately heavy, particularly if government were to collect some of the necessary information as part of its normal statistical service.[3] The basic requirements are: estimates of regional final demands; estimates of regional I-O coefficients; and, if the point estimate LSG model (the Leontief-Strout gravity model; see below) is used, a set of base-year interregional trade flows. An interregional model consisting of the national economy disaggregated into its component regions is much cheaper to construct than development of individual region models which are subsequently aggregated. Moreover, it would be very difficult to co-ordinate the construction of the latter, and inconsistencies and differences in methodology could well make the tables produced impossible to link together for the purposes of interregional analysis.

Third, interregional models have wider applications than the single region model. Polenske (**202**, 1969) lists the following potential uses for an interregional I-O model: studies of shifts in the location of industrial activity and employment; estimation of regional and industrial differences in production techniques; establishment of regional accounts; regional impact studies; regional economic development programmes; transportation planning; and civil defence planning. These broad categories mask individual applications

[3] Governments could perform this task much more easily than private research agencies, but seem reluctant to do so. One explanation is that: 'The general tendency within government agencies is to fund short-term projects which are to give answers to specific policy questions while neglecting to build or maintain an up-to-date data base' (Polenske, **202**, 1969, p. 12). There are problems, such as the reconciliation of available regional data with national data and the need to adhere to disclosure rules, but these are not difficult to solve.

that can be tackled only with an interregional model. Obvious examples include: calculation of the effects on different regions of changes in central government spending (particularly military expenditures, aerospace programmes or other major capital projects); evaluating the effects of interregional shifts in industrial location; measurement and forecasts of export markets for a region; estimation of the effects of freight rate changes on regional production and trade; calculation of 'spillover' effects of expanded development in rich regions on poorer regions and of interregional feedbacks.[4]

The major problem in the development of interregional I-O models arises from the fact that I-O analysis itself has no mechanism for explaining trade patterns, yet the derivation of interregional trade flows is the key distinctive feature of the interregional model. There is a wide spectrum of models that differ in their treatment of regional trade from the single region model at one end of the spectrum to the 'ideal' interregional model at the other. The single region model treats imports as a single row in the I-O table and exports as a single column in the final demand segment. The determinants of the size of regional exports and imports are not considered in the model, and the regional trade estimates are obtained directly from survey data.[5] When the single region model is used for projections, changes in exports are handled as either an assumed or given change in final demand while imports are assumed to account for a fixed proportion of total inputs into each sector, the proportion being determined from the imports/total input relation in the original transactions table. The 'ideal' interregional I-O model treats equi-

---

[4] A special variant of the interregional model is where a subregional-regional-interregional framework is used for examining the links of a small region with the wider region of which it forms a part and for measuring the impacts of the outside world on the small region. For a study demonstrating the utility of such a framework see Dolenc (56, 1968), in which he adopts a three-region scheme of this kind (Bucks County, the rest of the Philadelphia SMSA, and the rest of the world). See also Isard and Langford (117, 1971, pp. 137-41).

[5] Where non-survey techniques are used, a theory of interregional trade based on maximising local use of local output normally underlies the operations. Exports are treated as surplus production while imports fill the gap between local requirements and local production (see Chapter 6, pp. 118-26).

valent industries in separate regions as if they were individual sectors. Thus, such a model contains *nz* sectors where *n* is the number of industries and *z* the number of regions in the system. Interregional trade coefficients are bound by the same restrictive assumptions as intraregional production coefficients. Between these two extremes there are alternative methods of estimating interregional trade flows that can be used to implement an interregional I-O model. These are more economical in their data requirements than the full inter-regional model, yet avoid the 'partial' character of the single region model.

The 'ideal' interregional model

The full-scale interregional I-O model aims at treating *z* regions ($z \geqslant 2$) in equal detail. A complete interindustry matrix is specified for each region, and in addition interindustry flows in each direction between regions are recorded in a set of interregional matrices, with one matrix for each pair of regions. Thus, a complete four-region interregional model would contain a total of sixteen sub-matrices — four intra-regional matrices on the diagonal and twelve interregional matrices. This enables each economic activity to be identified by industrial group $(1, \ldots, i, j, \ldots n)$ and by location, i.e. by region $(1, \ldots r, s, \ldots z)$. The aggregate interregional technical coefficient matrix has $(nz)^2$ separate cells. Each region has a $n \times n$ matrix representing its own industrial structure and $z-1$ other $n \times n$ matrices illustrating the interindustry inter-regional trade relationships.

Abstracting from industry and product mix and from regional differences in production techniques, any sector *i* in one region could be identical in structure and composition to industry *i* in any other region. The distinctive feature of the 'ideal' interregional model is that it treats these apparently identical sectors as distinguishably separate industries. The very fact of their being produced in separate regions makes them different. In Isard's words:

any given good or service produced in any region must be taken as a unique commodity, distinct from the same good or service produced in any other region. Thus, for example, if states are designated as regions, Pennsylvania brick becomes a commodity different from New York brick or California brick ... the number of industrial categories in a territory is multiplied by the number of regions, if each region engages in each activity (Isard, **107**, 1951, p. 320).

In consequence, the interregional-interindustry coefficient is put on the same basis and is bound by the same assumptions as the local interindustry coefficients; both are treated as the standard input coefficients of Leontief models. Thus, any change in final demand *directly* calls for a proportional change in each of the inputs — not only each local industry input but also in each industry input from the other regions of the system.

This point has profound implications. The normal assumption of fixed and constant production coefficients has repercussions on interregional-interindustry relations since they imply fixed supply areas or channels for each sector. This means that purchasing industries are unable to substitute physically similar but regionally differentiated inputs. As we shall see, trade coefficient stability is a critical assumption if interregional I-O models are to be made operational. In this particular model, however, the stability assumption is even more restrictive since it is not simply a question of the proportion of inputs imported from a given region or the imported proportion of a purchasing industry's total inputs remaining constant. Instead, the model implies that the proportion of a given input (i) imported from a particular region (r) for use by a specific purchasing sector (j) located in a specific region (s) should also be constant. This assumption, in effect, freezes the spatial structure of the interregional system as well as the technological structure in each regional economy.

The interregional model can be expressed by modifying the usual I-O equation (Gross Output = Input Requirements + Final Demand) in the following way:

$$X_i^r = \sum_j^n \sum_s^z X_{ij}^{rs} + \sum_s^z Y_i^{rs} . \qquad (4.1)$$

There are nz equations of this type. The output of each industry in each region is seen to be equal to its sales to all industries and final demand sectors in all regions (including its own). The individual interregional interindustry trade coefficients are derived from the observed flows X_{ij}^{rs} and from observed outputs X_j^s, i.e.

$$a_{ij}^{rs} = \frac{X_{ij}^{rs}}{X_j^s}. \qquad (4.2)$$

Substituting (4.2) into (4.1), we obtain:

$$X_i^r = \sum_j^n \sum_s^z a_{ij}^{rs} X_j^s + \sum_s^z Y_i^{rs}. \qquad (4.3)$$

It is clear that measurement of the a_{ij}^{rs}s is the key to the empirical application of this model, and in order to derive these we have to measure interregional trade flows by region of origin and destination *and* by industry of source and purchasing sector. No country as yet possesses interregional trade statistics capable of this degree of disaggregation. Accordingly, the 'ideal' interregional model is non-operational and is likely to remain so for many years to come. Moreover, the crucial importance of the stability assumption in regard to interarea interindustry coefficients means that even if the mammoth task of obtaining point-estimates of all the necessary coefficients could be successfully executed we could not use these for projections without supporting evidence, e.g. estimates for another year. This is because the coefficients must not merely describe interregional trade at a given point in time but also reflect relatively constant interregional input requirements links. Even if data were available, the model could only be used for short-run analysis, where there was stability in the relative supply prices of each output produced in several regions, and in an economy characterised by excess capacity in all sectors. However, this last assumption while closing the door on one kind of coefficient variation creates the conditions for another. For if there are capacity constraints in any part of the system, supply channels are likely to change during an expansionary phase in order to ensure that input requirements are met; on the other hand, if we assume excess capacity in all sectors in all regions there will be strong pressure for nearby locally produced inputs in sectors operating below full capacity to be substituted for imported inputs (e.g. because local producers with their lower transport costs may undercut their more distant rivals). For all these reasons, Isard's interregional I-O model is primarily useful as a reference norm for theory rather than as a feasible empirical technique.

The closest empirical approximation to the full interregional model is a two-region model for California-Washington recently developed by Riefler (see Riefler and Tiebout, 211, 1970). This was made possible by the fact that survey-based I-O tables were already available for California and Washington (twenty-two and thirty-one sectors respectively), and that in the Washington study an import matrix and an export matrix were also available. Thus, many of the initial data requirements were easily accessible. The import and export matrices showed imported inputs and export sales by sector of origin and sector of destination from and to the rest of the world. The import matrix, in particular, revealed the dangers of making proportionality assumptions about the ratio of imported to domestic inputs across a row, since the ratio of imported to total non-value-added inputs varied widely from one input to another and between purchasing sectors. Given these different trade coefficients (m_{ij}s) between Washington and the rest of the world, estimation of the m_{ij}^{cw}s merely required the assumption that a constant proportion of a particular input imported by each sector came from California. The same procedure was adopted with the export matrix: it was assumed that a constant percentage of a particular Washington output exported to each sector went to California. The California-Washington import shares and the Washington-California export shares were estimated from trade flow data derived from three basic sources: ICC (Interstate Commerce Commission) rail statistics; water shipments estimates by the Corps of Engineers; and Census of Transportation data. With the aid of the local input coefficients and the newly derived interregional trade coefficients a table containing a 53×53 interindustry matrix and nine final demand sectors were developed; the rest of the world was treated as exogenous.

Apart from the general technique itself, the study included some tests on trade coefficient stability. There were imperfections in the tests: they were based on rail shipments, and the entrepôt activities of Washington and California in international trade could mean that any instability might have been due to instability in foreign trade coefficients rather than in interregional input trade coefficients. Nevertheless, the tests suggested strong evidence of variation in trading patterns over time. 1961 input trade coefficients were used to predict 1955 tonnage movements between Washington and California. The percentage deviation between predicted and actual terminations of California output in Washington ranged from four to seventy-one per cent; the Washington-California deviations ranged between zero and 55 per cent. Out of twenty-seven commodity groups tested, only eight sectors had an error of below 10 per cent while sixteen sectors had an error of less than 20 per cent.

Even the California-Washington model falls far short of the interregional model as conceived by Isard. The two western States have important links with other regions of the United States, yet all these links were aggregated into the 'rest of the world'. Moreover, interregional interdependence was severely limited by the assumption that the rest of the world sector was exogenous. Yet despite this simplification, the data requirements of the model are still considerable. First, very few regional I-O studies have included an import and/or export matrix. Second, many countries including the United Kingdom still lack the data from which gross interregional commodity flows might be derived. Further research into bilateral models of this kind is desirable and would be useful, but the ideal interregional model remains as far away from implementation as ever.

The intranational model

Although the intranational model developed by Leontief (**140**, 1953) does not itself determine interregional trade flows, it provides a useful starting point to a discussion of operational interregional models. By dividing the sectors of the economy into industries that figure in regional trade (called *national* industries) and industries that sell all their output locally (*local* industries), the model explicitly recognises the importance of regional trade. Moreover, it concentrates attention on extraregional or national impacts on regional economic activity. This model is also capable of describing a special kind of interregional system in that the classification of sectors can be extended (national, regional, subregional, etc.), and the analysis adopted to studying a hierarchy of regions from the nation down to urban areas. Finally, as Polenske (**201**, 1966) argued, the intranational model is a very convenient framework on which to graft alternative assumptions about the determinants of inter-regional trade.

The model can be summarised as follows. Let the n sectors of the economy be divided into two sub-sets: local industries which sell their output only in the region where the goods are produced and national industries which export to other regions besides the region of production. In the latter, therefore, production and consumption are balanced only in the national economy. The output of local industries is distributed (directly and indirectly) to two outlets: regional final demand for local products and to satisfy the direct and indirect requirements of national industries located within the region. If the subscript N represents the subset of national industries and L represents local industries, the aggregate matrix of technical coefficients can be partitioned as follows:

$$A = \begin{bmatrix} A_{NN} & A_{NL} \\ A_{LN} & A_{LL} \end{bmatrix}$$

Only the lower two sub-matrices are used in the model, for each region's share of national industries is assumed to be for each industry a fixed proportion of national output. The model can be expressed by two equations:

$$X_N^r = \lambda_N^r \, X_N^n \tag{4.4}$$

$$X_L^r = (I\text{-}A_{LL})^{-1} \, Y_L^r + (I\text{-}A_{LL})^{-1} \, A_{LN} \, X_N^r \tag{4.5}$$

We assume that the following are either given or have been estimated: the I-O coefficients, the national outputs of national industries, regional distribution shares of national industries (λ_N^r), and regional final demands. Given these variables, we can solve the two equations to derive each region's output of both national and local industries.

The intranational model does not fulfil all the conditions for a general equilibrium model (even within the framework of its restrictive assumptions) because it determines only the regional distribution of outputs whereas a general equilibrium solution must also determine the spatial distribution of goods, i.e. interregional trade flows. However, any of the methods for predicting interregional trade discussed below could be combined with the intranational model, or indeed with many other types of I-O model. At this juncture it is necessary to mention only two alternative simplifying assumptions which stem directly from the intranational model itself. The first of these, a suggestion by Brodersohn (**29**, 1965, p. 26) is 'that the demand for these "national" commodities is allocated by region in the same way as the output of the same'. When there is more than one purchasing sector this implies the additional assumption that each industry within the region has the same trade coefficient for a given input as the average for the region as a whole. The Brodersohn suggestion is very easy to implement since the λ^r_Ns have the dual function of allocating both output and consumption to regions. Thus, if region r produces x per cent of total national output of sector i then x per cent of the total consumption of i in each region is assumed to be purchased from region r. There is no justification for believing that this assumption will produce a reasonable simulation of interregional trade flows. The second possibility is Leontief's own suggestion that the imports of a commodity into a region 'will most likely come from the nearest surplus area' (Leontief, **140**, 1953, p. 95). If strictly applied, this might produce a skeletal framework of dominant interregional flows but would not capture the full complex network of interregional commodity movements. Moreover, to the extent that drawing requirements from nearby supply areas reflects the influence of distance and transport costs, the assumption may be regarded as a crude antecedent to the gravity trade model developed by Leontief a decade later.

The Chenery-Moses model

This method of predicting interregional trade flows used by Chenery (**40**, 1953) and by Moses (**185**, 1955) was the standard technique employed before the development of gravity and linear programming models. It is similar in practice to the Brodersohn variant of the intranational model in that it assumes that each region imports a fixed proportion of its requirements of a given commodity from a particular export region. It varies, however, in its method of estimating these fixed trade coefficients since in the Chenery-Moses formulation the coefficients are derived from base-year interregional trade flow estimates not from the constants λ_n^r. The implication of the model is that if region r imports x per cent of its requirements of commodity i from region s, then each industry j in r will also import x per cent of its i inputs from s. Thus, interregional trade flows are defined in terms of commodity coefficients rather than interindustry coefficients thereby assuming that each local sector follows the average import pattern of the region as a whole. The advantage of this assumption from the point of view of implementing the model is that where commodity flow data exist or can be estimated these usually specify only the regions of origin and destination and do not trace inter-industry flows.

The trade coefficients are derived simply by dividing a region's purchases of a commodity from a given region by total regional consumption of the commodity. Thus the trade coefficients all add up to the unity, i.e.

$$t^{1r} + t^{2r} + \ldots + t^{rr} + t^{sr} + \ldots + t^{zr} = 1. \quad (4.6)$$

Predictions of future interregional trade flows for interregional I-O projections are obtained by multiplying the base year trade coefficients by forecasted regional consumption of each commodity. The strict application of this model assumes that the base year trade coefficients remain unchanged, though Moses accepts that if changes in these coefficients can be predicted or if evidence is available that suggests the need to adjust individual coefficients (because of known capacity constraints, significant changes in relative regional costs, etc.) then new coefficients may be substituted.

The essential ingredients for application of the Chenery-Moses model are: (1) the availability of base-year interregional trade estimates by commodity and by regions of origin and destination; and (2) the reliability of the assumption of stable trade coefficients. The latter is of general importance in many of the trade distribution models and will be discussed separately. The former is also a relevant data requirement in some of the other models, but it is convenient to mention one or two of the problems here. The main stumbling block is how to obtain sufficient data from the meagre sources of information available to construct an interregional trade matrix ($z \times z$) for each commodity. The information which is collected very often refers to one transportation mode (e.g. the ICC Waybill data or the Corps of Engineers water shipments in the United States, or the 1962 Road Goods Survey in the UK [Ministry of Transport, **254**, 1967]) and is often unreliable due to sampling errors. Where sampling is used, the errors frequently prohibit the commodity and regional disaggregation needed for the trade matrices to be usable in the Chenery-Moses model. For example, the eleven to fifteen commodity groups used in the freight flow estimates of the Ministry of Transport (UK) are too highly aggregated for interregional I-O analysis, while the interregional disaggregation (78, 101 or 107 zones depending on the year and mode of the information) is much greater than is necessary for this purpose.[6] The commodity groups used in interregional trade statistics are only very rarely consistent with I-O industrial sectors.

If interregional trade flow data are not available in a form which is usable in interregional I-O analysis, the question arises as to whether they can be estimated by indirect methods. For example, the national coefficient adjustment techniques (i.e. the location quotient and the commodity balances approaches) described in Chapter 6 can also be used for obtaining estimates of interregional trade. These indirect estimates, however, have major defects. They refer to net trade flows whereas gross flows are required in the interregional I-O model. Cross-hauling may be very important[7] particularly with the level of aggregation used in I-O sectors.

---

[6] Although some information has been collected in the 1967-8 road freight survey on thirty commodity classes, this refers only to tonnages moved and will not produce interregional flow matrices for the thirty commodities.

In a 14-region model for fruit and vegetable shipments as a whole, Polenske (**201**, 1966) found that cross-hauls accounted for 2.2 per cent of shipments by rail and 21·3 per cent by road (13·8 per cent for rail plus road).

Moreover, these techniques yield trade flows which do not specify regional origin of imports or regional destination of exports, but merely a sector inflow or outflow for each region of the system. Thus, except in a two-region I-O model, some additional allocation procedure will have to be adopted to assign imports to regional source and exports to regional destination. Linear programming or gravity techniques could be used for this operation. Nevertheless, it is clear that too many arbitrary assumptions and adjustments are involved to use indirect estimates of interregional trade flows in a model of the Chenery-Moses type. The potential sources of error are too great — in the LQ or commodity balance procedure itself, in the neglect of cross-hauls, in the regional assignment solution, and in the stable trade coefficient assumption.

As pointed out below, there are no overwhelming theoretical reasons why trade coefficients should remain stable so that the reliability of the stability assumption is a matter for empirical testing. Moses's own preliminary tests indicated a substantial degree of variation, while Polenske's tests (**201**, 1966) on aggregate fruit and vegetable data and on two commodities (apples and potatoes) and at two levels of regional aggregation (fourteen and six regions) found that estimation errors in the Chenery-Moses model were higher than for other models tested. While it is true that the data requirements of the Chenery-Moses are economical, Polenske also tried an analogous technique which needs the same amount of basic data. This alternative technique she described as the 'fixed row coefficient model', whereas the Chenery-Moses model incorporates a fixed column coefficient assumption, where the coefficients in question refer to the inter-regional trade matrix for each commodity. The former differs from the latter by dividing each *row* in the trade matrix by region r's production of the good so that

$$t^{r1} + t^{r2} + \ldots + t^{rr} + t^{rs} + \ldots + t^{rz} = 1. \quad (4.7)$$

In other words, whereas the Chenery-Moses approach distributes regional consumption between domestic supplies and imports from each other region the row coefficient technique distributes regional production by domestic sales and exports to other regions.

The main feature of the row coefficient model, that the

proportion of the output of industry i in region r sold to region s remains constant irrespective of changes in the level of demand in any of the regions, is theoretically implausible, and infringes the Walrasian assumptions of input-output models that output changes are generated only by shifts in demand and price changes by shifts in supply. It is not surprising, therefore, that in her tests on the Japanese interregional model Polenske found that the row coefficient model performed almost consistently less well than either column coefficient (i.e. Chenery-Moses) or Leontief-Strout gravity models (Polenske, 204, 1970). On the other hand, in her earlier work on fruit and vegetables shipments (Polenske, 201, 1966) the row coefficient assumption worked relatively better. The critical question is whether changes in output have more or less impact on the regional distribution of shipments than fluctuations in total demand. Two possible explanations were suggested for the fruit and vegetable results: the strong interest of producers in retaining market links with each major consumer market, leading to rationing of available supplies in periods of low output; the indifference of consumers towards the regional origin of the goods consumed, leading to more regional substitution and hence variation in the import coefficients.

Of course, substantial variation in the row coefficients will have repercussions on the column coefficients, and *vice versa.* Variations, particularly random variations, in several cells of the interregional trade flow matrix will tend to invalidate both the column coefficient and the row coefficient assumptions. This is exacerbated by the degree of interdependence between exports (row values) and imports (column values) due to the facts that total interregional trade must be in balance (i.e. total exports = total imports for any commodity, though any individual region may have a positive, zero or negative trade balance) and that each bilateral export flow is also an import flow from the other region's point of view. The interdependence between rows and columns also makes economic sense in that changes in supply (output) and changes in demand (consumption) are interdependent and this supply-demand interaction will have repercussions on the structure and distribution of interregional trade. For these reasons, although one assumption may give better results than another, we should not expect the row coefficient and the Chenery-Moses models to diverge very widely in their predictive power. If one fails very badly, so should the other.

Linear programming transportation model[8]

The linear programming transportation model may in some cases be an appropriate technique for the derivation of inter-regional commodity flows. It calls for a different set of information inputs than some of the other models: regional production of each commodity, regional consumption of each commodity (D_i^r), and average transport costs per unit between region r and region s (T_i^{rs}). As with many of the regional trade distribution models, the linear programming solution provides no guidance as to sector destinations unless additional assumptions are made. The linear programming transportation model enables us to estimate interregional shipments given the above data requirements where inter-regional trade is assumed to take place so as to minimise total transport costs:

$$\text{Min} \sum_{r=1}^{z} \sum_{s=1}^{z} T_i^{rs} . X_i^{rs} \qquad (4.8)$$

subject to
$$\sum_{s=1}^{z} X_i^{rs} = X_i^r$$

$$\sum_{r=1}^{z} X_i^{rs} = D_i^s$$

where
$$X_i^{rs} \geqslant 0.$$

The best simulations of trade flows via linear programming methods are obtained in the case of shipments of a homogeneous commodity between spatially separated markets (quasi-points). In such a case, the number of flows is more likely to be reduced to a minimum giving rise to an optimal

---

[8]This section deals only with linear programming methods of determining interregional trade flows. There is a more general relationship between I-O and linear programming, but this is discussed separately in Chapter 10.

pattern of trade. But the linear programming transportation model is a most unsatisfactory way of distributing trade in an interregional I-O model. There are several reasons for this conclusion. First, the data problems are more serious. Unless some crude surrogate for transport costs is used, such as distance between the central points (or primary cities) of each pair of regions, it is not easy to obtain data for transport costs. This is particularly so when we take account of the facts that regions are spatially differentiated with many possible origins and destinations and that all transportation modes must be jointly taken into account for interregional I-O purposes. Secondly, commodity groups for which data are available are frequently a conglomerate category of heterogeneous goods, and this lack of homogeneity is even more evident in I-O sectors.[9] Broadly speaking, the more heterogeneous the commodity or industry group, the weaker the predictive power of the linear programming model (O'Sullivan, **193**, 1971). Third, like so many of the trade distribution models, there is no allowance for cross-hauls between regions.

Finally and most important, the model predicts an even more unrealistic pattern of trade than results from a no cross-hauls assumption. Because it is an optimising model it reduces the *number* of trade flows so as to minimise transport costs, and consequently the interregional trade matrix predicted by the model contains far too many zero cells. A property of the LP transportation model is that the solution contains the same number of non-zero trade flows as there are effective constraints. With z origins and z destinations, the number of constraints and hence the number of trade flows is equal to $2z-1$. This means that only $2z - 1/z^2$ of the total cells in the interregional trade matrix contain a positive trade flow. The proportion of cells *actually* occupied will be far higher than obtained via the LP solution.[10]

[9]Homogeneity is, of course, an important criterion for aggregation in an I-O sectoring scheme, but homogeneity in input patterns does not imply a homogeneous product from the viewpoint of interregional trade.

[10]O'Sullivan's tests on a 78^2 matrix showed an average of 28·8 per cent of cells actually occupied (range 9-61 per cent) compared with 2·5 per cent predicted by the LP model and 40 per cent (range 21-77 per cent) compared with a predicted 8·2 per cent in a 24^2 matrix (O'Sullivan, **193**, 1971). Moreover, these results overestimate the number of zero cells in the actual trade matrix because they refer to one mode of transport only − by road.

Gravity models

Gravity models have been used to analyse and predict inter-regional commodity flows (see for example O'Sullivan, **192**, 1970) and have also been specifically incorporated in an interregional I-O framework (Leontief and Strout, **149**, 1963; Wilson, **267**, 1968; Polenske, **206**, 1970; Edwards and Gordon, **62**, 1970). The rationale underlying the gravity approach is that the spatial movement of goods is directly related to the level of demand in the region of destination but is inhibited by the 'friction of distance'. If base-year interregional trade flows are available, a generalised production and attraction constrained gravity model may be used. This can be expressed as:

$$X_i^{rs} = k_i \, X_i^r \, D_i^s \, d^{rs\,(-\alpha_i)} \qquad (4.9)$$

subject to
$$\sum_{s=1}^{z} X_i^{rs} = X_i^r$$

$$\sum_{r=1}^{z} X_i^{rs} = D_i^s$$

where k_i = constant

α_i = exponential parameter to be fitted

D_i^s = demand for commodity i in region s.

Given X_i^{rs}, X_i^r, D_i^s and d^{rs}, k_i and α_i can be estimated by regression analysis.[11] The estimated values of k_i and α_i may then be combined with predicted future values of regional outputs and regional demands to obtain estimates of future interregional trade flows. The values of α_i can vary widely

---

[11]The regression equation takes the form

$$\log \frac{X_i^{rs}}{X_i^r D_i^s} = a - b \log d^{rs},$$

where $a = k_i$ and $b = \alpha_i$ (see O'Sullivan, **192**, 1970). Sometimes, it is useful to replace the constant k by two constants, say g^r and h^s (where $k = g^r h^s$), which reflect the relative supply position of region r and the relative demand position of region s respectively.

from commodity to commodity.[12] One reason for this is intercommodity differences in transport cost/value per ton ratios, since the size of α_i tends to be an inverse function of the value per ton of commodity i.

This type of gravity model may be compared with linear programming methods of deriving estimates of interregional trade flows. The gravity model, though requiring much the same kind of information, may be less demanding in its data requirements in that distance is much easier to measure than unit transport costs. On the other hand, the linear programming transportation model does not require base-year trade flows, whereas the gravity model in the form described above does; however, this is not an inevitable distinction since the Leontief-Strout gravity model can substitute exogenous measures of transfer cost parameters for base-year trade flows. The computational problems involved are much simpler with the gravity than with the LP model, though economy in computation is much less of an advantage nowadays than in the early years of computer development. More important is the fact that the gravity approach gives a more realistic simulation of interregional trade with two-way flows between regions and with the pattern of trade reflecting actual, empirically observed behaviour rather than optimising principles. Despite this, it does not follow that the gravity approach always produces better results. O'Sullivan (**192**, 1970) found that correlations between actual and predicted flo٧٠s were much higher in the LP than in the gravity model for nine out of eleven commodity groups.[13] However, the

---

[12] O'Sullivan's estimates ranged from $-0\cdot77$ to $-1\cdot64$ and those of Edwards and Gordon from $-0\cdot48$ to $-2\cdot22$.

[13] A major qualification on statistical grounds to the value of this finding should be noted. The comparison was based on multiple correlation coefficients obtained for the linear programming case by regressing actual flows against the linear programming solution and for the gravity model by fitting the log-linear version shown on p. 70, n. 11. This procedure did not permit the actual trade flows to be compared with the expected trade flows generated by the two models. The linear programming goodness of fit is overstated since perfect correlation would imply a linear regression slope equal to unity through the origin (and the test adopted does not measure the deviation from this), while that of the gravity model is understated because the tests refer to how relative distance affects $X_i^{rs}/X_i^r D_i^s$ rather than to how mass and distance variables are capable of predicting the value of each bilateral trade flow. I am indebted to Ian R. Gordon for this observation.

gravity models performed best for miscellaneous, heterogeneous commodity groups, whereas LP solutions are more satisfactory when dealing with single homogeneous goods. This suggests that gravity techniques may be the more appropriate method of estimating interregional flows between I-O sectors.

There are many types of gravity model, and several of these might be used to estimate or predict interregional trade. Perhaps the most useful, however, is that devised by Leontief and Strout specifically for an interregional I-O model. Their approach has two distinctive virtues. First, they incorporated it in an I-O model which simultaneously determines regional outputs and interregional shipments. Second, one of their versions of the model avoids having to measure interregional trade even in the base year.

There is no need in the Leontief-Strout model to assign the imports of goods to particular using industries, since the model is based on an assumption that does not distinguish between local supplies and supplies from other regions.

> The regional origin of the particular batch of a given kind of good absorbed by its users in one particular region is as irrelevant to them as the ultimate regional destination of his output is to a producer. It is as if the producers of a specific commodity or service located in one particular region had merged their output in a single regional pool, and the users of that commodity or service located in a given region had ordered and received it through a regional demand pool. All interregional movements of a particular commodity or service within a multiregional economy can thus be visualised as shipments from regional supply to regional demand pools of that good (Leontief and Strout, **149**, 1963, p. 120).[14]

This assumption serves two very useful purposes. The first is the point already referred to, i.e. if regional origin does not matter to users, it is unnecessary to make a distinction between local and imported requirements. Second, it enables us to interpret regional outflows as varying directly with the level of output in the region of origin while inflows vary directly with regional consumption. This makes it easier to

---

[14]This assumption is, however, characteristic of many other trade flows estimation methods, such as the Chenery-Moses and the linear programming models.

specify the interregional commodity flows equation which is
the central feature of the model.

The model can be summarised in the following set of
equations:

$$X_i^r = \sum_{j=1}^{n} a_{ij}^r X_j^r + Y_i^r \tag{4.10}$$

$$X_i^r = \sum_{s=1}^{z} X_i^{rs} \tag{4.11}$$

$$D_i^s = \sum_{r=1}^{z} X_i^{rs} \tag{4.12}$$

$$X_i^{rs} = \frac{X_i^r \cdot D_i^s}{X_i^n} \cdot Q_i^{rs} \tag{4.13}$$

Moreover, if the interregional system is closed we may also
write

$$\sum_{r=1}^{z} X_i^r = X_i^n = \sum_{s=1}^{z} D_i^s. \tag{4.14}$$

Equations (4.11), (4.12) and (4.14) are matters of definition,
equation (4.10) expresses the usual I-O relationships while
equation (4.13) is the gravity trade model used for determining interregional shipments. Q_i^{rs} is a parameter reflecting
transfer costs between region r and region s for commodity i.
Although (4.13) is a non-linear equation it is homogeneous
of the first degree. This is an important property from the
point of view of computations. We know from the linear
homogeneous equation (4.10) that a proportional change in
each of the nz final demands will be accompanied by an
equal proportional change in all regional outputs and inputs,
while the homogeneity of (4.13) ensures that if all regional
outputs and inputs change in the same proportion interregional shipments will also change by that proportion.

The Leontief-Strout gravity I-O model does not require
a huge input of data. Provided that final demands, I-O

coefficients and the trade coefficients (Q_i^{rs}) are known, regional outputs, regional consumption and interregional flows can be determined. These interregional flows are more satisfactory than in any of the other models examined in the sense that provided regions r and s both produce and consume a given good shipments will occur in both directions. The critical problem in empirical application of the model is the measurement of Q_i^{rs}. There are two possible methods. First, if data on base year trade flows are available Q_i^{rs} can be derived empirically from equation (4.13), and the Q_i^{rs} values obtained used to estimate trade flows for future years (this is what Leontief and Strout call the point-estimate model).[15] However, even if there are no base year trade flow estimates at hand, Q_i^{rs} may be measured by resorting to exogenous estimates of transfer costs. Leontief and Strout suggest that Q_i^{rs} can be estimated as

$$(C_i^r + K_i^s) \, d_i^{rs} \, \delta_i^{rs} . \tag{4.15}$$

The term δ_i^{rs} is given a value of 1 or 0 depending on whether or not the good is exported from region r to region s. C_i^r and K_i^s are parameters representing the relative positions of region r as a supplier to other regions and of region s as a user, and their values are derived statistically. The most important variable d_i^{rs} is a measure of the inverse of the per unit transport cost for commodity i. However, where data shortages prevent an estimate of actual transport costs,

---

[15]Polenske (201, 1966) argued that the point-estimate model did not yield consistent estimates of future interregional trade flows. Her proposed solution was to modify the base-year values of Q_i^{rs} by introducing two new variables, γ_i^r and ϵ_i^s, estimated from the equations

$$\sum_{r=1}^{z} (\gamma_i^r + \epsilon_i^s) \, Q_i^{rs} X_i^r = X_i^n$$

$$\sum_{s=1}^{z} (\gamma_i^r + \epsilon_i^s) \, Q_i^{rs} D_i^s = X_i^n .$$

In her tests of various multiregional trade models on fruit and vegetable shipments, Polenske found that this modified version of the Leontief-Strout gravity model predicted best of all and also did very well in forecasting the year-to-year direction of changes in shipments. The standard Leontief-Strout model was the second-best predictor of interregional trade flows.

Leontief and Strout suggest that the reciprocal of distance may be used. In such circumstances the burden of inter-commodity variations in Q_i^{rs} shifts to the C_i^r and K_i^s para-meters. It is apparent that this format of the Leontief-Strout gravity model is closely analogous to the production and attraction constrained gravity model described above.

There have been few tests of the Leontief-Strout gravity model. Leontief and Strout themselves presented some partial tests of the usefulness of their model in predicting rail shipments of coal, cement, soyabean oil and steel shapes. Even for predictions only two and four years distant from the base year, the estimation errors were very high. More recently, Polenske (**204**, 1970) has tested the full Leontief-Strout gravity I-O model with the aid of the 1960 Japanese interregional I-O tables ($z = 9$; $n = 10$). Given final demand changes for 1960-3, the model was used to estimate regional outputs and interregional trade flows for 1963. The accuracy of the estimates of the latter was impossible to test since there were no interregional trade estimates for 1963, but the predictions of national and regional outputs were testable. The model overestimated actual 1963 total Japanese production by 3.6 per cent while the range of variation for total regional outputs was $+16.0$ to -4.8 per cent. [16] Although these errors appear quite large, they are in part explicable by factors other than the gravity model, e.g. technological change was rapid in the early 1960s yet 1960 technical coefficients were used in the predictions. The model clearly needs further testing before a definite appraisal of the usefulness of gravity techniques in inter-regional I-O models can be made.

The stability of interregional trade coefficients

If interregional I-O models are to yield reasonable predictions of changes in output in response to changes in final demand, it is important that the interregional trade coefficients should be stable. If they are unstable, the actual regional distribution

---

[16] The range of variation in predictions of regional sectoral outputs was much wider particularly for primary industries (agriculture, mining) but also for the main manufacturing industries (metals, textiles and chemicals).

of outputs and the predicted distribution may vary widely.[17]

Although we can list sets of theoretical assumptions that will lead to trade coefficient stability, there is no guarantee (or even likelihood) that these assumptions hold. For example, we might assume that traded goods are homogeneous to ensure that shifts in trade coefficients do not take place as a result of product mix. But how often can we rely on sectoral disaggregation being fine enough to give I-O sectors the property of homogeneity? We could assume no changes in relative regional costs of production or in relative transport costs between regions, and in this case the assumptions may be reasonable provided we stick to short-run analysis. But can we always assume excess capacity in each industry in each region, excess capacity in each bilateral transport channel and unemployed labour in each region? These are vital assumptions since otherwise capacity constraints and bottlenecks will lead to shifts from one supply source to another. Or consider another situation: if regional production and consumption centres coincide yet are far apart from centres in other regions and if unit transport costs are heavy then interregional trade coefficients are likely to be stable even in the face of shifts in relative costs. On the other hand, the trade coefficients of a small region with many alternative suppliers outside her boundaries will tend to be unstable particularly for goods where the transport cost/value ratio is low. Finally, if we make an assumption of complete regional specialisation it is clear that trade coefficients will be stable because there is only a single source for the input in question.

These comments are merely illustrations of the fact that we can develop theoretical models which predict coefficient stability or alternative models predicting instability according to taste. The question of trade coefficient stability is not a theoretical point but an empirical problem. One approach to this is to supply a long list of plausible but insufficiently

---

[17] Of course, it does not necessarily upset the models if trade coefficients do vary provided that the variations are predictable so that new coefficients can be substituted. However, changes in trade coefficients are notoriously difficult to predict compared with changes in input coefficients. In this chapter we concentrate on the importance of stable trade coefficients if interregional models are to be useful as a short-run analytical tool. Methods of forecasting longer-term changes in trade coefficients are discussed separately in Chapter 9, pp. 175–83.

tested empirical generalisations as to why interregional trade coefficients should remain stable (see for example Hochwald *et. al.,* **100**, 1960). Such generalisations might include the following:

(1)   the comparative stability of the relative prices of goods that figure prominently both in interregional and intraregional trade;

(2)   the similarity between consumer price indices in different regions;

(3)   the reluctance of industries to alter sources of supply for high transport cost inputs;

(4)   habit and custom, as expressed, for instance, in an unwillingness to change suppliers in response to minor price differentials;

(5)   the breakdown between local supplies and imports may reflect quality or other differences in the inputs from the two sources, i.e. another manifestation of the product-mix problem.

These points are not very convincing, at least without more thorough empirical evidence. In any event, they do not all guarantee trade coefficient stability.

Probably the only way to test the hypothesis of interregional trade coefficient stability is by direct measurement of the coefficients over time. Unfortunately, there are very few tests of this kind. Moses (**185**, 1955) carried out some limited tests on five broad commodity groups for 1947, 1948 and 1949 in his three-region model of the United States. When 1949 coefficients were used with 1947 data, the average error in predicting the fifteen total regional shipments was 4 per cent, and it was 12 per cent for individual interregional flows. While admitting the existence of variation in the coefficients Moses's conclusion was 'that they have exhibited sufficient stability to warrant their being subjected to further statistical evaluation on various levels of regional and commodity aggregation' (p. 826). This is perhaps rather optimistic, particularly since we would expect to find relative stability in supply channels when the national economy is divided into a few, very large regions (Isard, **107**,

1951, p. 322, n. 16). As pointed out above (p. 61), the more recent tests by Riefler and Tiebout indicate even wider degrees of error at the individual interstate shipments level. Since all the tests refer to very brief time intervals, they cast doubt on the underlying assumptions of interregional models even for short-run predictions. The failure hitherto to find strong support for the coefficient stability hypothesis must be kept in mind whenever interregional I-O models are employed.

Are interregional feedbacks important?

For certain kinds of analysis, such as tracing the effects on each region of an increase in national growth, an interregional I-O model is essential. A more debatable question is whether or not it is necessary to employ an interregional model when our primary concern is measuring economic impacts on a particular region. In other words, what do we lose by using the time- and data-saving single region model? This problem is not peculiar to regional input-output analysis alone. The choice between a regional and an interregional approach has plagued regional income analysts since Metzler (**164**, 1950) first presented the theoretical demonstration of the difference between the simple regional income multiplier and that which allows for interregional feedback effects.[18] In the latter case, an increase in income in region r will lead to an increase in r's imports from some or all of the other $z-1$ regions in the system, and the induced expansion in their exports will have a multiplier effect on their levels of income. Their higher incomes will be associated with rising imports, and some of the increased imports will take the form, either directly or indirectly, of expanded exports from region r. The crucial point is whether these feedback effects are quantitatively significant or not. The aggregate nature and crudity of the data have not made it easy to resolve this problem with Keynesian multiplier models. A wide divergence of views prevails: Brown, (**31**, 1967) for instance, argued that the multiplier was 'only marginally increased by putting in

---

[18]Chipman (**43**, 1950) also made the same points simultaneously and independently.

the effects of repercussions', while Steele (**229**, 1969, and **284**, 1972) held that, on the contrary, interregional feedbacks were important (his estimates of feedback multipliers were 4-12 per cent higher than simple multipliers). Since input-output models are currently in more widespread use for estimating income multiplier effects at the regional level, the question of the size of feedbacks in such models is clearly of some importance.

The measurement of feedbacks requires full specification of both intraregional and interregional trade matrices.[19] In a multiregional model (for expositional purposes let us assume $z = 2$) the coefficient matrix may be partitioned, i.e.

$$A = \begin{bmatrix} A^{11} & | & A^{12} \\ ---- & + & ---- \\ A^{21} & | & A^{22} \end{bmatrix}$$

and the usual input-output equation $(I - A)X = Y$ can be written as

$$(I - A^{11})X^1 - A^{12}X^2 = Y^1 \qquad (4.16a)$$

$$(I - A^{22})X^2 - A^{21}X^1 = Y^2 \qquad (4.16b)$$

Solving these simultaneous matrix equations yields the following solution for X^1:

$$X^1 = [(I-A^{11}) - A^{12}(I-A^{22})^{-1}A^{21}]^{-1}Y^1 + [(I-A^{11}) -$$
$$A^{12}(I-A^{22})A^{21}]^{-1}A^{21}(I-A^{22})^{-1}Y^2 \qquad (4.17)$$

and similarly for X^2. Since in the measurement of interregional feedbacks we are interested only in the changes in final demands, we may treat X^1, Y^1, Y^2 as if they were $\triangle X^1$, $\triangle Y^1$ and $\triangle Y^2$. Also, since the objective is to find the effect on X^1 of changes in final demand from within the region (i.e. $\triangle Y^1$) we assume $\triangle Y^2 = 0$ and drop the second term in the above equation. Moreover, we know that in the

---

[19]Of course, in practical terms the interregional trade matrices may have to be constructed with the aid of one of the simplifying interregional trade models discussed earlier in this chapter. As a result, purchasing sectors may not be specified and these matrices will have non-zero elements only on the diagonal, thereby assuming that imports are distributed to local industries in the same way as local inputs.

single region model the change in gross output is shown as

$$\Delta X^1 = (I - A^{11})^{-1} \Delta Y^1 . \qquad (4.18)$$

Accordingly, assuming a given change in final demand in Region 1 the change in output due to feedback will be

$$\left\{ [(I-A^{11}) - A^{12} (I-A^{22})^{-1} A^{21}]^{-1} - (I-A^{11})^{-1} \right\} \Delta Y^1 .$$

The size of the feedback is clearly very important in any decision about the need to use interregional models to measure impacts on the individual region. The empirical research on this question is primarily by Miller (175, 1966, and 176, 1969) though Riefler and Tiebout (211, 1970) also had some brief observations to make. Miller's tests were carried out under varying sets of assumptions about the nature of final demand changes, the types of region examined (though in the context of a two region model) and the techniques for measuring interregional trade. The results did not appear to vary a great deal in response to changes in the initial assumptions. A basic distinction may be drawn, however, between the case of a two-region model where there are leakages to a third outside region (e.g. the rest of the world) and the case where the regions in the model form a closed system of completely interconnected regions. In the first case, Miller found that feedbacks were very small − on average, the single region model underestimated the change in gross output by only one-half of 1 per cent. Of course, these results might vary according to the degree of interdependence between and the relative sizes of the two regions. In their California-Washington model Riefler and Tiebout (pp. 144-6) found that interregional linkages raised output in Washington as a consequence of a final demand change there by 4·3-5·0 per cent, though California's output rose by only 0·3-0·8 per cent (with two conspicuous exceptions[20]) due to linkage effects in response to changes in California final demand.

The more precise test of the scale of interregional feedbacks, however, is with the closed system without outside leakages. The results here were rather different and showed

---

[20] The exceptions were primary metals and paper products. These industries purchased relatively high proportions of their inputs in Washington State.

that feedbacks were more significant. The average error was about 7 per cent, and was once again invariant to the type of final demand change (e.g. whether this was confined to one sector or spread equally over all industries). Miller's second set of experiments was more comprehensive in its testing of the closed system. A clear finding was the (not surprising) conclusion that the size of the feedback depended upon the degree of interregional interdependence (or its converse, the degree of self-sufficiency). The larger and more self-sufficient a region is, the less necessary it is to allow for interregional linkages. Miller even suggested a simple rule of thumb to determine *a priori* the magnitude of feedbacks: a region which supplies 10 per cent of its own needs will underestimate gross output changes by 10 per cent if it ignores feedbacks, while a region with 90 per cent self-sufficiency will underestimate output changes by 2 per cent; between these limits, a 1 per cent decline in error is associated with each 10 per cent increase in self-sufficiency.[21] Clearly, more empirical tests are needed on the validity of this proposition.

A very recent study of a closed interregional system reinforces the argument that, at least in a closed system, feedback effects are too large to be ignored (Greytack, 77, 1970). The tests were carried out on a completely regionalised United States economy disaggregated into a system of eight regions with twenty-three industries in each region. Although there were drawbacks in the data, national interindustry coefficients were used in each region and a variety of sources and estimation methods used to derive the trade coefficients, the results were very clear-cut. Greytack's major findings were that interregional feedback effects accounted for a sizeable proportion of the total impact of a unit of each industry's production on the aggregate level of output in the region (on average, about 27 per cent) and that neglecting interregional feedbacks in the calculation of regional impact multipliers produced on average error of 21·4 per cent. Even more troublesome was that the nature of the error in the regional *v.* interregional multiplier estimates was not primarily due to systematic bias, and therefore

[21]A related point is that the size of feedback effects is not independent of the degree of regional aggregation.

it was impossible to adjust for the errors automatically. In this particular case, applying the optimal linear correction reduced the root mean square error by only 27 per cent. For closed systems without outside leakages, the pendulum is swinging in favour of the need to take account of inter-regional feedbacks.

The evidence is thus rather inconclusive. However, where the interregional models available are of a type with leakages outside the system, there is probably little gain in using the more complicated and data-hungry interregional model as opposed to the single region model, at least when we are concerned merely with estimating the overall impact on an individual region of changes in its own final demand. It is, of course, extremely difficult to develop closed interregional models, and in an economy such as the United Kingdom for instance leakages into foreign trade can be very heavy. Moreover, the need to employ an interregional model will depend very much on the scale of region studied and on how heavily it is engaged in interregional trade. Because of limited resources at the local level, there is a strong argument for interregional models to be developed by government or other national agencies so that they are available to be grafted on to sub-regional analyses and forecasts as required. Even if it is decided that the type of region and structure of the system make it acceptable to use the single-region model, caution must be exercised in how it is used. The small errors due to the neglect of feedback quoted by Miller refer to average errors over regional output as a whole. If the objective is to measure impacts on one or more specific sectors, a single region model ignoring feedbacks may give very misleading results.

PART TWO: Data problems

5 Data Collection and Preparation of the Transactions Table

The earliest regional input-output studies employed national input coefficients, but from the late 1950s an increasing proportion of studies have used industrial survey methods to draw up a transactions table from primary source data. Although there has been some revival of secondary data techniques in recent years that usually adopt certain adjustment or reduction procedures to convert national coefficients, primary data methods remain the recognised methodology for local input-output studies. They have the advantage that they do not assume, implicitly or explicitly, that regional production functions are similar to national and they reduce, though fail to eliminate, 'industry-mix' and 'product-mix' problems. On the other hand, they are more costly in the use of both money and time. A survey-based table may cost ten times as much and take eight to ten times as long to prepare as a secondary data table. The other major difference between survey (primary) and non-survey (secondary) models is their relative effectiveness in the measurement of inter-regional trade flows. In the former both intra- and extra-regional trade flows are estimated directly from actual inter-industry transactions data. In the latter, however, the input-output coefficients are conceived as technical coefficients rather than trade flow coefficients. Interregional trade flows are estimated residually as a by-product of the adjustment process on the national coefficients. This usually involves some limiting assumption, e.g. maximising local trade, which can often lead to very inaccurate estimates of interregional trade.

The aim of this chapter is to describe some of the main procedures involved in the collection of data and preparation of the table for a survey-based input-output model.[1] A rational sequence of stages in this process could take the following form:

(1)   delimitation of the study area;

(2)   objectives of the research;

(3)   secondary data search and description of the structure of the regional economy;

(4)   listing the population of firms and establishments by industry;

(5)   the sectoring scheme and aggregation;

(6)   development of control totals;

(7)   selecting the samples;

(8)   questionnaire design and preparation; type and nature of information required; selection of base year;

(9)   conduct of the survey;

(10)   processing the data;

(11)   preparation of the transactions table; input-output conventions; 'arbitraging';

(12)   consistency checking.

These steps will be discussed in turn. The level of the analysis is in general rather than in very specific terms, since this book is not intended as a manual on regional input-output techniques.

Delimitation of the study area

This is often a non-question, since many regional input-output studies are commissioned or sponsored by regional or national government agencies, and the study area is pre-

---

[1]For a more detailed discussion of some of the problems that arise in collecting the data for and constructing a survey-based input-output table see Isard and Langford (**117**, 1971).

determined as an existing administrative unit. However, where there is flexibility in selecting and delimiting the study area, there are several economic considerations to bear in mind. For instance, it is important that interregional trade coefficients should be stable if a regional input-output model is to be used for forecasting or economic impact analysis. Stability in trade coefficients implies fixed supply areas, and in an ideal world the 'regions' of an input-output analysis would conform to a supply area. Of course, even in this ideal world there is an arbitrary element in bounding the region since supply areas will be of different size for different commodities. Another not unrelated factor is that the study region should not cut across the local economic structure. This prescription favours the homogeneous region concept. An obvious illustration is that the study area for input-output analysis should avoid covering only a half of a crop-growing area, coalfield or steelmaking belt. Similarly, in a 'closed' input-output model (i.e. where households are endogenous) homogeneity of consumption patterns is a desirable feature to be taken into account in the choice of area.

If homogeneous regions are good candidates for input-output models, strongly nodal regions may be poor candidates unless the boundaries of the region conform closely to the outer limits of the gravitational field of influence of the dominant node, and even then an important condition must be that this 'force field' should not overlap with that of a node outside the region. Moreover, a strongly nodal region may be characterised by rapid change and flux within the region as nodes rise and fall in relative importance and as polarisation towards the nodes alters the spatial balance and distribution of economic activities within the region. The dynamics of intraregional change may be reflected in instability in interindustry relationships, and such instability will seriously weaken the utility of the input-output tool. The best way to handle a nodal region with input-output techniques may be to adopt a regional-subregional model which measures the flows between the poles and other parts of the region as well as between industrial sectors.

An important, if almost self-evident, point is that the delimitation of the study area is not independent of the objectives of the research. For example, a regional input-output model used for measuring tax impacts should be applied to geographical areas that coincide with fiscal units, whereas an urban input-output model might employ areal subdivisions that break a broad city-region down into the central city, the suburbs and the rest of the region. Similarly, where the input-output table is drawn up as an adjunct to regional policy the study area could well be a 'planning' or 'programming' region, i.e. a geographical area over which economic policy decisions apply.

The size of the selected area may have a feedback effect on the relevance, validity and effectiveness of the input-output model. It is arguable that a larger region makes a more appropriate object for an input-output analysis on at least two grounds: *ceteris paribus,* the larger the region the smaller the ratio of extraregional to total flows, and regional trade flows are more difficult to measure and probably more variable than intraregional flows; larger regions will tend to be more diversified and the local interindustry matrix should consequently exhibit more interdependence and fewer zero cells than in a small region. On the other hand, a small region is easier to cover using primary survey data both because the geographical area to be researched will tend to be smaller and because its economic structure will be simpler. It is doubtful whether there are scale economies in the construction of survey-based input-output tables; indeed, it would not be surprising if research costs increased more than proportionately to increases in the size of the region. However, it is debatable whether very small regions (e.g. small town communities) make suitable areas for an input-output analysis, partly because the ratio of final demand to total output will tend to be high in such regions, partly because most of the interindustry transactions will be in effect interregional flows which are much more difficult to trace. Hence a small area table may be much less reliable.

Objectives of the research

The research objectives of any input-output project will undoubtedly influence the nature and type of information required and thereby dictate the scale and organisation of the data-collection process. For instance, taking an extreme case, where a project is concerned not only with measuring exogenous changes on a major region of the national economy but also with estimating the impact of growth and decline in this region on the rest of the economy, an interregional model with its huge data and resource requirements may be needed. Interregional models will also be obligatory for evaluating the effects of changes in central government spending (e.g. defence costs) or in government location policies on all regions in the economy. At the other extreme, if the analyst is concerned with measuring the impact of expansion in a key industry on a small region, a highly aggregated single region model of the TAP (Technique for Area Planning) variety or on the lines discussed by Doeksen and Little (55, 1968) may be sufficient for the purpose (for further details of the use of simplified aggregate models see Chapter 7, pp. 131-8). However, where survey methods are used it is not easy to construct highly aggregated tables, and sophisticated sampling procedures may be needed to produce accurate results. Generalising from these two points, the research objectives have implications for the extent of disaggregation of regional trade flows and for the size of the local interindustry matrix. In some cases, for example when attention is focussed on intraregional changes, a detailed interindustry matrix will be needed, but regional trade can be handled with a single import row and export column. In other situations the emphasis of the research will be on relationships with other areas outside the region's boundaries, and a 'dogleg' table will be required with full-blown export and import matrices; the interindustry matrix, on the other hand, could be either very small or, more usually, the same size as the trade flow matrices. These two very dissimilar types of table will have quite different meanings in terms of data collection. The research effort needed to provide complete trade matrices will be enormous unless non-survey techniques are used to apportion total imports and exports among sectors; apportionment via primary data could call for industrial surveys in *other* regions as well as in the study region.

Sometimes the objective of a regional input-output model is to provide a basis for regional forecasting. In this case the degree of detail required in the forecast will dictate the degree of disaggregation in the table. Forecasts which incor-

porate projections for individual industries at the minimum
list heading or SIC four-digit levels will demand a very large
table. But if the input-output model is to be used for aggregate economic forecasts, then a simple table may be more
than adequate. Williamson (**265**, 1970) showed that very
small tables (even 6 X 6) could yield fairly acceptable forecasts at the aggregate level though not necessarily for
individual sectors (see Chapter 7, pp. 134-8).

Secondary data search and description of regional economic structure

Once the decisions on the study area and the research objectives have been taken, the analysts may begin the process of
collecting the data for the construction of the table. The
first phase in this process is so obvious that it hardly needs a
mention. A primary data table does not mean that available
secondary information should be ignored. Published statistics
will be valuable in several ways, even though they rarely
yield direct information on interindustry transactions. They
enable us to have a clearer picture of the structure of the
regional economy (e.g. its industrial composition) and this
helps us to assess the scale of the surveys needed and gives
some preliminary clues about the ultimate shape and
structure of the table. They are very useful indeed for the
estimation of control totals (see below), a crucial step in
construction of the table for sectors where sampling procedures are used. For several sectors of the economy, central
and local government and agriculture are typical examples,
published data may be quite extensive, and the effort needed
for surveying these sectors is then substantially reduced. Even
in regions where published data are sparse, it is usually possible to obtain detailed employment statistics by individual
industry and even this frugal information provides a rough
guide to the region's economic structure. Moreover, for some
of the exogenous final demand sectors and the primary
input rows there is often no alternative to published information; central government spending in the region and tax
payments may be most easily obtained in this way. Also,
ratio and apportionment techniques where regional totals
are estimated as shares of the national may be useful for

filling in some of the data gaps for sectors too insignificant and too costly to survey. To sum up, the search for and use of secondary data is an essential and valuable part of the research effort even in the most primary-data-based input-output study.

Listing the population of firms and establishments by industry

The first step in collecting unpublished data must be to trace the sources from which these data will be obtained. In effect, this means tracing all the establishments in both the private and the public sectors throughout the region; this must be done even for sectors where very small samples are to be used since we cannot draw a satisfactory sample if our knowledge of the population as a whole is imperfect.

There are many possible sources for lists of firms, though their availability varies from region to region. Several sources will be normally used in an attempt to obtain a comprehensive master list. In some circumstances lists of firms by industry may be obtained from government departments, though in the United Kingdom the disclosure rules of the Statistics of Trade Act of 1947 frequently even apply to the release of simple information of this kind. Where households are to be surveyed, electoral lists give a fairly comprehensive coverage. For business firms industrial and trade directories may be used where available. Such lists may be incomplete (this is in fact a characteristic of virtually all lists of firms), particularly in this respect — that some areas of the region, especially metropolitan areas, may be covered much more comprehensively than other areas, e.g. rural areas. Chamber of commerce lists are a similar though generally less complete source. Lists of all commercial and industrial purchasers of electricity, gas or water may be obtained from the public utility companies serving the region; although coverage particularly of electricity consumers will be almost complete, it may be difficult to assign the names and addresses to industries. If this is so, additional information will be necessary from other directories.

Perhaps the most common source is the Yellow Pages of a classified telephone directory. One defect of this source is obvious to everyone who has ever used the classified directory.

The trade classifications in telephone directories are frequently difficult to follow, and certainly bear no relation to standard industrial classifications or to the industrial sectors that might be used in an input-output model. Other defects are: possible non-ownership of telephones by very small firms (e.g. tradesmen, small retail shops); lags in entries; the fact that some firms use only the white pages; the entries of some firms, again the smaller ones, could be listed under the owner's name rather than under the business title. Furthermore, there is no reason why the area covered by the directory should coincide with the boundaries of the study area, and some effort may be involved in deleting firms located outside the region.

Assuming that a master list has been obtained from one or more of these sources, it is often desirable to check the accuracy of the lists with the aid of small cluster surveys. A number of small zones in the study area are selected, visited and all addresses and nature of business of all firms found in the sample zones are recorded and then checked against the master list for completeness and correct industrial assignment. Such a survey will reveal whether further work on the list is needed. Finally, a serious drawback of lists obtained from directories and similar sources is that a list in itself provides insufficient information for sampling in sectors where samples are to be used. It is important to have some knowledge of the size distribution of firms in each industry, and these are most easily obtained via the official employment agencies. In the United Kingdom, for example, each employment exchange of the Department of Employment and Productivity has a list of all firms with more than five employees in its area. These lists are drawn up as part of the official employment returns, and although they are only updated once a year and they omit the very small firms they are very useful indeed as a basis for sampling, assuming that access to the lists can be obtained.

Sectoring and aggregation

The number of sectors in an input-output table will be determined by a host of factors such as costs and resources, research objectives and data availability. The usual starting point is the economy's standard industrial classification (SIC four-digit level for the US, and minimum list heading for the UK) since this enables the maximum use to be made of the secondary data available. Adjustments are then made, involving more disaggregation in some cases but less in others, to reflect more precisely the region's industrial structure, to avoid disclosure and to economise on data collection. Because of the differences in industry definitions (industry-mix), the greater the degree of disaggregation the better. The Phila-delphia Input-Output study, for instance, contained 496 sectors — a finer breakdown than the national four-digit codes — of which 361 were in manufacturing and 74 in wholesale and retail distribution (Isard *et al,* **106,** 1966-8). However, this was exceptional, and in most regions data collection costs, the intended use of the model and disclosure problems restrict the model to the forty- to eighty-sector range. In the 1963 Washington study, to take a well-known example, sixty industries were chosen including one 'unallocated' or 'dummy' sector. This was a maximum size given the budget constraint and the volume of available data. The sixty industries were then aggregated into twenty-seven in the published table, partly to avoid disclosure, partly because aggregation improved the table's accuracy.

The number of sectors ultimately selected is not inde-pendent of the criteria used for delimiting each sector. The main criterion is that of homogeneity. By homogeneity in this context we do not necessarily mean the homogeneity of individual products, but in the sense of industries having similar sales and purchases patterns. Bramhall (**28,** 1961) listed several sectoring criteria: the output (commodity, service or imputed value) produced and delivered to other units should be homogeneous; the units (firms, establish-ments, etc.) of a sector should be oriented towards the same social goals or motivating values; the quality of each input required to produce one unit of output should be substan-tially the same for each unit within a sector and should be invariant with changes in final demand (this is the homo-geneity described above); and, finally, regional shipments from the units of each sector should vary linearly with changes in demand in receiving regions. How far the sectors of the economy satisfy these criteria determines how endogenous the sectors are, and how appropriate it is for them to be placed in the matrix rather than in the final demand segment of the table. In fact, few sectors in an input-output study will perfectly satisfy all these criteria, and the less homogeneous input-output sectors are the more inaccurate will input-output forecasts be.

In some cases practical considerations force the analyst to sacrifice homogeneity. In heavily industrialised regions, for instance, agricultural output will be so small a proportion of total output that, despite its marked heterogeneity both from the point of view of products and input patterns, it may be grouped into one or two sectors only, to economise on survey costs. Also in some complex multiproduct industries, of which chemicals is a typical case, subdivision into more homogeneous sectors may be impossible because the cost structures of individual products are frequently masked by the commercial accounting practices adopted.

Apart from homogeneity criteria, the sectoring scheme will be influenced by the structure of the region and the objectives of the study. Generally speaking, the industries in which the region specialises will be more disaggregated than other industries. Thus, the table may contain several agricultural sectors in a rural region, a highly disaggregated manufacturing sector in an industrialised region, and so on. Research objectives frequently dictate how far final demand is split up into component sectors. In an input-output model concerned with government impacts, the public sector will tend to be highly disaggregated. In the Clinton County, Pennsylvania study (Gambles and Raphael, 66, 1965) for instance, government accounts were divided into seven sectors, five in the internal matrix and two exogenous in final demand. Similarly, in an input-output model emphasising export base theory, final demand 'exports' may be subdivided in exports to the nearest dominant region, other interregional exports, foreign exports and non-commodity export sectors such as tourism and out-commuting workers.

Development of control totals

Control totals of gross output will be needed for each sector in the input-output model. In some cases, particularly where

100 per cent coverage of establishments is obtained, the control totals are merely used for consistency checking. However, where interindustry transactions are estimated via sampling of firms, control totals are imperative in order to 'blow up' the sample data into comprehensive interindustry transactions flows for the sector as a whole. The most readily available source of control totals is a production census. However, use of this requires the study region to conform to a census region and also demands that the sectoring scheme should closely follow the Standard Industrial Classification. Where these conditions are satisfied, the base year for the input-output table will usually be the same as a production census year in order to reduce interpolation errors.

Where census data are not available control totals have to be estimated from whatever sources can be obtained. The West Virginia study, for instance, used employment and earnings data from the state's Department of Employment Security and tax data on business and occupations from the State Tax Commission. Employment statistics are the traditional, if very imperfect, source for sectors where no output data exist. For some sectors – agriculture being a common example – control totals are easily accessible from the published statistics of government and official agencies. Apart from total output measures, control totals are desirable for individual components of output such as consumption, investment and exports. These are much more difficult. Estimates of regional consumption may be derived with the aid of cross-section budget studies, though the sample of the Family Expenditure Survey in the UK is probably too small for this purpose. Regional investment estimates are notoriously difficult to obtain in the absence of survey data. Regional exports and imports estimates have the additional disadvantage that there are no matching entries in the input-output table that allows them to be checked. Furthermore, there are no direct methods available to measure regional trade from secondary sources. The standard procedure is to use a variant of the commodity balance approach (Isard, **108**, 1953), i.e. exports – imports = production – consumption, and then to manipulate other sources of information in order to gross up the net trade balance estimate to derive gross exports and gross imports. In view of the sparsity of published or otherwise accessible data on interregional trade (the ICC waybill data and the Army Engineer Corps water shipments data in the US and the British Rail and the Road Goods Surveys in the UK are all severely deficient), the residually estimated control totals are of little value. As one analyst has put it:

> To assume that the regional trade balances can be indirectly established as residuals from a set of data the accuracy of which can be only partially checked corresponds to imagining that national accounts could be established without utilizing foreign trade statistics which, instead, usually constitute one of the most reliable bodies of facts (Cao-Pinna, **34**, 1961, p. 313).

The necessity for control totals — to blow up sample data, to check the accuracy of survey results, to fill in gaps in the chain of coefficients needed for each industry, to be used in conjunction with national coefficients as a basis for estimating rows and columns for sectors where survey data cannot be obtained — clearly indicates that the dichotomy between secondary data input-output tables and primary data tables is a false one. Unless every firm and household in a region is to be surveyed the maximum use has to be made of secondary data in order to construct a table. The efforts of the input-output analyst in the search through published and unpublished but fugitive data will be worthwhile no matter how intensive the surveys are intended to be. In some cases, maximum exploitation of available secondary information will mean the difference between the feasibility of implementing an input-output model and failure due to too high costs.

Selecting the samples

Assuming that coverage of *all* firms and establishments in a region by survey is impossible,[2] and that the research objectives suggest that a primary data table is essential, the key to economy of resources in the construction of a regional input-output table is efficient sampling. An extreme example of how sampling may drastically reduce the scale of an input-

---

[2] A complete census is occasionally possible in a small region e.g. the Kalamazoo input-output study (Hochwald, *et al.*, **100**, 1960).

output survey was the West Virginia study (Miernyk and Shellhammer, **170**, 1968, and **171**, 1970). A master list of 26,692 non-agricultural establishments was reduced to 12,402 by elimination of all firms with less than four employees; sampling reduced the establishments surveyed to 406, only 3·3 per cent of the population. Although random samples were drawn in some sectors, in many cases stratified sampling procedures were adopted in order to ensure that both large and small establishments were represented. In coal mining, for instance, the sample covered less than 1 per cent of establishments but more than 50 per cent of output. The size of sample ratio varied from 0·2 to 33·3 per cent. To protect against non-response each size group in each sector was over-sampled, and replacement establishments were chosen on a random basis until the desired sample size had been attained. Larger samples (in terms of output and employment) were drawn in key industries in the regional economy where interindustry transactions were expected to be important, such as (in West Virginia's case) coal, chemicals and primary metals.

The West Virginia sample illustrates what can be achieved with sensible sampling methods. The small size of the overall sample was attainable for two reasons: the exclusion of the very small establishments; and the fact that most of the sector samples passed tests on their representativeness. The firms of less than four employees were omitted for several reasons: tests of the sample's effectiveness would not have been possible for small firms; most of these establishments were in retail trade and other service sectors which do not produce very meaningful input coefficients even when perfect data are available; it was believed that more could be discovered about sales from small to large firms from the purchasers than from the sellers. To test the selected samples, a second random sample, identical in size to the first, was chosen for each sector after the survey was complete. The tests were limited since the only data available for all establishments consisted of annual average earnings. However, according to both t and F tests, the differences between the two sets of samples were not significant in the great majority of cases. In fact, 87 per cent of gross output was accounted for either by satisfactory samples or by reliable published data.

It is possible, of course, that the size distributions of establishments and the industrial composition in the region may rule out such a small sample as was achieved in the West Virginia study. In other studies more comprehensive surveys have been undertaken. In the Clinton County study (Gambles and Raphael, **66**, 1965) all financial institutions, utilities, department stores and government units were interviewed, as were 20-50 per cent of firms in the commercial sectors. Even so, the total sample size was only 550 firms, but this is explained, of course, by the small size of the region. In the 1963 Washington State study a stratified sample by industry of 3,000 business establishments was used, supplemented by 150 personal interviews with the heads of the larger business firms in the state. Although the response rate was less than 20 per cent of the firms approached, the coverage factor (i.e. the proportion of each industry's employment or output accounted for by completed questionnaires) was about 44 per cent of non-agricultural activities, and in key sectors such as aerospace, aluminium and chemicals the coverage factor was almost 100 per cent.

In the Philadelphia study (Isard *et al.,* **106**, 1966-8) rather different principles were adopted. The aim in this case was to minimise the number of establishments surveyed compatible with satisfying specific standards. These standards were to sample each four-digit SIC industry represented in the region, to ensure that the sample should exceed 25 per cent of the industry's employment and to include at least three firms in each sector. The larger firms were preselected because most of the region's industries had a highly skewed size distribution. The sample size was increased in those cases where preliminary analysis suggested that the sampled establishments were very heterogeneous. Also, central Philadelphia establishments were somewhat over-represented in the samples because of their proximity to the research headquarters and the need to minimise interview costs. The result was that in manufacturing industry completed questionnaires were obtained for 921 establishments, 15·4 per cent of establishments in the metropolitan area but covering 52·6 per cent of regional manufacturing employment; in construction, a notoriously difficult sector to survey, the coverage factor was considerably lower — only 10·6 per cent of employment.

These examples could easily be multiplied several fold. They show that input-output analysts tend to adopt somewhat different sampling procedures, and that it is difficult to deduce general principles. What is clear in all cases is that a balance has to be struck between reliable estimates and coverage and the universal need to hold down survey costs.

A few generalisations are possible. First, there is an element of choice and flexibility in sample survey designs. For example, one possibility is to sample the key industries in the regional economy (e.g. Moore and Petersen, 181, 1955) leaving adjusted national coefficients to deal with the rows and columns for other sectors. Alternatively, the analyst may systematically sample each industry in the region. A further possibility is to confine distribution of a long detailed questionnaire to a carefully selected sample of firms in major industries, but to augment this with a smaller and briefer mail questionnaire to all firms in other industries, though this raises problems of how to make inferences about the sales and purchases patterns of non-respondents.

Second, different sampling methods may be necessary for different sectors. Stratified sampling by sector and size of firm is frequently used for the manufacturing and commercial sectors. Drawing the sample may be difficult for industries with a relatively small number of firms, say ten, but where costs rule out 100 per cent coverage. A general convention is to tend to preselect the larger establishments in a particular industry, partly because they are more likely to be able to provide more detailed information, but mainly because they account for a higher proportion of the total interindustry flows and it is the *size* of the flows that determine the values of the coefficients. For some sectors a full count of establishments may be possible if co-operation is achieved, e.g. central and local government; for others, such as agriculture and distribution, published data may be available in sufficient quantity to cut down the data collection task substantially. Occasionally, it is necessary to survey households particularly in order to obtain information about direct imports of consumer goods, though if there is evidence of homogeneity in household expenditure patterns a sample of two hundred to five hundred may be more than adequate.[3]

Third, the type of sampling undertaken very often depends on cost. In some respects, random sampling would be preferable but this is often ruled out on cost grounds since it involves having a larger sample (if the random sampling error is approximately inversely proportional to the square root of the number of units in the sample, the easiest method of improving accuracy is to increase the sample size). If costs make this impracticable, then various procedures may be adopted to reduce the size of sample required to ensure a given degree of precision, such as stratification, the utilisation of supplementary data, adoption of a variable sampling fraction and multistage sampling. Finally, it is scarcely necessary to stress that an essential prerequisite of sound sampling is that the sampling frames (e.g. lists of firms) should be complete.

This discussion of sampling problems has inevitably been scanty, and has had to be confined to the barest of generalisations. It would be beyond the scope of this book to venture further into the analysis of this complex subject. However, it is clear that employment of a skilled sampling specialist on any primary data input-output project can save a great deal of time, resources and money on the surveys.

Questionnaire design and preparation; type of information required; selection of base year

The design of questionnaires is a fine art in itself. However, the information required in an input-output survey is largely of a hard data kind where nuances of question phrasing are rarely called for. The principles of input-output questionnaire design are fairly clear-cut: brevity (not always possible); clarity in the questions, with plenty of explanatory notes as required; definitions of terms such as 'capital', 'profit', 'taxes' provided to avoid ambiguities; recognition that these terms can vary in meaning from one sector to another, as

---

[3]In the Clinton County Study 476 households (about 5 per cent of the total) were sampled. Urban households were selected at random from the telephone directory while rural households were selected by means of a stratified sample from randomly selected blocks, each one square mile in area.

indeed can output, which is measured differently in producing industries from the service trades, and this suggests the need for custom-built questionnaires for each sector. This desideratum has other favourable consequences; for instance, with individual questionnaires for each sector it is possible to specify each type of material input appropriate to that sector, and this increases the efficiency and detail of the response. Because purchasing conventions and types of material used differ from one sector to another, individual questionnaires for each sector avoid confusion and make for greater clarity.

The length of survey questionnaires depends on the type of information required for the input-output table, and the information needed depends on the purpose of the study – how aggregate the model is, whether a regional or inter-regional table, whether a static or a dynamic table, etc. The following gives some indication of a standard list of information requirements: annual expenditures on material and inter-mediate inputs, heat, light and power, transport costs, rents and rates, taxes, wages, profits and miscellaneous expenditures; annual sales to various types of purchasers, such as local businesses, businesses in other regions, overseas buyers, wholesalers and retailers, and households; annual expenditures on new capital plant and equipment, plus changes in inventories and depreciation expenses on plant and equipment. It is usual to ask for information in current money values (where 'current' equals the base year), though occasionally physical input and output data is obtained. Wherever appropriate, the distribution of sales and purchases between local and out-of-region receipts and expenditures is requested. For service sectors gross margins are frequently used as a measure of output. Particular situations may call for variations on these standard information requirements. For example, if the input-output model is to be used to determine the impact of changes in defence spending, the questionnaire will specifically ask for sales data to defence-related activities, including the geographic distribution of sales to defence prime contractors. The detail required on capital account will be much greater in a dynamic model where information will be needed for constructing a table of capital coefficients; this will also necessitate requests for estimates of 'potential capacity'.

An important question to be considered when constructing an input-output table is the base year to which the data refer. Obviously, *ceteris paribus* there should be a preference for the most recent year for which information can be made available. This preference may be overridden, however, by a less recent year if this makes possible the use of published or otherwise extant information that would greatly simplify the data-collection task. Hence, production census years have considerable attraction for input-output tables. In the Philadelphia input-output study 1959 was chosen despite being an off-Census year because there was a great deal of data available as a result of the Penn-Jersey Transportation Study. Another problem experienced in the Philadelphia study was the four-to-five year time lag between the year of the table and the year of data collection; this can create all kinds of difficulties such as the changes that take place in the sample frames over a five-year period. Finally, accounting years can vary widely for different establishments and especially between sectors. Minor distortions due to this factor can be eliminated in the 'arbitraging' process during the construction of the table. More serious maladjustments due, for instance, to wide seasonal differences in sales levels can be handled by correcting the accounting year data to either a calendar year or a standard accounting year basis.

Conduct of the survey

Survey information for input-output tables may be collected either by mailed questionnaire or by personal interview. The complexity of the information required, the lower response rates and the dangers of receiving incorrect information rule out the former except in very rare cases where a simplified type of table is to be constructed, e.g. the Hansen-Tiebout 'rows only' model (Hansen and Tiebout, 79, 1963), or collecting data on firms in minor sectors in the TAP study where major-minor transactions would be picked up via the detailed interviews with all firms in the major industries (Bonner and Fahle, 24, 1967).

The personal interview technique is quite a long drawn out process. After the samples have been selected, the first step would be to send letters to the senior manager of the establishment from the head of the research project, the head of the institution carrying out the project, and the head of any government or public agency either sponsoring the project or strongly associated with it. These letters would explain the objectives of the project, its nature and request the firm's co-operation. It is also useful at this or a later stage to send an explanatory brochure describing the structure and uses of a regional input-output table. Several days later, a member of the research team will arrange an interview by telephone. At the interview the researcher will take along the appropriate questionnaire, acquaint the respondent with its details, fill in the non-statistical information, and discuss any problems arising from the questionnaire. He will then leave the questionnaire behind with printed instructions and a return mail envelope so that the respondent can complete it and return when he has had time to consult his records and files. After a period of around one month, if the questionnaire has still not been returned, the respondent will again be contacted by mail. If the questionnaire is not then returned within, say, a further three weeks, the researcher will contact the respondent by telephone to urge response and to offer any further help required. When the questionnaires have been returned, receipt is acknowledged with a letter of thanks. Each returned questionnaire is scrutinised for internal consistency and edited if necessary. Any queries arising out of the information supplied will be taken up with the respondent.

This broad sequence is only a general guide, and departures from it will be quite frequent. For instance, with very large firms and non-business organisations it may be necessary for the researcher to help directly in the extraction of data from files. Also, the interview process needs to be prefaced by considerable preparation. This includes the training of interviewers on the methodology of input-output, the interpretation of company accounts and on the interview itself. Different types of researcher and interviewer will be required for different sectors. For example, it is quite common to employ graduate students in business or economics for a period of several months to collect data from the industrial sectors; a household survey, on the other hand, may be manageable with wives of members of the faculty over a much shorter period; or again, establishments requiring data extraction by the research team can probably be dealt with best by full-time research assistants on the project. Another essential preliminary task is to carry out a pilot survey to test the questionnaire; needless to say, the pilot firms will have to cover many sectors, and where several types of questionnaire are involved (e.g. thirteen were used in the Clinton County study) the pilot survey will inevitably be quite extensive.

In carrying out the survey, it is customary to assign responsibility for particular sectors to particular interviewers, each of which would be under the overall control of an experienced researcher. In a large, sprawling region, however, it may be necessary to divide the region into several geographical blocks and give a researcher responsibility for obtaining all information from *all* sectors in that block. The interviewers need to be flexible, and if hard data on particular questions are unobtainable after probing it is acceptable for them to ask for 'guesstimates' on the missing items. It is important, of course, for the researchers to be persistent in pursuit of a high response rate in order to reduce the problems of non-response bias. There are many reasons why firms may refuse to co-operate: too busy, overloaded with too many questionnaires and other requests for information from government, universities and other bodies, veto by out-of-region headquarters, lack of tact and diplomacy in the initial approach, and fears that information supplied will not be kept confidential (particularly important in highly competitive industries or in firms sensitive about their profits). These difficulties have to be combated as best they can, but sound background public relations, willingness to take time in explaining the purposes of the project and courteous persistence in requests for information can help to raise the response rate.

Processing the data

There is little to be said on this question, other than the fact that it is desirable to assemble the data by hand, desk calculator and counter sorter rather than by computer. There are several reasons for this: the need to fill gaps in the returned questionnaires and to make adjustments for inconsistencies; the desirability of the analyst acquainting himself with the details of the data to improve his judgement when 'arbitraging' in the construction of the table; the wide variety of sampling ratios from sector to sector which makes it easier to 'blow up' the data to gross flows with simple statistical aids rather than standard computer programmes. Consequently, it will be unusual to do more than transfer the questionnaire data to punch cards for simple processing. The closer the analysts keep in contact with the raw data the more satisfactory will be the final input-output table. This follows from the fact that judgement and subjective evaluations are involved in reconciling row and column entries, making minor adjustments in individual cell entries and other elements in the arbitraging process.

Preparation of the transactions table

Estimates of total gross flows and the interindustry transactions that make them up are obtained from assembling the survey data, either by direct summation in sectors where complete counts were achieved or by 'blowing up' the sample results with the aid of independently measured control totals. In a comprehensive regional input-output study two sets of tables will be obtained initially, one based on interindustry sales and the other on interindustry purchases. The specific cell entries may diverge, i.e. the row (sale) entry may be different from the column (purchase) entry, but these may be reconciled by 'arbitraging' – exercising judgement, additional field surveys in tricky cases and by estimating which of the two entries is more reliable. Miernyk and Shellhammer (170, 1968) suggest a 'reliability quotient' to deal with the latter. This quotient is based on several factors: the proportion of total sales accounted for by the sample; the accuracy of the sector controls totals; the homogeneity of output within the sector; the representativeness of the sample as determined by t and F tests; and the interviewer's judgement about the reliability of the purchasing department's data compared with sales data in each firm. Sales can then be reconciled with purchases by reconciling the most reliable cell first and proceeding until the least reliable cell is agreed upon last.

This procedure makes it unnecessary to resolve the controversy about whether or not sales data are less reliable than purchase data. Harmston and Lund (**80**, 1967) argued that the cells should first be filled with purchase entries on the grounds that these are easier to allocate among industries and that the US Treasury Department's income tax reports were a source of purchase data. This conflicts with the Hansen-Tiebout justification of their 'rows only' model that firms are better informed about their sales destinations than their purchase sources.

In constructing the table there are a number of conventions that ease the preparation task and avoid what would otherwise be serious problems. Strictly speaking, the input-output table ought to be constructed in physical units in order to reflect technological relationships. However, money values are normally used. They are easier to obtain, they provide a common measure and they have the considerable advantage that they permit us to sum down a column as well as across a row. It is also customary to measure inter-industry flows at producers' prices. This strengthens the constant coefficients assumption, since it implies that trans-actions data will not be affected by changes in the geographical distribution pattern (i.e. destinations of output). It also helps to avoid double counting of transport and distribution costs.

The estimation of coefficients in producers' prices (i.e. fob prices) is no easy matter since transport costs have first to be removed. The Philadelphia study, for instance, resolved the problem by using OBE (Office of Business Economics) transport margins by type of commodity. However, the use of aggregate data of this kind can lead to serious inaccuracies. As Isard and Langford frankly admitted (**117**, 1971, p. 7): 'In retrospect, we should have derived transport margins directly from primary data, differentiated by transport mode, and we also should have obtained, at least for motor freight transportation, two margins, one for interregional shipments and one for intraregional shipments.'

The output of wholesale and retail trade and of many service industries is defined as gross margins (i.e. operating costs plus profit). It is desirable that these margins should be measured via sample surveys rather than by applying national averages, since trade sector margins may vary substantially between regions. Inventories in raw materials should be treated separately from stocks of work-in-progress, and are assigned to the producing industry in order to avoid disturbing the balance between column and row sums. Another device is the use of 'dummy' industries, one to represent unallocated inputs and others to deal with 'pseudo-sectors' in which the input coefficients have little meaning. Examples of the latter in the US 1958 table included 'business travel, entertainment and gifts', 'office supplies' and 'scrap and secondhand goods'.

A more serious problem is what to do about secondary products. Many firms produce goods that do not belong to the industry to which the firm in question has been assigned. For an accurate input-output table all similar products should be added to the output of the appropriate industry regardless of the sectoral classification of the producers. This is not always possible. The US national table treated secondary products in most cases as a sale from the producing industry to the primary industry, but this involves double counting. Where secondary products accounted for a substantial proportion of the producer's output and differed markedly from the primary product, both the secondary output and its associated inputs were subtracted from the producing industry and added to the primary industry. Sometimes the secondary products problem is ignored even though it involves a radical departure from the homogeneity of output assumption. In the Philadelphia study, for example, secondary products were left as part of total output and were not transferred to any other industry, apart from the exception of five establishments where output was divided into two to deal with heterogeneous input structures and output mixes.

Another set of conventions relates to the treatment of imports. Imports for final use can be directly assigned to final demand. Imports for intermediate use, however, fall into two categories: commodities not produced domestically (non-competitive imports) and commodities produced domestically (competitive imports). The former are entered directly as the inputs of the purchasing industries, but the latter are added to the output of the corresponding domestic industries and to their sales to actual purchasers of imported goods.

Finally, intrafirm transactions even though they are not registered in the market must be included in the table in the intrasector cell. Also, it may be necessary once the trans-actions table is constructed to apply a computer summation routine in order to aggregate sectors and reduce the size of the table. Reasons for this may include masking the identity of individual firms, making the table more manageable in size, and improving its accuracy and utility if the aggregated table conforms more to the constant coefficients assumptions.

Consistency checks

The huge data requirements of a regional input-output table, the reliance for many sectors on survey samples, and the exercise of judgement involved in the arbitraging and adjust-ment process might give rise to fears of cumulative errors in the transactions table were it not for the fact that there are consistency checks available virtually at every stage. There are checks possible on the sample populations if cluster field surveys in depth are undertaken. We have already referred to Miernyk's suggestion of testing the selected sample of firms against a second test sample. Similarly, in the Philadelphia study ratios for each establishment sur-veyed were compared with the corresponding ratios for the sample as a whole, the regional industry and the national industry. These ratios referred to output per head, inputs per unit of output, material costs per unit of output, heat, light and power per unit of output, and wages per unit of output. Where control totals are specifically estimated for sector outputs in the project, there may be independently estimated secondary estimates available for comparison. Consistency checks on final demand items are much more difficult, but the accuracy of export data may be checked in some circum-stances against available marketing information, while sales to final demand may frequently be checked against purchasers' records. This last point is merely a specific case of the general internal consistencies of the input-output table itself. If both sales and purchase data are gathered, these provide some check on each other since one industry's purchase is another's sale after allowing for transport costs and trade margins (a problem that is resolved if all items are based on producers' prices). Even more important as an aid to con-sistency checking is the overall balance of the input-output table itself. Because the input-output table is a logically consistent accounting framework, it is a sound guarantee of the reasonableness of the final results. We know that each row sum (total sector sales) should be the same as each column sum (total sector purchases), and that even though individual row and column totals in the final demand and value added quadrants of the table do not balance, the *aggregate* identity of final demand and value added is a useful additional check. If in order to achieve accounting balance in the constructed table it is necessary to make *large* adjustments to individual items in the table, this provides reasonable grounds for suspicion of major errors earlier in the project.

6 Data Reduction Methods in Regional Input-Output Analysis

Introduction

The implementation of a regional I-O model is invariably a compromise between the desire for theoretical satisfaction and comprehensive data coverage, on the one hand, and the need to economise on time and resources on the other. At one end of the spectrum we have a full-scale interregional model with direct estimates not only of each local I-O coefficient but also of each interregional trade coefficient both by origin and destination and by supplying and purchasing industry, so that a model of n sectors and z regions will have $(nz)^2$ cell entries. At the other end of the spectrum we collapse the interregional system into a single region model with a single row for imports and a column for exports representing flows from and to the 'rest of the world', and estimate the regional transactions table by multiplying estimates of regional outputs by the matrix of national I-O coefficients obtained from the national table. Neither of these extremes is permissible: the first is still unattainable though huge financial resources and simplifying estimation procedures for interregional trade flows may make it feasible in the near future (e.g. the HERP programme); the second is now accepted as being almost useless, unless we can assume that the region in question is a mini-carbon-copy of the national economy and does not engage in interregional trade. Clearly, these assumptions cannot be made.

Most regional I-O studies fall somewhere between the two extremes. There are several non-exclusive steps that can be taken to simplify the data collection task and to reduce the undertaking to manageable proportions. These include:

(1) aggregation of the interregional system into two, three (typically the study region, all other regions of the system, and the foreign trade sector) or more regions;

(2) methods to calculate interregional trade flows without having to trace the individual firm's non-local sales and purchases;

(3) using secondary data (i.e. national I-O coefficients and other published information) to derive local I-O coefficients from adjusted national coefficients;

(4) simplification of the table via reduction in its size, compounding of sectors, a 'rows only' table, adoption of non-square matrices in a commodity-industry model, and other techniques to reduce the data burden.

The first of these procedures has already been discussed (see Chapters 2, pp. 22-5, and 4, pp. 60-1), while the second was treated in detail in Chapter 4. It is only mentioned here in so far as it overlaps with (3), i.e. one method of converting national to regional coefficients is to estimate import requirements (m_{ij}s) directly, subtract these from the national coefficients and derive the local input coefficients as a residual. In this and the next chapter attention is primarily focussed on (3) and (4) — methods of adjusting national coefficients and resort to simplified I-O tables.

Why unadjusted national coefficients cannot be used

Since most countries (at least those with a demand for regional I-O studies) already have one or more national tables and a certain amount of regional output and/or employment data, the information is usually available to adopt short cuts in the construction of regional I-O tables. In most of the early regional studies, national I-O coefficients were used in their unadjusted form. Dictated by the state of knowledge at the time and limited financial resources, this step cannot be justified theoretically and is now rarely used. There are several reasons for this. First, there is the industry-mix problem and the related question of product mix. A sector which is defined, say, as 'engineering' for the nation may include a quite different conglomeration of industries than that included within the category 'engineering' in any particular region. The trouble lies in the imprecision of the concept of the 'industry'. It is true that industry mix differences can be minimised if the national tables are disaggregated to very fine industry detail (four hundred to five hundred sectors, for instance), but such tables are rare. To the extent that a sector at the regional level contains different industries from that in the nation then its input requirements pattern is likely to vary from the national. The product-mix problem arises because even within a precisely defined industry firms may produce a different range of products or, at least, the same range in varying proportions. The I-O sector invariably produces more than one commodity, and since it is most improbable that very different products will require the same inputs in the same proportions the failure to satisfy the single product industry assumption implies variation in coefficients between areas. Firms in a given national industry will tend to produce a much *wider* variety of products than firms classified in the same industry in a region. Thus, regional technical coefficients will vary from national coefficients, though the dissimilarity will be reduced the finer the degree of industrial disaggregation and the larger, the more industrial and the more diversified the regions under study.

The second major difference between national and regional coefficients reflects the fact that regional economies are much more open than nations. The regional propensity to import includes imports not only from abroad but from other regions, and consequently will be far higher than the national propensity to import. Even in an economy as deeply involved in international trade as the United Kingdom the national propensity is only about 0·2, whereas estimates for the regions fall within the range 0·55-0·74.[1] Similarly, interregional

[1] These estimates are very approximate. They also exclude Scotland, where unnaturally low estimates were obtained. See Steele (**229**, 1969, p. 285). More recent estimates by Steele (**284**, 1972) indicate a range of 0·44 to 0·82.

exports are much larger than foreign exports. Also, an inverse relationship tends to exist between the size of a region and its involvement in interregional trade. Consequently, it is not permissible to take over the national coefficient as a regional coefficient without making adjustments for interregional trade. The point is that the national coefficient is a technical coefficient whereas the regional coefficient in a regional I-O table expresses the relationship between *local* inputs and output. Thus

$$a^r_{ij} = r_{ij} + m_{ij} . \qquad (6.1)$$

This specifies the total technical coefficient, a^r_{ij}, for the region as the sum of regional inputs, r_{ij}, plus imported inputs (from other regions as well as from abroad) divided by the output of sector j. Furthermore, since sector j is a regional industry, then product and industry mix as well as the two other points considered below mean that a^r_{ij} is not necessarily equal to the national direct coefficient. In other words

$$a^n_{ij} \neq a^r_{ij}.$$

The trouble with nonsurvey techniques of estimating regional I-O coefficients is that none of those currently in use successfully correct for *both* these types of difference between regional and national coefficients, i.e. (1) interregional trade influences and (2) the host of factors that may lead to a divergence between a^n_{ij} and a^r_{ij}.

There are two other major sources of variation between national and regional coefficients (and between the coefficients of different regions), and these have received less attention in the literature. The first of these is differences in regional price levels. These are relevant because I-O coefficients are expressed in monetary rather than physical terms. Probably wage differentials are the major source of regional price variation, and it is quite easy to correct for these. The second may be much more serious, though it is difficult to be certain since the problem is shrouded in mystery. This is the question of whether there are regional differences in production functions even after making allowances for industry and product mix. There is a lack of research in this area. Minasian's (177, 1961) analysis of US manufacturing industries did not reject the hypothesis of linear homogeneous production functions between regions. More recently, however, Karaska (125, 1968) has provided evidence which casts some doubt on the assumption of identical production functions between regions. He pointed out that I-O coefficients are not real technological coefficients, but averages of the production functions for many different firms. He went on to demonstrate with the aid of survey data relating to individual firms *within* a region (the Philadelphia area) that I-O coefficients varied widely between firms.[2] The coefficient of variation for technical coefficients at the four-digit SIC level ranged from 11·16 per cent to 55·82 per cent for different industries, and increased markedly with industry aggregation and when local coefficients were analysed. If there are wide differences between the production functions of firms in the same industry within a region, then it is probable that there will be differences in the production function of that industry from one region to another, unless the industry happens to contain a similar distribution (by size and other characteristics) of firms in every region. This condition is unlikely to hold except by chance. In other words, if there is evidence of wide differences in technical coefficients between firms in the same region, we would be very surprised to find no differences in industry technical coefficients among regions.

Conversion of national to regional coefficients

There are several kinds of procedure that can be selected for the adjustment of national I-O coefficients for regional tables. These can be classified into four broadly separate groups. They comprise:

(1)   *ad hoc* adjustments;

(2)   regional weights and aggregation techniques;

---

[2]Examination of coefficient variation correlated against selected variables revealed that the latter were unimportant apart from an inverse relationship between a small variation in I-O coefficients and a large value for the chief input and a high ratio of total material inputs to value-added. Karaska concluded (p. 225) that 'a complicity of factors accounts for the variation in production functions of firms in an I-O system. No single variables explain variation in Leontief coefficients, and the multiple association of certain selected variables likewise fails to explain a large portion of variation'.

(3)   methods of adjusting a^r_{ij} $(=a_{ij}{}^n)$ to separate out r_{ij} and m_{ij};

(4)   estimation of non-local requirements and determination of r_{ij} residually.

These alternative approaches will be discussed in turn.

(1)   *Ad hoc adjustments*

This method uses a variety of information sources and judgemental influences to adjust the national I-O coefficients so as to reflect regional interindustry relations. Since all relevant facts are brought into consideration in the adjustment process and, in the end, the degree of adjustment relies on subjective evaluation, this approach is unsystematic and arbitrary. This kind of analysis was adopted in Moore and Petersen's Utah study (181, 1955). They obtained a crude transactions table by using national coefficients to obtain sector columns from control totals. They then adjusted the row and column distributions for each sector in the light of regional production processes, marketing practices and product mix. Some of the alterations affected individual entries, others affected groups of entries. In addition, they made adjustments for interregional trade, though here use was made of one of the standard techniques discussed under (3) below.[3] Although in some respects *ad hoc* methods could result in a more realistic regional I-O matrix, the subjectivity involved when changes are made in individual cells makes it difficult to test the accuracy of the table in the absence of a survey-based matrix for comparison. If a survey-based table were available it would undoubtedly contain all the information used in the preparation of an *ad hoc* adjusted table, and much more besides, so that the comparison would not yield an independent test. The only other possible evaluative test for *ad hoc* adjustments is to assess the forecasting power of the table, though Miernyk (169, 1968) has argued with convic-

---

[3]This was a variant of the supply-demand pool technique. The method assumed that local goods would satisfy input requirements wherever possible. Unusable surpluses were assumed to be exported and the gap between local supply and local requirements filled by imports. The authors argued that these assumptions were permissible in Utah because local output was given a locational advantage due to the 'considerable space buffer' around Utah.

tion that though a non-survey table can provide a reasonable description of a regional economy it is virtually useless for projection purposes.

(2) Regional weights and aggregation techniques
This technique allows the analyst to take account of differences in regional and national industrial structures. Shen's study (**223**, 1960) is a pioneering effort in this field. The technique involves taking a highly disaggregated national I-O table and using regional weights to group sectors into a more aggregated regional table. Shen's aggregation was based on regional industry value-added weights, because output and shipments data were too incomplete. Since value-added approximated wages, the I-O coefficients reflected the influence of regional labour-output coefficients and wage rates. In many cases significant differences were found between the regional and national coefficients, and this suggests that the method adjusts for the effect of regional industrial composition.

More recently, Czamanski and Malizia (**51**, 1969) have carried out a more ambitious study though on similar lines. They constructed a 1963 table for Washington State derived from the 1958 US national table, and compared the results with the table based on the 1963 survey. Many more adjustments were made than in the Shen study. Aggregation into a regional table used several kinds of regional weights — sales, receipts, value added and value of shipments. In addition, adjustments were made for domestic imports and for relative price levels between 1958 and 1963. Several simplifying assumptions were necessary. Tertiary sectors were excluded via aggregation, a step which was criticised by Miernyk, since these may be very important analytically, e.g. capacity constraints in electricity supply. Price differences were assumed to operate uniformly along rows. Wherever one product is substituted for another due to demand or industry mix differences, it affects all users to the same degree. Finally, changes in the degree of fabrication uniformly affect all productive processes. The corollary of these latter two assumptions is that differences in sales patterns and in technology operate uniformly along rows and columns respectively. The results of the comparison with the survey-based table were not very encouraging. Reasonable estimates could be obtained only if primary sectors and industries in which Washington was highly specialised were left out and their coefficients estimated by direct survey methods (these sectors accounted for 28 per cent of regional gross output). Miernyk concluded ('Comments', p. 82) that the study showed 'that short-cut methods do not work'. This is a harsh judgement. There is further scope for refinement of Czamanski's techniques especially as and when new data become available. Furthermore, there are alternative non-survey techniques which may be more successful. These are treated below.

The most recent attempt to employ aggregation and weighting methods, again using the Washington State economy, is by Walderhaug (283, 1972). He found that about 270 of the 367 industries in the US 1963 national table were represented in the Washington economy, and aggregated these into the 27 industries of the Washington survey table, weighting the columns of input coefficients by estimates of gross regional output in each industry. In most cases the differences between the synthetic and survey-based I-O flows fell within an acceptable range (and could be reconciled by 'arbitraging'), and many of the exceptions were due to the poorer quality of the *survey* coefficients. Walderhaug argued that an informed local analyst would be able to detect, and correct for, unrepresentative national coefficients due to product mix or technology. One particularly interesting suggestion was the hypothesis that it is a single or relatively few *large* establishments in the region that embody a technology different from the national average, and that it would be worthwhile to survey these on an individual basis. This is consistent with the case for 'mongrel' studies (using a mix of survey and nonsurvey methods) argued at the end of this chapter.

(3) *Location quotient and commodity balance approaches*
Several simple non-survey techniques have been developed that are very economical in their data requirements. These procedures have the defect that they normally assume that national and regional *technical* coefficients are identical ($a_{ij}^n = a_{ij}^r$). However, by dividing the regional technical coefficients into two separate trade components – the local

I-O coefficients r_{ij} and the requirements from outside the region m_{ij} – they produce estimates of the former that are much closer to the regional I-O matrix obtained by survey data than they are to national coefficients. On the other hand, they all tend to overestimate intraregional interdependence and to ignore cross-hauling. To remedy this imbalance much more refined procedures have to be adopted or alternative approaches to estimating interregional trade flows have to be employed. In general, these alternative techniques, the Leontief–Strout gravity approach for instance (see Chapter 4), need considerably more data though less than when comprehensive survey methods are employed.

The non-survey techniques described in this section fall into two categories.[4] The first group is based on the location quotient concept, while the second derives from the regional commodity balances approach developed by Isard (**108**, 1953). The location quotient is a measure comparing the relative importance of an industry in a region and its relative importance in the nation. Thus for industry i

$$LQ_i = \frac{X_i^r / X^r}{X_i^n / X^n} , \qquad (6.2)$$

where X represents output, and superscripts r and n the region and the nation respectively.[5] There are several variants of the LQ approach to estimation of regional I-O coefficients.

Simple LQ method. If $LQ_i \geqslant 1$, we make $r_{ij} = a_{ij}^n$. If regional final demand is given or estimated, then exports of industry i may be computed as a residual. On the other hand, if $LQ_i < 1$ it is assumed that imports are needed, and regional I-O coefficients for row i are estimated by multiplying the national coefficient by the location quotient, i.e.

$$r_{ij} = a_{ij}^n \cdot LQ_i . \qquad (6.3)$$

Imports of product i are estimated as the quantities required

---

[4]The analysis in this section owes a large debt to the work of Schaffer and Chu (see Schaffer and Chu, **220**, 1969, and **221**, 1969; and Schaffer, **219**, 1970).

[5]Employment or some other indicator is sometimes used instead of output.

to satisfy regional production requirements. On the assumption of identical national and regional technologies and no product or industry mix problems

$$m_{ij} = a_{ij}^n \ (1 - LQ_i). \tag{6.4}$$

In common with all the LQ procedures, this technique allows the national coefficients to be revised downwards but not upwards.

Purchases only LQ method.　The simple LQ approach is satisfactory only if the needs of local industries for output i relative to the needs of national industries for i are the same as the ratio of total regional to total national output. If this condition does not hold, a modification to correct for this is to make the reference base in the LQ not total regional and national outputs but only the outputs of those industries purchasing inputs from industry i. Thus

$$LQ_i' = \frac{X_i^r/X^{\prime r}}{X_i^n/X^{\prime n}} , \tag{6.5}$$

where the prime shows that only purchasing industries are summed together. The method of obtaining the local coefficients is exactly the same as in the preceding case. The purchases only LQ technique was tried with some degree of success by the CONSAD Corporation in their study of the regional impact of federal procurement (**48**, 1967).

The expenditure location quotient method. It must be obvious by now that there is a wide variety of location quotients, and that each of these may be used to adjust the national I-O coefficient in the usual way (i.e. if

$$LQ_i \geqslant 1, r_{ij} = a_{ij}^n \text{ if } LQ_i < 1, r_{ij} = LQ_i. \, a_{ij}^n).$$

One variant, which we shall call the expenditure location quotient, is very important in economies heavily engaged in international trade. This quotient was suggested by Stilwell and Boatwright (**234**, 1971) in their attempt to measure interregional trade flows in the United Kingdom. It has never been used to adjust I-O coefficients, but it is a very relevant quotient in a country such as the United Kingdom.

What the expenditure LQ method does is to substitute a new denominator in the quotient measure, where this denominator corrects for the existence of foreign trade and, in particular, for the fact that the contributions of international imports and exports vary from sector to sector. The technique simply involves adjusting the percentage shares of each industry in national output by subtracting estimates of export production by industry and by adding in estimates of international imports by industry. The assignment of foreign imports to industries raises technical and measurement problems, but to a greater or lesser degree depending on the quality of available statistical data these can be solved. The result of the technique is to convert an industrial distribution of output vector into a vector reflecting the industrial distribution of domestic expenditure. At the regional level, the expenditure LQ enables us to compare regional production with estimated regional expenditures.[6] If output falls below expenditures in the region, we can adjust the national I-O coefficient downwards to recognise the fact that imports are needed to satisfy requirements. The expenditure LQ method is the closest of all the LQ procedures to the commodity balances and supply-demand pool techniques described below.

Cross-industry quotient method. Whereas the simple LQ approach establishes import needs in constant proportions for the appropriate rows, use of the cross-industry quotient enables import proportions to vary within the rows. The CIQ compares the proportion of national output of selling industry i in the region to that of purchasing industry j,

$$CIQ_{ij} = \frac{X_i^r/X_i^n}{X_j^r/X_j^n}. \tag{6.6}$$

If $CIQ_{ij} \geqslant 1$, $r_{ij} = a_{ij}^n$. Since the output of industry i is greater than that of industry j in the region compared with the nation, it is assumed that regional industry i can supply all the requirements of regional industry j. If $CIQ_{ij} < 1$,

[6]Of course, if regional expenditures can be measured directly instead of assuming identity of regional and national industrial shares, the inaccuracy of the technique is reduced.

$r_{ij} = CIQ_{ij} \cdot a_{ij}^n$. In the former case, regional gross flows are the local *purchasing* industry's share of national gross flows but where $CIQ_{ij} < 1$ regional gross flows are the local *selling* industry's share of national gross flows. Exports and imports are estimated as residuals.

It is well known that LQ techniques involve a great many unrealistic assumptions: similar regional consumption functions, production techniques and industry mixes compared with the nation. A more serious weakness in the present context (and this applies even more strongly to the CIQ technique) is that interregional flows disappear too easily. The overstatement of self-sufficiency is a difficult problem particularly in very open regions. The CIQ approach has an advantage compared with other LQ techniques since it enables us to differentiate between trade coefficients for different using industries of inputs from sector i. On the other hand, the CIQ technique takes no account of the weighting of each of the two industries relative to the total output of all industries. Round (**214**, 1969) in an unpublished paper, has suggested that the addition of new parameters (reflecting scale economies and specialisation, the existence of some imported inputs in all small supplying sectors and transport costs) may eliminate many of the defects of the LQ groups of non-survey techniques. However, it may be difficult to incorporate the influence of these parameters in practical studies.

The second group of non-survey techniques starts essentially with methods to derive the balance of trade for individual sectors and then uses these results to estimate the regional input-output coefficients. The origins of techniques of this kind are found in Isard's regional commodity balances approach (**108**, 1953). The method simply involves subtracting total regional requirements from total regional output in each industry so as to obtain a net surplus (or deficit). Regional output is either given or estimated. Requirements consist of two components — inputs and final demand. Estimates of inputs are obtained by multiplying regional industry outputs by national input-output coefficients, while final demand vectors are estimated as the region's share of national final demand vectors. Total regional requirements of product i are obtained when we sum the elements in each row.

Supply-demand pool method. This approach merely involves extending the commodity balance technique to construct regional interindustry tables. Where the commodity balance shows a surplus, imports are assumed zero, exports are assumed equal to the surplus, and the national I-O coefficients are substituted for regional coefficients. On the other hand, if the commodity balance shows a deficit, exports are set at zero, imports are computed as the difference between regional input requirements and locally available requirements plus imports for final demand, and regional coefficients are estimated as

$$r_{ij} = a_{ij}^n \cdot \frac{X_i^r}{D_i^r}, \tag{6.7}$$

where D_i^r represents total regional requirements (for inputs and final demand) of product i. Thus, the regional coefficient is obtained by multiplying the national coefficient by the ratio of regional supply to regional demand of the producing sector i. This method allocates local production where adequate to meet local requirements. However, if local output is inadequate the technique allocates to each purchasing sector j its share of regional output i, based on the requirements of j relative to total requirements for i (D_i^r).

A modified SDP method. There are several variants of the SDP approach. For example, Kokat (**131**, 1966) suggested an alternative which adjusts the SDP technique for the case in which regional final demands are predetermined. In the net exports case, the procedure is the same as with the standard SDP method. The main difference arises when there is a net deficit. Imports are assumed to enter the region as inputs but never for final demand. Regional flows are computed as

$$X_{ij}^r = X_j^r \cdot a_{ij}^n \cdot \frac{(X_i^r - Y_i^r)}{(D_i^r - Y_i^r)}, \tag{6.8}$$

where Y_i^r equals regional final demand for sector i. Thus, each purchasing industry j obtains its share of regional output i available for intermediate use, based on the needs of the purchasing industry itself relative to the needs of all purchasing industries.

RIOT simulator. Schaffer and Chu (**220**, 1969) have developed an iterative technique which in addition to assuming national production technology attempts to distribute local production initially according to the national sales pattern and then according to local needs. The first step is to compute required inputs for producing regional output of j by using national I-O coefficients while regional final demands are estimated as a proportion of national final demand. Second, regional sales are initially distributed according to the national sales-distribution pattern. Then we compare requirements and allocations and construct for each row i a pool of surplus available for reallocation and a pool of needed reallocations. For industries with exportable surpluses (pool > needs), each buying industry receives all its requirements of product i and the excess is exported, i.e. as with the SDP approach. In industries where outputs are insufficient to meet local needs (pool < needs), on the other hand, the pool is spread via an iterative process among industries according to relative need until the pool diminishes to zero. Finally, imports are computed as the difference between total requirements and regional flows ($D^r_{ij} - X^r_{ij}$).

Since this second group of survey techniques follows the principles of the commodity balances approach, the methods described suffer from the same defect as the LQ techniques, i.e. they ignore the existence of cross-hauling. To obviate this properly, it is probably necessary to make a direct attack on the interregional flows measurement problem by adopting a gravity approach *à la* Leontief–Strout, a constrained linear programming solution or some other technique that will yield two way flows between each pair of regions. ns.

Since all non-survey techniques discussed in this section are equally defective from a theoretical point of view in that they are all based on the assumption of maximum local trade, ranking in order of merit has to be based on how the results stand up to tests. Tests have been carried out on some of these non-survey techniques by Hewings (**91**, 1969, and

94, 1971), Schaffer and Chu (221, 1969) and Schaffer (219, 1970). Since there are no survey-based regional I-O tables in the UK, Hewings judged non-survey techniques by their ability to predict for the West Midlands 1958 Census of Production outputs from a 1954 base. Although no single technique yielded the best predictions consistently, the results were moderately encouraging.[7] In particular, output in larger sectors was predicted more accurately than in smaller sectors. Schaffer and Chu were able to compare the coefficients, income multipliers and imports and exports obtained from their simulated regional I-O table using alternative non-survey techniques for Washington State in 1963 derived from the 1958 United States table with the 1963 Washington survey-based table. Four techniques were considered: LQ, CIQ, SDP and RIOT. In addition, Schaffer (219, 1970) compared these results with the US national table. The more recent tests involved a thirty-three-sector model, while Schaffer and Chu's earlier analysis was on a twenty-three-sector model. There were some differences in the quality of results between the two sets of tests, but the more recent study in general fares best. The conclusions may be summarized as follows:

(1) All the techniques yielded a regional table which is closer to the survey-based table than it is to the US national table.

(2) The CIQ method appeared to yield the best estimates of imports and exports.

(3) All the techniques predicted imports much better than they predicted exports, but even the least unsatisfactory method severely underestimated exports (producing an estimate only 75 per cent of the survey value). Moreover, only CIQ gave an estimate of exports for each industry and the other methods only yielded an export estimate when local output is big enough to supply all local requirements.

(4) Regional I-O coefficients were found to be much lower than national coefficients. The weighted average total was closer to the survey value with the RIOT technique, but all the techniques estimated regional production coefficients that were correlated with survey coefficients for most

---

[7] It is only fair here to mention that Round (273, 1972) has criticised the mechanics of Hewings's approach quite severely.

sectors. Chi-square tests showed that non-survey methods could yield coefficient values similar to survey coefficients for sixteen industries.

(5)   Output (or column) multipliers were much closer to survey than to national results, with RIOT giving the best estimate of the mean value. On the other hand, when individual sectors were considered, survey-based multipliers were underestimated at low values and overestimated at high values whereas the national multipliers, though much larger, varied consistently with the simulated values.

(6)   Estimates of income multipliers were much higher than in the survey model and substantially lower than national income multipliers.

Taken as a whole, the results were quite favourable considering that 1958 US table was too highly aggregated to permit much adjustment for product-mix differences in the simulations and the fact that no weighting techniques were adopted to take account of price changes and other sources of regional-national variation.

(4)   *Direct estimation of imports*

This method of estimating regional I-O coefficients requires more resources and data than those discussed in the previous section, and is practical only for a single region study. On the other hand, imports are very important at the regional level, they are often used in further processing, and it could be argued that an attempt to estimate these directly is worth the extra effort when we consider the inadequacies of non-survey methods of estimating interregional trade. Su (236, 1970) has proposed a technique which determines the r_{ij}s residually after imports into the region have been estimated by direct survey methods. This enables the analyst to construct an import requirements matrix which Su regards as too important for regional I-O analysis to be collapsed into a row vector of non-competitive imports as in national tables. At the same time, the technique is simpler to apply than a comprehensive survey since it is unnecessary in this model to obtain independent estimates of the local coefficients. On the other hand, even this approach abstracts from differences between national and regional technology, product mix and industry mix.

If we obtain a regional matrix of I-O coefficients derived from the national table by simple aggregation (A), we may write:

$$A = R + M + \epsilon , \qquad (6.9)$$

where R = matrix of regional coefficients illustrating local requirements

M = matrix of imports
ϵ = matrix of random disturbances.

Assuming that ϵ is negligible, then we obtain our regional coefficients matrix residually as

$$R = A - M . \qquad (6.10)$$

The matrix multiplier obtained by this approach is $(I - A + M)^{-1}$ and this is $\leqslant$ the usual Leontief inverse $(I - A)^{-1}$. Income multipliers estimated by this approach thus tend to be smaller than in other regional I-O studies because the leakages have been estimated more precisely.

The survey information needed for this technique is very simple, and does not even require firms to supply absolute figures of their purchases (assuming that the little information needed to weight each firm in its sector totals can be obtained). Firms are merely asked to identify the *proportion* of required inputs for each sector imported from other regions or abroad in their total inputs of that sector. When the individual percentage figures are obtained ($P_{ij} = m_{ij}/a_{ij}^r$), they are multiplied into the corresponding elements of the A matrix thereby yielding estimates of the m_{ij}s. In a similar manner, each element of R can be approximated by multiplying $(I - P_{ij})$ by the corresponding elements of matrix A.

As an alternative to this 'imports only' approach, Schaffer (**219**, 1970) has suggested an 'exports-only' survey which is a variant of the SDP method though requiring a minimum of survey data. It is, in effect, a more simplified derivative of the Hansen - Tiebout 'rows only' approach (**79**, 1963) discussed below (see Chapter 7, pp. 131–3). The information required from firms is not difficult to obtain: their SIC code to permit assignment to sectors, annual sales value, and the proportion of sales to purchasers outside the region. Regional production coefficients are then calculated as

$$r_{ij} = a_{ij}^n \cdot \frac{X_i^r - E_i^r}{D_i^r}, \tag{6.11}$$

where E_i^r represents regional exports of commodity i. This approach meets export requirements first and allocates the remainder of regional output to satisfy local needs in proportion to requirements. Unlike the other non-survey techniques this method permits the national coefficient to be adjusted upwards in some circumstances. Preliminary tests on Washington State suggested that the 'exports only' approach yielded results just as good as, perhaps even marginally better than, the other data reduction techniques. However, a possible drawback to both these latter techniques arises from the well known fact that interregional trade coefficients are much more unstable than technical coefficients. Consequently, there is a more serious risk that the import requirements matrix or the export proportions obtained might be atypical. This is not an overwhelming objection, but perhaps suggests that special care should be taken in selecting the year for collecting the survey data.

Conclusions

It would be foolish to pretend that non-survey techniques provide a better approach to the construction of regional I-O tables than survey techniques. In particular, in the present state of the art it still requires survey data to ensure that a regional model makes allowance for the possibility of divergence between regional and national production functions and it is easier with a survey-based model to deal with the vexing problems of product and industry mix. Moreover, Miernyk and others have argued that a non-survey model is of little use in regional projections, largely on the grounds that forecasting requires adjustments in the I-O coefficients over time and/or capital coefficients data, and since these require knowledge of the technological practices of individual firms a survey approach is essential. On the other hand, non-survey methods are cheaper and a regional table can be constructed in a short space of time. Moreover, in cases where comparisons are needed, as with an interregional model, development of regional tables from a similar data base and with consistent sectoring offers considerable advantages. Goldman ('Comments' on Czamanski and Malizia, **51**, 1969) has argued that the importance of interregional models provides the main justification for non-survey techniques since the survey approach is too expensive to pursue for all regions, especially in a country with as many regions as the United States. The results of the tests on non-survey techniques hitherto are not too discouraging. They at least suggest the value of further research into the refinement of these techniques, the development of new approaches and a more thorough testing of the techniques already in use.

Finally, it is possible that there is a middle way in the choice of method. Many of the tests on non-survey techniques highlighted their inability to produce reliable estimates of I-O coefficients for certain sectors, for instance, the failure for primary industries and industries highly specialised in the region in the Czamanski-Malizia study. A crucial next step in regional I-O research is to use a non-survey technique systematically to estimate the elements in the I-O matrix but to replace the entries in the rows and columns relating to a few critical key or problem industries with survey-based estimates. A mix of the two approaches could reduce the resources needed to construct a regional table to perhaps 20-25 per cent of the full survey cost. The real problem, and a serious one, is how to devise procedures for *a priori* identification of the sectors in which surveys ought to be carried out. In the absence of a survey table already available, it is impossible to pinpoint these sectors by a comparison of survey and non-survey estimates. Some industries are obvious candidates for preselection: leading sectors in the regional economy; new or rapidly expanding sectors especially in circumstances where an economic impact evaluation is a primary objective; industries where product-mix and industry-mix problems are clearly present from information available about the differences between regional and national industrial structures; industries where cross-hauling is known to be extensive; and, more generally, industries where the non-survey regional coefficient varies considerably from the national coefficient. There is no study completed or even under way which has effectively employed a mix of survey and non-survey methods systematically or on any scale, and it is probable that a regional table constructed on these lines might require more 'arbitraging' and balancing than is usually necessary. Nevertheless, a mongrel study of this kind might well represent a more effective and balanced compromise between the present extremes of cheap but possibly unreliable non-survey methods and prohibitive surveys. It is surely a fruitful line of inquiry for future research.

7 Simplified Forms of Regional Input-Output Tables

An alternative approach to reducing the data needs of a regional model via non-survey techniques is to simplify the structure of the I-O table itself. Simplification can take many forms: obtaining information about sales or purchases only rather than both; using a rectangular I-O matrix with number of columns not equal to rows (hybrid model); compounding less important sectors together (e.g. 'minor' sectors as in the TAP study, or service industries); a general reduction in the size of the table via aggregation. There is no very clear distinction between these procedures, many of them are very similar and several could be described as an amalgam of economic base and input-output models.

The intersectoral flows approach

The most important example of the first type of simplification is the intersectoral flows (or 'rows only') model developed by Hansen and Tiebout (**79**, 1963). The basic differences between their approach and the usual I-O procedures were: first, that employment was used as the unit of measurement rather than monetary values; second, firms were asked to provide the *proportions* of their sales to specified final demand sectors and local industries, and no information on inputs was requested. All sales flows were converted to employment, and this implied a type of value-added approach in contrast to the gross flows traced in a standard I-O table. The objective of the study was to derive employment multipliers for California and three of its sub-regions, and to use these to determine the relative impacts on employment of shifts in the various final demand sectors. The chief advantage of the method was its cheapness. Much of the non-manufacturing information required and employment data for manufacturing firms were obtained from other sources, and so the only additional information needed was the percentage breakdown of sales of manufacturing firms. This was easily obtained from a mail questionnaire to a sample of two thousand firms including a complete coverage of establishments employing more than a hundred people; over five hundred responses were received. The rationale of asking for sales breakdown was based on the assumption that firms are more familiar with the destination of their outputs than with the origin of their inputs, especially when regional disaggregations are needed.

Once the basic data were obtained, the method involved two stages. The initial allocation assigned employment in each industry sector to seven final demand sectors and to twenty-five local industry groups, thereby giving a table with industry groups as rows and final demand sectors and industry groups as columns. Employment summed across each row equalled total employment in the industry. From this table employment input coefficients could be derived which are similar to the usual I-O direct requirement coefficients. The second step involved tracing the interindustry output flows to the final demand sectors, i.e. by collapsing the entries in the industry groups columns into the final demand columns. This was achieved by allocating inputs to an industry, shown in one of the industry columns, in the same fashion as that industry's employment is allocated to the final demand sectors and industry groups (i.e. across the row). Of course, this first round still leaves some employment assigned to industries rather than to final demand, but via an iterative process all employment originally allocated to local industries could be assigned indirectly to the final demand sectors.

These two stages give a direct employment estimate and an indirect employment estimate in each industry group for each final demand sector. Via aggregation of all industry groups it is possible to derive several employment multipliers: (1) direct (since this is the employment directly assigned to final demand, it always equals unity); (2) direct + indirect; (3) direct + indirect + induced (short run), obtained by making local consumption endogenous as when we derive Type II multipliers in standard I-O analysis; (4) direct + indirect + induced (long run), obtained by considering all final demand sectors as endogenous with the exception of private and government exports. For California State as a whole, the direct + indirect multipliers fell within the range 1·02-1·46 for different final demand sectors while the direct + indirect + induced (short run) multiplier fell within the range 1·93-2·76. Although it is obvious that this model cannot generate much of the useful information obtained from a traditional I-O model, its benefits suggest that it is worth serious consideration. It is inexpensive, it is very simple to operate and its main product − employment multipliers − is possibly one of the more useful tools in regional economic analysis.

Technique for Area Planning

Another method of making the data collection task more manageable is to carry out a detailed comprehensive survey only for certain sectors and to rely on mail questionnaires and compounding of transactions to cope with the less important industries. *Technique for Area Planning* (E.R. Bonner and V.L. Fahle, **24**, 1967) is a good illustration of this approach. The basic principle of the technique is a division of a region's industries into major sectors, for which data are collected individually, and minor sectors, which are compounded as far as 'minor X minor' transactions are concerned with the household sector. Thus, full interindustry transactions are traced for the major sectors only. Details of 'major X minor' transactions are obtained from the detailed surveys of the former, while the only survey information obtained from the minor sectors themselves (via mail questionnaire) refers to sales to exports and purchases from imports. Much of the data needed for the minor sectors' internal transactions can be obtained from published or other sources instead of a direct approach to establishments, though clearly there is a need for flexibility here according to the type and quality of accessible information in the study region.

The major sectors would include the leading sectors in the region in terms of size and growth rate (whether positive or negative) and would clearly contain the main export industries. Since the main export industries are analysed in detail while many of the remaining industries are aggregated, there is close kinship between TAP and the disaggregated basic-service models suggested by Garnick (**67**, 1969). In a study of eighteen service (or residentiary) industries in 167 nodal regions covering the whole of the United States, Garnick showed that at each point in time the residentiary sectors seemed to move in approximately fixed proportions across regions. This suggested it was unnecessary to have much inter-industry detail in service industries in regional I-O models, and these findings support the argument in favour of TAP and similar techniques.

The main support for TAP must depend on the extent of the sacrifice in precision paid for simplification. Bonner and Fahle tested the technique in seven areas where comprehensive regional I-O tables were available.[1] In most cases multiplier values derived from the modified TAP table were close to the estimates yielded by a comprehensive transactions table, and economic impact estimates were generally within 5 per cent of those obtained by more traditional I-O methods. On the other hand, the tests showed that TAP results became more inaccurate with an increase in regional size and diversification. The authors concluded that regions with an index of regional specialisation of less than ±0·20 were not suitable candidates for the TAP approach.[2]

Hybrid models

One method of simplifying the task of constructing a regional I-O table is not to reduce the number of firms approached but to provide a simpler questionnaire which is easy to complete

[1] The areas were: Fulton County, New York; Clinton County, Pennsylvania; Mobile, Alabama; Sabine-Neches, Texas; Boulder, Colorado; Kalamazoo and St Louis.

[2] The index of regional specialisation is computed by comparing the percentage shares of total employment for each industry in the region and the nation, summing up the positive *or* negative differences between regional and national percentages, and dividing by one hundred.

thereby increasing the probability of a high response rate. A direct way of achieving this is to ask for a less detailed breakdown of inputs. This suggests the possibility of a hybrid I-O table which has much fewer rows than columns. A model of this kind has been tested by Williamson (**265**, 1970). Suppose the regional economy is grouped into n sectors. Each of these sectors could be surveyed, but the analyst might request that inputs be recorded and classified in a smaller number, say $n/2$, of broader industrial groups. In such a model the direct requirements would be broken down among the $n/2$ broader groups of local suppliers while estimates of subsequent requirements to satisfy the demand for first round inputs would be based on multipliers calculated from a $n/2 \times n/2$ matrix of the broader groups. As with all modified tables, the proof of the pudding is in the eating. Tests on the predictive power of the hybrid model for twenty-year employment projections by Williamson showed that its forecast deviated from that of a standard I-O model by only -0.2 per cent, though individual sector forecasts varied more widely.[3] Where cost considerations dictate a mail questionnaire survey without interviews the hybrid (rows $\neq$ columns) model is a feasible alternative to the intersectoral flows approach.

Reduction in the size of the input-output model

Selection of an appropriate level of aggregation is a problem facing all I-O analysts. For instance, aggregation techniques are one method of adjusting national coefficients for a regional table.[4] Occasionally, aggregation is dictated in a regional table in order to prevent disclosure of information by individual firms. Sometimes, however, aggregation of sectors prior to data collection is a means of reducing the costs and simplifying the construction of a table. The crucial

---

[3] The range of forecasts deviated by -8.7 per cent to $+8.0$ per cent from standard I-O forecasts.

[4] Incidentally, the proper way to carry out such aggregation is to convert the national into a regional matrix of the same size and then to aggregate, not to aggregate the national table *first* and then convert it to a corresponding regional table. The former procedure yields a regional table weighted to take account of regional industrial mix, while the latter approach merely gives a more aggregate impression of the national industrial structure. Barnard and Charlesworth (**14**, 1970) criticise Peterson and Wykstra (**199**, 1968) for aggregating prior to converting.

question is once again the loss in predictive efficiency. Williamson (**265**, 1970) found that the long range (twenty-year) employment forecast of a 6 X 6 model differed by +4·9 per cent from a 12 X 12 model forecast. A recent study by Doeksen and Little (**55**, 1968) took aggregation to the extreme. They recognised that a large model was necessary if the study was concerned with the detailed inter-industry structure – for example, if one of the objectives was to seek out sectoral capacity constraints. However, for economic impact studies where the main focus of interest is the broad effects of expansion in one or two sectors a much smaller model may be quite acceptable. Doeksen and Little (p. 134) argue that:

When data and research funds are limited, a small aggregated model will yield multipliers for a specific sector which are similar or nearly identical to those obtained from a large disaggregated model. . . . This study shows that the size of the model has little or no effect on the size of a sector multiplier.

The striking feature of this study was the extent of the aggregation. Three sectors were randomly chosen as a focus of interest, and the remaining sectors aggregated, two each time, until the model was aggregated down to a four-sector model (the three preselected sectors and one other representing all remaining sectors). Four models were analysed: two hypothetical twenty-five-sector models selected by Monte Carlo random number techniques and two actual models – a twenty-seven sector Washington State table and a twenty-nine-sector model for Oregon. Both output and income multipliers were calculated. The results were surprising. There was little difference in the multiplier values as the degree of aggregation was altered. The smaller multipliers changed only at the third decimal place, though rose slightly as model size decreased. The larger multipliers, on the other hand, tended to fall a little with increasing aggregation. Income multipliers in general tended to increase slightly as the model size decreased. Finally, zero regression coefficients were obtained when size of the model and size of the multipliers were compared. If results of this kind were universal, it would suggest considerable scope for economies in economic impact or new plant feasibility studies.

However, it may be premature to rejoice too soon. Two major problems remain. First, how representative are these results? We shall come to this in a moment. Second, assuming a high degree of aggregation are the data for the aggregated sectors available and if not how can they be obtained? In the above study, an existing table was scaled down via aggregation. Presumably, however, the case for a small model rests on economy in data collection where no large table exists. If the data for the highly aggregated sectors have already been published or are easily accessible from official sources in sufficient detail to yield estimates for imported purchases and export sales (sales to and purchases from the preselected key sectors will be obtained from the survey), there is no problem. In most cases such data will not be available. If so, there arises a critical sampling problem. If, say, twenty-five or more sectors have been aggregated into one, how can a sample be drawn which adequately depicts its row and column transactions without descending to the detail involved in the construction of a standard size I-O model? True, this exaggerates the problem a little since with a high degree of aggregation a much higher proportion of transactions will be internal to the aggregated sectors. Nevertheless, a survey of highly aggregated sectors raises, unless the sampling fraction is very large, awkward problems of statistical inference.

Is it possible to generalise from the Doeksen-Little results? In a recent paper Hewings (**93**, 1971) has taken this analysis much further. In the first place, he carried out tests on the 1963 Washington table which supported Doeksen and Little's findings. Multiplier values for individual sectors remained realtively stable during the course of aggregation, and the variation which did take place was independent of either the degree of aggregation or the method of aggregation. The sectors with large multipliers experienced a slight fall in multiplier values as aggregation was carried out; initially low multipliers, on the other hand, tended to increase slightly during aggregation. Second, he argued that the effects on gross output values as the matrix is aggregated are perhaps more important than variations in impact multipliers. Accordingly, he carried out a series of tests on the Washington table of theorems developed by Morimoto (**183**, 1970). These theorems stated conditions for the absence of 'aggregation bias', i.e. the difference between outputs observed in an aggregated matrix and those in an unaggregated matrix:

(1)   the aggregation bias is zero if final demands are proportional to those of the base period;

(2)   if some sectors are not aggregated and the change in final demands occurs in the unaggregated sectors, the first order aggregation bias disappears irrespective of how the remaining sectors are aggregated.

The correctness of the theorems was demonstrated by the tests. Hewings's conclusion was that:

If one's interest is confined to a small number of sectors, as would be the case in measuring the impact of a new plant or industrial complex upon a regional economy, one could safely use a very highly aggregated matrix provided one postulated no changes in the final demands of the sectors which were aggregated together.

PART THREE: Applications

8 Economic Impact Analysis

The effects of any final demand change, real or simulated, in a regional I-O model can be treated as an economic impact on the region. I-O multipliers offer a short-cut method of calculating these effects when aggregate measures of impacts are sufficient, though there may be no alternative to a detailed examination of the interindustry matrix if the disaggregated impacts on particular sectors are required. However, economic impact analysis usually implies something more specific than any final demand change. It may refer to the introduction of a new plant into an area, the growth of a new industry, expansion of a dominant factory or other commercial establishment, a public investment project, an inflow or cutback in central government spending in the region, the establishment or withdrawal of defence contracts or a defence base and similar developments. In most of these cases economic impact analysis shows the relevance of I-O models as a tool of analysis for regional policy (or for measuring the regional implications of a national policy change). But the I-O model is only a tool, and is no substitute for a regional development strategy. Its neutrality and value-free character is demonstrated by its appeal to analysts in market economies and centrally planned economies, in capitalist and socialist economies alike. For an economic impact study to give useful answers to policymakers, we must be certain of the questions we wish to ask of it. This means that the goals of regional policy must be known. On the other hand, it is possible to measure economic impacts without the analysis having policy implications.

The measurement of impacts

The most important prerequisite for an economic impact study is the availability of appropriate income and employment multipliers derived from the inverted coefficients matrices of a regional (or local) I-O table.[1] Given this basic information, the main additional requirement is forecasts of final demand changes in the sector (or sectors) under study. The projection techniques used for estimating the future demand changes will vary widely according to the nature of the analysis. For instance, projections of a regional industry's exports may be obtained from a national demand study; in estimating the local impact of a university, future expenditures may be obtained via a regression analysis relating expenditures to full-time student numbers (see Bonner, **25**, 1968); sometimes, hypothetical final demand changes spanning a number of sectors may be simulated; the repercussions of a change in the level of central government spending may be based on actual planning decisions to expand or contract a specific spending programme. These few examples are merely illustrative. Clearly, there are a great many alternative final demand changes that could be introduced, and these may be derived by employing sophisticated forecasting techniques, by simulation experiments, by examining the effects of known and planned intentions and so on. Once the final demand change has been given or estimated, and assuming that if expansion is involved the sector concerned can cope without adding to its productive capacity, the procedures for measuring output, income and employment impacts are straightforward. Let us consider for example the measurement of direct, indirect and induced effects. The total income change is obtained by multiplying the Type II income multiplier for the sector by its direct household coefficient and then multiplying the product by the final demand change. The increased production needed in each sector to support a given increase in final demand is derived by multiplying the final demand change by each coefficient in that sector's row in the expanded inverted matrix. The employment created can be estimated by multiplying total production requirements from each sector (as obtained from the previous set of calculations)

[1] See Chapter 3, pp. 31–52.

by its employment-production coefficient and summing the results.[2]

Calculation of income and employment impacts in this manner is a simple operation once a regional I-O model is available and the relevant inversion routines have been carried out. This approach has now replaced the earlier impact study methodology found in the work of Isard and Kuenne (110, 1953) and Miller (174, 1957). These studies used the national coefficients of the US 1947 national table, and employed a variety of techniques (location theory, interarea commodity flow data, informed judgement, etc.) to estimate the fraction of inputs imported. Iterative solutions were adopted to project future output, and national employment-production coefficients were used to convert output forecasts into employment terms. This method has been superseded because of the development of regional tables and the growth of computer capacity. However, the Isard-Kuenne analysis had one distinctive feature that is still of some value. In their evaluation of the impact of steel on the Greater New York-Philadelphia region, they explicitly took into account the steel-fabricating industries that were closely linked to steel itself. In effect, they grafted agglomeration aspects of location theory on to a regional I-O framework. The expansion in output and employment of steel-using activities was forecast prior to any I-O operations, and was included in the regional bill of goods. Thus, this approach suggested that it was possible to measure the impact of expansion in a group of closely interrelated sectors as well as in one industry alone.

Not all regional economic impacts can be assessed simply by working through the effects of final demand changes. This procedure is appropriate when the development takes the form of expansion or rundown within a sector already in the region. But there are other types of change which need a

---

[2] As pointed out in Chapter 3, the Type II employment multiplier for sector j is expressed as

$$\frac{\sum_{i=1}^{n} b_{ij}^* \pi_i}{\pi_j}$$

different treatment: the entry of new firms with activities closely related to, but different from, those of existing firms; the growth of a firm or industry engaged in producing import substitutes; or the introduction of an industry entirely new to the region. The impacts of development of this kind can manifest themselves in ways other than a rise or fall in the level of sales to final demand and its effects; for instance, they may alter the coefficients in the direct coefficients table. An obvious case is where the growth of import substitutes alters the relative size of the r_{ij} and the m_{ij} in the total a_{ij}. The introduction of a new sector into the regional economy, however, usually calls for a new row and column to be added to the interindustry matrix.

If measurement of an impact involves changes in the direct coefficients table this will normally be connected with changes in the geographical distribution of sales and purchases rather than with changes in input requirements pattern for technical reasons. It is quite possible, of course, that the analyst may wish to assess the impact of a firm new to the region but producing goods similar to those already produced in the region. For this reason, it would seem appropriate for the activities of this new firm to be treated as an addition to the output of that sector. Yet the new firm may be much more efficient than existing firms and its input requirements pattern may be quite different. If its interindustry purchases were added to the sector's total purchases and the new firm absorbed as part of the sector, the direct coefficients table would be altered. However, this procedure would be justified only if a further change in final demand for the sector as a whole would not disturb the new direct coefficients table. Since the new firm is, by assumption, more efficient than existing firms, it is most unlikely that this condition would hold. Accordingly, the new firm might have been treated more satisfactorily if (despite the character of its output) it had been regarded as a new sector with an additional row and column. Whether the departure from homogeneity in regard to input requirements is sufficient to require this may be in part a matter of judgement.

Changes in direct coefficients due to regional trade adjustments will, however, be more common. An interesting example quoted in the TAP (Technique for Area Planning) study (**24**,

1967) is the introduction of a radio assembly plant into an area with a thriving electronics industry but without assembly facilities. The plant is assumed to have the same input pattern as the sector as a whole apart from purchases of electronic components. The immediate impact of the firm will be that output of electronics components previously exported will now become an intrasectoral transaction. However, more fabrication in the form of radio assembly will be done in the region and this will raise the value of electronics exports. Thus, in this case the location of the new plant will increase local purchases for the region's electronics sector and will raise total output, and these changes will show themselves as higher intrasectoral sales and increased exports. Estimation of the plant's total impact will require a new direct coefficients table to be constructed and then for this table to be inverted to obtain new direct, indirect and induced coefficients. The projected increase in electronics exports sales as a result of the new plant will be used to estimate the overall effect on regional output and income.

Where the impact source to be investigated takes the form of expansion in a particular industry or introduction of a new plant to produce import substitutes, a technique suggested by Little and Doeksen (155, 1968) may be useful. Dealing with import substitution by reducing imports and raising local purchases by an equivalent amount is in itself inadequate if it fails to take account of interdependence among sectors. Little and Doeksen's method involves the use of what they call the 'leakage coefficient'. In its extreme form (i.e. when it is used as a measure of total import leakages) the leakage coefficient is computed by subtracting the income multiplier estimated from the standard I-O table from a hypothetical multiplier derived from a modified I-O table. In this modified table imports are added to entries in the endogenous portion of the table. To do this properly requires knowledge of the distribution of each industry's imports to supplying industries so that the imports by any sector can be apportioned to the appropriate column in the table. The hypothetical I-O table thus obtained assumes zero imports. It is expressed in coefficient form and inverted in the usual way to compute the hypothetical multipliers both on a sectoral and aggregate basis. Of course, estimation of the impact of expanded output in a sector competing with imports or of the introduction of a new plant producing import substitutes does not require adjustments in each entry of the table. But the leakage coefficient approach can be adapted to the problem of eliminating either imports in a single sector, in whole or in part, or imports in a group of sectors. In an import substitution impact study the leakage coefficient is used as a measure of the increase in the value of the multiplier. It involves comparing the results from a pre-impact I-O table with those derived from a simulated post-impact table. The latter requires the specification of the interindustry input requirements of the import substitute firm in detail.

Measurement of the impact of a new plant in a new industry is easy conceptually, since it merely involves adding a new row and column to the I-O table, but is difficult in practice. This is because the new row and column need not only estimates of the plant's forecasted output but also of its sales and, more difficult, its purchases pattern. When the establishment of a plant is certain and imminent, the required information may be obtained from the company involved. Where this is not possible (e.g. in a simulation study), estimates of input requirements would have to be obtained from pilot plants, engineering studies or even from I-O data derived from national or other regional tables. Resort to data of this kind presents problems on how to distribute inputs between local and out-of-region sources. Miernyk and Shellhammer (170, 1968) suggested that inputs not produced in the region should be assigned to imports, but this probably leads to an underestimation of the new firm's total impact. Once the row and column have been constructed, the new expanded matrix is inverted and the impact of the plant's output worked out in the usual way.[3]

Defence impacts

The greatest impetus to regional economic impact analysis has probably been the investigation of the regional effects of defence and space-related expenditures in the United States.

---

[3]Even if an I-O table is not available in the study area, it may be possible to obtain a reasonable estimate of the new plant's overall impact by constructing a very small I-O model of three or four sectors (Doeksen and Little, 55, 1968).

A contributory factor in this has been the increasing volume of information made available over the last decade by the US Department of Defense and NASA and analysed in detail by regional scientists (for example, Isard and Ganschow, 111, 1962; Isard and Karaska, 112, 1962; Dyckman, 59, 1965; Weidenbaum, 264, 1966; and Karaska, 123, 1966, and 124, 1967). The most important consideration, however, has been the size of military spending and the space programme, the fact that their distribution has been regionally concentrated so that many local areas and even regions depended vitally on the scale of spending being sustained, and the fears (and hopes) of what might happen to the American economy if a massive defence cutback were to occur.

Many of the initial inquiries into the effects of military spending and changes in its scale of activity (for instance, Leontief and Hoffenberg, 142, 1961) concentrated on measuring the impact at the aggregate national level. Such an approach is inadequate in itself since the brunt of defence-space impacts falls on individual regions and localities. This is partly because the military-space-industrial complex affects certain industries and not others, and the geographical distribution of the affected industries is by no means uniform. At the national level, it is not beyond the capability of modern macroeconomic management to ensure that a large cutback in the defence-space sectors is roughly offset by expansion of demand in other sectors. At the local level, however, the structural readjustments could be much more painful. Transfers from military to non-military spending do not merely imply shifts of resource between industries but also involve variations in relative regional growth rates. Moreover, since disarmament could form part of a package involving tax cuts and possibly a relaxation of monetary policies and since these associated changes also have differential effects on particular industries, the consequencies of a defence cutback on a particular region may depend on its industrial structure at large not solely on its dependence, direct and indirect, on defence contracts. Of course, virtually all changes in final demand in government expenditure have a regional dimension. What gives defence-space expenditures special significance are their high regional concentration and the fact that changes in the level of spending could be proportionately much larger and more sudden than in other components of final demand. Also, even though the central government may assume responsibility for compensatory action to offset defence cut-backs, the measures taken have to be implemented at the regional and local level.

The measurement of defence impacts raises problems that are rarely found, at least to the same degree, in other economic impact studies. These problems primarily relate to data limitations and the interpretation of data. For instance, information about particular kinds of defence expenditure may be classified on security grounds and not released for analysis. Although the US authorities have been more forth-coming in recent years, there is in the United Kingdom still no published information available on the regional breakdown of expenditures though scraps of information have occasion-ally been made available to researchers for specific purposes. Moreover, a very high proportion of defence spending in manufacturing consists of subcontracting (perhaps one-half of the total in the United States), and most of the data available relate to prime contracts. Although NASA has released some information on sub-contracts, this has been analysed primarily in interregional rather than in interindustry terms (Karaska, 124, 1967; Krumme, 133, 1970). The high incidence of sub-contracting in defence-space manufacturing makes it par-ticularly difficult to trace through the interindustry flows without a detailed survey of the subcontractors themselves. This is aggravated by a tendency for many large defence contractors to operate in more than one industry and in more than one region, and to be conglomerate organisations with divisions, subdivisions and ties with other firms in different areas of the economy. A byproduct of this situation is that subcontracting flows occur not only between industries but both between regions and within the same corporation. To the extent that the multiplant firm creates difficulties for data collection in regional I-O analysis, these difficulties are multiplied in defence impact evaluations.

Another general problem in regional I-O analysis, product mix, is more intractable in the defence-space sector. Both the final products and the intermediate inputs into each product are highly specific, and are not adequately described in terms of I-O sectors. This suggests a need for finely disaggregated industrial sectors, particularly in such fields as scientific instruments. More important, however, is its implication that defence products manufactured in different regions and described under the same broad heading may have very dissimilar input patterns. As a consequence, it would be very dangerous to use national I-O coefficients for defence-space sectors as proxies for local coefficients. This view is supported by an analysis of actual interindustry purchases for the defence sector in Washington State by Gordon (**74**, 1966) that showed that these differed greatly from hypothetical purchases based on using US coefficients. In addition, the industry-mix problem may be serious, because firms engaged in defence and aerospace activities may also be involved in other sectors with a quite different pattern of interindustry relationships.[4]

Despite these difficulties, there is no practical alternative to using an I-O model for estimating regional impacts of defence expenditure. It is true that in a recent study Billings (**21**, 1970) has argued that impact income and employment multipliers estimated with the aid of an economic base model give reasonable measures of the total direct, indirect and induced effects of defence expenditure.[5] But, as the author himself accepted, only an I-O model can produce the disaggregated output, income and employment impacts that may be necessary for either diagnostic or prescriptive action. Moreover, the I-O table used in this comparison had only fourteen sectors and some of the coefficients used were derived from the national table. The comparison might have been less favourable had a more disaggregated model been employed.

In the defence sector, the sum total income effects can be split up and made comparable with the traditional tripartite division of income effects in I-O models. The direct impact takes the form of prime contract awards; the indirect effects

---

[4] Krumme (**133**, 1970, pp. 237-8) suggested that: 'There is some reason to believe that these early-round indirect coefficients of the aerospace segments of the industries may be atypical compared with the remainder of the respective industries, and that the marginal additions to the coefficients in later rounds become more typical.

[5] This study referred to Arizona. The aggregate income multiplier for the I-O model was 6·5 per cent greater than the economic base multiplier, while in employment terms the gap narrowed to 4·7 per cent.

work through subcontracts and purchases of supplies by the prime contractors; the induced impacts are connected with regional consumption, business and local government investment decisions. Much of the early work was on direct impacts only, yet in defence-space activity a high proportion of the impacts may be indirect.[6] Moreover, because the defence-space sector may be by far the largest employer in a particular locality the induced effects are often too substantial to be ignored. In such areas, for instance, regional and local governments may be highly dependent on defence spending via induced effects. This dependence can have important long-term planning implications for government spending, with respect for example to the provision of schools, hospitals and other social services. For these reasons, the I-O model represents the only feasible approach to the measurement of defence impacts at the local level. This is not to say that it is an ideal instrument. The magnitude of induced, and to a lesser extent indirect,[7] income changes in part reflect the growth of non-manufacturing industries in response to expansion in the defence sector. Because of the difficulties of measuring output in many of these industries, the absence of technical factors that stabilise intersectoral relationships in manufacturing, and the possible irrelevance of linearity assumptions, the I-O approach may yield less satisfactory forecasts for service sectors than for manufacturing.

What the I-O model will show, of course, is the full impact that the defence-space industry may have on a local economy. Peterson and Tiebout's survey (**198**, 1964) revealed that 41·6 per cent of manufacturing employment in Los Angeles was tied directly or indirectly to defence-space expenditures. The size of indirect and induced effects means that the share of defence expenditures in gross regional output can give a very misleading impression of the dependence of a region on defence activities. In Washington State, for instance, defence-space expenditures (primarily on manufacturing rather than installations, with aerospace the leading industry) accounted for only 4·5 per cent of gross output in

---

[6] In a survey of Los Angeles-Long Beach referring to 1960-1 Peterson and Tiebout (198, 1964) found that the ratio of direct to indirect defence-space employment was 54·7 to 45·3.

[7] Direct effects on non-manufacturing sectors may also be important in some regions, e.g. where military contracts are awarded to R and D institutes.

1963. This did not mean, however, that the regional economy could easily absorb the impact of its withdrawal. Indirect and induced income changes almost doubled the direct impact (the Type II multiplier for aerospace was 1·90), a large number of jobs was involved, and defence activities are geographically concentrated in and around Seattle. Even if regional economies are sufficiently diversified for any defence cutback to be offset by expansion in other sectors (as argued by Hughes [104, 1964] with respect to Massachusetts and New England), the readjustments may nevertheless be slow and painful – spells of unemployment and forced migration, idle industrial capacity, falling tax revenues for local governments, loss of trade in service industries, and so on. The I-O simulations indicating that the slack from a withdrawal of defence contracts ought to be taken up fail to reveal the transitional difficulties because they assume that the adjustments are instantaneous.[8]

Apart from the data problems, the procedures are similar with the defence-space sector as with other industries when we are concerned with the measurement of impacts within the single region. If faced with a discontinuous shift in the level of defence spending, the more crucial problems are likely to arise at the interregional level. This is because defence-space activities are disproportionately concentrated in certain regions, while the expanding non-military sectors that could replace them may have locational advantages only in other, possibly distant, regions. Thus, changes in the composition of final demand from defence-space to other activities will not only involve shifts of resources among industries but also within regions. The magnitude of these shifts can be appreciated only by implementing an interregional I-O model. The pioneering study in this context was by Leontief and associates (144, 1965) in which the simplified intranational model (see Chapter 4, pp. 61–3) was used, though a similar exercise could be carried out with the aid of the more ambitious US interregional model recently developed at Harvard (HERP).[9]

---

[8] This assumption can be avoided if a dynamic I-O model is available, or possibly even with a comparative statics model if iterative procedures and a period analysis are linked together.

[9] For another version making use of Harris's multiregional model (83, 1970) see Udis (282, 1970).

The intranational model consisted of forty-one national industries and seventeen local industries, and the US economy was divided into nineteen regions. A 20 per cent across-the-board cut in all kinds of military purchases was simulated for 1958, and it was assumed that this was offset by a compensating across-the-board increase in non-military final demands (an expansion of 1·8 per cent). The two changes were balanced so as to leave the aggregate level of employment unchanged, and since wages per unit of output were higher in military than in non-military sectors, civilian demand had to expand by 7·6 billion dollars to offset a defence cut of 6·3 billion dollars. The simulation required three stages. First, conventional I-O calculations were made to estimate the direct and indirect effects of the assumed shift from military to non-military final demands on the total output of all goods in the country at large. At this stage, the household sector was treated as a component of final demand. Second, changes in the outputs of national industries predicted by the first phase were allocated regionally on the assumption of uniform percentage changes in each region. This step assumed foreknowledge of output and employment of national industries prior to the shift, and this regional distribution was obtained by the simplifying assumption that regional shares in the national output of each national industry were proportional to their shares in its production capacity. The third and final stage determined the distribution of changes in the output of local industries through separate I-O calculations. Local industry output was distributed in three ways: deliveries to military and non-military final demand within the region; inputs to national industries in the region; inputs to local industries themselves. A distinctive feature of this stage was that the household sector was now treated as a local industry and as endogenous within the interindustry matrix. This change in the treatment of households is important as an internal consistency check, since if regional inputs into the household sector were separated out and summed for the economy as a whole they should match the private consumption vector of final demand used in the first stage.

As pointed out by Tiebout (**249**, 1965), the most rapid rates of regional growth in the United States since the end of World War II have been experienced by peripheral regions in the far West and the South East, and a major factor in this performance was specialisation in defence-space activities. This view was confirmed by the Leontief study. The simulation indicated that employment would contract in ten out of the nineteen regions. The largest loss would have been California (−1·85 per cent) and the largest gain in Minnesota and the Dakotas (+1·54 per cent), though since these were net changes they under-estimated the readjustments required. The most striking result of the analysis was the lack of correspondence between the regions dependent on defence spending and those dependent on civilian demand. The former group included the Western, South-Western and South-Eastern states, and the latter group the Mid-West, the Great Lakes region, the North Atlantic and New England states. Clearly, the problems of readjustment consequent upon a defence cutback would be much more serious in the first group of regions. However, the importance of interregional analysis of this kind is not to bring out this obvious fact but to enable the analyst to predict and prescribe for the readjustments necessary in each region as a consequence of any projected shift in the level of defence-space expenditures.[10] The approach is equally applicable to other fields, such as changes in the level or distribution of government spending as a whole, forecasting the regional effects of national growth or predicting the consequences of interregional locational shifts.

Qualifications

Economic impacts can be measured, as we have seen, in several different ways. Which of these is appropriate will depend upon the purpose of the study, and this will vary according to circumstances. In most cases it is probable that

[10] Such readjustments are likely to involve changes in other fields of government expenditure. This was a major finding of the inquiry into the impact of the Vietnam war on the Philadelphia economy in 1968 (Isard and Langford, 116, 1969, and 117, 1971): 'One clear lesson learned from this application is that when any Federal government program . . . is changed in magnitude, whether contracted or expanded, there must be concomitant changes in other government programs as well, whether they be tax programs, social welfare programs, or environmental conservation programs' (Isard and Langford, 117, 1971, p. 19). Moreover, such compensatory measures leave the regional economy quite different in structure from that supported by military expenditures.

an economic impact analysis will be linked with regional development policy, and the aims of the analysis will be determined by broader policy objectives. The I-O model itself is merely a tool of analysis, and is neutral from the point of view of regional policy. Thus, an economic impact analysis can only reveal the best, or a preferred, alternative if policy goals are closely specified. For example, if maximising employment is the dominant goal the measurement of impacts will focus on employment multipliers. But policy objectives may be more complex. For instance, if limited resources are a constraint the size of the initial capital invest-ment may be an important factor. In selecting one from many feasible alternatives, conflicts may arise because, say, the sector with the lowest capital-output ratio (and the lowest initial capital investment) might also have a very low employment multiplier. [11] Another factor in the decision could be expectations about demand for the products of the sectors being considered. Which of several sectors should be selected, or whether new industries are to be preferred to expansion in existing industries, will depend on whether policy objectives favour stability or growth, emphasise employment creation or income growth, on how important it is to save investment resources, and so on. The I-O model and the economic impact analysis cannot resolve these questions; they can only help to supply the right answers once the questions have been resolved.

Some regional objectives may cover aspects of development on which an economic impact analysis based on I-O models can throw no light. For instance, the creation of external economies may be a factor affecting the selection of a new industry or justifying the encouragement of expansion in a particular sector yet these effects cannot be captured by an I-O model. For example, Bonner's study of the impact of the University of Colorado (25, 1968) excluded its role as a magnet for attracting other industries and the development of contacts between university and industry scientists and technologists. Moreover, the conclusions drawn from an economic impact study are bound by the assumptions of I-O model. If these assumptions do not apply, the con-

---

[11] In the majority of cases we might expect the sectors with high capital-output ratios to have the lower employment multipliers.

clusions may be invalid. These assumptions include the absence of price reactions to increased output, no substitution effects which modify the structure of the I-O table, and no investment capacity or labour supply constraints in any sector of the model. These qualifications do not reduce the usefulness of economic impact analysis, but merely remind us of the obvious point that the techniques should not be applied mechanistically.

9 Regional Forecasting

Introduction

Since a major spur to the growth of regional economics is interest in regional policy, and since an important prerequisite for implementing a successful regional policy is good-quality economic forecasting, it is scarcely surprising that the development of satisfactory regional forecasting techniques is a vital task for regional economists. In the absence of further theoretical advances and the provision of more data the use of more complex econometric forecasting techniques is not yet practicable,[1] and input-output models are probably the most useful forecasting tool currently available.

It would be too much of a digression to discuss the problems of regional economic forecasting in detail. However, a few remarks are not out of place. There are at least three crucial factors that make regional more difficult than national economic forecasting:

(1)   the shortage of past and current time series data;

(2)   the 'openness' of regional economies;

(3)   the implication of the fact that regional strategies are predominantly long-term.

The first problem is critical since the absence of full sets of

---

[1] However, as first steps in such attempts see F.W. Bell (17, 1967), L.R. Klein (129, 1969) and N.J. Glickman (73, 1971).

regional income accounts rules out the type of forecasting technique used at the national level. Since consideration of input-output methods assumes the prior existence of at least one and preferably two or more input-output tables, the additional data requirements for input-output forecasting are not excessive. Second, the open character of regional economies is a severe obstacle to accurate forecasting, partly because interregional flows are much larger than international flows but mainly because these flows are neither controllable nor easily measurable compared with flows between countries. The input-output approach has no advantages in the prediction of regional trade. It is arguable that of all coefficients in the input-output model changes in the regional trade or supply coefficients are the most difficult to predict. Whether input-output models have any serious *disadvantages* in this respect probably depends upon the empirical (and unknown) question of whether or not interregional trade is unstable. If there were a high degree of instability in regional trade flows this would suggest the need for a more flexible approach to forecasting than that obtainable with input-output analysis.

Third, the fact that the more important regional problems are questions of long-run changes in structure and growth rates and that regional policy tends to be geared more to the long, hard task of bringing the lagging regions up to scratch than to, say, the regional effects of short-period recessions means that long-term forecasts are the most valuable. This complicates the regional forecasting problem: first, the techniques of short-term forecasting have been sharpened in response to national economic needs and are more highly developed than those for assessing secular change; second, it is inherently more difficult to make long-term forecasts, since in the longer run parameters that can be treated as constant in a short-term projection period tend to change in value, frequently in ways that are hard to predict. Although static models have dominated regional input-output applications, input-output can be used for long-term forecasts as easily as most alternative techniques available. Indeed, the input-output model offers a choice from short-term forecasts with a static model (constant input coefficients, projected changes in final demand) through medium-term forecasts with comparative static formulations (variable input, and possibly trade, coefficients) to long-term forecasts with dynamic models (variable input coefficients, endogenous capital coefficients) or even longer-term projections using a dynamic model with changing capital coefficients (and if required with matrices of variable labour coefficients).

There is obviously some affinity between impact analysis discussed in Chapter 8 and input-output as a regional forecasting device; indeed, it may be impossible to draw a clear distinction between them, particularly when the projection period is short. However, the following working definition may be adopted: in economic impact analysis we are concerned with predicting the impact of expansion (or decline) in one or a few sectors, the introduction of new firms or industries, simulation and feasibility experiments, etc.; in regional forecasting our main preoccupation is with predicting over-the-board changes in final demand (though we are likely to be interested in individual sector forecasts that go to make up the overall projection) or in even more general terms forecasting the growth of the regional economy. Moreover, although economic impact studies may involve the adjustment of a few input coefficients they usually work with a single I-O table, and hence are usually confined to evaluating short- or medium-term impacts. Regional forecasting will be more effective when more than one I-O table is available, when many more coefficients are adjusted or introduced, and when the projection period is long rather than short. Thus, the typical economic impact analysis will be an evaluation of the short-run effects of expansion in a small part of the regional economy (a group of industries, a single industry, even one or two firms) while the typical regional forecasting model will look at long-term future change in the region as a whole.

The ingredients of a regional I-O forecasting exercise may be made up of several components, the choice of which depends upon the length of the forecast period and the objectives and character of the projection. Not every forecasting study will require all the potential ingredients found in a dynamic I-O model of the following type (see Almon, **3**, 1963):

$$\mathbf{X} = A\mathbf{X} + G\dot{\mathbf{X}} + \mathbf{Y} \qquad (9.1)$$

where G = capital coefficients matrix and $\dot{X}$ = vector of changes in gross output.[2] The requirements for forecasting are:

(1)   regional projections of final demand and its components, including stepwise changes as well as a terminal period forecast;

(2)   the input coefficient matrix, A;

(3)   the regional capital coefficient matrix, G;

(4)   predictions of changes in the A matrix;

(5)   predictions of changes in the G matrix;

(6)   decomposition of the A matrix into two components, the intraregional coefficient matrix ($\sum\limits_{j=1}^{n} r_{ij}$) and the import coefficient matrix ($\sum\limits_{j=1}^{n} m_{ij}$, or more usually a vector m_j);

(7)   estimates of imported capital coefficients which have to be combined with the investment effects of G to yield total expansion investment requirements;

(8)   forecasts of shifts in import/local shares of inputs both for intermediate goods in general (6) and for expansion capital goods (7); this is the general problem of forecasting regional trade coefficients.

At one extreme, a forecast may merely require final demand projections to be postmultiplied by the Leontief inverse matrix of a 'single snapshot' table to produce estimates of gross output changes, (stages (1) and (2) only). At the other extreme, in a fully dynamic forecast all stages (1) to (8) may be involved. Many forecasts will fall somewhere between the two extremes. Stages (2) and (6) are discussed in other parts of this book. In the present chapter the order of analysis and discussion will be as follows: (*a*) regional pro-

---

[2] Gross output is, of course, a function of final demand so that the above equation can be rewritten as

$$X = (I{-}A)^{-1}Y + (I{-}A)^{-1}G(I{-}A)^{-1}\dot{Y}.$$

jections of final demand; (*b*) predictions of variations in input coefficients (the essential ingredient of comparative static forecasts); (*c*) forecasting shifts in regional trade which will affect the regional trade flow coefficients; (*d*) analysis of the repercussions arising from the introduction of the capital coefficients matrix into the input-output system (dynamic models). In the same way as we may attempt to forecast investment requirements in order to identify any productive capacity constraints that may abort a dynamic forecast, it is possible to construct a labour coefficients matrix (and where appropriate to predict changes in the cells of this matrix to take account of labour productivity changes) in order to ascertain whether there are any labour supply bottlenecks. This possibility, though quite feasible in practice, will not be discussed in detail on the ground that there are more direct methods of forecasting manpower requirements and investigating future labour demand-supply disequilibria than that offered by I-O models.

Regional projections of final demand

The common core of any econometric forecasting model is projections of the independent variables. In I-O models if input, trade and capital coefficients are treated as the model's structural parameters, then final demand is the sole independent variable (or rather set of variables). To provide reliable forecasts of final demands it is arguable that what is needed are full sets of regional income accounts available on a time series basis. However, if such accounts did exist it is likely that a rather different forecasting model from input-output would be adopted. In their absence fairly crude methods of projecting final demand have to be used. Since projections of regional consumption, investment, government spending and exports would be essential components of virtually any regional forecasting model, we are dealing in this section with considerations much broader than those peculiar to I-O techniques. Nevertheless, since final demand projections are necessary if regional I-O tables are to be used as a forecasting device some attention must be given to the problem.

A possible advantage of I-O forecasting techniques is that

some model variants may be adopted that economise on the task of projecting final demand. This is because the openness of the model can be reduced by transferring some components of final demand into the interindustry matrix (Hoch, 99, 1959; Tiebout, 251, 1969). The most obvious method is to construct a dynamic model in which exports and central government spending are alone retained in the exogenous final demand segment of the table while consumption and investment are made endogenous, i.e. consumption is expressed as a function of income, investment as a function of output.[3] The theoretical drawback of such procedures is, of course, the fact that it neglects the autonomous element in consumption and investment. The forecasting model becomes, in effect, little more than an export base projection model embellished by tracing through interindustry repercussions.[4]

A contrary argument is that the more 'closed' models are less reliable for forecasting because the individual components of final demand are harder to predict than final demand as a whole. For instance, forecasting regional exports is so much more difficult than forecasting national exports since with the latter we have reliable time series of exports as well as useful information on trends in international trade. There are no equivalent data available on regional exports and interregional trade. A somewhat different argument, though in support of the same point, is that the more we close the model, the narrower the forecasting base, the greater the model's instability and (probably) the more unreliable its projections. Not least among the reasons for this is the likelihood of offsetting trends in certain components of final demand — local consumption and exports, central government spending and local government spending, for example. Reducing the exogenous variables to one runs against the tide of econometric forecasting techniques which tend either to include large numbers of independent variables in multiple regression analysis or to adopt a complex multivariate simultaneous equation approach.

Miernyk (173, 1970) has argued, and most I-O forecasting

---

[3] Such formulations usually include local government spending and any other local demand sectors in the matrix.

[4] This conclusion is scarcely surprising if the arguments in Chapter 3 are accepted.

practitioners would appear to agree, that final demand on current account is easier to project at the regional than at the national level. This is based on the assumption that a region's major industries serve national markets, in which case national projections for these industries can be used as benchmarks. By appropriate adjustments regional projections may be derived not only for the national market sectors themselves but for other supplying industries directly and indirectly tied to them. Of course, this approach presupposes the existence of national projections – a not unreasonable assumption given the greater experience and more effort put into national forecasting. Given this assumption, the regional economist escapes from having to project each regional final demand independently.

In the West Virginia model two alternative projection methods for final demand were employed. Both are almost naively crude, but are fairly typical of the approaches used in other I-O forecasts. In the first projection, each sector in the region was assumed to maintain its 1965 share of national markets at the end of the forecasting period (1975), and national rates of growth in final demand (derived from studies by Almon, 4, 1966, and by the Bureau of Labor Statistics) were applied to the regional sectors. The second method retained the national forecasts as the benchmark but used shift and share analysis to allow for regional variations in their share of national final demand over the forecast period. There is a growing and controversial literature on shift and share techniques (for a few recent contributions see Houston, 103, 1967; Brown, 30, 1969; Mackay, 158, 1968; Stilwell, 232, 1969, and 233, 1970; Buck, 32, 1970; Paris, 194, 1970), and probably on balance the critical bombardment is beginning to reflect on the value of the technique. Nevertheless, it is an improvement on constant-share assumptions. However, there is some evidence that the shift component is unstable overtime (Brown, 30, 1969), and if this is the case projections using this approach may be unreliable. Its advantage is in the economy of its data requirements, and it may also appeal to some because it is neutral in terms of economic theory.

Reliance on national projections as a basis for forecasting regional final demands is characteristic of most attempts to project final demand as a whole. Such techniques are crude, but they are easy to implement and they are likely to be widely used until we have much more regional data and more sophistication in regional forecasting methodology. When we disaggregate final demand and attempt to make projections for individual components, there is a wider choice of approaches available though none of these are fully satisfactory. An interesting procedure to deal with personal income and consumption forecasts was adopted by Tiebout in his income and output projections for Washington State, 1963-80 (Tiebout, 251, 1969).[5] This is to make a distinction between the increase in personal income due to the growth in per capita income of existing regional residents (*intensive growth*) and the increase in income due to the growth of employment (typically associated with in-migration) and output without any per capita growth effect (*extensive growth*). This distinction may be of critical importance in consumption forecasts: extensive growth implies new residents who may be assumed to spend similarly to existing residents, hence the average propensity to consume is the appropriate coefficient; intensive growth, on the other hand, means rising incomes for existing residents, and thus the marginal propensity to consume is relevant. In regions where the marginal and average propensities differ the accuracy of the forecast will be improved by drawing the intensive-extensive growth distinction. Even in cases where the marginal equals the average propensity to consume the allocation may still be useful because of a differential between the marginal and average propensities to consume *local* goods. Thus, rising per capita incomes may be associated with increased purchases of imported goods (i.e. lower marginal propensity to consume local goods) or, conversely and more rarely, with import substitution. Even if this methodology is not adopted, it is probable that forecasts of regional consumption will follow similar lines in that such forecasts will normally be derived from projections of regional population and income.[6] Thus, a main virtue of Tiebout's methodology is that it offers a

[5] A similar technique was adopted on Tiebout's advice in the Boulder, Colorado, study of the economic impact of the space programme (Miernyk, 168, 1967).

[6] For example, Hoch's (99, 1959) forecasts of household expenditures in the Chicago region were based on three sources: population forecasts, projections of long-term growth in real income per capita and budget studies used to relate consumer spending by industry to total consumption.

systematic treatment of variables that have to be included in a consumption forecast in any event.

Investment and exports are two items of final demand that cannot be projected via the use of national-shares methods. The obvious reason is the fact that regional growth differentials are largely explained by variations between regions in rates of investment and in export performance. A major weakness in techniques of regional forecasting is that no satisfactory method exists of forecasting regional investment and exports. It is true, of course, that part of the problem can be handled by making them endogenous. Thus, induced investment can be treated as a simple function of income (Tiebout, 251, 1969) or, more satisfactorily, in a dynamic model as a function of changes in output or capacity. Exports to other regions can also be made endogenous if we develop a fully fledged interregional model in which exports to each region are treated as a function of income in the region of destination. Moreover, if we adopt the traditional I-O convention of regarding competitive imports as negative entries in final demand, final demand projections will require us to forecast imports to final consumers as well, and this task would also be greatly simplified in an interregional model. Apart from noting the enormous task that empirical implementation of an interregional model especially in a forecasting context implies, the main point to observe is that if we project regional trade in this manner we have moved into the field of forecasting variations in regional trade flow coefficients – a subject which is treated separately below (see pp. 175-83). Furthermore, closing the models in this way can offer only a partial solution since autonomous investment (not to mention replacement investment)[7] and foreign exports have still to be forecasted independently.

Long-run projections of autonomous investment and regional exports are very much the same problem since a primary need in both cases is prediction of locational shifts into and out of the region. As R.B. Williamson has recently

---

[7]Replacement investment is not too difficult to forecast particularly if data are available on the age distribution of the capital stock and on the probabilities of future technical obsolescence. Also, there are alternative rules-of-thumb available for projecting replacement investment of which straight-line depreciation methods are the simplest.

reminded us (**266**, 1971, p. 4), Isard's comparative cost analysis, despite being very complicated to implement, is an incomplete technique for forecasting industrial location patterns. In any event, since many location decisions are based on neither profit-maximising nor cost-minimising strategies it is doubtful whether locational changes can be predicted by reference to economic factors alone. *Faute de mieux*, we may have to make do with unreliable trend assumptions (e.g. Hoch, **99**, 1959) or alternative forecasts using a range of feasible projections.

The least unsatisfactory approach to regional export forecasting is to break the problem down to the individual sector level. There is little alternative to detailed analysis of the export prospects of individual regional industries which may also involve obtaining projections from individual firms and making forecasts for each regional market separately. However, there are one or two simplifying procedures that may be adopted. For instance, Artle (**6**, 1965, p. xxxiii) argues that it may be permissible to concentrate on the large export sectors and to hold export ratios for industries with low export/output ratios (i.e. below some appropriate cut-off point — 5 or 10 per cent) constant over the projection period. National data, such as estimates of income elasticities of demand for particular products, may be useful provided that they are employed as a feasibility check rather than as a basis for 'regional shares' projections. Moreover, in industries where production is heavily concentrated in one or two regions (e.g. particular types of capital goods and consumer durables), regional export projections may well approximate to national demand projections. Of course there are complications. This approach may be easier to carry out for individual commodities or products and to aggregate these into I-O sectors may give rise to delicate weighting problems. Nevertheless, these *ad hoc* painstaking methods are likely to yield better results than any general technique. For example, there have been experiments based on making benchmark estimates of 'production *minus* local requirements' for each industry (in effect, variants of Isard's commodity balance approach) and using these as a forecasting base, but they are grossly unreliable. On the same lines, changes in location quotients where these exceed unity provide an unsatisfactory projection technique for regional exports. In particular, a rising location quotient is not a conclusive signal of export expansion, for changes in location quotients reflect variations in output in other regions as well, making it impossible to disentangle the export effect.

Forecasting the government spending component of regional final demand can also create problems. It may be a partial solution to make local government spending endogenous, but this step cannot be adopted for central government spending. It is true that certain items of government spending are related to population provision so that regional population forecasts have an obvious value. Income trends within a region may be useful too. It is less easy, however, to make projections for central government capital spending as a whole and for its regional distribution. In the United States for instance, the regional distribution of expenditures on the defence-space linked sector would be of crucial importance, but it is notoriously difficult to project long-term trends in sectors with this degree of volatility. This illustrates, if as an extreme case, a general problem with projections of government spending in regions: the fact that we are usually concerned in regional analysis with long-term forecasts and change whereas government spending plans can be greatly affected by the pressures of short-run political decisions. However, once again, there are redeeming simplifications. For instance, it is still a safe generalisation that the long-term trend of government expenditure, even in real terms, will be upwards, partly because rising incomes and the proliferation of private wants create a demand for more public wants (e.g. the growth in car ownership and the demand for roads). Furthermore, in countries with an equity-biased regional policy there are grounds when using regional share projections to allow for increasing shares of central government spending in backward regions.

All this indicates that there is still much progress to be made in the field of projecting regional final demand changes, and clearly if we cannot attain a high degree of reliability in the forecasts of final demand there is not much to be gained from I-O forecasting.[8] However, if appropriate projection

[8] Of course even if this were the case it does not rule out other uses for regional I-O models such as simulation experiments, feasibility studies, working out the regional effects of foreseeable changes in GNP, etc.

techniques can be devised their value can be tested in some degree by 'backcasting' before policy judgements are made on the basis of their predictions. Finally, if there are known defects in the projection techniques available to forecast regional final demands we can be consoled by the fact that probably the same, or similar, defects exist in our alternative methods of regional forecasting.

Forecasting changes in technical coefficients – comparative statics

Even if we can satisfactorily forecast changes in final demand there must be doubts about post-multiplying these by an unchanged inverse matrix as the projection period lengthens. It is an axiom of forecasting methodology that as the forecasting interval increases we must progressively reduce the number of both structural constants and exogenous variables in the model. In input-output analysis the interindustry matrix is the main set of structural constants. To use input-output techniques for forecasting regional change for anything longer than a very short time period we need to investigate the possibility that the interindustry coefficients may change, and for this we need to forecast what the direct transactions table will look like at the terminal date. In this way we move from statics to comparative statics, but not yet to dynamics.[9]

To recapitulate on points discussed in Chapter 6 (see pp. 112-15), input coefficients are more difficult to estimate at the regional than at the national level since it is not merely a question of finding the appropriate value for the technical coefficient (a_{ij}^r) and seeing whether this varies from the national coefficient (a_{ij}^n) but also of splitting total input requirements between local supplies and imports. Thus,

$$a_{ij}^r = (r_{ij} + m_{ij}) \underset{\neq}{=} a_{ij}^n . \qquad (9.2)$$

These two problems need to be treated separately and in this section we shall confine our attention to the technical coefficient (a_{ij}^r), leaving the difficulties arising from changing

[9] Dynamics requires us to investigate the capacity-creating effects of regional expansion. See below, pp. 183-92.

proportions of local and imported inputs for analysis in the next section. If there are snags in estimating the regional input coefficient for a single year, the multiplication of these difficulties when we move into a forecasting context scarcely requires emphasis.

Before looking at the methods available for forecasting changes in regional technical coefficients, it may be useful to offer a few comments on the problems of input-output coefficient variation in general, not least because some of the techniques used in regional studies make use of national projections and because the technical and conceptual questions are essentially the same in both cases. There are at least four main reasons why national input-output coefficients vary over time: relative price changes, product-mix variations, technical change and economies of scale.[10] Relative price changes influence the coefficients primarily via the substitution of one input for another, but they can also have some impact via differential movements in output prices (i.e. the coefficient denominators). The 'relative price-substitution' effect is the reason why input coefficients in current prices are more stable than in constant prices, and hence are easier to forecast (Tilanus, **252**, 1966; Sevaldson, **222**, 1963). Input and output prices usually tend to move in parallel since prices of output depend largely on the prices of its cost components. The main factor, however, is that inputs whose relative prices are falling tend to be substituted for those with rising relative prices, and consequently substitution tends to stabilise the value of inputs in each cell. The closer the elasticity of substitution is to unity, the greater the stability.

The product-mix cause of variation in coefficients arises out of the aggregation procedures inevitable in input-output analysis. To make input-output tables manageable we are forced to adopt a sector classification that, no matter how finely disaggregated we try to make it, necessarily groups

---

[10] At the regional level, input-output coefficients may change because of localisation economies (i.e. external economies due to agglomeration of establishments in the same industry) and urbanisation economies (external economies due to agglomeration of unlike activities), but both these can be subsumed under scale economy effects. The questions of import substitution and replacement of local supplies by imports are, as we have seen, a separate problem since they affect the value of r_{ij} rather than a'_{ij}, but these two can largely be explained by relative price and/or scale effects.

together different products within an individual sector. If the outputs of these products grow or decline at different rates, the input-output coefficients will change unless we continuously alter the weights attached to each constituent in the sector. To do this we have to project the growth rates of each constituent product. Product-mix effects can change the coefficients even in the absence of technical change, though proper coefficient adjustment will probably require us to modify the detailed coefficients for anticipated technical changes before adjusting for product-mix variations.

Technical change is the most important source of variation in input coefficients and the most difficult to forecast. We can deal with economies of scale quite briefly since (apart from the external economy effects at the local level) these are only likely to be important in the early stages of an industry's growth except when they are interrelated with technological advances. Moreover, their influence should be easily measurable from engineering cost functions data. Anticipating the effects of technological change, however, is much more complicated. Long-term projections may necessitate 'technological forecasting', a field of inquiry in its own right which may in some forms be akin to futurology. Long-term technical changes have two effects: bringing about changes in the coefficients; revolutionising current products and processes in a way that requires the creation of *new* input-output sectors and hence makes almost all pre-existing coefficients redundant (Aujac, **10**, 1971). Although the latter effect rules out direct intertemporal comparisons of input-output tables, it is not impossible in theory to take it into account in an input-output forecast by adding new rows and columns, particularly if interindustry projections are based on 'drawing-board' engineering and technical information rather than on observed empirical data. Fortunately, most projections will relate to a shorter forecast period in which we can keep the number of sectors constant.

A priori, we might expect the impact of technical change to be very sudden and to lead to marked instability in the technical coefficients. In practice, this rarely happens and changes in input-output coefficients due to technical advances occur very slowly. There are obvious reasons for this. First, although the replacement of an old technique (or material) by a new one may look very sudden, it takes time for the innovation to diffuse through the economic system as a whole. Second, if most technical progress is 'embodied' in capital accumulation, the national rate of gross investment acts as a constraint on the diffusion of technical change. As for methods of forecasting the impact of technological change on input-output coefficients at the national level, there are two main approaches. The first relies on technical and engineering data, industry experts and technical feasibility studies. This method may be appropriate in certain sectors undergoing rapid but foreseeable technical change such as electricity generation or steel. The danger is that the analyst may underrate the gap between 'best-practice' and 'average' technology, and overadjust the coefficients. The second approach is to make what Almon (4, 1966) calls 'judicious extrapolations' based on a comparison of the coefficients in two or more past input-output tables but introducing adjustments for anticipated technical changes where appropriate. The latter is the technique employed by Mrs Carter in her studies of structural change in the US economy based on the 1947 and 1958 input-output tables (A.P. Carter, 37, 1970). Such an approach would also involve, if we are concerned with forecasting, derivation of best practice coefficients from sample information or experts' judgement to predict the average interindustry relations of the future (Carter, 35, 1963, and 36, 1967). This is the most recommended technique, given the current state of the art, for regional coefficient forecasts.

It should be noticed that although it is analytically simple to separate the individual factors behind coefficient variation, it is often very difficult to do this operationally. To the extent that it was possible to isolate separate causes, Mrs Carter found that in the United States between 1947 and 1958 the impact of new techniques was more important than substitution effects (Carter, 37, 1970). A recent study of Ireland (1953-8), however, indicated that input substitution and product-mix variations were more important (McGilvray and Simpson, 163, 1969). Clearly, the relative impact of each source of variation may differ between countries, within a country and over time.

Perhaps a more important question from the viewpoint of

regional forecasting is whether technical coefficients remain stable over time. Arguments have already been mentioned why coefficients may change less than *a priori* expectations might suggest. Obviously, they change and the tendency to change will increase with the length of the projection period.[11] Yet careful studies (Carter, **37**, 1970; Sevaldson, **222**, 1963; and at the regional level Miernyk, **169**, 1968) have indicated a high degree of coefficient stability over time, with large variations being both exceptional and predictable.[12] Indeed, Carter showed that in the United States the major changes in coefficients did not relate to intermediate input requirements at all but to primary inputs; the labour coefficients decreased over time in almost all sectors. The changes in input coefficients that did occur tended to be fairly universal and hence more easily predictable: across-the-board parallel changes in rows of coefficients; an increase in the dependence of most sectors on the general co-ordinating sectors, i.e. producers of services, communications, energy, transport and trade; across-the-board decline in the relative contribution of basic material inputs; a convergence in the input structure patterns of the major industrial groups.

There are several alternative methods of forecasting coefficient changes at the regional level. Most of these are crude, very imperfect and rely heavily on the analyst's judgement. The one exception, the ideal solution of having annual consistent regional tables stretching over a long period to provide a satisfactory base for projecting future trends, is as yet impracticable. At the other extreme, we might rely on blind faith and assume that the coefficients will remain constant. The empirical evidence at the national level supporting stability is hardly strong enough to justify such optimism, however, and except for very short-term forecasts it will be necessary to investigate at least the possibility of variation. Thus, 'the problem in this case is not in trying to overcome

---

[11] According to Rey and Tilanus (**208**, 1963), the prediction error for all industries combined arising from the use of base year coefficients increased proportionally to $\sqrt{t}$, where t equals the forecast period.

[12] It is only fair to mention the existence of evidence on the other side (Rey and Tilanus, **208**, 1963; McGilvray and Simpson, **163**, 1969). Coefficient instability in the Netherlands may be explained in part by the high proportion of foreign trade, while the Irish evidence is weakened by the poor quality of the data available.

the constant input coefficient requirement; it is in trying to determine how coefficients will vary or what their values will be at certain points in time' (Harmston and Lund, **80**, 1967, pp.39-40).

Each method varies in data requirements. The simplest is to assume that national and regional coefficients are identical (a_{ij}^n d_{ij}^r) and to use national forecasts of changing structural relations to predict how the regional coefficients will change. An improved variant of this which requires a survey-based regional table is to obtain national projections of changes in coefficients and to assume that these apply proportionally to the regional technical coefficients independently estimated (this method was adopted by Tiebout [**251**, 1969] in his projections for Washington State).

Where two or more regional tables exist, two further methods become feasible. The first is to use marginal flow coefficients which measure the ratio of the changes in inputs to the changes in outputs, i.e.

$$a_{ij}^*(t) = \frac{X_{ij}(t) - X_{ij}(t-k)}{X_j(t) - X_j(t-k)} \tag{9.3}$$

where a_{ij}^* = the marginal input coefficient and k = time period between the two input-output tables. Tilanus's (**253**, 1967) test of this technique on Netherlands data showed that mean square prediction errors increased by 25 per cent when marginal coefficients were used instead of average. He argued that this could well have been primarily due to the fact that measurement errors in average flows are compounded when differences between two flows are used to estimate marginal coefficients. He did not suggest that his tests affected the theoretical advantages of using marginal coefficients, but rather that direct research into the technological developments of individual sectors might be a better method of attempting to estimate them. The second approach using the same body of information is to compare the average coefficients for two tables and to use this as a basis for forecasting a third direct coefficients table for the terminal date of the projection. The predictions will call for a mix of extrapolation, analytical judgement and reliance on industry experts and other sources of technical information.

In a great many cases, however, two regional tables will not be available. Assuming the existence of a single survey-based regional table and all the primary data going into its construction, how can we project the average coefficients from this table to the terminal year? Liebling (Comment on Isard and Smolensky, **120**, 1963) argued that, since over a ten to twenty year period technological change can be expected to bring about considerable changes in direct input coefficients, attention should be focussed in long-term projections on the most modern rather than on the average technology. This provides the key to the best practice technique adopted for regional forecasting by Miernyk (**169**, 1968, and **167**, 1970).

The first step is to compute the average input coefficient for the base year from a sample survey. The next stage is the identification and selection of a sub-sample of 'best-practice' establishments in each sector. Several criteria could be adopted for identifying the best-practice firms; in the West Virginia study four measures were used — establishments with low ratios of employment/gross output, labour costs/gross output and depreciation/gross output and with a high profit/gross output ratio. The 'best practice' coefficients of today (period t) are assumed to approximate the average input coefficients of period $t + k$. If the terminal period for the forecast equals the base year plus k, no further adjustments are required. If not, further adjustments will be needed by linear extrapolation or interpolation as appropriate or by relying on engineering productivity data and relative price data to extrapolate beyond k. However, before this can be done the time interval k itself must be estimated. There is no clear link between age of establishment and efficiency, so we cannot solve the problem by the simple assumption that the best practice establishments are k years younger than the average. A better solution is to apply national rates of change in input coefficients, where several national tables exist, to the regional coefficients as a guide to determining k; the relative differences between regional average and best practice coefficients are expressed as percentages of the national rates of change and the results averaged to obtain a rough estimate of k. Of course this procedure is an alternative to using the national coefficients as surrogates for regional coefficients, and implies that national and regional rates of change in the coefficients are more comparable than the coefficients themselves.

Another technique for projecting input-output matrices, frequently used at the national level but never to my knowledge adopted in a regional application, is what is called the RAS method. Basically, this is a mechanical method of adjustment where row and column multipliers[13] are used to project an initial matrix, usually with very limited information. In the strict case the sole information available is the original matrix and row and column control totals for a later year; in modified forms, the analyst may have at his disposal the matrix and a series of control totals, or two independent matrices for separate years. The minimum-information RAS methods tend not to work very well, probably because the method spreads any changes evenly along rows and down columns and such spreading may be inappropriate. Better results are obtained if a more flexible approach is adopted in which the mechanics of adjustment are moderated by making use of external data, each set of which may only affect a single row or column at a time (Lecomber, **280**, 1971).

Trade coefficient projections

It is widely known that the effects of changes in trade coefficients, especially in an expanding region, can have a bigger impact on the structure of the regional economy than changes in technical coefficients due to technological change or product mix. For this reason a regional I-O forecasting model will need to incorporate some attempt at projecting changes in trade coefficients. We have already briefly discussed the question of trade coefficient stability (see Chapter 4, pp. 75-8) in the context of developing interregional models for short-run analysis. Our focus here is on long-run projections, but it will be necessary to extend our earlier discussion

[13] It is common to treat the row and column multipliers as a function of time. However, exponential functions are unsatisfactory because they lead to column sums of matrices rising through time at an increasing rate and linear functions may result in many negative elements. The better solution is to dampen both rising and declining trends in the multipliers, though choice of the particular function is arbitrary.

on whether or not stability exists. The problems are readily identified; unfortunately, the solutions are not. As we shall see, a satisfactory forecasting technique for predicting changes in trade coefficients has yet to be devised. The main problem is to estimate for each pair of interindustry relations the future breakdown between the proportion of inputs supplied domestically and those imported from outside the region; adjustment of direct consumption coefficients (and in a dynamic model, the capital coefficients) for import substitution or replacement of local suppliers by imports will also be required, though the problem here is more straightforward.

At the outset, a major obstacle is the lack of sufficient data to provide an adequate forecasting base. Even if a survey-based regional table exists the only information on imports it is likely to provide is a single row vector of imports by sector of destination. Interregional trade flow data are very sparse indeed: in the United States sample ICC waybill data for rail, Corps of Engineers water shipments information and patchy road freight data for certain commodities; in the United Kingdom the position is much worse with inadequate rail and road freight surveys only available in recent years and for very broad commodity groups. Apart from comprehensive interregional models which require precise specification of each m_{ij}^{rs}, the main requirement in regional I-O analysis is for flows by *sector* origin and destination yet available data refer to *regional* origin and destination and are for commodities that may be difficult to make consistent with I-O sectors. It is arguable, therefore, that a good start to forecasts of trade coefficients would be to construct a disaggregated import matrix ($n \times n$ sectors) for the study region by means of survey information; since only *proportions* of inputs imported would be needed such a survey should be relatively simple to undertake (Su, **236**, 1970).

We could argue indefinitely about the stability or instability of trade coefficients without coming to a settled conclusion, but a brief review of some of the main influences is a useful introduction to assessing the forecasting requirements. Important potential sources of instability are differential relative price changes between regions and capacity constraints. In regard to the first, the question is whether relative price variations between regions are large and, even if they are, does the differential induce much substitution of imports for local supplies, or *vice versa*? Regional price data are very scarce, and since price differentials primarily reflect cost differentials the question boils down in part to the unsettled point of whether or not regional production functions are identical. The answer is probably negative since there is a fair amount of evidence, if largely impressionistic, of changes in interregional competitiveness. We would expect such changes to lead to interregional substitution, and perhaps a fundamental reason why our forecasting methodology in this respect is so weak is that I-O frameworks are poorly equipped to handle substitution effects. Second, capacity constraints can affect coefficients drastically since, where they are strong, large upward shifts in imports may be needed to satisfy otherwise infeasible final demands. But since our primary concern is with longer-term projections, this source of instability should not be too serious since in the long run capacity ought to be more elastic.

On the other hand, there are *a priori* arguments favouring stability. Customer loyalty, habit or inertia may slow down reactions to changes (e.g. in prices) which might be expected to alter the balance between local and imported requirements. This may be buttressed by explicit management policy. Thus, Gordon (74, 1966) reported in his study of the defence industries in Washington State that large industries very often maintained a fairly constant in-state procurement ratio in the face of marked changes in product mix, output volume and price changes. Stabilising actions of this kind may be reinforced by component substitution by subcontractors and by promotional activities and pressure exerted by regional and local governments.

The size and structure of the system of regions may also affect the question of trade stability. For instance, in a large country made up of sparsely populated regions with widely dispersed regional production and consumption centres trading patterns will tend to be more stable than in small system of highly urbanised regions where each main local supplier may be faced with several alternative competitors near at hand over regional boundaries. Moreover, much depends on whether the regions on which the I-O tables are based are functional economic regions or were initially drawn up for administrative convenience. If the delimitation of regions disregards nodality criteria trade flows may be highly unstable.

The empirical evidence on trade coefficient stability was quoted in Chapter 4 (Moses, 185, 1955; Riefler and Tiebout, 211, 1970; see also Isard's study of cotton shipments, 108, 1953); it is unnecessary to repeat it. There are insufficient case studies available to settle the question, but the results hitherto are not very encouraging to the trade stability hypothesis. However, these studies have been concerned with short-run variations, and year-to-year changes are not necessarily inconsistent with long-term stability.

It is apparent from the foregoing comments that data limitations and ignorance about the direction of changes in trade flows make projections of trade coefficients a difficult task, perhaps the most troublesome of all the elements in a regional I-O forecasting model. Before discussing potential approaches to the problem, it should be noted that the factors influencing stability mentioned above provide some clues as to what to look for. For example, where regional cost and price data exist they may be very useful in predicting shifts between local requirements and imports, in the short run via changes in relative outputs and in the longer run by locational shifts into or out of the region. If formalised, this amounts in effect to a comparative cost analysis. Similarly, a close investigation of capacity constraints may signify even a long-run increase in an import coefficient. For instance, it may be known that a major industry in the region will experience a substantial increase in demand and be equally clear that local suppliers cannot supply the required increase in inputs because of, say, a chronic and permanent shortage of skilled labour or exhaustion of a local natural resource. Even evidence of local inertia and habit in maintaining traditional trading relationships may be useful in forecasting, since a sociocultural analysis of the character and behaviour of local entrepreneurs and managers may be helpful in estimating future responses to relative price changes in inputs. Finally, the size and location of the study region may indicate the scope for future import substitution; for instance, substitution possibilities may be dampened in a small region close to other large regions who are already supplying inputs.

In Chapters 4 and 6 various indirect techniques for deriving regional trade flows — location quotient methods, linear programming, gravity models — were examined, and it is pertinent to ask whether these are of any value in forecasting trade coefficients. All have the drawback that they only yield estimates of trade flows by commodity or industry of origin. Further operations are needed to apportion imports between purchasing sectors, and often the simple procedure of assuming imports have the same sector distribution as local inputs is adopted. Even apart from this defect, these indirect techniques are unsatisfactory as forecasting devices. The location quotient methods are invariably based on an assumption of maximum local production which leads inevitably to underestimates of interregional trade flows. Moreover, it is very doubtful indeed whether the concept of 'maximum local production' has any meaning in the long run when capacity constraints are much less serious. At first sight, linear programming and gravity models offer more promise. For instance, given data on regional outputs, regional consumption and transport costs (or alternatively on regional final demands, regional production costs and transport costs) we can determine an optimal allocation of trade flows via linear programming; then given projected values for these variables we can devise the optimal trade flow for the target year, and from this information work out changes, if any, in the trade coefficients. Deficiencies in linear programming techniques for estimating trade flows (data problems; no cross-hauls; highly aggregated commodity groups; and reduction of the *number* of flows) have already been discussed in Chapter 4. Gravity models may also have some application in forecasting trade coefficients. However, in their case base year interregional trade flow estimates will usually be needed in order to estimate the distance/transport cost exponents.[14] Forecasts of regional production and demand and, if transport costs are used instead of linear distance, of future transport costs may then be used to predict trade flows for the terminal year of the forecast period. There is a very serious objection to both the linear programming and gravity model techniques when employed for this purpose. This is that in

---

[14]In the Leontief-Strout formulation (see pp. 74-5), however, the transport cost parameters can be determined exogenously.

most formulations the initial data requirements involve forecasts of regional gross outputs, the variables which are the
very object of the forecasting exercise![15] Of course it is
possible to obtain independent estimates of regional outputs
and to check these against the outcome of the I-O forecasts
when these have been run, but this is scarcely satisfactory.

There is no clear-cut technique available for directly forecasting changes in sectoral import coefficients. The best we
can do is rely on parts of location theory, analysis of long-run
trends, feasibility studies of import substitution and other
technical and marketing information supplied by industry
experts, *ad hoc* adjustments, the exercise of judgement and
sheer improvisation. The closest procedure to a method,
adopted by Tiebout (**251**, 1969) in his projections for
Washington State 1963-80, deserves full marks for ingenuity
but is no more scientific than the alternatives. His adjustments
were based on the hypothesis that as a region grows and its
demand for a product increases relatively more of the product
will be produced locally. Given this assumption, the next
step was to compare the study region with a *larger* (in
terms of output) region similar in economic structure (in
this case the choice was the extended San Francisco Bay
area of California, for which an I-O table for 1964 was already
in existence). The allocation of a_{ij} between r_{ij} and m_{ij} was
adjusted with the aid of this table and an import flows matrix
for Washington State.[16] Of course, these adjustments were
not automatic. Each import was examined individually and,
with the aid of the San Francisco Bay data in mind, it was
considered whether it was likely to have a larger or smaller
share of total requirements by 1980, and if so the magnitude
of the change was estimated.[17] Clearly, the analyst needs to
exercise a wide degree of judgement. However, the flow-by-
flow analysis ensures that possible changes in coefficients
as a result of foreseeable events are not unwittingly over-
looked. For instance, in the Washington projections the
regional coefficients (r_{ij}) in food processing and forest pro-

[15] Of course in certain variations of the gravity model it is possible to determine
gross outputs and trade flows simultaneously, though this method would require
very accurate projections of regional final demand.

[16] Unpublished, prepared by P.J. Bourque.

[17] Direct consumption coefficients were adjusted for import substitution in
the same way.

ducts were revised downwards because projections of local outputs of agriculture, fishing and logging revealed local supply constraints.

Given that we have to rely on analysis of locational shifts, examination of possibilities of exploiting scale economies and other *ad hoc* methods of identifying trade coefficient changes, the magnitude of the problem is not as huge as might appear on first sight. It may be relatively easy to predict changes or their absence in certain sectors. This is best understood by referring to Leontief's intranational model (see Chapter 4, pp. 61-3) with its hierarchy of goods with market areas of different size and varying degrees of prominence in inter-regional trade. Some sectors will be so heavily localised that the study region may be either virtually the sole producer or a non-producer; if the scale of production is very large relative to regional demand the scope for import substitution may be non-existent. At the other extreme, there are purely local sectors (particularly in the service industries) while imports are negligible. In addition, in some sectors bulk commodities (coal, cement, building stone, etc.) figure prominently. Such goods can normally be transported only short distances, and shifts in non-local supplies may be fairly predictable since the main factor influencing them will be variations in transport costs, and these can often be anticipated.

Some changes in the ratios of local to imported requirements may be foreseeable by looking at the relationship of projected increases in final demands to intermediate input (and primary input) requirements from local industrial sectors. Capacity constraints that cannot be overcome within the forecast period or the presence of excess capacity may indicate the likelihood of, respectively, a rise or fall in the import coefficient. The major difficulties arise when we try to anticipate the possibility of import substitution and its effects, particularly for sectors where the import coefficients are currently very high. Such possibilities are more difficult to foresee at the regional than at the national level, firstly because non-local suppliers may be nearer and secondly, and more important, because regional authorities lack the tariffs and protectionist devices to ensure that import substitution possibilities are not thwarted by more effective extraregional competition.

Sometimes import substitution will be associated with the entry of new industries into the region; on other occasions it will be based on expansion in existing industries that have hitherto operated only on a very small scale. In regard to new industries, it may be helpful to search for obvious gaps in the region's economic structure; this is most easily done by perusing the current I-O table for 'weak interdependencies'. However, identification of gaps does not necessarily imply that import-substitution industries will develop, particularly within the forecast period. There is little alternative to a full-scale locational and/or comparative cost analysis. Even this provides no clear-cut answer, since although observing locational shifts into or out of the region may give a crude guide to future changes in import propensities, they are not immediately helpful on the magnitude or the speed of such changes. In some cases, for example when a substantial expansion in a major industry is planned and it is expected that this will have a direct agglomeration pull on other sectors,[18] the impact will be predictable. However, such cases are rare. Projecting the import substitution effects of the *feasible* but uncertain location of new industries in a region will usually be highly speculative compared to most tasks of standard forecasting practice.

Forecasting import substitution as a consequence of exploitation of economies of scale in local industries will tend to be much easier, partly because such opportunities are infrequent. They are more likely to occur in a rapidly growing and relatively underdeveloped region, except for the occasional instance of a relatively new firm expanding its operations to optimal scale. The prerequisite for import substitution on these grounds is a sufficient increase in regional demand to switch the balance of advantage in favour of local firms, i.e. so that scale economies plus transport cost savings offset the previously lower costs of imports. It should be noted that import substitution of this kind is not necessarily confined to manufacturing; the growth of local construction firms to replace out-of-region contractors is a typical example in other sectors. The main problem is that the import substitu-

[18]The Isard-Kuenne (110, 1953) analysis of the location of a new steel mill in the greater New York-Philadelphia region probably falls into this category.

tion process may be discontinuous, and it is not easy to evaluate whether substitution will occur within the forecast period. One possibility is to monitor this by adopting iterative solutions rather than 'one-shot' projections. For example, we could prescribe benchmark values for local production and use these as a guide as to whether import coefficients should be changed. If the benchmarks are exceeded in any of the interim years of the projection period, we could then rerun the projections with new adjusted import coefficients (Artle, 6, 1965, pp. xxxi-xxxiii).

Dynamic models

If it is desired to use an input-output framework for long-run regional forecasting, it is necessary to employ a dynamic model. For short-run projections it is sometimes permissible to use the standard static model by deriving forecasts for regional gross outputs by using the original inverse matrix and by projecting changes in final demand. For medium-term forecasts the interindustry matrix would be adjusted by allowing for changes in the input coefficients and possibly for shifts in regional trade coefficients. At best, however, this must still be treated as comparative statics. A truly dynamic model must allow for the structural relations between stocks (capital) and flows (output) and take explicit account of the fact that substantial increases in output will create additional capacity requirements so that projected changes in final demand will not only require more intermediate goods but also investment goods from all appropriate sectors in the economy. This has two further repercussions. First, investment must be taken out of the final demand sectors of the economy and treated separately. Second, since investment goods have the property that they do not have to be used up or 'consumed' in the current time period (with the possibilities of unused capacity and building ahead of demand) the time dimension has to be formally introduced into the dynamic model, whereas even with the comparative statics formulations the temporal aspects are merely implicit and have no operational significance.

The theoretical development of dynamic I-O models owes most to Leontief (141, 1953, and 145, 1966, pp. 145-51) with important refinements by Dorfman (**57**, 1954 and **58**, 1958). Empirical implementation at the national level has been taken furthest by Almon (**3**, 1963, and **4**, 1966), but the much trickier problem of making a dynamic I-O model operational at the regional level relies a great deal on the work of Miernyk (**170**, 1968; **171**, 1970 and **173**, 1970) and Bargur (**13**, 1969).

The basic additional ingredient to the I-O structure when the model is dynamicised is a matrix of capital coefficients (G) in which each entry (g_{ij}) represents the *stock* of industry i used per unit of output of industry j over time period t. The increase in the capital stock necessary to meet an increase in output is endogenous to the model. In Leontief's formulation

$$X_i = \sum_{j=1}^{n} a_{ij}X_j + \sum_{j=1}^{n} g_{ij}\dot{X}_j + Y_i, \qquad (9.4)$$

where $\dot{X}_j$ = rate of change of output of industry j. Time is treated as continuous in this variant, a fact that makes it difficult to implement empirically. Thus, it is more usual to adopt a form of the model that uses discrete period analysis, i.e.

$$X_i^t = \sum_{j=1}^{n} a_{ij}X_j^t + \sum_{j=1}^{n} g_{ij}(X_j^t - X_j^{t-1}) + Y_i^t \qquad (9.5)$$

or in matrix form

$$\mathbf{X}^t = (I{-}A)^{-1}\mathbf{Y}^t + (I{-}A)^{-1} G\Delta\mathbf{K} \qquad (9.6)$$

where $\Delta\mathbf{K}$ represents the difference between required capacity in year t and actual capacity in $t{-}1$ if we assume a direct correspondence between output and capacity. This is a determinate system but a simplified one; it assumes no disinvestment (what Leontief called 'irreversibility') and does not allow for the existence of excess capacity in various time periods. To permit the latter the simple dynamic I-O model has to be transformed into a more complex linear programming model (see Dorfman *et al.*, **58**, 1958). In such a model it may be efficient to build capacity ahead of demand, and optimisation procedures have to be used to solve the choices among output and resource allocation alternatives. The details and consequences of this transformation need not concern us here.[19]

From a theoretical point of view, the construction of a dynamic model creates few problems. Equation (9.6) above represents a set of n linear difference equations from which the system can be solved. In regional models, however, it is necessary to take notice of the fact that regional economies are 'open'. This means an additional complication, since net investment may take place with the aid of imported capital goods as well as those produced by local industries. In other words

$$\mathbf{I}_e = (I-A)^{-1} G\triangle\mathbf{K} + \hat{M}_c\triangle\mathbf{K}, \qquad (9.7)$$

where $\mathbf{I}_e$ = total net (expansion) investment and $\hat{M}_c$ = a diagonal matrix of imported capital coefficients.

The more serious difficulties arise when attempts are made to implement a dynamic I-O model at the regional level. The problems are many: general data scarcities particularly with respect to capital stock measures; how to separate net and replacement investment; the relationship of capacity to output, and the definition of capacity; a mechanism for determining the rate of imported capital.

The data availability question has not been too troublesome in the United States at the national level, building up on Grosse's pioneering work (Leontief *et al.,* **141**, 1953, pp. 185-242), which estimated capital and inventory coefficients for a vast range of industries. More recently, there have been detailed studies of marginal capital coefficients in one or two industries (see A.P. Carter in T. Barna (ed.), **35**, 1963), though regional estimates have been rather rare. Important work has been carried out for West Virginia by Miernyk and his associates (**170**, 1968) and for California by Zuzman and Hock (**269**, 1965). For most countries regional capital stock data can be derived only by extensive survey methods. The capital coefficient matrix for a region will have to make a distinction between the relationship of fixed capital to output and that between inventory requirements and output. Each entry in the capital coefficient matrix g_{ij}

---

[19] The nature of the relationship between input-output and linear programming models is discussed in Chapter 10.

represents the amount of total capital goods including inventories produced by industry i in order to allow industry j to expand output by one unit. If the marginal equals the average capital coefficient, we may write:

$$g_j = \sum_{i=1}^{n} g_{ij} = \frac{\sum_{i=1}^{n} S_{ij}}{X_j} = \frac{S_j}{X_j}, \qquad (9.8)$$

where S = capital stock.[20] The total of column j in the capital coefficient matrix shows the total capital requirements from all industries for industry j to expand its output by one unit, and represents therefore the capital-output ratio of industry j. This may be defined as the ratio of the total cost of capital goods to the value of output at capacity, or the quantity of capital required per unit of capacity.

This definition draws attention to two crucial points — the precise conceptualisation and measurement of the numerator and the denominator in the capital-output ratio. The proper value for the numerator which measures expansion investment requires us to subtract replacement capital from total investment and to transfer this to the final demand segment of the table, while in the denominator the appropriate measure is that of 'capacity output' rather than current output.

To differentiate between expansion and replacement investment exactly is not possible in most cases, because like for like replacement is relatively rare. This is due to technical change. However, there is no reason to suspect that the separation of expansion from replacement investment is a more intractable problem than others created in input-output analysis as a result of technical changes, for example, variations in input-output coefficients themselves or in capital coefficients. In many public sectors it may even be impossible

---

[20] Alternatively, marginal capital coefficients may be estimated directly from

$$g_{ij} = \frac{S_{ij}^{t} - S_{ij}^{t-1}}{X_j^{t} - X_j^{t-1}}$$

The trouble with this method is that measurement errors in the average stock and flow data are compounded when differences between them are used to estimate marginal coefficients.

to separate out capital transactions from current transactions, and because of this the government sectors are frequently retained in final demand – a procedure that provides a simple solution at the expense of completeness of the dynamic model. If the investment data are obtained by survey methods, as is frequently the case in regional studies, the distinction between expansion and replacement investment has usually to be left to the judgement of the respondents. This may be the best policy especially if cross-checks exist from secondary data, e.g. the West Virginia study used the National Planning Association's (**190**, 1966) national estimates as a check. If the questions are phrased and understood correctly, for instance, by asking firms what investment would be necessary to increase capacity output by 10 per cent, 15 per cent, 20 per cent, etc., the respondent's own estimate of expansion investment may be the most accurate available. Questions of this type have the advantage that they measure the marginal capital coefficients needed for forecasting purposes directly. However, they do not offer an escape from the most troublesome aspect of the capital coefficient measurement problem – how to treat capacity.

The capacity problem has two dimensions: the definition of capacity, easier in some sectors than in others; determination of the level of output or capacity which triggers off new investment. There is no unique definition of capacity. For instance, some economists speak of 'normal capacity' which may vary from one sector to another, while others have defined capacity as that level of output which corresponds to the bottom point of the average cost curve. In the two regional studies to be implemented empirically, the West Virginia and the California water resources analyses, the following similar procedures were adopted. Capacity was defined as *potential output* (Miernyk), or by Bargur as the maximum output that can be achieved with current technology, i.e. assuming no idle capital and the most efficient and full use of machines and buildings. Measurement of capacity should present few problems for manufacturing or even for construction and mining, but in many other sectors, particularly service industries, the concept is not very meaningful. For instance, it is quite possible in the retail sector to find new investments in additional shopping facilities taking place even when there is considerable spare capacity among existing establishments. Certainly, most retail establishments could increase their turnover substantially without adding to their fixed capital stock.[21] The co-existence of new investment and excess capacity in retail trade reflects the importance of competition and the opportunities opened up at new locations.

This leads on to the second problem, the fact that even if capacity is measurable it remains difficult to identify when expansion investment will be triggered off. The simplest, but scarcely justifiable, solution is to assume that the change in capacity is equal to the change in output, but this ignores the existence and *need* for excess capacity in some sectors and neglects the possibility that it may be possible to raise output (within certain limits) without having to increase the capital stock. A more satisfactory solution is to identify the relationship between expansion investment and the degree of capacity utilisation. For instance, in a given sector the normal capacity utilisation may be defined as when output is, say, 90 per cent of full capacity (i.e. potential or maximum output). Increases in output below the 90 per cent ratio have no effect on investment, but if output exceeds this level of expansion, investment is triggered off and the capital coefficient immediately comes into operation to derive investment requirements. This type of model is quite likely to yield reasonable results in capital-intensive, oligopolistic industries, less so in competitive service industries. Thus, for the retail trade sector it may be an improvement to relate 'expansion' investment to local population and income trends rather than to capacity. Although refinements of this kind may make the model untidy, particularly from the point of view of computation, e.g. if they require equation (9.7) to be modified, they may improve its predictive ability.

Imported expansion capital is usually treated simply as a row vector (i.e. out-of-region sector origins are not identified) and converted into a diagonal matrix for computation. The coefficients are estimated from survey data. However, where the dynamic model is used for long-run forecasting it will be necessary to estimate shifts in imported capital coefficients, and it is difficult to see how this could be done without

[21] However, increased sales might necessitate more investment in inventories.

identifying sectors of origin and types of capital goods unless crude projections of import shares are made. In general terms, the problems of forecasting changes in trade coefficients are similar for imported capital as for general trade coefficients, and the latter have been discussed earlier. Perhaps they are more difficult. For example, technical change probably has a bigger impact on regional trade in capital goods, while price differentials are less likely to be useful as a guide for predicting trade shifts because of the importance of quality and specialisation differences in regard to capital equipment.[22] On the other hand, the production of many types of capital goods is heavily localised so that for some capital goods industries in some regions imports may be either zero or account for total supply.

A further obstacle to implementation is that in a long-run forecasting context it will be necessary to project changes in the capital coefficients since it is arguable that these will bear the brunt of technological change. Even if technological change can be forecast some technique will be necessary to spread these changes over the projection period. In addition, capital coefficients will be affected by economic conditions (e.g. changes in factor price ratios) or by changes in the distribution of capital (e.g. in the ratio of finished goods inventories to total capital or in the ratio of building and works to machinery and equipment). If past time series of net capital formation and output changes are available, they may provide some pointers to projecting capital coefficients in a given direction, e.g. a trend towards greater capital intensity. Moreover, it may be possible to derive projections from national studies since it is a reasonable working assumption that technical and economic changes affecting the ratio of investment to capacity move in a similar direction, if not at the same rate, over the national economy. Of course, it will be necessary to make adjustments for local and imported supplies at the regional level. Needless to say, work on projecting marginal capital coefficients for individual regions is still in its infancy.

Finally, some comment is needed on the practical attempts

---

[22] A contrary argument is that quality and specialisation factors could make for trade stability because of the difficulties of substitution for a highly specialised product.

to implement a dynamic regional input-output model. The Californian dynamic interregional input-output programming model for California and the Western States (Bargur, 13, 1969) was an ambitious model with a limited purpose – to prescribe general policy recommendations for the efficient use and management of water resources. Only a scaled-down version of the model was made operational, but even with a highly aggregated eleven-sector model a three-period forecast spanning a decade (1963-72) involved 190 constraints. Despite the short planning horizon and the simplifications introduced into the model, it was felt that the model yielded practical results by way of fixing shadow prices for water and making sensible decisions about interregional water transfers. The Californian study illustrates very well the gap between the analytical refinement of dynamic models and the quality of the data fed into them, and this suggests that the main priority should be for improved data rather than for more work on theoretical developments.

The West Virginian model was more on the lines of equations (9.6) and (9.7) above with alternative procedures used to project the relationship between investment and capacity. Although a simpler model than that used in the Californian study it was given a much wider application – a ten-year projection of output in the West Virginian economy and estimation of the investment requirements needed to fulfil this output. Additional uses included the construction of employment projections for fifty-eight occupational groups (this required the addition of a matrix of labour coefficients), estimating the impact of a change in residential construction, evaluating the effects on business of changes in state tax structure, and simulation experiments on new activities. The designers of the model freely admit its limitations, particularly the difficulties of relating investment to output in certain sectors. The most interesting aspect of the results (since the projections extending to 1975 cannot be tested directly) was a comparison between the predictions of the dynamic model and those of a comparative statics model which retained investment as an exogenous component of final demand but allowed for change in the input-output coefficients via annual linear interpolations between the base year matrix for 1965 and the projected input-output matrix for 1975. The dynamic model has the advantage not only that it is more satisfying theoretically but also that there is a consistency check on investment available from the identity between capital sales and capital purchases (both of which are generated by the model) whereas the static model merely includes sales on capital account.

However, a comparison of the projections obtained from the two models does not provide a clear-cut case for using the more complex and data-hungry dynamic model. The aggregate output forecasts differed by only 1 per cent, although there were wide differences for some sectors (32 per cent for 'other transportation', 5-13 per cent for construction sectors, 6 per cent for logging, 13 per cent for furniture and 5 per cent for fabricated metals). Since all these sectors were involved in new investment and the dynamic forecast was higher in every case, it suggests that the static model may tend to underestimate sales on capital account. This is confirmed by the tendency for these sectors to show considerably higher capital requirements estimates with the dynamic than with the comparative static model despite the fact that the latter yielded higher forecasts of expansion capital overall. The dynamic model, however, yielded higher estimates for *imported* capital. Despite Polenske's objection (**203**, 1970) that these results fail to provide sufficient justification of the advantages of dynamic over comparative static models, it is a reasonable inference that the case would swing more and more in favour of dynamic applications as the projection period lengthens. In other words, the similarity between the aggregate projections of the two models may reflect the relatively short ten-year forecasting period.

As a final note of qualification, it must be admitted that 'dynamic' input-output models are only dynamic in a restricted sense. Although they take account of the fact that substantial increases in output will generate additional capacity requirements which in turn will induce further growth in output, they fail to accommodate the feedbacks that investment has on regional productivity (e.g. labour coefficients) and on interregional competitiveness. Nor is it easy to use a dynamic input-output model to handle the dynamic effects of labour market adjustment (e.g. migration), to deal with agglomeration economies, or to forecast economic fluctuations. It may be feasible in the future to refine input-output models to take account of some of these effects, though it would probably be easier to adopt some alternative type of dynamic regional econometric model which does not suffer from the inflexibilities of input-output analysis.

Conclusions

It is clear from the preceding analysis that there is still much work to be done in refining the techniques for regional input-output forecasting. We would argue that such efforts would be worthwhile. Support for this view is easily obtained. Almon (4, 1966, p. 137), for instance, has argued that input-output forecasting is suitable for regional applications because its emphasis on forecasts of the markets to which an industry sells and detailed knowledge of its material requirements is at the heart of locational and regional problems. Tiebout's (251, 1969, p. 340) argument is that a regional input-output forecasting model is a very flexible instrument since it can easily accommodate modifications of the data, improvements in the analysis behind individual components of the model and even *ad hoc* adjustments. It provides, in effect, the basis of a 'projection process' rather than a rigid technical straitjacket, despite its obviously technical ingredients. On the other hand, there are signs in recent years that as data gaps are filled more and more attention is being given to devising more complex regional econometric forecasting models. One reason for this is that input-output models cannot easily accommodate some key aspects of regional economic analysis. For instance, the tendency for industries and people to migrate between regions in search of higher returns cannot be handled very satisfactorily with input-output analysis, but requires operational models of industrial location and population migration decisions. It is interesting, however, that a recent attempt to implement such a model (Harris, 83, 1970) incorporates an input-output framework (using national coefficients) to forecast intermediate requirements but adds to it via introducing separate location and migration equations and by using a linear programming transportation model to determine interregional trade flows.

The true test of regional input-output forecasting techniques is their predictive ability. Unfortunately, it is not yet possible to apply this test since the major refinements in regional input-output forecasting methodology (projecting coefficient changes, implementing a dynamic model, etc.) are of such recent origin that the only projections including them still refer to the future (e.g. the West Virginia projections refer to 1975, Washington State to 1980). Back-casting offers some scope for limited tests, of course, but since data often exist for past values of coefficients such tests are not very helpful for evaluating projected coefficients, particularly since efforts to project coefficients backwards in time are in such circumstances a waste of resources and may be coloured by knowledge of the directly estimated coefficients. Such projections that do exist are of the economic impact variety (e.g. Bonner's [25, 1968] projection of the expansion of the University of Colorado up to 1980) or merely involve forecasting the effects of final demand changes on a purely static model. A pioneering example of a test that went beyond this stage was carried out by Hoch (99, 1959) in the Chicago area. Using 1947 as a base he compared forecasts for 1954 with actual production in that year, and tried alternative models with varying degrees of model closure and with both constant and variable trading pattern assumptions. All the models predicted total production within 4-5 per cent of the actual level, but no particular formulation emerged with a clear-cut superiority. It will be interesting over the next few years to judge the accuracy of the projections of the more recent refined models, not only as predictors of total output but also to evaluate the reliability of each component (final demand, input coefficients, trade flow coefficients, capital coefficients, etc.).

10 Regional Input-Output and Linear Programming

The input-output model is not only a descriptive technical device it is also value-free and neutral from the point of view of policy – hence its appeal in planned and market economies alike. It tells us what is, rather than what should be. Moreover, its neutrality does not prevent the I-O table being put to practical use in economic impact studies, forecasting and other applications. Yet these uses are meaningful only if the restrictive assumptions of the models are not infringed. The strength of I-O analysis – its description of interindustry relations, its technical aspects and its value-free character – is also, when viewed from another perspective, its weaknesses. I-O models operate much less effectively when the parameters change. They do not include a mechanism for handling substitution effects both in regard to inputs in technological processes and to trading patterns. They do not recognise that an increase in final demand may be aborted because of capacity constraints or other bottlenecks somewhere in the economic system.[1] When considered as a planning tool, the neutrality

[1] This particular criticism has been voiced very strongly by Rosenbluth (212, 1968, pp. 12-13): 'The popularity and fascination of I-O analysis is, I think, largely due to the fact that it always gives the planner a sensible-looking answer, no matter how unreasonable the question. No matter how strange the hypothetical 'bill of goods' may be, the I-O model will always come up with a unique set of industry output levels which will produce exactly the required final bill of goods, with no shortages or surpluses. Is it not strange that an economic system so dominated by internal rigidities as the Leontief system is should function in this apparently flexible manner.' Rosenbluth also speaks of 'the sleight-of-hand of the interindustry system' and 'the straitjacket of a square matrix of I-O coefficients'.

of I-O analysis is a doubtful advantage at a time when governments are being recommended to introduce a stronger 'goal-oriented' content into the planning process. Finally, if economics is concerned with finding efficient means to achieve chosen ends in a world of scarce resources, it is arguable that a technique which leaves economic choice out in the cold, as I-O analysis does, is grossly deficient. Yet all these potential weaknesses of I-O models are easily remediable if we convert our I-O models into linear programming models. This is relatively easy to do because both I-O and linear programming are blood relations in the family of linear economic models.[2]

Some of the advantages of and uses for linear programming versions of I-O models are implicit in the above comments. Since regional planners, particularly those working in backward regions, are always faced with problems of scarcity and with how to economise on scarce resources in order to achieve their objectives most effectively, the usefulness of an approach which allows for the possibility of economic choice is obvious. Linear programming recognises that there are many feasible production possibilities but enables the analyst to choose one that either maximises a desired benefit or minimises losses. It also is a very flexible approach, since there are many possible objectives which could be optimised both of a general or a very specific nature. Thus, the objective function (i.e. the linear function to be maximised or minimised subject to stated linear inequalities, named the constraints) could refer to maximisation of GRP (gross regional product), minimisation of interregional transport costs, minimisation of investment in a particular sector subject to satisfying future demands, minimisation of labour costs and many others. The structure of the objective function will depend on the uses of the model, whether it is for economic forecasting, resource allocation in space and/or overtime, an optimal investment programme or for analysis of resource utilisation and investment requirements in particular industries.

There are several types of problem where the linear pro-

---

[2] Dorfman *et al.* (58, 1958, p. 4) point out that: 'I-O analysis may be thought of as a special case of linear programming in which there is no scope for choice once the desired pattern of final output has been determined.'

gramming approach to I-O analysis is particularly relevant. Five possibilities, by no means an exhaustive list, will be mentioned here. First, if it is proposed to employ I-O techniques within a policy objectives framework a linear programming model is a method capable of combining analysis of the technical interindustry relationships and pursuit of goals. For example, an interregional programming model might be applied in which the objective was to maximise the sum of gross regional products, subject to certain specified equity constraints. These equity constraints could take the form that final demands in the prosperous regions should be limited in some way; for instance, Mathur (**161**, 1971) suggested that final demand might be made proportional to regional population. Although a goal-oriented content to the model could affect the nature of the objective function, goals are frequently fed into the programme as constraints as in the example above.

Second, a programming approach may well be preferred if the analyst wishes to avoid the restrictions imposed by assuming fixed I-O coefficients, unchanging location patterns and fixed trading relationships. In particular, it is possible to explore the substitution implications of relative price changes by running and rerunning the model with different sets of prices. This is straightforward, because prices are usually considered as given in optimisation models of this kind. This point highlights a general drawback to linear programming techniques: their inability to yield a fully determinate general equilibrium solution and their need to treat demand considerations in a simplistic manner. Thus, solving the objective function usually requires us to specify such data as the prices of output, primary factors (e.g. labour) or transport rates; in a general equilibrium framework these would be variables rather than predetermined parameters. Moses (**187**, 1968) draws attention to two types of programming models: one (e.g. Henderson, **88**, 1958; Moses, **186**, 1960; Hurter and Moses, **105**, 1964) specifies minimum prices for primary factors of production and transport costs, assumes perfectly inelastic demand for each good in each region and is concerned with minimising the costs of producing and transporting a fixed set of final demands; the other (e.g. Stevens, **230**, 1958) specifies final goods prices, assumes demand to be perfectly elastic, and aims to maximise the value of all regional final outputs subject to each region consuming a minimum amount of each final good. Neither approach is satisfactory.[3] There have been studies (Samuelson, **216**, 1952; Smith, **226**, 1963; and Takayama and Judge, **240**, 1964) which have employed programming techniques to devise a spatial price equilibrium and have taken account of the interaction of supply and demand functions, but these analyses have not included interindustry relationships but have, in fact, taken regional production levels (though not total regional supply) as given.

This is a useful juncture to interpose a reference to the *dual*. Each linear programme expressed in its original form (the *primal*), e.g. a maximising problem, has a direct converse called the dual, in this case a minimising problem. The dual will provide an alternative, and in some circumstances a simpler, solution. It is relevant here because the dual of an output-maximising problem will yield a set of 'shadow prices' or accounting prices for inputs that will minimise resource costs. Shadow prices for inputs (labour, capital, water, etc. according to the problem)

minimise the total resource valuation without giving rise to un-imputed profits in any possible use of the resources. The system of valuation is reminiscent of the operation of a competitive market in which resource users are forced by competition to offer to resource owners the full value to which their resources give rise, while competition among the resource owners drives down resource prices to the minimum consistent with this limitation (Dorfman *et al.*, **58**, 1958, pp. 43-4).

Shadow prices can thus be of great practical use to the planner because they can provide an instrument for simulating the market mechanism in an environment where a competitive market is absent in order to enable decentralised decision-making units to make optimising decisions. The use of shadow

---

[3] Consider, for instance, Kuenne's (**135**, 1963, pp. 432-3) comment on the Stevens-type models: 'If minimal final goods consumption levels are set, and prices are found which meet these minima, no assurance exists that it is a better solution than some other set of final goods prices also meeting the constraints but yielding different supply patterns. In short, the absence of the ability to handle demand relationships in these programming models requires the injection of arbitrary price or other assumptions of necessity unsatisfying'.

prices for water resource management projects has been an obvious application in the regional field.

These advantages of programming models over traditional I-O models cannot be regarded as a criticism of the latter. The Leontief assumptions rule out both the possibility of substitution of inputs in technology and relative price changes. In Leontief models there is one, and only one, efficient solution; hence the question of optimisation does not arise.

The third possible use for linear programming is found in interregional I-O models where a variant of the traditional linear programming transportation problem can be adopted to derive estimates for interregional trade flows. This use, which was discussed in Chapter 4, refers to trade flows for particular commodities and says nothing about interindustry relationships. It takes as given regional production and consumption levels and unit transport costs for each commodity and is grafted on to I-O techniques only by assuming that imports are distributed among consuming sectors in the same way as local supplies. The problem is, therefore, merely to find a network of trade that will satisfy regional requirements with the minimum total expenditure on transportation. There is a great deal in favour of integrating the linear programming transportation model with interregional I-O analysis in a meaningful way. The latter normally treats interregional trade patterns as a datum. The difficulty with this is obvious if a capacity constraint develops anywhere in the economy. If the required output of a single regional industry is greater than that region's capacity to produce the good, then the whole final demand programme becomes infeasible. In the real world this is nonsense if the good is transportable and other regions have excess capacity. However, if optimisation and substitution possibilities are introduced by converting the model into a programming technique, we can get round this objection by having the model determine all outputs and trade flows simultaneously. The trick for doing this is simply to assume that inputs into transportation are the same as inputs into all production. This ensures that the objective of minimising transport costs implies more general efficiency criteria. Minimising transport costs involves minimising the inputs required for transport, and this in turn implies the minimisation of total inputs required in producing and delivering all final demands in each region. This will clearly lead to optimisation of *both* production and trade.[4]

Fourth, a programming approach is virtually obligatory for dynamic I-O models.[5] This conflicts with Leontief's own analysis, since he attempted to make his dynamic system determinate by assuming no disinvestment and no idle capacity. His dynamic system took the form of a set of difference *equations*, rather than the inequalities traditional in linear programming. Dorfman *et al.* (58, 1958, p. 266) argued that this gives a false determinacy to the system, since the existence of a uniquely determinate solution is logically incompatible with the characteristics of a dynamic model. Even if we retain the assumptions of fixed I-O coefficients and fixed capital-output ratios, the introduction of the time dimension and stocks of capital make a choice – between capital investment and production for consumption and between working at full capacity or leaving some of the capital stock idle – necessary in every time period, whether the choice is made by explicit planning decisions or via a market mechanism. Goods produced now can be stored for later use, or resources can be devoted to investment to permit future production. Some of the capital stock may be kept idle, or the distribution of output may be adjusted to achieve full capacity everywhere in the system. In a dynamic model capital stocks can be treated as additional primary factors, and they do not have to be produced and used within the production period. Instead, the rate of investment may be adjusted over time so that the capital stock accumulates in an efficient manner, e.g. to maximise the rate of growth of GRP over the planning period. Similarly, if the dual is applied, it is inappropriate to allow shadow prices calculated on the basis of present scarcities to guide decisions over the period. This is because current decisions may reduce the relative scarcities of the scarce resources so that the current shadow prices cease to be relevant, and what is needed is the time path of

[4] In the Moses model (186, 1960) discussed below only substitution between regions is considered in order to ensure that the model, despite its huge data requirements, could be applied empirically. However, its adaptation to allow substitution between industries and between alternative technological processes in the same industry presents no difficulty from a conceptual point of view.

[5] The use of dynamic I-O models in regional forecasting is discussed in Chapter 9, pp. 183-92.

shadow prices. This too implies choice and optimisation over time, not a 'one-shot' determinate solution.

Fifth, and finally, programming models may be a particularly useful device for achieving an efficient allocation of a productive factor or resource in scarce supply. Ideally suited to handle such problems as how to optimise the use of resources between industries and regions in an economy characterised by a shortage of labour (or capital), the main application of this type of approach in a regional context has been in the water resources field in relatively arid regions, e.g. the south-western states of America (see Lofting and McGauhy, **156**, 1968, and Bargur, **13**, 1969). A very simple static single region programming model for allocating water might take the following form:

$$\text{Max } Z = \sum_{i=1}^{n} Y_i \qquad (10.1)$$

subject to:

$$X_i - \sum_{j=1}^{n} a_{ij} X_j \geqslant Y_i \qquad (10.2)$$

$$\sum_{i=1}^{n} \omega_i X_i \leqslant W_0 \qquad (i = 1, \ldots, j, \ldots n). \quad (10.3)$$

The as represent the usual interindustry coefficients, W_0 is the total amount of water available and the ωs are the water input coefficients per unit of output. The constraints are expressed as inequalities since an optimal solution might include the possibility of surplus output and even unused water.[6] It is possible to express the constraints as equations, but this is unduly restrictive since it eliminates some possible solutions at the outset. From a computational point of view, the inequalities present no problem since all we have to do is to introduce a 'slack' variable which converts the expression

---

[6]This is largely due to the discontinuities implicit in the use of linear coefficients. The problem does not arise in the marginal analysis of the traditional microeconomics of resource allocation unless marginal revenues minus marginal costs are negative in all sectors.

into an equation. Thus, inequality (10.2) above becomes

$$X_i - \sum_{j=1}^{n} a_{ij} X_j - \theta_i = Y_i , \qquad (10.4)$$

where θ_i is the slack variable which allows for the possibility that production may exceed requirements. The economic significance of slack variables is that, particularly in programmes where final demands are specified and especially in an interregional system, the optimal solution to a linear model will almost always involve unused capacity at some higher-cost producing locations. If surpluses are permitted then any given bill of goods can be produced in a great variety of ways, and we must choose an optimal solution from the many feasible solutions. The statistical significance of slack variables is that by converting linear inequalities into sets of linear equations, they enable the programme to be solved with the aid of standard methods of solution.

To revert to water resources problems, the model described above is almost crudely simple, and not typical of the situations with which most water resources analysts have to grapple. First, many water resource needs have to be coped with by multiregional authorities and in many cases an interregional model is necessary to allocate resources efficiently. Second, stock-flow relationships are relevant to analysis of water resource needs, and since the demand for water is functionally related to the growth of the regional economy analysts are usually primarily concerned with the future requirements for water rather than the current situation. Hence, a dynamic analysis is usually obligatory. Since we wish to examine interregional programming and dynamic models in a more general context, these extensions will not be analysed here.[7] It should be noted, however, that in a dynamic analysis special attention may be paid to a separate water projects construction sector, and the programme might include other objectives such as minimising investment in this sector over time subject to satisfying specified water requirements. Third, the provision of water, particularly for direct

---

[7] Bargur (**13**, 1969) has proposed an interesting dynamic interregional programming model for water requirements in the ten Western States. His model includes production, capital, employment and water constraints.

use by populations or for agriculture, is not merely a question of quantity but also of quality. The pollution of water may affect both output and costs, and can be dealt with either by translating changes in water quality into quantity terms (i.e. by computing new water input coefficients) or by introducing water treatment investment constraints (for an analysis of the importance of water quality in I-O models, though not of the linear programming variety, see Miernyk, 172, 1969).

Before discussing examples of interregional linear programming models in more detail, there are two general observations that require comment at this stage. Linear programming models may be easier to implement at the national than the regional level, because some typical constraints (e.g. the availability of labour, imports) mean much more in the national economy. This is yet another consequence of the 'open' character of regions which enable them to attract labour, capital and other imported inputs from other parts of the system. National constraints of this kind are much tighter and easier to identify. The problem is not insuperable at the regional level but it is often necessary to introduce additional variables or procedures to restrict inflows of resources. Considering imports for instance, appropriate import prices may be selected and the model then computed so as to minimise the cost of imports. An alternative is for a trade balance constraint to be imposed on the region so that its imports are limited by its capacity to export. Of course these problems need not arise in an interregional as opposed to the single region model, because the objective function in an interregional programming model will normally have direct implications for interregional resource flows. For example, in an income-maximising model factors will move to the locations where their shadow prices are highest subject to demand constraints, and interregional factor and commodity movements will be determined in a transport-cost-minimising model though at a low level.

A factor of considerable importance for the utility of linear programming models is their very heavy data requirements. This restricts the scope for empirical implementation. For instance, in dynamic interregional models concerned with optimisation in n sectors over z regions and over k time periods there will be nzk variables and constraints; in a fifty-industries, ten-regions model a ten-year programme with annual solutions will imply five thousand variables and constraints. To permit operationality it is common to simplify the programme either by reducing its scale or by adopting a sub-optimising solution. At one extreme, we might employ the procedure of Chapter 4 (pp. 68-9) and use the linear programme merely to solve interregional trade flows in an interregional I-O model in which both regional outputs and demands are precisely specified beforehand. The aggregate model in this case is not really concerned with optimisation at all. In a fully developed linear programming I-O model a common solution is to limit the number of sectors in which output levels are optimised by predetermining output in the remaining sectors according to a simple allocation rule. For instance, Mathur (**161**, 1971) separates out natural resource industries and their production is distributed between regions according to predetermined proportions; Moses (**186**, 1960) treated the service industries as non-optimising sectors and determined their outputs in each region by multiplying their national outputs by a set of constants representing each region's shares of national output averaged over preceding years. Assumptions of this kind may be a necessary compromise if a model is to be put to practical use. Most interregional models permit locational and trade pattern substitution but do not allow for technological substitution between and within industries. Although the latter would be included in a super-optimisation model, this goes beyond input-output economics since technological substitution of this type involves too radical a departure from Leontief assumptions.

The first attempt to implement an interregional I-O linear programming model empirically was made by Moses (**186**, 1960) more than a decade ago. The data related to the United States in 1949, the model was static and highly aggregated (nine regions and twenty industries). Labour is treated as the sole primary factor of production and the objective function of the model is to minimise the total amount of labour used directly and indirectly in producing *and* transporting the goods needed to satisfy final demands in each region. The constraints in the model are as follows: regional final demands are given, and supply must equal demand for each product in each region;[8] there are capacity limits on the output of each regional industry and on the transport sectors; there are limited supplies of the primary input, labour, in each region, and the labour is assumed to be homogeneous and perfectly mobile within but not between regions; flows between each pair of regions, including the intraregional flows, must be zero or positive. The model can be written as follows:

$$\text{Min } Z = \sum_{i=1}^{n} \sum_{r=1}^{z} \sum_{s=1}^{z} (1_i^r + 1_i^{rs}) X_i^{rs}, \qquad (10.5)$$

where 1_i^r = labour inputs in production per unit of output and 1_i^{rs} = labour inputs in transporting per unit of output from region r to region s, subject to:

$$X_i^r + \sum_{s=1}^{z} X_i^{sr} - \sum_{s=1}^{z} X_i^{rs} - \sum_{j=1}^{n} a_{ij} X_j^r = Y_i^r \qquad (10.6)$$

$$\sum_{i=1}^{n} \sum_{s=1}^{z} (1_i^r + 1_i^{rs}) X_i^{rs} \leqslant L^r (s = 1, ..., r, ...z) \qquad (10.7)$$

$$X_i^{rs} \geqslant 0, \qquad (10.8)$$

where L^r = total labour supply of region r. Solving the system yields the shipments of each good for each pair of regions including the intraregional flows. Regional outputs can then be obtained by aggregating shipments from each region, i.e.

$$X_i^r = X_i^{rr} + \sum_{\substack{s=1 \\ (r \neq s)}}^{z-1} X_i^{rs}.$$

Since they are the sum of regional outputs, national outputs can also be derived. Total transport costs can be determined by multiplying total shipments of each good by the appro-

---

[8] This is unusual in a linear programming formulation since it rules out all possible solutions involving surplus output anywhere in the system. There is nothing to prevent the more usual inequality being adopted, i.e.

$$X_i - E_i + M_i - \Sigma a_{ij} X_j \geqslant Y_i$$

where E = exports and M = imports.

priate unit shipping costs.

There are two aspects of the analysis that require comment: the treatment of transport in the matrix and the procedures used to implement the model. Each regional I-O table differs from the usual national matrix by eliminating the transport sector row and by substituting for the transport column several columns for each good and between each pair of regions. The justification for no transport row is that variations in the distance that inputs have to travel in order to reach the user have no effect upon industry output. The number of transport columns in each regional table is equal to the number of regions multiplied by the number of producing industries. The transport industry's output is multidimensional because transport's input requirements may differ for hauling given weights of different goods and even for hauling a given weight of a given commodity between different pairs of regions. Since changes in both the commodity and geographical composition of trade may take place between one period and another, multiple columns for transport enable the effects of these changes on all regional outputs to be taken into account. Thus, the regional interindustry matrices in this model assume an unusual rectangular form with $n \times n (1 + z)$ cells. In Moses's application of the model data shortages made it impossible to adopt this approach, and in the end transport was left out of the matrix altogether.[9]

The implementation of the model was carried out via an iterative process of the following kind. First, the national outputs of all industries — both optimising and non-optimising, i.e. service industries — were determined by solving a national I-O system. The national outputs of the non-optimising industries were then allocated to regions using share techniques. The next step was to estimate the amount of optimising goods each region required because of its having been assigned certain outputs of non-optimising industries, and this was obtained by multiplying the latter by the appropriate technical coefficients. The intermediate requirements of optimising goods thus obtained were added

[9] Of course transport costs for each good between each pair of regions were used in the optimisation of interregional trade flows.

to each region's final demand for these goods to give the first-round total requirements of optimising goods. Linear programming transportation procedures were then applied to find the pattern of shipments (and hence output) which minimises total labour and transport costs for satisfying the first-round total requirements subject to capacity constraints: these were called the first-round shipments. These were then multiplied by the appropriate technical coefficients in order to determine the second-round requirements of optimising goods. They were added to the first-round total requirements, and the optimising procedure was applied yet again. The process was continued until the sum of regional outputs for each optimising sector approached within 1 per cent of the values determined in the initial solution of the national I-O system. In the Moses study the process necessitated seven iterations.

It is clear that ingenious though this implementation was, it falls short of the conceptual analysis of the model: it was impossible to apply the method proposed to deal with the transport sector, certain industries had to be allocated to regions mechanistically without optimisation, and national coefficients had to be used for all nine regions in the absence of regional tables. Nevertheless, it did prove possible to derive meaningful results from the study. In addition to the obvious results — estimates of interregional trade, regional outputs, etc. — the study produced two findings of more general interest. First, two optimisations were run, one aimed at minimising labour costs only and the other minimising the sum of labour and transport costs. Comparison of the results showed that transport costs had a significant effect on the system, and the analysis could also be used to identify the transport cost advantages and disadvantages of particular regions. Second, the model could be employed to examine the locational advantages of particular regions in respect to particular industries, via the use of quasi-rents to indicate short-run regional comparative advantage. Quasi-rents were assumed to appear when regional requirements for any good could not be entirely satisfied from the most efficient source, and were earned by those industries in each region which operated at full capacity and, because some local demand was satisfied by higher cost imports, would have produced at a higher rate if additional capacity had been available. The quasi-rents earned by each industry in each region reflected the general inter-dependence of the interregional system as a whole since their levels depended upon the level and spatial distribution of all final demands, the level and spatial distribution of all capacities, all labour costs, and all transport costs.

The missing ingredient from the Moses model is a dynamic content. This deficiency has been remedied by analyses by Bargur (13, 1969) and Mathur (161, 1971). The Bargur model dealt with the problem of water requirements in the Western states of the USA and was concerned with maximisation of gross regional product (GRP) over the planning period.[10] Mathur's approach is much closer to the Moses model, since it is concerned with minimisation of transport costs and hence of total costs (assuming input homogeneity) in an inter-regional system, the main difference being the introduction of capital coefficients and a growth rate. Growth is handled by use of Leontief trajectories where each trajectory is defined by a vector of final demand and the rate of growth of that final demand. The total output vector as well as the corresponding capital vector also grow by the same rate of growth. Growth in the aggregate economy can be represented by a vector addition of such trajectories. Computationally, growth can be handled by adding the growth rate multiplied by the capital coefficients to the I-O coefficients, and then operating with the new augmented coefficients in place of the original ones. For a particular growth rate, the model can be written as:

$$\text{Min } Z = \sum_{i=1}^{n} \sum_{r=1}^{z} \sum_{s=1}^{z} T_i^{rs} X_i^{rs} \qquad (10.9)$$

subject to

$$X_i^r + \sum_{s=1}^{z} X_i^{sr} - \sum_{s=1}^{z} X_i^{rs} - \sum_{j=1}^{n} (a_{ij}^r + y\, g_{ij}^r) X_j^r \geqslant Y_i^r \qquad (10.10)$$

$$X_i^r = P_i^r X_i^n \qquad (i = 1, 2 \ldots k) \qquad (10.11)$$

---

[10] For a description of the general dynamic linear programming I-O model for a single region see Bargur (13, 1969), pp. 29-33.

$$\sum_{r=1}^{z} X_i^r \leqslant X_i^n \tag{10.12}$$

with the additional optional constraint

$$\sum_{s=1}^{z} \sum_{i=1}^{n} X_i^{rs} - \sum_{s=1}^{z} \sum_{i=1}^{n} X_i^{sr} = 0, \tag{10.13}$$

where T_i^{rs} = transport cost for shipping one unit of commodity i from region r to region s.

y = growth rate in output

g_{ij}^r = capital coefficients for region r.

X_i^n = national output of industry i obtained by solving the dynamic model for the national economy.

P_i^r = share of national production of natural resource industry i ($i = 1, ..., k$) assumed to come from region r.

This is a standard transport cost minimisation programme which also implies optimisation of production. Its most distinctive feature is the amendment of the production inequality (10.10) to allow for growth in the economy and, in particular, for the capital-creating effects of expansion.[11] Equation (10.11) reflects the fact that the location of natural resource industries falls outside the optimisation procedure, and their distribution among regions is predetermined using a straightforward shares allocation method. The meaning of (10.12) is obvious. As for (10.13), it is clear that there is no inherent reason why interregional trade should balance since an imbalance does not lead to balance of payments problems of the kind experienced in international trade. However, to permit long-run imbalances may result in chronic stagnation and persistent out-migration from some regions of the system,[12] and a balance of trade constraint may be a useful

[11] Mathur, in fact, expresses (10.10) as an equation (as in the Moses model). If this is treated as a balance equation it requires a solution for only z-1 regions since output for the zth region can be obtained as a residual.

[12] For an analysis of regional balance of payments problems see Richardson (**209**, 1969, pp. 259-70).

buttress for equity objectives.

One of the main virtues of this model is that it was empirically testable. Mathur implemented the model at a five-region, twenty-seven-sector level for India using I-O data for 1959. Ten of the industries were assumed to be natural resource industries with their location pattern assumed proportional to their current production. As in most interregional applications, data shortages necessitated the assumption that both I-O and capital coefficients were the same in all regions. Solutions were obtained for three growth rates (0, 10 and 15 per cent) both with and without the trade balance constraints. The results showed, quite convincingly within the limitations imposed by the data, that the optimum pattern of production is highly sensitive to changes in the rate of growth and to imposition of the trade balance constraint. The results varied from sector to sector. For instance, certain heavy industries (iron and steel, cement, glass, jute and wood products) were insensitive and could be described as locationally inelastic. Other industries (petroleum, fertilisers) were sensitive to variations in the growth rate, and yet others (transport equipment, rubber and leather, textiles, paper, non-electrical equipment) were violently sensitive to imposition of a trade balance constraint. The reason for the latter is that without a trade balance constraint all these industries were almost completely concentrated in the East region (Assam, Bengal, Bihar and Orista). With a zero growth rate the costs of maintaining balanced regional development in the trade sense were 5 per cent additional transport requirements, though the higher the growth rate the lower the proportionate increase in transport costs. Finally, several industries (aluminium, electrical equipment, chemicals and food industries) were sensitive to both the growth rate and the trade balance constraint. These may be regarded as the 'footloose' industries, and their optimal spatial distribution alters drastically with variations in the growth rate. The upshot of this analysis is that it is dangerous to plan the optimal location of industries on the basis of static prescriptions, such as regional comparative advantage, without regard to the expected growth rate of the economy.

Important though these empirical applications are, there is little doubt that further work remains to be done in this field particularly with interregional models. Data shortages are probably the most crucial restraint on future research. The theoretical advantages of linking regional I-O with linear programming techniques, however, need little stress. If I-O is to become much more of a practical tool for regional planners and policymakers, a programming approach offers the considerable advantage of being able to feed policy goals and objectives directly into the analysis. As such programmes need not be concerned solely with efficiency criteria since, for example, equity objectives might be included in the constraints or in final demand specifications, the integration of linear programming and I-O offers an immediate answer to critics who derive I-O analysis as an interesting but useless technique.

11 Input-Output and the Environment

Introduction

Pollution, the creation of waste residuals and deterioration in the quality of 'free' environmental resources (water, air, land, etc.) are becoming problems of increasing concern to planners and policy-makers. Many of these problems (air pollution, water quality, recreational resources, and many more) crop up primarily at the urban and regional level, and are beginning to figure prominently in policy discussions related to improving levels of regional and metropolitan welfare. In very recent years there have been a few attempts to integrate analysis of environmental and ecological factors with input-output models of the conventional economic system, though with one or two exceptions most of these applications have referred to the national economy.

The use of I-O models in environmental applications is at first sight surprising. Many of the relationships between the ecological and economic systems are non-linear, and fixed coefficients assumptions may be less appropriate than in inter-industry relations. To take a simple example, levels of air pollution are not a linear function of the number of motor vehicles in use. Moreover, ecological inputs and outputs — the use of common property resources, e.g. streams and rivers as inputs, the use of environmental media or 'sinks' in which to dispose of wastes, and the output of pollutants from the production process — have no market price because they can neither be made subject to the laws of property rights nor exchanged in a market. Although most of these environmental inputs and outputs can be measured in physical terms they can only be assigned monetary values by allocating shadow prices to them. This makes it difficult to incorporate them in an I-O framework because I-O tables are usually expressed in monetary flows and are to some extent descriptive accounting devices that depend upon the aggregation of all the elements in columns and rows. Some qualitative environmental factors — for instance, the aesthetics of urban design — have to be excluded altogether from analysis based on I-O concepts. On the other hand, measurable (i.e. material) environmental inputs and outputs can, as we shall see, be made consistent with I-O accounting by drawing upon materials balance equations derived from the law of conservation of mass.

Despite these difficulties, it can be shown that an I-O approach is helpful in the analysis of environmental resource and waste-creation problems, though it is clear that there are many other methods of analysis. One possible reason for neglecting I-O methodology might be the belief that pollutants and other waste products are rare exceptions to the market exchange economy, occasional externalities that can be handled on an *ad hoc* basis. However, a recent contribution by Ayres and Kneese (11, 1969) has firmly established that waste residuals are a general feature of the production process and need to be handled in a general equilibrium framework, though the traditional Leontief assumption of no joint products is obviously inapplicable when industries produce pollutants as well as commodities.

Much of the analysis that follows treats environmental problems within general I-O models that could well refer to a national economy or even a closed economy. Since the problems are essentially similar regardless of the geographical unit involved and the integration of the economic and ecological systems within an I-O structure is a complicated enough question as it is, this procedure is permissible. However, there is one point about regional applications of such models that requires emphasis, and not surprisingly this arises from the openness of regional economies and the existence of interregional trade. Ecological inputs are usually, particularly in a growing economy, scarce environmental resources that are transferred at a zero price but yet have considerable positive value; ecological outputs, on the other hand, tend to be unwanted pollutants and other waste residuals that are also transferred at a zero price but have high negative value. Thus, welfare will tend to be increased *ceteris paribus* the more a regional community can economise in the use of its 'free' inputs and the smaller its volume of ecological outputs. It follows that on ecological cost grounds imports can be regarded as desirable, particularly of goods that are profligate in the use of environmental resources or create huge amounts of waste residuals during their production; the sole exception to this generalisation is products that pollute most as they are consumed (e.g. motor vehicles). Conversely, the export of goods that incur high ecological costs in their production has an adverse effect on welfare since non-residents thereby enjoy the benefits accruing from the consumption of such goods at well below their real *social* costs of production. The introduction of ecological aspects adds a new dimension to regional balance of payments criteria. However, taking into account all the objectives that might be included within a regional balance of payments policy, it is improbable that ecological cost savings will be regarded as more than a marginal factor. Nevertheless, they might have some influence, for instance in the selection of industries for import substitution. Of course, any distortions on resource allocation and welfare due to non-marketable ecological inputs and outputs can be reduced if we can assign prices to environmental resources and taxes on waste outputs.

The Cumberland model

John H. Cumberland (**50**, 1966) was the first economist to include environmental effects in an extended interindustry model, and his work is the only study of those considered to be concerned solely with regional analysis.[1] His approach was to add rows and columns to the traditional input-output table to identify environmental benefits and costs associated with economic activity and to distribute these by sector (see Fig. 12). Row *R* measures the environmental effects of any development project or programme, and consists of monetary esti-

---

[1] See also a later paper by Cumberland (**278**, 1971).

mates of any environmental benefits by sector, as shown in row Q, minus estimates of environmental costs by sector, row C. The entries in column B represent the costs which would have to be incurred by the public and private sectors of the regional economy in order to neutralise adverse environmental effects and to restore the environment to its base period quality levels. Both the rows and columns should be disaggregated into subsectors for each environmental and resource factor either considered relevant or for which estimates can be obtained, e.g. water, air, land or open space, ecological balance, etc.

This model is ambitious because unlike most of the others it attempts to place monetary values on environmental effects rather than measuring them in purely physical terms. This is a difficult task since many impacts of development on the environment are largely qualitative, while those which are measurable (e.g. pollutants discharged per unit of air or water, noise levels, area of open space per household) need monetary

Fig. 12. Cumberland model

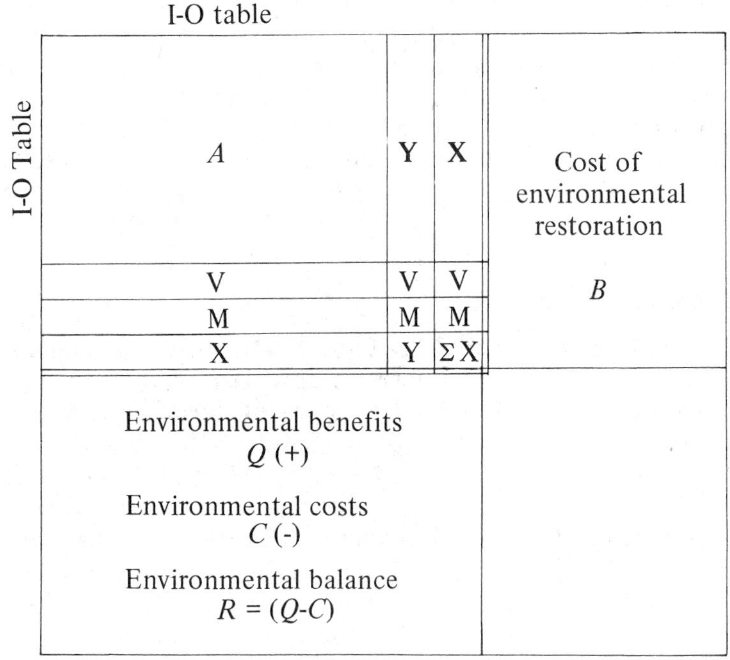

I-O table

I-O Table		A		Y	X	Cost of environmental restoration
		V		V	V	B
		M		M	M	
		X		Y	ΣX	
	Environmental benefits $Q\ (+)$					
	Environmental costs $C\ (-)$					
	Environmental balance $R = (Q\text{-}C)$					

weights to convert them. However, the costs of pollution control can be used as pricing guidelines. Also, it may be possible to impute prices to resources formerly regarded as 'free goods' which become scarce as consumption increases. Nevertheless, 'guesstimates' and subjective judgement in assigning monetary values will inevitably be required. This difference in accuracy between monetary measures of inter-industry economic flows and environmental effects is sufficient justification for the environmental repercussions being placed outside the traditional input-output table. Of course, where regions enforce air and water quality standards inputs purchased for pollution treatment purposes will already be included in the conventional interindustry matrix. But the existence of separate environmental balance rows and columns allows explicit analysis of the external economies and dis-economies that are so important in any discussion of the environmental consequences of regional development.

An important characteristic of this model is that it does not incorporate the flows into the economy from the environment and *vice versa* into an input-output framework in an integrated manner since neither B nor R is linked to par-ticular values for the interindustry flows between economic sectors. Thus the environmental rows and columns do not measure environment-industry coefficients. Rather they refer to the environmental effects of a specified regional develop-ment project or programme. In other words, Cumberland intends his extended input-output model to be used as an aid to a goal-oriented regional policy or development programme and not as a general interindustry analytical tool. Since in regard to environmental criteria, 'a proposed development project can potentially be capable of making a positive contribution to the development and welfare of a region only if the total environmental gains (Q) from the project to one or more sectors exceed the total environmental losses (C) of all sectors'[2] (Cumberland, p. 89), it is clear that this model is much closer to a cost-benefit evaluation of environmental effects than to an analysis of the inputs and

---

[2] It should be noted that a development project may increase welfare even if the cost of environmental quality restoration (B) exceeds the net environmental benefits (R), provided that gross environmental benefits are used to compensate the sectors adversely affected.

outputs of ecological commodities. Nevertheless, this study was important as a pioneering conceptualisation of the improvement in regional analysis gained from linking input-output analysis with evaluation of environmental repercussions.

The Isard-Daly models[3]

Daly (**52**, 1968) and Isard (**119**, 1969) have developed essentially similar approaches to the problem of how to incorporate the environment within an input-output framework. Conceptually, their models are comprehensive in that they show the interactions both within and between the economic and the environmental systems. This contrasts with the Ayres-Kneese study which treated ecological resources and wastes only as they entered and left the production process. The essential feature of the analysis is a general input-output

Fig. 13. Isard-Daly models

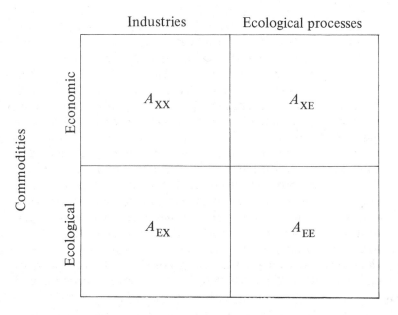

---

[3]The discussion in this section owes a lot to P.A. Victor's critique of Daly and Isard. See Victor (**258**, 1971), Ch. 2, pp. 30-44.

flows matrix which includes both economic activities and environmental processes. The aggregate matrix is partitioned into four sub-matrices as in Fig. 13. The diagonal matrices contain the coefficients representing the internal structures of the economy and the environmental system, whereas the off-diagonal matrices illustrate the flows from the environment to the economy and *vice-versa*.

The model illustrated in Fig. 13 is, in fact, very similar to that proposed by Isard. It is a commodity-by-industry (ecological process) model with rectangular matrices. Commodity flows are measured along the rows starting from basic trading commodities such as wheat and cloth at the top of the table and moving via borderline commodities such as crude oil down to ecologic commodities such as plankton and fish. Activities are measured in the columns ranging from industries such as agriculture and textiles at the left of the table through petroleum refining and sport fishing to ecological processes such as plankton and fish production. This format is theoretically more satisfying than that of Daly, who uses a highly aggregated industry-by-industry model (agriculture, industry and households) to represent the economic system. The ecological system is broken up by Daly into life processes (animal, plants and bacteria), non-life processes (physical and chemical reactions in the air, water and earth) and the sun as the source of primary energy.

The use of square matrices implied in the industry-by-industry and the highly aggregated process-by-process sectoring schemes is inappropriate when the economic-ecological model is intended for analytical purposes. First, the assumption of one-product industries (or processes) is logically inconsistent with such a model. If the generation of wastes and pollutants is a general concomitant of economic production, then each industry will have at least two products, its main output and the waste product. Furthermore, within the ecological system each of the processes included in the input-output table hides a wide variety of 'products' and 'outputs'. The solution is to allow more commodities than industries (processes) as in Isard's formulation. Second, Daly sums across the rows of his table in order to calculate technical coefficients and this involves adding together both economic and ecological outputs from the same industry. This must not be done, however, since market prices cannot be directly assigned to ecological outputs as these are not distributed through a market. Once again, this particular problem is obviated by using a commodity-industry model. Isard did not need to derive the coefficients from the input-output table because he hoped to use production coefficients obtained directly from technical data and actual experience in industries and processes.

Even in the improved Isard version, there are two critical problems that stand in the way of attempts to implement the model. First, there are data shortages. The A_{XX} matrix can be obtained by traditional input-output techniques (though using the commodity-industry variants), and there is a considerable volume of technical data available, though much of it is fugitive, on the flows of ecological resources into the economy (A_{EX}) and on the flows of ecological outputs (usually wastes and pollutants) from economic activities back into the environment. Where are the data, however, that will yield production coefficients for the A_{EE} matrix, the internal relationships within the ecological system itself? Our knowledge of these interrelationships is very skimpy indeed. Moreover, the absence of monetary valuations that would enable us to aggregate widely heterogeneous ecological commodities into a single measure of output of an ecological process is a technical obstacle, though not an insuperable one, in the way of estimating input-output coefficients. This leads on to the second main problem that cannot be solved satisfactorily until more information is available. Is the assumption of fixed proportions in input-output relations less justified in the ecological system (and in the economic-ecological interactions) than in the economic system itself? There is some evidence that throws doubt on fixed coefficients. For instance, ecological processes are very often non-linear. The causal chains and interdependencies are of a cumulative nature (see Kapp, 121, 1970), and exponential functions are more common in the technical literature than linear. Furthermore, it is doubtful whether the quality of 'free' environmental resources remains stable over time. Rapid variations in quality of, say, water inputs could require adjustments in industrial production processes and infringe the assumption of invariant production functions. On the other hand, these problems are more likely to arise in a dynamic model (though it might be argued that such a model is essential for analysis of ecological processes), and there is insufficient evidence to establish that linearity and stability assumptions are any more heroic for the ecological than for the economic system.[4]

The Leontief model

The founder of input-output analysis in the western world, Leontief himself, has recently described a model in which environmental pollution is integrated in a standard type of input-output table (Leontief, **148**, 1970). Although such a model might take many forms, e.g. depending on whether households as well as industries generate pollution and on how pollution control is financed — whether by direct payments by households, taxation or industry eliminating pollution at its own expense, there are all variants of the type of model shown in Fig. 14.

Fig. 14. Leontief model

Outputs Inputs and pollutants' output	Sectors			Final demand	Gross output
	1	2	Pollution abatement		
1	X_{11}	X_{12}	X_{1PA}	Y_1	X_1
2	X_{21}	X_{22}	X_{2PA}	Y_2	X_2
Physical output of pollutants	X_{1P}	X_{2P}	$-X_{PA}$	Y_P	X_P
Value added	V_1	V_2	V_{PA}	V_Y	V
Gross sales	X_1	X_2	X_{PA}	Y	X

[4]For a more extended discussion of Isard's views on the relevance of input-output frameworks for dealing with environment quality problems see Isard and Langford (**117**, 1971, ch. 15) and Isard *et al.*(**118**, 1971).

The problem facing the analyst who wishes to include the impact of environmental pollution in an input-output model is that the generation and distribution of pollutants are primarily non-marketable transactions. Thus, flows of pollutants have to be measured in physical terms via detailed analysis of technical relationships. However, if we wish to go beyond describing the effects of pollution and prescribe policies, e.g. measures to reduce the adverse effects of pollutants, the introduction of cost and pricing questions is inevitable. The Leontief model shows how these factors can be taken into account within the framework of a standard input-output model. In Leontief's words (148, 1970, p. 262): 'The technical interdependence between the levels of desirable and undesirable outputs can be described in terms of structural coefficients similar to those used to trace the structural interdependence between all the regular branches of production and consumption. As a matter of fact, it can be described and analysed as an integral part of that network.' Moreover, this integration with interindustry analysis is fully achieved in the sense that any reduction or increase in the output of pollutants can be traced to changes in final demand and/or in the technical structure.

The modifications required in the standard input-output table are really quite modest. In Fig. 14 the interindustry flows table is highly simplified by assuming only two industrial sectors and one pollutant, say air pollution; however, multiplicity of sectors and pollutants does not alter the analysis in substance. The distinctive features of this input-output table are the row that represents the physical output of pollutants and the column representing the pollution abatement industry. Since the former is in physical units whereas the rest of the table is in monetary values, the pollutant's output row must be exempt from vertical summations. The pollution abatement industry, on the other hand, can be treated in the same way as other industries, and requires inputs from them. However, there is no intraindustry coefficient and indeed no input row for the pollution abatement industry itself, reflecting the fact that its output is used to offset pollution generation in the economy as a whole irrespective of its source and is not sold as inputs to other industries. In the version of the model described in Fig. 14 it is assumed that the costs of pollution abatement are paid for directly by households;[5] an alternative version in which individual industries finance pollution abatement themselves would require an input row for the pollution abatement industry though households would still pay for it indirectly via higher prices. The other peculiarity of the pollution abatement industry in the Leontief table is that its output is recorded twice – in physical terms (i.e. amount of pollutants eliminated = negative output of pollutants) in the pollutant output row and in monetary values in the usual fashion at the bottom of the industry's column (i.e. in terms of the cost of inputs from other industries and value added). This double valuation of the output of the pollution abatement industry enables the monetary cost of eliminating each unit of pollutant to be estimated directly.

Further light on the meaning of Fig. 14 can be shed by use of some simple accounting identities. Summing the columns and rows of the basic input-output table (i.e. leaving aside the pollutants row), we obtain:

$$X = X_1 + X_2 + V = X_1 + X_2 + X_{PA} + Y . \qquad (11.1)$$

Thus
$$V = Y + X_{PA} \qquad (11.2)$$

$$\therefore Y = V - X_{PA} . \qquad (11.3)$$

The introduction of the pollution abatement industry financed from households upsets the traditional identity of value added and final demand ($V = Y$). Sales to final demand are reduced below the level of value added by an amount equal to the expenditure of resources on pollution abatement.

As for the output of pollutants we do not sum across the row in the usual way. The total gross output of pollutants is made up of the pollution generated by each industry

$$X_P = X_{1P} + X_{2P} . \qquad (11.4)$$

What counts from the point of view of evaluating environmental disturbance, however, is the impact of pollution on society as a whole, or in input-output terminology the deliveries of pollutants to final demand or the net output of pollutants. This is equal to the gross output of pollutants

---

[5] In effect, these costs can be treated as a subtraction from final demand.

minus any elimination of pollutants as a result of pollution abatement activities, i.e.

$$X_P = X_P - X_{PA}$$
$$= X_{1P} + X_{2P} - X_{PA} . \qquad (11.5)$$

Thus, for the pollutant row the key entry is found in the final demand column which represents the net impact of pollution on the economy and is obtained by summing the positive and negative outputs of pollutants generated by each industry including pollution abatement. The entry in the gross output column, X_P, is significant only as an indicator of the maximum amount of pollution that would be created if unchecked. The row for pollutant output can be regarded as a kind of externalities row in the input-output table. Its existence, however, has repercussions on the rest of the table because dealing with externality problems usually requires economic resources.

The Victor model

The latest version of an environmental I-O model has been developed by Victor (**258**, 1971). His approach is more general than the Leontief approach, more in keeping with traditional I-O accounting conventions than Cumberland's, and less ambitious than Isard's and Daly's. His model corrects critical deficiencies in the Daly model and clarifies points that are only implicit in the Isard study. Its more limited aims compared with these latter two analyses are reflected in the absence of a subsystem showing the interrelationships within the environment itself, on the grounds that data shortages make it impossible to operationalise such a subsystem at present. Accordingly, the model includes only flows of 'free goods' from the environment into the economy and of waste products from the economy to the environment, but the benefit accruing from its more modest scope is that the model can be implemented. Thus, Victor argues (**258**, 1971, p. 11) that his work is 'the first study in which comprehensive estimates of material flows are used to extend I-O analysis in order to quantify some of the more obvious links between the economy and the environment of a country'.

Victor uses a forty-commodity - sixteen-industry model

for the economic system as his basic framework, thus profiting from the advantages of a commodity-industry approach for ecological analysis: the fact that all production involves wastes so that each industry is characterised by joint products; and that each commodity does not have to be measured in the same units so that the economic data in the model can be expressed in monetary units whereas the ecological data are expressed in terms of weight. This is an extremely useful device when most ecological commodities, e.g. pollutants, are not exchanged in a market and have no explicit price. Thus, his I-O table is divided into two sectors, the economic sector which is a standard commodity-industry table expressed in monetary values and the ecological sector expressed in weight terms. The latter is broken down into subsectors reflecting land, air and water respectively. The other main feature of the model is that the accounting identities characteristic of I-O tables are also found in the ecological sector because the use of physical data enables the author to adopt the materials balance equation approach stressed by, among others, Ayres and Kneese (11, 1969). We can treat each production process as an inflow of raw materials and energy and a subsequent outflow of useful products, waste products and energy. The law of conservation of mass implies that if there is no change in inventories during the process the combined mass of material inflows equals that of material outflows. More precisely, in a closed economy when there is no change in the mass of capital equipment, inventories of finished and semi-finished products, and consumer durables, the mass of ecological inputs to an economy must equal the mass of its ecological outputs. This is the materials balance equation.

Victor's I-O table with its economic and ecological sectors is shown in Fig. 15. A conventional commodity-industry table is augmented by additional columns representing ecological outputs and additional rows for ecological inputs. The model is described by nine matrices, eight vectors and one scalar Of these, four matrices and two vectors refer to the ecological sector. The notational code is described overleaf.

(a)   *Economic Sector*

   Matrices

   Z = inputs of economic commodities to industries.

Fig. 15. Victor model

| | | Economic sector | | | | Ecological sector | |
		Commodities	Industries	Final demand	Gross output	Out-puts	Totals
Economic sector	Commodities		Z	Y	**X**	R	
	Industries	U			**T**	Q	
	Value added		V_Z	V_Y	**V**		
	Totals	**X**	**T**	**S**	**W**	**P**	
Ecological sector	Inputs	N	M				**L**

Y = final demands for economic commodities by categories of final demand.

U = outputs of economic commodities by industries.

V_Z = expenditure on primary inputs by industries.

V_Y = expenditure on primary inputs by categories of final demand.

Vectors

X = sums of rows in matrices Z and Y showing domestic supplies of economic commodities.

T = sums of rows of matrix U showing total gross outputs by industries.

V = sums of rows in matrices V_Z and V_Y showing total expenditures by primary inputs.

X´ = sums of columns of matrix showing total outputs

by economic commodities; this is the transpose of vector **X**.

$\mathbf{T'}$ = sums of columns of matrices Z and V_Z showing total economic inputs of industries; this is the transpose of vector **T**.

$\mathbf{S}$ = sums of columns of matrices Y and V_Y showing total expenditures by categories of final demand on economic commodities and primary inputs.

Scalar

$\mathbf{W}$ = sum of elements of vector **S**, and is also equal to the sum of elements of vector **V**. The equality of **W**, **S** and **V** reflects the identity of gross domestic expenditure (final demand) and gross domestic product (primary inputs).

(b) *Ecological Sector*

Matrices

R = outputs of ecological commodities discharged as a result of final demand for economic commodities.

Q = discharge of ecological commodities by industries.

N = inputs of ecological commodities used in conjunction with the final demand for economic commodities.

M = inputs of ecological commodities used by industries.

Vectors

$\mathbf{P}$ = sums of columns of matrices R and Q showing total outputs of ecological commodities.

$\mathbf{L}$ = sums of rows of matrices M and N showing total inputs of ecological commodities to industry and final demand.

The table now yields several self-evident accounting identities:

(a)   *Economic sector*

Each element of vector		Sum of *corresponding* (row or column) elements of matrix (or matrices)	
T	$=$	U	(11.6)
X'	$=$	U	(11.7)
X	$=$	$Z + Y$	(11.8)
S	$=$	$Y + V_Y$	(11.9)
V	$=$	$V_Z + V_Y$	(11.10)
T'	$=$	$Z + V_Z$	(11.11)

In addition

$$Y = U - Z \tag{11.12}$$

$$\text{and } W = S = V \tag{11.13}$$

(b)   *Ecological sector*

Each element of vector		Sums of *corresponding* (row or column) elements of matrices		
P	$=$	$Q + R$	ecological outputs	(11.14)
L	$=$	$M + N$	ecological inputs	(11.15)

In addition

$$P = L \qquad \text{materials balance equation[6]} \tag{11.16}$$

Victor's work extends far beyond the simple accounting model described above, since he attempted to apply his model empirically with the aid of available data on waste products and environmental resources (in practice, only water) assembled and collected for Canada in 1961. These waste products and 'free' ecological resources were assigned to thirty-one categories and were then introduced into the economic input-

[6]This identity depends, of course, on the assumptions stated above (p. 225): a closed economy and no accumulation of mass in the economy itself.

output model with its sixteen industries and forty commodities according to industry of use or generation. The quality of much of the data used was very imperfect, but the importance of the study lies in its methodology rather than in the precision of its results. With the aid of this information Victor was able to undertake several applications. He developed a set of ecological impact tables (with and without import leakages) which show the direct and indirect effects on individual ecological inputs and outputs attributable to the production of one dollar's worth of each commodity delivered to final demand. Second, by applying a set of shadow prices representing the social valuation of the ecological commodities he showed how the impact tables could be used to derive an estimate of the ecological costs of producing and consuming each economic commodity. There are two obvious methods of deriving these social valuations: assessing the extra payments made by households, firms and government because of the use or generation of ecological commodities (e.g. water treatment costs, cleaning costs, medical bills); and the superior method of evaluating the compensation that would have to be paid to people whose welfare had been reduced as a result of the use or production of ecological commodities. The latter method is superior because it allows for estimates of environmental damage that do not directly induce the expenditure of economic resources. On the other hand, it is more subjective and ingenious techniques have to be adopted to derive appropriate compensation values. In his study, Victor did not in fact take this final step of imputing monetary valuations to ecological costs but instead relied on weights derived from technical information to obtain *relative* evaluations of the ecological costs of producing and consuming one dollar's worth of each commodity. He found, however, that the ranking of commodities according to ecological costs was rather insensitive to changes in the values attached to the social weights.

Only one or two of his detailed results can be quoted here. Assigning an index of 1·0 to the most ecologically costly commodity-petroleum, the next most costly commodities were coal (0·968), vehicles (0·357) and paper products (0·147). No other commodity had an index higher than 0·062. Using these weights, he estimated that the total ecological costs of production of economic commodities in Canada in 1961 amounted to $3,415,000 \times 10^9$. Victor was also able to disaggregate his physical weight estimates of ecological inputs and outputs by province, a useful step since different direct and indirect inputs and outputs of ecological commodities will result from different patterns of regional final demand. Finally, Victor employed a linear programming version of the commodity-industry I-O model to find out what would have happened to the index of ecological costs in 1961 if the use of the private car had been reduced by 50 per cent in Canada and replaced by public transportation. The answer was a decline of 9·04 per cent. Interesting though these results are, they are overshadowed by the more significant general contribution of Victor's study – his demonstration that implementation of an environmental I-O model is empirically feasible.

Conclusions

In this chapter we have briefly examined the role of I-O models in the analysis of environmental and ecological problems as reflected in four alternative I-O accounting frameworks. We have not extended the discussion into the much broader questions of pricing and environmental control, apart from incidental comments on the Leontief model. Our aim has been merely to show that the environmental disturbances and scarce-resource-use problems that figure increasingly in regional and urban development questions can be analysed with the aid of I-O models.

The conclusions on the alternative formulations examined are already implicit in the comments on the individual models. Cumberland deserves credit for the first attempt to incorporate environmental evaluations in a regional interindustry study, though his treatment of environmental relationships was closer to a cost-benefit analysis and he did not use linear I-O coefficients in the environmental sector itself. Leontief's model is interesting as an attempt to retain as much of the traditional I-O table format as possible, in its emphasis on dual (monetary *and* physical) measures of output in the pollution abatement industry, and in its explicit introduction of prices into the model as a method of eliminating pollution.

On the other hand, the I-O table then becomes clumsy and difficult to use for accounting purposes and, more important, the model is partial in scope because it excludes the 'free' environmental inputs from the analysis and concentrates solely on pollutants. The approaches of Isard and Daly are much more comprehensive in that they deal not only with ecological inputs into and outputs from economic production but also present a conceptual framework for analysing the interrelationships internal to the ecological system itself. The Daly model has serious theoretical and practical weaknesses, but these are largely eliminated in the Isard commodity-industry and commodity-process model which permits industries to have multiple outputs and does not require the aggregation of monetary and physical values.

The main drawbacks of the Isard model are that it remains doubtful whether the cells in the ecological system's submatrix can be adequately quantified and it is possible that the fixed input coefficients assumption may be even less valid than in the economic system. Given these doubts and the relative scarcity of data on relationships within the ecological system as opposed to interactions between it and the economy, there is much to be said in favour of a more modest approach sacrificing comprehensiveness for the sake of operationality. Victor's study achieves an admirable compromise between the theoretical ideal and the practical requirements for empirical application. He drops the internal matrix of the ecological system, but retains the commodity-industry table of the Isard model. Moreover, he is able to make his analysis of ecological inputs and outputs conform to the principles of consistent I-O accounting by adopting the materials balance concept. He does not attempt to integrate the economic and the ecological sectors in his I-O table into a framework that permits summation over the two sectors by expressing all inputs and outputs in monetary values. However, his analysis of the relative ecological costs of producing and consuming individual commodities is only a short step away from absolute monetary valuations of such costs. Victor wisely takes the view that this final step should await more and better quality data. His prime achievement is to translate the conceptual framework for environmental I-O analysis into a form that is empirically workable. There is now no reason, other than the costs of data collection, why future I-O studies, particularly urban and regional applications, should not explicitly consider the impact of ecological inputs and outputs on growth and welfare.[7]

[7]For a broadly based discussion on environmental pollution which encompasses an input-output approach see Herfindahl and Kneese (**279,** 1971).

12 Urban Input-Output Models

Although there have been several empirically implemented urban input-output models (for example, Hirsch, **95** and **96**, 1959, and **97**, 1963; Berman, **19**, 1960; Artle, **6**, 1965; Karaska, **122**, 1966), these have not been very different from area input-output applications on a larger scale. Several of the studies included interesting conceptual suggestions (Hirsch, **97**, 1963) or contained useful supplementary analysis of a non-input-output kind (Artle, **6**, 1965), but the actual input-output tables themselves were almost identical to the standard regional or national table. In particular, the usual format was a high degree of disaggregation in the local interindustry matrix but with outside trade merely treated as an inport row vector and an export column vector of final demand. Yet it is arguable that the economic development, fiscal and planning problems facing urban communities call for modifications to and refinements of traditional input-output methodology if it is to be of maximum utility to metropolitan areas. Furthermore, although there are no applied examples to my knowledge, an interurban input-output model parallel to Isard's interregional model offers considerable advantages for the analysis of a regional system of cities and their interrelationships.[1] The full potential of input-output techniques in the

---

[1] Isard himself recognised the possibilities of using this approach in an *intra*urban context. He argues (Isard and Langford, **117**, 1971, p. 16) that 'it is not too bold to move ahead to develop a pure interregional model for improvement of intrametropolitan analysis and greater understanding of internal interdependencies'.

study of urban economics has yet to be realised.

At first sight there are several reasons why input-output analysis might not appear very relevant to analysis of urban economic problems. Agglomeration and scale economies are almost universal characteristics of the urban economy and are not easily made compatible with the linearity assumptions of input-output models. Similarly, space and locational features are important features in the city yet, as Kuenne (135, 1963) pointed out, input-output models are essentially space-less. Most urban problems call for long-term solutions whereas input-output techniques work best when they deal with short-run changes. In the urban context, however, long-run population, employment and output projections will be needed to aid decision-making. But as we have already seen (Chapter 9) major obstacles arise in attempting to apply input-output techniques for long-term projections purposes − namely, the stability or instability of technical coefficients and, even more critical, of trading coefficients. Although input-output is primarily a neutral technique from a policy point of view, it can be used for policy purposes if a linear programming version is adopted. But even a linear programming input-output decision model is of little use in an urban area if the area is not covered by a single decision-making unit, and for most countries this condition is rarely fulfilled. Even in a non-policy context the ideal unit for a subnational input-output study would be a fairly homogeneous, clearly bounded geographical area, and few cities can be described in this way.

Although some of the above objections may restrict the scope for input-output analysis in the urban field, they do not challenge its basic usefulness. A more difficult objection arises from an inevitable feature of urban economies − their small geographical size. A well known precept in urban and regional economics is that the smaller the area in question the higher the proportion of external trade to total output. It follows that in a city a high proportion of output will go to final demand (exports) and a substantial share of inputs will not pass through the interindustry matrix (i.e. imports). An economy in which intermediate demand accounts for only a small proportion of total output does not appear an obvious candidate for an input-output study. This argument is not as strong, however, as it seems. This is because the conventional division between intermediate and final demand is not very useful in urban analysis. There is a great deal to be said in favour of using a closed model in which many items usually considered as part of final demand are treated as endogenous. Such items include household demand,[2] private investment and certain items of government spending (e.g. local government expenditures). This reflects the importance of specialisation in exports and, to a lesser degree, of central government income transfers as generators of urban expansion. Conversely, households and local government sectors are often treated as components of the endogenous segment of the economy because their activities are, in cities, closely tied to the general level of economic activity in the area.

By closing the model to an appropriate degree we obviate the problems arising from a high ratio of final to intermediate demand as well as gain a model which has the advantage of explaining more of the key urban variables within rather than outside it. On the other hand, since measures of trade external to the city are less precise than measures of interindustry flows, these benefits may be offset by the reduced accuracy of urban input-output tables. If final demand is pruned down until it virtually comprises merely exports, the final demand percentage of total output may become fairly small even in an urban area. Moreover, the percentages may vary considerably from sector to sector. For instance, Hirsch's study of St Louis (**95**, 1959) revealed an average export/output ratio of 26 per cent, even though the most predominantly export sector ('other transport equipment') exported 97 per cent of its output. The wide intersectoral variations may be revealed most easily by drawing up the input-output tables in a 'triangularised' form, i.e. rows of sectors with a high degree of interdependence on the input side, but with large sales to final demand and hence less inter-dependence on the output side, are placed at the top of the table, while sectors with high

---

[2] To include households among the city's endogenous sectors it is necessary to assume that employees in the different production sectors spend their income in the same way.

output but low input interdependence are placed at the bottom.[3]

In this discussion of urban input-output we have chosen to concentrate on three major issues: the use of input-output techniques to evaluate the impact of the introduction of a new plant, or more generally any final demand change, on the local government fiscal sector; the explicit introduction of space, e.g. physical space requirements of business firms, in an input-output framework; and the value of interurban models. However, prior to this, there are several *ad hoc* comments on urban input-output applications that require a brief mention.

For instance, a feature that distinguishes urban centres from other geographical units is that they usually import labour inputs from outside their boundaries as commuters. It is unsatisfactory to aggregate these with other kinds of inports, so that a useful modification to the standard table is to disaggregate imports into 'labour' and 'other goods and services'. When the model is used for prediction, this raises the interesting question of whether or not we would expect the labour import coefficient to be stable. *A priori*, labour supply constraints within the city itself may suggest a rise in the labour import coefficient during a phase of urban expansion. As in most similar situations in input-output models, we are not, however, bound by constant coefficient assumptions if evidence is available to make the appropriate adjustments and if iterative solutions are adopted.

In urban input-output models we should not be too surprised to discover that the household coefficients are relatively small, and that income multipliers are low. These are merely manifestations of the fact already observed that cities are usually closely integrated with the region and nation that contains them and that this integration shows itself in high imports and high exports. This, in turn, suggests the advantages of using complete export and import matrices rather than column and row vectors to analyse a metropolitan area's external trade. A city's geographical sources of supply and markets may be at least as important as sectoral origin and

---

[3]Triangularisation of an input-output table presents practical problems since the relative size of cell entries has to be taken into account as well as the fact of zero and non-zero entries.

destination in projections of metropolitan change and implementation of urban policy decisions. However, cost and data constraints would normally prohibit the construction of trade matrices for a single urban area unless it was in the context of developing a comprehensive interurban model. Artle in his study of Stockholm (6, 1965) merely drew a distinction between the rest of Sweden and foreign countries in his analysis of Stockholm's external trade, though he did divide trade with Sweden into two sectors — agriculture and all other industries. Gottlieb (75, 1960) suggested the desirability of a central city, suburban (or regional), and 'rest of the world' subdivisions, requiring a system of 9 (3 × 3) matrices. However, even a simplified structure of this kind has yet to be implemented.

Some interesting problems arise in regard to the appropriate degree of disaggregation in urban input-output applications. The treatment of imports and exports already discussed is merely one example. Another is how far to disaggregate sectors in the interindustry matrix. It is well known that certain service industries are found in virtually all urban areas (distribution; local government services; professional services such as lawyers, doctors, and accountants; hotels and entertainment; and so on), and there is probably some substance in the generalisation that these sectors have very similar structures in most cities and that their coefficients are probably very stable. If this is the case, it may be both efficient and economical to adopt a highly aggregated sectoring scheme for such service activities and to concentrate resources on a finely disaggregated sectoring of manufacturing industries. In an urban model it may also be desirable to disaggregate the household sector and government. Particular types of households have differential effects on retail distribution, transportation demands, the demand for homes and many other dominant metropolitan activities. Where households are endogenous, it may be helpful to introduce additional rows and columns to reflect separate household groups by income, social class, race or family size. Of these possibilities, the income-size classification is probably most important in an urban study because so many of the crucial urban demands—for space, public transport, cultural and leisure facilities, etc.—are functionally related to income levels. As for government expenditure, Artle suggested a fourfold division: non-defence current account; defence spending (a predictable category in a work with an introduction written in 1964 in California); government subsidies and transfer payments; and capital spending on roads, streets, public buildings, etc. This last category is obviously of crucial importance in a city since urban infrastructure spending can generate urban growth (though it may also, in part, be induced by previous levels of activity). In this sense it is not merely an important component of government spending but a decision variable capable of influencing the levels and spatial distribution of subsequent economic activity.

The incompatibility between urban external and agglomeration economies and linear input-output models has already been noted. Although this restricts the potential of input-output analysis in the urban economy, there are some remedies available to deal with the problem. Firstly, though the input-output table offers no hope of measuring external economies, the interdependence between sectors is clearly shown up in the table and this interdependence is very often indicative of the agglomeration advantages gained from the location of interdependent industries in the same area. In other words, the input-output table may guide the analyst to particular industries which are sources of or beneficiaries from external economies. Second, in cases where a triangular input-output system is adopted, it is possible to introduce non-linear relationships, since the hierarchical ordering characteristic of the triangular input-output table permits systems of non-linear equations to be solved sequentially. If non-linearities can be handled, the analysis of scale economies and indivisibilities is not ruled out. Finally, although no urban model has been calibrated which allows for the measurement of environmental benefits and general amenities it is now conceptually possible and empirically feasible to analyse the effects of pollution (external diseconomies) on an urban area with the aid of an input-output framework (this merely requires reduction to the urban level of one of the approaches outlined in Chapter 11).

There have been two attempts to show how an evaluation of the impact of urban economic activity on the quality of life might be carried out using an input-output framework

(Bergmann, **270**, 1969, and Hirsch, Sonenblum and St Dennis, **272**, 1971). Bergmann's model relates to what she calls social, environmental and governmental (SEG) problems, examples of which include the economic wellbeing of Negro residents, air pollution and the fiscal sufficiency of the urban core. Hirsch classifies quality of life indicators into five urban subsystems: the natural environment (e.g. quality of air, water); the spatial environment (e.g. arrangement of work-places and residences); the economic environment (e.g. poverty); the public service environment (e.g. education, medical care); and the socio-cultural environment (e.g. availability of theatres, museums, concert halls).

Bergmann's approach is to link an SEG accounting system to the urban input-output model. The former consists of two matrices: a behaviour matrix which represents the behaviour of firms in matters that affect SEG indices, and an impact matrix which attempts to measure the effects of activities in the behaviour matrix on these indices. When the two matrices and the inverse input-output matrix are multi-plied together, we obtain an industry effect matrix which when multiplied by the final demand vector estimates the economy's impact on the SEG indices. The difficulty with this approach is that some of the impacts are non-measurable (though others may be translatable into income-equivalents), and hence it is necessary to assign weights to each aspect of business behaviour affecting the SEG measure in order to aggregate the impacts into an overall index of SEG wellbeing. In effect, Bergmann uses constant linkage coefficients (which is one of three approaches discussed by Hirsch), although the types of relationships involved are unlikely to remain con-stant either as output changes or over time.

Hirsch discusses three alternative procedures that enable quality of life measures to be related to the market valuation data of the input-output model. First, there is the linkage technique that links the indicators to input-output sector outputs via the use of linkage coefficients (e.g. pollution coefficients such as pollutants per unit of output). This approach may be suitable where there are no feedbacks between quality of life indicators and input-output sectors. Where feedbacks are important, a dummy sector technique may be employed in which 'dummy' industries representing imputed sets of transactions for the relevant industries are included in the endogenous matrix. This approach, which is similar to Isard's treatment of environmental pollutants discussed in Chapter 11 (pp.218-21), is particularly appropriate for indicators associated with the natural and spatial dimensions of urban quality. The third approach, the disaggregation technique, is to disaggregate input-output sectors so as to correspond with specific indicators. This is especially feasible in the case of the household and government sectors. For instance, household incomes and government welfare, health and education expenditures (using input criteria as surrogates for quality, e.g. hospital beds per capita, size of classes) can be translated into indicators of the quality of life. These sectors in the standard input-output table, however, will be too aggregated. It will be necessary to disaggregate households at least by income class, while the linkage technique could also be used, e.g. to relate data on income distribution to spending on cultural activities. Elsewhere (**271**, 1968) Hirsch suggested how the local government sector might be broken down into five categories; in the more recent paper he suggested education, health, welfare, public safety, fire, recreation, direct highway transit, and water and sanitation utility sectors. Some of these activities might be dealt with in the endogenous segment if they are affected in some consistent manner by the producing sectors (e.g. public safety, roads, transit and fire protection); others would have to be handled, as suggested above, by the use of linkage coefficients between public service expenditures and output (or failing this, input) quality measurements.

Hirsch and his associates recognise the limitations of input-output frameworks for analysing quality of life indicators: the difficulty of measuring indicators of the socio-cultural environment; the weakness of linearity assumptions in analysis of the spatial and natural environments; the prevalence of externalities in quality of life indicators making it difficult to assign prices; most of the indicators refer to stock concepts but input-output analysis mainly provides estimates of changes in indicators.

To turn to one of the major themes of this chapter, input-output techniques can be employed to show whether a given urban industrial development will increase or reduce the net fiscal resources available to the area. This is an important question, since almost all urban governments are hard pressed financially, and need to give attention in any policies to promote economic expansion in their area to the question of whether or not net fiscal resources will be improved. Of course, while any type of urban economic development will broaden the tax base, all forms of economic expansion also generate public expenditure requirements, either directly or indirectly via the demands of the newly employed for housing, education and social services. It is by no means clear that the net effect will always be positive, and it will certainly vary in magnitude from one type of development to another. For instance, in his study of the finance of local education in the United States, Hirsch (**98**, 1964) found that expansion of industries with high wage, low employment characteristics was most likely to have a positive net fiscal resource impact.

An input-output framework is useful in a fiscal impact study since the indirect and induced public expenditure effects of any development project attracted to a city can be a large component of the total impact. This is because we must take into account the new labour force and residential development associated with the new enterprise, as well as the output impacts of the enterprise itself. The general principles that impinge on a net fiscal resources impact study are almost self-evident. Clearly, an urban government will find new activities more satisfactory *ceteris paribus* if they pay sufficient taxes to cover their associated direct, indirect and induced public expenditure requirements and if their labour force has average income levels sufficiently high to cover its demands on public and social services. In this respect, activities generating large per capita personal income impacts are particularly welcome since the aggregate income effect will tend to be greater than the employment and population effect, and this, in turn, usually implies that the ability to pay for public services will exceed the need and demand for them. Another consideration is that in the introduction of a new plant into a region it is necessary to distinguish between the initial construction impact and the longer-run operations of the plant. While the former can be treated analytically as an addition to regional final demand, the latter will involve either an increase in the activity levels of an existing industry or a new row and column in the input-output table. The influence and timing of both phases must be allowed for in evaluating the fiscal impacts, as well as the size of the labour force, its wage levels and geographical source (local residents, commuters from outside the city boundary, or in-migrants), and its housing and public service requirements. For example, if a high tax, low wage plant employs commuters from other areas, this may shift part of the public expenditure burden to other local governments.[4]

From the local fiscal impact viewpoint, the criterion is whether the direct, indirect and induced effects of any anticipated development reduce the local government per capita deficit (or increase the per capita surplus); alternatively, whether the development, given the prevailing tax rates, permits a higher level of public services per capita, or, with given expenditure levels, allows tax relief. However, this does not imply that maximisation of the fiscal residue should be the major objective of urban development policies. For example, it may be rational and consistent with community preferences for an urban government to reject a development that would reduce tax rates on the grounds, say, that its presence might have serious adverse environmental effects.

What are the alternative methods of dealing with local fiscal impacts in an input-output model? Cumberland's treatment (**50**, 1966) is the simplest, though it has the disadvantage that the local government sector is not endogenous to the system. His table includes the tax revenue flow row in the value added quadrant, and a local government expenditures column in the final demand quadrant. In practice, the revenue row will be disaggregated with a separate row for each tax since development affects each source of revenue differently. Similarly, the expenditure columns may be disaggregated to identify individual spending categories so that the impact of development on each may be estimated. The method involves *ad hoc* estimation of net tax revenues and expenditures before and after development, where adjustments are made for each aspect of the development (con-

---

[4] In a few cases, however, this may be offset by having to provide subsidised public transport services for commuters.

struction, operation, the labour force and its indirect demands for housing and public services, etc.). Finally, the expenditure and revenue comparisons are further adjusted for population change in order to measure the per capita local government revenue and expenditure repercussions of development. It is obvious that this method of dealing with local fiscal impacts is merely an adjunct to an input-output approach rather than an integral part of it.

Hirsch (**97**, 1963) outlines two methodologies to deal with the problem, one of which he calls a modified balanced regional input-output model and the other a two-stage model. The latter has close similarities with the above treatment since traditional employment, output and income input-output multipliers are used for estimating the tax base and the activities requiring public services. In addition, fiscal side calculations can be made to derive revenue and expenditure estimates. This needs a little more explanation. On the revenue side, the approach starts with estimates of the direct employment, output and income anticipated from the entry of the new plant. Combining these with the standard urban employment, output and income multipliers obtained with the aid of the input-output table produces estimates of new direct, indirect and induced employment, output and income. Housing cost coefficients and output-property coefficients can then be used to translate direct, indirect and induced changes in income per household and output into assessed valuations of residential property and industrial and commercial property respectively. The prevailing property tax rate (or rate poundage) can then be applied to the assessed valuations to yield estimates of property tax (rate) payments. Other sources of local government revenue can be handled in similar fashion: sales tax payments related to direct, indirect and induced personal income (in cities where sales taxes operate); local government receipts related to output; user charges related to income; and so on.

On the cost side, Hirsch's approach makes the simplifying assumption that local government services are person- rather than plant-oriented. It is assumed that the average person in a given urban area requires a fixed amount of local services *in toto* — taking account of public service requirements not only in relation to the household and dwelling but also workplace and private consumption. Thus, the estimates of changes in public service costs are derived from forecasts of population increase associated with the new development.[5] Aggregating the various local government tax payments and subtracting from this total the derived estimates of local government expenditure costs enables the local government net fiscal resources impact to be measured.

Hirsch's alternative solution to the problem incorporates the local government sector into the input-output model itself.[6] The local government row is divided into two. The first row shows local government service costs and reflects the costs incurred by the urban government in supplying services to local beneficiaries on an industry basis. The sectoral allocations require the analyst to impute costs to industries. The second row measures 'local government fiscal resources', i.e. the difference between local government tax receipts from a given local industry and the costs of servicing that industry, with all indirect effects ignored. Industries that pay more for services than they receive are described as having a positive local government fiscal resource status. The local government column is also split into two. The first column shows the sales of local industries to local government, while the second column is primarily for balancing entries (which may be zero) and represents the central government subsidy (or in the United States context, the state and federal subsidy).

The direct, indirect and induced service cost changes associated with specific industrial developments can be obtained by multiplying the inverse matrix values of the local government service cost row by the anticipated final demand changes. Similarly, the values of the local government fiscal resources row of the inverse matrix can be used to obtain estimates of local government net fiscal resource status. This is an absolute measure of the fiscal implications of a given industrial development policy on the urban area's local fiscal position. Both estimates considered together indicate the policy's relative impact on urban government net fiscal

---

[5] For some items of public services slight modifications may be needed, e.g. education costs may be related more to anticipated changes in the school population than in the population as a whole.

[6] For a more recent study on similar lines which disaggregates urban government into five sectors see Hirsch (**271**, 1968).

resources. These impact estimates can be used as one element in the determination of a selective urban development promotion policy.

In an urban input-output model it is virtually obligatory to do something about the abstraction from space characteristic of input-output theory. The spatial dimension is of critical importance in the urban economy,[7] and the urban planner will be closely concerned with such problems as the demand for additional land for population and industry, increases in floor-space requirements, the impact on urban transport of expansion and structural change in the urban economy, changes in the intra-urban location of industry and other spatial problems. The industrial and sectoral interdependencies found in the traditional input-output table will be of some value to the planning function, but it might be argued that a more explicit introduction of spatial elements into the input-output tables would increase their usefulness. There are several ways in which this might be done, though some approaches merely supplement the input-output approach rather than being integrated into it, while others are so heavy in their data requirements that they are non-operational. A simple, if incomplete, solution is to supplement the basic input-output table with flows of rental space (as measured by the monetary value of rental services) which can be used in conjunction with floor-space or areal data so that the monetary units of the basic table can easily be converted into the physical terms that planners require (Artle, **6**, 1965).

At the other extreme, it is conceptually possible to construct an intraurban model in which the urban area is divided up into a large number of zones. In such a model space would need to be introduced in at least two ways: the demand for urban land in each zone; the transportation flows of goods and people between zones. The former could be handled with a linear programming model which optimised the use of vacant land over the urban area and assigned industries to zones according to their ability to pay rent; this might maximise aggregate rent-paying ability on the lines of the Herbert-Stevens residential distribution model (**90**, 1960). The input-output table would be grafted on to this land allocation

[7]For a general discussion of the role of location factors in urban accounts see Harris (**82**, 1964).

model, since the analysis would need to take account of indirect and induced as well as direct land requirements of specific sectors by dividing forecast output changes by sectoral output-floor space ratios. The second spatial aspect, the transportation flows, might be dealt with by using a variant of the Moses model (186, 1960), treating the transport industry's output as multidimensional to reflect the fact that input requirements vary for transporting people and different goods between each pair of zones in the city.[8] Neither of these approaches is implementable with present data, but the task may be less difficult than appears at first sight if highly aggregated zoning subdivisions were used. For instance, an elementary model may make a distinction only between the central core (CBD), the inner ring and the suburbs. Such a framework would be useful not only for predicting the impact of expansion in the city economy but also for evaluating the effects of location shifts from the central city to the suburbs.

Hirsch (97, 1963) proposed a less ambitious method of estimating land requirements or demands for floor space generated by changes in final demand. There is no reason why entries in the transactions matrix should always be expressed in monetary units. Row entries may be expressed in physical units provided that the same unit of measurement is used consistently along a given row, and of course provided no attempt is made to invert a matrix that contains both monetary and physical units. For example, a transactions matrix could be constructed with an acreage row; such a row may be treated as if it were exogenous without a column counterpart, though it may be convenient to include a corresponding column with zero entries.[9]

In many cases it may be useful to have several rows for land use, representing, for instance, floor space, car parking space and land available for expansion, all broken down by industry. Similarly, as in the model suggested above, it may be important if an industry's land requirements alter with

---

[8] For the Moses model see Chapter 10, pp. 204-8.

[9] This reflects the fact that land, like labour, is a stock rather than a flow. The use of rows *or* columns (or dummy rows or columns with zero entries) rather than the traditional row-column matrix is the most convenient way of accommodating stock and flow relationships within the same model.

its location to develop separate input-output matrices and acreage rows for industry in the core and in the suburbs, in other words to construct an intraurban model. The rows in the coefficient matrix for floor-space ratios will be expressed in terms of acres per monetary unit of output. The direct and indirect output changes per unit of final demand will be derived from the inverse matrix, and these can then easily be converted into direct and indirect acreage requirements; similarly, with direct, indirect and induced land requirements. The drawback to this approach, as Leven pointed out (**151**, 1961, p. 181), is that there is little justification for the assumption that production functions are linear and homogeneous with respect to land inputs.

The third important question for discussion is the utility of interurban models. As yet no such model has been implemented, a fact that is scarcely surprising in view of the heavy data requirements of such a model. However, the conceptual framework for an interurban model is easy to understand. It is analogous, at the regional level, to the 'ideal' interregional model developed by Isard (**107**, 1951; this was briefly discussed in Chapter 4, pp. 57-61). The essential features of the model are an interindustry flows matrix for each urban centre and an interurban trade matrix between each pair of urban centres (and presumably between each centre and the 'rest of the world' outside the system of cities). Given n sectors and z urban centres plus an additional region representing the rest of the world the system will consist of $(z + 1)^2$ matrices, each with n^2 entries.[10] For an alternative formulation, we may resort to the intranational model (also discussed in Chapter 4 pp. 61-3). This makes a distinction between industries that figure in trade outside each area and local industries which sell their output only locally. Since many sectors in an urban area will be of the latter variety (most retail trade, primary and secondary education, local government, etc.), this type of model with its relative economy in data is very appropriate to urban analysis.

Whatever the model used, it is reasonable to assume that it

---

[10]In practice the off-diagonal entries in the interurban trade matrices may often be zeros, reflecting the fact that it is customary to neglect sectoral origins and destinations when we specify geographical origins and destination.

will be unnecessary to have as high a degree of sectoral disaggregation as is found in an interregional model. First, service industries are fairly dominant in urban economic structures, and these exhibit fairly stable interindustry relationships which are also rather similar over a wide range of sectors. Second, within an interurban system substantial cross-hauls of a particular manufacturing commodity are rare, and there is some degree of manufacturing specialisation between centres. Each city will not have a long list of manufacturing industries characteristic of, say, a highly diversified regional economy. Third, there is a growing amount of evidence (Williamson, **265**, 1970; Doeksen and Little, **55**, 1968; Hewings, **93**, 1971; see also Chapter 7, pp. 135-8) that, within certain limits, the size of the model does not have much effect either on multiplier values or on individual gross output impacts. The interurban input-output model may be quite satisfactory even if each urban economy is subdivided into a mere dozen sectors. Assuming that the system itself is unlikely to contain more than eight or ten towns and cities, this reduces the overall scale of the interurban model to a manageable size.

What are the advantages of an interurban model? In the most general terms, such a model will throw a great deal of light on the links that bind the cities of a regional system together and on the interdependence between sectors both within and between centres. More specifically, the interurban input-output model will permit tests of the stereotyped theories used by spatial analysts to explain urban systems: central place systems, growth pole-zone relationships, principles of the urban hierarchy, etc. For example, if the growth pole-zone hypotheses are valid, we would expect the leading cities to have their major industries selling high proportions of their output to final demand, while the smaller dependent centres in the broader growth zone would specialise in industries supplying inputs to major industries in the growth pole (very often the leading city), thereby exhibiting a high degree of interurban interindustrial interdependence,[11] and/ or in service sectors supplying direct to local households.

---

[11] To show this, full specification of the interurban trade flow matrices will be required.

These characteristics, if they exist, would be most easily shown up in sets of interurban tables constructed in triangularised form. Triangularised tables have considerable advantages for comparisons of this kind; in Leontief's words (**143**, 1963, p.151) they emphasis the 'dependence and independence, hierarchy and circularity (or multi-regional interdependence) . . . the four basic concepts of structural analysis'.

It is probable that an interurban model would be more useful for describing these structural and hierarchical relationships within a regional system of cities than for forecasting. Because of the magnitude of external economies of scale and agglomeration economies in a fast-growing urban economy, the linearity assumptions of the input-output model may give misleading results if we attempt to predict the impact on urban gross outputs of final demand projections.[12] Although the interurban model may have pedagogic value in showing how stimuli exogenous to the region are traced through the system of cities, it may be simpler and no less accurate to use an input-output table for the region as a whole as the main forecasting tool, and then to employ *ad hoc* apportionment techniques specifically adjusting for external economy effects in certain cities in the region. Doubts about their utility for forecasting could well be the limitation of interurban models which, combined with their expense, has delayed practical applications.

---

[12] However, we should note here the observation (p. 238 above) that a triangular input-output system may be able, on statistical grounds at least, to accommodate non-linearities, thereby allowing us to introduce scale effects.

13 Conclusions

The purpose of this book has been to examine the relevance of input-output techniques to regional economics. Despite their obvious limitations – such as the reliance on linear relationships in an area where agglomeration economies may be important or their frequently heavy data requirements – regional input-output models have several compensating virtues. They can be implemented empirically; they represent, at least when interregional models are constructed, a general equilibrium approach; and they are neutral from a policy point of view, though this fact does not prevent their having extensive policy applications. Moreover, although a possible criticism of the use of input-output models in a regional context is that space is an absent dimension it is easy to use input-output tables to show the impact of spatial shifts in economic activity, i.e. changes in industrial location. Furthermore, the consistency checks inherent in input-output accounts improve the reliability of the models for analysis. Finally, if multiplier analysis is a valuable tool in regional economics, there can be little doubt that the disaggregated interindustry multipliers derived from input-output models yield the most accurate results.

Although the choice of input-output model will be governed by the objectives of the study, interregional models are the most satisfying theoretically, partly because they permit us to trace changes in final demand through the system of regions as a whole, partly because they offer the possibility of explaining production and trade simultaneously. A problem in this latter respect is that the input-output model itself contains no mechanism for explaining trade patterns, yet deriving interregional trade flows is obviously a crucial element in an interregional model. The solution is to graft on either additional assumptions or a subsidiary model for this purpose. Of the main alternatives – row coefficient, column coefficient, linear programming, standard gravity and Leontief-Strout gravity models – all but the third and last require base-year trade flows as a datum. Apart from this, the gravity approaches are probably the most suitable for dealing with heterogeneous input-output sectors. If time and resources permit, the effort involved in developing an interregional model can be worthwhile since such a model is the best instrument available for handling certain specific problems: measuring the regional impact of central government expenditures; evaluating the effects of locational shifts; working out the repercussions of changes in regional development policy, and so on.

When faced with the problem of preparing an input-output table for a single region the analyst will usually have a strong preference for a survey-based model. Although the data collection task is costly and fraught with difficulties, sufficient experience has been gained particularly in the United States to make this a fairly straightforward operation provided that the time and cost constraints are not severe. Even where time and money are short, there is still some scope for using input-output techniques since new developments have made secondary data methods more reliable and there are numerous simplification procedures possible in the construction of the table which ease the data collection task. As yet, there are insufficient tests available on the reliability of secondary data models, but it is unlikely that they will ever be more than a second-best option. On the other hand, there is considerable scope for a mix of primary and secondary data methods in which rows and columns developed for key sectors from industrial surveys are integrated into a predominantly secondary data table. Obviously, the value of this approach requires as a prerequisite a finely disaggregated and reliable set of national input-output coefficients on which to apply the reduction techniques. The simplified forms of regional input-output model (the intersectoral flows approach, TAP and small scale models) are probably less reliable, but they can be used when approximate aggregate results are needed. These simplified models employ the same theoretical principles as standard input-output models, but in practice many of them have close affinities to a disaggregated economic base approach. Their use is justified only in cases where time and resources forbid a more comprehensive approach.

Considerable emphasis has been placed in this book on the applications of input-output techniques at the regional level in economic impact studies, regional forecasting, policy-oriented problems requiring linear programming versions of an input-output model, and in the economic analysis of environmental resources and pollution and of urban problems. Of these, economic impact analyses are the simplest and most common. Given sets of income and employment multipliers derived from the input-output table and independent forecasts or simulations of final demand changes, measuring the consequences of any foreseen or desired change is a simple operation. The method is useful for evaluating the output, income and employment repercussions including all inter-industry effects of exogenous changes in final demand sectors, expansion in an existing regional industry, the introduction of a new plant into the region or of changes in the level of government defence or other spending. In many cases, however, economic impact analyses can degenerate into academic exercises unless they are linked with a policy strategy. Thus, the input-output model on which economic impact analysis is based may be most useful when it forms one component of a decision model in which regional policy goals are precisely specified. The impact study measures the consequences of change, but what consequences are desirable is unclear without explicit policy objectives. Another more direct solution, discussed below, is to adopt linear programming versions of input-output models that convert the latter into optimising procedures.

Possibly the most important application of regional input-output models is as a technique for forecasting. Regional forecasting is vital since virtually any regional analysis or policy design involves looking at what might happen in the future. Given the shortcomings of theory and data limitations, input-output techniques are at present more satisfactory than more sophisticated econometric methods as a forecasting device. This statement is not intended to imply that no problems arise in the use of input-output models for forecasting. Indeed, there are severe gaps in our expertise, and these occur at the practical more than at the conceptual level. The overall forecasting requirements are: projections of regional final demand; an input-output coefficient matrix; a regional capital coefficient matrix; predictions of changes in the input-output matrix; predictions of changes in the capital coefficient matrix; decomposition of the input-output matrix into regional (local) requirements and import coefficients; estimates of imported capital coefficients; shifts in the imported/local shares of all inputs and capital goods, i.e. forecasted changes in regional trade coefficients.

These estimates permit a variety of forecasting procedures: a *static* forecast of the type examined under economic inpact analysis where the sole requirements are an input-output matrix and a forecast of changes in final demand; *comparative static* forecasts which accommodate changes in both the technical input and in the regional trade coefficients; and *dynamic* forecasts that, via the introduction of a capital coefficient matrix, explicitly allow for the capacity-creating effects of new investment. Dynamic forecasts are theoretically the most satisfactory of these, and the case for employing them increases, not unexpectedly, with the length of the projection period. The practical difficulties, however, are not solely confined to the implementation of dynamic forecasts. Even with static models it is not easy to predict the changes in final demand that are essential ingredients in the forecast. Ratio and apportionment techniques are quite commonly used, but even the most popular of these (shift and share projections) are not fully satisfactory. Theoretically, the ideal procedure would be to disaggregate final demand into its individual components. However, a major weakness in regional input-output forecasts is the lack of a satisfactory method of forecasting regional investment and exports. The solution of making them endogenous (by treating investment as induced and by employing an interregional model in which interregional exports will be determined within the system) is obviously only a partial one. Turning to comparative static forecasts, the complications become more serious. Although estimation of 'best practice' coefficients can be recommended for predicting technical coefficient changes at the regional level (despite their implication that national and regional rates of change in the coefficients are closer together than the values of the coefficients themselves), it is more difficult to select a suitable procedure for predicting changes in the regional trade coefficients. This is a particular manifestation of the general proposition that input-output models are not equipped to handle substitution effects. Since 'maximum local production' hypotheses, linear programming and gravity models are not feasible in this case, primarily because the initial data requirements normally include forecasts of regional gross outputs, i.e. one of the objectives of the forecasting exercise, *ad hoc* methods such as marketing forecasts have frequently to be relied upon. A 'naive' solution to the dilemma is to assume that trade coefficients are stable, but the sparse empirical evidence available is somewhat discouraging to the trade stability hypothesis. However, all the tests hitherto have dealt with short-run changes rather than with the question of long-run stability.

A major potential source of trade coefficient instability is capacity constraints in local industries which can result in a situation where in the short run an increasing proportion of rising demand may be satisfied via imports. In the long run, on the other hand, import substitution due to capacity constraints should not be a serious problem. In this sense, long-run projections using dynamic models may be easier to implement than comparative static forecasts. The key elements in a dynamic input-output forecast are that investment *must* be treated separately from final demand and that the time dimension has to be introduced explicitly since investment goods do not have to be used up in the current time period. The problems of implementation are practical and empirical rather than conceptual and theoretical. They include how to draw a distinction between expansion and replacement investment, the definition of capacity, identifying the appropriate level of capacity that triggers off new investment in each industry, the difficulty of predicting variations in imported capital coefficients and so on. More experience is needed with dynamic regional input-output forecasts and more tests of their predictive power required before it can be accepted that these problems have been satisfactorily solved.

The value of linear programming input-output models is that they add an efficiency-optimising procedure to the standard input-output approach. By permitting the analyst to exercise economic choice they directly introduce policy decisions into the analytical framework. Although demand considerations are treated in an over-simplified manner, linear programming formulations have considerable theoretical advantages. If inputs into transport can be assumed identical to inputs into production, the traditional transport-cost-minimisation objective function involves minimising all costs and this leads to optimisation of production and trade. Moreover, it is unnecessary for the model to be concerned solely with narrow measures of economic efficiency. An earlier statement (Chapter 10, p. 211) may bear repetition:

A programming approach offers the considerable advantage of being able to feed policy goals and objectives directly into the analysis. As such programmes need not be concerned solely with efficiency criteria since, for example, equity objectives might be included in the constraints or in final demand specifications, the integration of linear programming and input-output offers an immediate answer to critics who deride input-output analysis as an interesting but useless technique.

The major obstacle to wider application of linear programming input-output models at the regional level is that they are greedy consumers of data, and the limited volume of data available may limit the scope for present and future studies. The few analyses that have been undertaken have had to adopt severe simplifying assumptions in order to reduce the data input need for implementation.

A new field for the application of input-output techniques, but one which clearly holds considerable promise at the regional and urban levels, is in the analysis of environmental resources and pollution. Pioneering work in this area has been carried out by Cumberland, Daly, Isard and Leontief. The most recent contribution by Victor achieves the translation of a conceptual framework for environmental input-output analysis into a form that is empirically feasible. The main features of his model consist of exclusion of the elusive *intra*sectoral flows within the ecological sector itself, adoption of the materials balance approach popularised by Ayres and Kneese and deployment of a commodity-industry model which permits horizontal summation of *physical* units of ecological commodities.

Urban economics is a neglected field for the application of input-output techniques. Although input-output tables have been constructed for urban areas, these have usually been miniature versions of the standard regional input-output table without any specifically urban content. There are undoubtedly difficulties in the way of urban applications. For example, in most cases it would be necessary, in order to maximise its utility, to link an urban input-output model to the pursuit of urban planning goals, and this requires injecting a policy orientation into the model.[1] As we have seen, a linear programming version may be able to take account of the policy goals aspect. However, even in a non-policy context the ideal unit for a subnational input-output study would be a homogeneous, clearly delimited geographical area, and few cities can be described in these terms. Another problem is that the small area of cities means a high ratio of external trade to gross output, and consequently interindustry flows at the urban level may be quantitatively less significant than the final demand components of gross output. The remedy in this case is to close the model by including certain sectors, local government and investment for instance, within the interindustry matrix. The linearity assumptions of input-output models are probably more serious when applied to urban problems. This is because of the importance of agglomeration economies in urban economic change. Although there are procedures for dealing with non-linearities in input-output models they are rather cumbersome. This is probably a major reason for the delay in applying input-output techniques at the urban level. Thus, it may be easier to use an input-output table for the region as a whole as the main forecasting tool and then to employ *ad hoc* apportionment techniques to derive urban economic forecasts making specific adjustments for external economy effects in individual cities. But these objections are not strong enough to justify the limited volume of research into urban input-output applications hitherto.

Several areas for development have been identified. First,

---

[1] For a simple but clear exposition see Artle (7, 1963).

an input-output framework would be useful for evaluating the impact of a new activity, or indeed any final demand change, on the urban government fiscal sector, particularly since it may be the indirect and induced repercussions that determine whether the entry of a new firm means a net revenue gain or loss to the local exchequer. Second, it is possible to introduce space and location (e.g. via the use of floor-space indices) into an urban input-output model to take account of the physical space requirements (including the indirect and induced requirements) of business firms. Third, the construction of interurban input-output models may be valuable for throwing light on the interdependencies between urban areas within a region. These may be easier to build than interregional models since small size (sector) models may be permissible, partly because the predominant service industries probably have similar structures in different cities and consequently can be aggregated together, partly because manufacturing specialisation is higher between cities than between regions and hence fewer key sectors are involved. Moreover, it has previously been shown (Chapter 7, pp. 135-9) that small scale models can predict quite effectively. Finally, although difficult to implement because of data problems, the attempt to construct an *intra*urban input-output model involving the subdivision of an urban area into the central city, the inner ring and the suburbs with matrices for each sub-area would be well worth making.

There have been scores of regional input-output studies in recent years particularly in the United States, but this does not mean that the scope for further work is exhausted. On the contrary, there is much to be done. Most of the studies hitherto have been stereotyped, involving the construction of a standard regional input-output table with its import row and export column with the aid of field surveys. There has been much less effort put into the implementation of interregional models or into evaluation of the reliability of the new secondary data adjustment techniques. In addition, there is a dearth of serious research into the wider applications of input-output techniques at the regional and urban level, apart from the measurement of defence-space sector impacts. Some of the possibilities have been discussed in Part Three of this book. It is clear that many problems arising from these applications remain unsolved, but since most of the obstacles are practical, solutions will be found through experimentation and experience in implementation rather than emerge from theoretical discussion. At the other extreme we must avoid the danger of treating input-output techniques as a 'master key' method capable of being applied to any urban or regional problem. There are many such problems for which input-output models are a singularly inappropriate technique. For example, the measurement of agglomeration and other external economies, explicit consideration of distance and other spatial variables, competitiveness and substitution in interregional trade, questions of this nature do not lend themselves to analysis via input-output techniques. But there are many other problems, only some of which have been discussed in this volume, where regional input-output models have considerable, if untested, potential. Further work in this field is much more likely to explore these new applications than to repeat the construction of the standard regional input-output tables that have become commonplace in the last decade.

Bibliography

The following abbreviations are used in the bibliography:

AER	American Economic Review
ARS	Annals of Regional Science
EJ	Economic Journal
Em	Econometrica
G & C	Growth and Change
HJE	Hitotsubashi Journal of Economics
JAIP	Journal of American Institute of Planners
JFE	Journal of Farm Economics
JPE	Journal of Political Economy
JRS	Journal of Regional Science
K	Kyklos
LE	Land Economics
OEP	Oxford Economic Papers
PF	Public Finance
PPRS	Papers, Peace Research Society
PPRSA	Papers and Proceedings, Regional Science Association
QJE	Quarterly Journal of Economics
RE & S	Review of Economics and Statistics
RES	Review of Economic Studies
RS	Regional Studies
RUE	Regional and Urban Economics
SA	Scientific American
SEJ	Southern Economic Journal
SJPE	Scottish Journal of Political Economy
US	Urban Studies
WBR	University of Washington Business Review
WEJ	Western Economic Journal

1   R.G.D. ALLEN, *Mathematical Economics,* 2nd Ed. (Macmillan 1959).

2   C. ALMON, Jr., 'Numerical Solution of a Modified Leontief Dynamic System for Consistent Forecasting or Indicative Planning', *Em,* 31 (1964), 665-78.

3   C. ALMON, Jr., 'Consistent Forecasting in a Dynamic Multi-sectoral Model', *RE & S,* 45 (1963), 148-62.

4   C. ALMON, Jr., *The American Economy to 1975* (Harper and Row 1966).

5   K. ARA, 'The Aggregation Problem in Input-Output Analysis', *Em,* 27 (1959), 257-62.

6   R. ARTLE, *Studies in the Structure of the Stockholm Economy: Toward a Framework for Projecting Metropolitan Community Development* (Berkeley 1965).

7   R. ARTLE, 'Public Policy and the Space Economy of the City', in L. Wingo (ed.), *Cities and Space* (Johns Hopkins 1963), 155-72

8   R. ARTLE, 'Planning and Growth – A Simple Model of an Island Economy: Honolulu', *PPRSA,* 15 (1965) 29-44.

9   H. AUJAC, 'La hierarchie des industries dans un tableau des échanges interindustrielles', *Revue Economique,* 11 (1960), 169-238.

10 H. AUJAC, 'New Approaches in French National Planning: Input-Output Tables and Technological Forecasting' Fifth International Conference on Input-Output Techniques (Geneva, January 1971).

11 R.U. AYRES and A.V. KNEESE, 'Production, Consumption and Externalities', *AER,* 59 (1969), 282-97.

12 R.W. BAHL and K.L. SHELLHAMMER, 'Evaluating the State Business Tax Structure: An Application of Input-Output Analysis', *National Tax Journal,* 2 (1969), 203-16.

13 J. BARGUR, 'A Dynamic Interregional Input-Output Programming Model of the California and Western States Economy', Contribution No. 128 (Water Resource Centre, California, June 1969).

14 J.R. BARNARD and H.K. CHARLESWORTH, 'The Kentucky Secondary Data Approach and its Potentials', *G & C,* 1 (1970), 33-8.

15 J.R. BARNARD, *Design and Use of Social Accounting Systems in State Development Planning* (Bureau of Business and Economic Research, Iowa University 1967).

16 J.R. BARNARD, J.A. MACMILLAN and W.R. MAKI, *Evaluation Models for Regional Development and Planning* (Institute of Urban and Regional Research, University of Iowa, W.P.2, 1968).

17 F.W. BELL, 'An Econometric Forecasting Model for a Region', *JRS*, 7 (1967), 109-27.

18 E. BENOIT and K. BOULDING, *Disarmament and the Economy* (Harper and Row, New York 1963).

19 B.R. BERMAN, 'Economic Projections for the Region as a Whole', in B.R. BERMAN, B. CHINITZ and E.M. HOOVER, *Projection of a Metropolis: Technical Supplement to the New York Metropolitan Region Study* (Harvard University Press 1960), 1-53.

20 R.B. BILLINGS, 'The Mathematical Identity of the Multipliers derived from the Economic Base Model and the Input-Output Model', *JRS*, 9 (1969), 471-3.

21 R.B. BILLINGS, 'Regional Defense Impact — A Case Study Comparison of Measurement Techniques', *JRS*, 10 (1970), 199-216.

22 J.C. BOLLENS, *Exploring the Metropolitan Community* (UCLA, Berkeley and Los Angeles 1961).

23 R.E. BOLTON, *Defense Purchases and Regional Growth* (Brookings Institution, Washington 1966).

24 E.R. BONNER and V.L. FAHLE, *Technique for Area Planning: A Manual for the Construction and Application of a Simplified Input-Output Table* (Regional Economic Development Institute, Pittsburgh, for Economic Development Administration, US Department of Commerce, Contract No. C-306-66, 1967).

25 E.R. BONNER, 'The Economic Impact of a University on its Local Community', *JAIP*, 34 (1968), 339-43.

26 P.J. BOURQUE, 'Income Multipliers for the Washington Economy', *UWBR*, (winter 1969), 5-15.

27 I.E. BRADLEY and J.P. GANDER, 'Input-Output Multipliers: Some Theoretical Comments', *JRS*, 9 (1969), 309-17.

28   D.F. BRAMHALL, 'Projecting Regional Accounts and Industrial Location: Reflections on Policy Applications', *PPRSA*, 7 (1961), 89-118.

29   M.S. BRODERSOHN, *A Multi-Regional Input-Output Analysis of the Argentine Economy* (Buenos Aires: Instituto Torcuato Di Tella, Centro de Investagaciones Economicas, October 1965).

30   H.J. BROWN, 'Shift and Share Projections of Regional Economic Growth: An Empirical Test', *JRS*, 9 (1969), 1-18

31   A.J. BROWN, 'Appendix on "Regional Multipliers",' N.I.E.S.R., *Economic Review,* 40 (May 1967), 33.

32   T.W. BUCK, 'Shift and Share Analysis – a Guide to Regional Policy?', *RS*, 4 (1970), 445-50.

33   B. CAMERON, 'The Construction of the Leontief System', *RES*, 19 (1950-1), 19-27.

34   V. CAO-PINNA, 'Problems of Establishing and Using Regional Input-Output Accounts' in W. Isard and J.H. Cumberland (eds.), *Regional Economic Planning* (OECD, 1961), 305-38.

35   A.P. CARTER, 'Incremental Flow Coefficients for a Dynamic Input-Output Model with Changing Technology', in T. Barna (ed.), *Structural Interdependence and Economic Development* (Macmillan, London 1963), 277-302.

36   A.P. CARTER, 'The State of the Arts in Projecting Input-Output Structures', HERP, Paper presented at Institute of Management Sciences (Boston, April 1967).

37   A.P. CARTER, *Structural Change in the American Economy* (Harvard University Press 1970).

38   M.K. CHATTERJI, 'An Input-Output Study of the Calcutta Industrial Region', *PPRSA*, 13 (1964), 93-102.

39   M.K. CHATTERJI, 'Local Impact of Disarmament, Foreign Aid Programs and Development of Poor World Regions: A Critique of the Leontief and Other Growth Models', *PPRS*, 4 (1966), 67-76.

40   H.B. CHENERY, 'Regional Analysis', in CHENERY, CLARK and CAO-PINNA, *The Structure and Growth of the Italian Economy* (US Mutual Security Agency Rome 1953), 97-116.

41 H.B. CHENERY, 'Interregional and International Input-Output Analysis', in T. Barna (ed.) *The Structural Interdependence of the Economy* (New York and Milan 1956).

42 H.B. CHENERY and P.G. CLARK, *Interindustry Economics* (Wiley, New York 1959).

43 J.S. CHIPMAN, *The Theory of Inter-sectoral Money Flows and Income Formation,* (Johns Hopkins Press 1950).

44 C. CHRIST, 'A Review of Input-Output Analysis', NBER, *Input-Output Analysis: An Appraisal* (Princeton 1955).

45 J.W. CLARK, 'Rail Freight Data: A Tool for Market and Regional Analysis', *SEJ*, 23 (1956), 134-41.

46 S. CLELAND, 'Local Input-Output Analysis: A New Business Tool', *Business Topics,* Michigan State University, 7 (1959), 41-8.

47 C.P. COHEN, P.W. SOLENBERGER and G. TUCKER, *Iterative and Inverse Techniques for Solving Large-Scale Multi-Regional Input-Output Models,* Reprint No. 17, HERP, (June 1970).

48 CONSAD Corporation, *Regional Federal Procurement Study* (US Department of Commerce Contract 7-35211, October 1967).

49 A.O. CONVERSE, 'On the Extension of Input-Output Analysis to Account for Environmental Externalities', *AER*, 61 (1971), 197-8.

50 J.H. CUMBERLAND, 'A Regional Interindustry Model for Analysis of Development Objectives', *PPRSA*, 17 (1966), 65-94.

51 S. CZAMANSKI and E.E. MALIZIA, 'Applicability and Limitations in the Use of National Input-Output Tables for Regional Studies', *PPRSA*, 23 (1969), 65-77, 'Comments' by M.R. Goldman, 79-80, and by W.H. Miernyk, 81-2.

52 H.E. DALY, 'On Economics as a Life Science', *JPE*, 76 (1968), 392-406.

53 G.B. DANTZIG, 'Programming of Interdependent Activities, Part II', *Em*, 17 (1949), 200-11.

54 H.C. DAVIS, *Economic Evaluation of Water, Part V, Multiregional Input-Output Techniques and Western Water Resources Development,* (Water Resources Centre, Berkeley, No. 125, 1968).

55 G.A. DOEKSEN and C.H. LITTLE, 'Effect of Size of the Input-Output Model on the Results of an Impact Analysis', *Agricultural Economics Research,* 20 (1968), 134-8.

56 M. DOLENC, 'The Bucks County Interregional Input-Output Study', *PPRSA,* 20 (1968), 43-53.

57 R. DORFMAN, 'The Nature and Significance of Input-Output', *RE & S,* 36 (1954), 121-33.

58 R. DORFMAN, P.A. SAMUELSON and R. SOLOW, *Linear Programming and Economic Analysis* (McGraw-Hill 1958).

59 J. DYCKMAN, 'Some Regional Development Issues in Defense Program Shifts', *PPRS,* 2 (1965), 191-203.

60 J. DYCKMAN and R.P. BURTON, 'Some Interregional (Intrastate) Problems in the California Development Plan Studies', *PPRSA,* 15 (1961), 45-56.

61 R.H. EDELSTEIN, *Methodology of Regional and Subregional Input-Output Studies,* (HERP 1968).

62 S.L. EDWARDS and I.R. GORDON, 'The Application of Input-Output Methods to Regional Forecasting: The British Experience', *Colston Papers,* 22 (1970) 415-30.

63 M.J. ELLMAN, 'The Use of Input-Output in Regional Economic Planning: The Soviet Experience', *EJ,* 78 (1968), 855-67.

64 J.C.H. FEI, 'A Fundamental Theorem for the Aggregation Problem of Input-Output Analysis', *Em,* 24 (1956), 400-12.

65 W.D. FISHER, 'Criteria for Aggregation in Input-Output Analysis', *RE & S,* 40 (1958), 250-60.

66 H.B. GAMBLES and D.L. RAPHAEL, *A Microregional Analysis of Clinton County, Pennsylvania* (PRAG, Pennsylvania State University 1965).

67 D.H. GARNICK, 'Disaggregated Basic-Service Models and Regional Input-Output Models in Multiregional Projections', *JRS, 9* (1969), 87-99.

68 D.H. GARNICK, 'Differential Regional Multiplier Models', *JRS*, 10 (1970), 35-47.

69 D.H. GARNICK, *et al., Toward Development of a National-Regional Impact Evaluation System and the Upper Licking Area Pilot Study* (US Department of Commerce, OBE, Regional Economics Division 1971).

70 R.C. GEARY, 'Towards an Input-Output Decision Model for Ireland', *Proceedings of the Statistical and Social Inquiry Society for Ireland,* 21 (No.2), 1964.

71 A. GHOSH, *Experiments with Input-Output Models* (Cambridge University Press 1964).

72 E.W. GILBOY, 'Consumption and Input-Output Analysis', in T. Barna (ed.), *The Structural Interdependence of the Economy* (New York and Milan 1956), 395-407.

73 N.J. GLICKMAN, 'An Econometric Forecasting Model for the Philadelphia Region', *JRS*, 11 (1971), 15-32.

74 G.C. GORDON, *A Study to Measure Direct and Indirect Impacts of Defense Expenditures on an Economy* (US Arms Control and Disarmament Agency, November 1966).

75 A. GOTTLIEB, 'Planning Elements of an Inter-Industry Analysis – A Metropolitan Approach', in R.W. Pfouts (ed.), *Techniques of Urban Economic Analysis* (Chandler-Davis 1960), 380-93.

76 R.E. GRAHAM, D. GARNICK and A. OLSEN, 'Economic Projections for Local Areas', *American Statistical Association, Proceedings of Social Statistics Section,* 62 (1967), 16-20.

77 D. GREYTACK, 'Regional Impact of Interregional Trade in Input-Output Analysis', *PPRSA,* 25 (1970), 203-17.

78 G. HADLEY, *Linear Programming*, (Addison-Wesley, Cambridge, Mass. 1962), 487-514.

79 W. LEE HANSEN and C.M. TIEBOUT, 'An Intersectoral Flows Analysis of the California Economy', *RE & S,* 45 (1963), 409-18.

80 F.K. HARMSTON and R.E. LUND, *Application of an Input-Output Framework to a Community Economic System* (Missouri University Press 1967).

81   F.K. HARMSTON, 'Use of an Intersectoral Model in Developing Regional Multipliers', *ARS*, 3 (1969), 1-7.

82   B. HARRIS, 'An Accounts Framework for Metropolitan Models', in W.Z. Hirsch (ed.), *Elements of Regional Accounts* (RFF, John Hopkins Press 1964) 107-207. 107-207.

83   C.C. HARRIS, Jr., 'A Multiregional, Multi-Industry Forecasting Model', *PPRSA*, 25 (1970, 169-80.

84   P.E. HART and A.I. MACBEAN, 'Regional Differences In Productivity, Profitability and Growth', *SJPE*, 8 (1961) 1-11.

85   L.M. HARTMAN, 'The Input-Output Model and Regional Water Management', *JFE*, 47 (1965), 1583-91.

86   J.M. HARTWICK, 'Notes on the Isard and Chenery-Moses Interregional Input-Output Models', *JRS*, 11 (1971), 73-86.

87   E.O. HEADY and H.O. CARTER, 'Input-Output Models as Techniques of Analysis for Interregional Competition', *JFE*, 46 (1959), 978-91.

88   J.M. HENDERSON, *The Efficiency of the Coal Industry: An Application of Linear Programming* (Harvard University Press 1958).

89   J.M. HENDERSON, 'An Economic Analysis of the Upper Midwest Region', Upper Midwest Economic Study, Technical Paper No. 1. (June 1961).

90   J.D. HERBERT and B.H. STEVENS, 'A Model for the Distribution of Residential Activity in Urban Areas', *JRS*, 2 (1960), 21-36.

91   G.J.D. HEWINGS, 'Regional Input-Output Models Using National Data: The Structure of the West Midlands Economy', *ARS*, 3 (1969), 179-91.

92   G.J.D. HEWINGS, 'Regional Planning: Problems in the Application of Interregional Input-Output Analyses to State Planning and Program Activities', *ARS*, 4 (1970), 114-22.

93   G.J.D. HEWINGS, 'Aggregation of a Regional Input-Output Model and the Effect upon Impact Analysis: A Comment', S.E. Kent Regional Input-Output Study, Discussion Paper No.4, Centre for Research in the

Social Sciences, University of Kent at Canterbury, (May 1971).

94 G.J.D. HEWINGS, 'Regional Input-Output Models in the UK: Some Problems and Prospects for the Use of Non-Survey Techniques', *RS*, 5 (1971), 11-22.

95 W.Z. HIRSCH, 'An Application of Area Input-Output Analysis', *PPRSA*, 5 (1959), 79-94.

96 W.Z. HIRSCH, 'Interindustry Relations of a Metropolitan Area', *RE & S*, 41 (1959), 360-9.

97 W.Z. HIRSCH, 'Application of Input-Output Techniques to Urban Areas', in T. Barna (ed.), *Structural Interdependence and Economic Development* (1963) pp. 151-68.

98 W.Z. HIRSCH, 'Fiscal Impact of Industrialization on Local Schools', *RE & S*, 46 (1964), 191-9.

99 I. HOCH, 'A Comparison of Alternative Inter-Industry Forecasts for the Chicago Region', *PPRSA*, 5 (1959), 217-35.

100 W. HOCHWALD, H.E. STRINER and S. SONENBLUM, *Local Impact of Foreign Trade* (N.P.A. 1960).

101 M. HOLZMAN, 'Problems of Classification and Aggregation', in Leontief, *Studies in the Structure of the American Economy* (OUP. 1953), 326-59.

102 E.M. HOOVER and B. CHINITZ, 'The Role of Accounts in the Economic Study of the Pittsburgh Metropolitan Region', in W. Hochwald (ed.), *Design of Regional Accounts* (RFF, Johns Hopkins 1961), 253-70.

103 D.B. HOUSTON, 'The Shift and Share Analysis of Regional Growth: A Critique', *SEJ*, 34 (1967) 577-81.

104 J.J. HUGHES, 'Disarmament and Regional Employment', *JRS*, 5 (1964), 37-49.

105 A.P. HURTER and L.N. MOSES, 'Regional Investment and Interregional Programming', *PPRSA*, 13 (1964), 105-19.

106 W. ISARD, T.W. LANGFORD, Jr., and E. ROMANOFF, *Philadelphia Region Input-Output Study* (Working Papers, Regional Science Research Institute, Philadelphia, 1966-8).

107 W. ISARD, 'Interregional and Regional Input-Output Analysis: A Model of a Space Economy', *RE & S* 33 (1951), 318-28.

108 W. ISARD, 'Regional Commodity Balances and Interregional Commodity Flows', *AER*, Papers 43 (1953), 167-80.

109 W. ISARD, 'Some Empirical Results and Problems of Regional Input-Output Analysis', in W. Leontief *et al.*, *Studies in the Structure of the American Economy*, (OUP 1953), 116-81.

110 W. ISARD and R.E. KUENNE, 'The Impact of Steel upon the Greater New York – Philadelphia Urban Industrial Region', *RE & S*, 35 (1953), 289-301.

111 W. ISARD and J. GANSCHOW, *Awards of Prime Military Contracts by County, State and M.A.s of the US, Fiscal Year 1960* (Regional Science Research Institute, Philadelphia 1962).

112 W. ISARD and G.J. KARASKA, *Unclassified Defense Contracts: Awards by County, State and M.A. of the US Fiscal Year 1962* (World Friends Research Center Inc., Philadelphia 1962).

113 W. ISARD and E.W. SCHOOLER, 'An Economic Analysis of Local and Regional Impacts of Reduction of Military Expenditures', *PPRS*, 1 (1964), 15-44.

114 W. ISARD and S. CZAMANSKI, 'Techniques for Estimating Local and Regional Multiplier Effects of Changes in the Level of Major Governmental Programs', *PPRS*, 3 (1965), 19-46.

115 W. ISARD, E. ROMANOFF and L. ALSPACH, *The Boston Regional Interindustry Study, 1958, Key Coefficients for the Industries* (Technical) Paper No. 2, Regional Science Research Institute, Boston Office (Cambridge 1966).

116 W. ISARD and T.W. LANGFORD, Jr., 'Impact of Vietnam War Expenditures on the Philadelphia Economy: Some Initial Experiments with the Inverse of the Philadelphia Input-Output Table', *PPRSA*, 23 (1969), 217-65.

117 W. ISARD and T.W. LANGFORD, Jr., *Regional Input-Output Study: Recollections, Reflections and Diverse Notes on the Philadelphia Experience* (MIT Press 1971).

118 W. ISARD, C. CHOGUILL, J. KISSIN *et al., Ecologic and Economic Analysis for Regional Planning* (Free Press, New York 1971).

119 W. ISARD, 'Some Notes on the Linkage of the Ecologic and Economic Systems', *PPRSA*, 22 (1969), 85-96.

120 W. ISARD and E. SMOLENSKY, 'Applications of Input-Output Techniques to Regional Science', in T. Barna (ed.), *Structural Interdependence and Economic Development* (Macmillan, London 1963) 107-18.

121 K.W. KAPP, 'Environmental Disruption and Social Costs: A Challenge to Economics', *K*, 23 (1970), 833-48.

122 G.J. KARASKA, 'Interindustry Relations in the Philadelphia Economy', *The East Lakes Geographer*, 2 (1966), 80-96.

123 G.J. KARASKA, 'Interregional Flows of Defense-Space Awards: The Role of Subcontracting in an Impact Analysis of Changes in the Levels of Defense Awards upon the Philadelphia Economy', *PPRS*, 5 (1966), 45-62.

124 G.J. KARASKA, 'The Spatial Impacts of Defense-Space Procurement', *PPRS*, 8 (1967), 109-22.

125 G.J. KARASKA, 'Variation of Input-Output Coefficients for Different Levels of Aggregation', *JRS*, 8 (1968), 217-27.

126 R.A. KAVESH and J.B. JONES, 'Differential Regional Impacts of Federal Expenditures', *PPRSA*, 2 (1956), 152-67.

127 C.D. KIRKSEY, *An Interindustry Study of the Sabine-Neches Area of Texas* (Austin 1959).

128 L.R. KLEIN, 'On the Interpretation of Professor Leontief's System', *RES*, 20 (1952-3), 131-6.

129 L.R. KLEIN, 'The Specification of Regional Econometric Models', *PPRSA*, 23 (1969), 105-15.

130   R.G. KOKAT, 'Some Conceptual Problems in the Implementation of the Maryland Interindustry Study', *PPRSA*, 17 (1966), 95-104.

131   R.G. KOKAT, *The Economic Component of a Regional Socioeconomic Model* (IBM Technical Report, 17-210, 1966).

132   T.C. KOOPMANS, (ed.) *Activity Analysis of Production and Allocation* (Wiley, New York, 1951).

133   G. KRUMME, 'Comments on Interregional Subcontracting Patterns and Bilateral Feedbacks', *JRS*, 10 (1970), 237-42.

134   R.E. KUENNE, 'Walras, Leontief, and the Interdependence of Economic Activities', *QJE*, 68 (1954), 323-54.

135   R.E. KUENNE, *The Theory of General Economic Equilibrium* (Princeton, 1963).

136   E. KUH, 'Measurement of Potential Output', *AER*, 56 (1966), 758-76.

137   T.H. LEE, D.P. LEWIS and J.R. MOORE, 'Multiregion Intersectoral Flow Analysis', *JRS*, 11 (1971), 49-56.

138   W.W. LEONTIEF, 'Quantitative Input and Output Relations in the Economic System of the United States', *RE & S*, 18 (1936), 105-25.

139   W.W. LEONTIEF *et al.*, *The Structure of the United States Economy*, 1919-39 (Harvard UP 1941).

140   W. LEONTIEF, 'Interregional Theory', in Leontief *et al.*, *Studies in the Structure of the American Economy* (OUP, New York 1953), 93-115.

141   W.W. LEONTIEF, 'Dynamic Analysis', in Leontief *et al.*, *Studies in the Structure of the American Economy* (OUP, New York 1953), 53-90.

142   W. LEONTIEF and M. HOFFENBERG, 'The Economic Effects of Disarmament', *SA*, 204 (April 1961) 3-11.

143   W. LEONTIEF, 'The Structure of Development', *SA*, 209 (September 1963).

144   W. LEONTIEF *et al.*, 'The Economic Impact – Industrial and Regional – of an Arms Cut', *RE & S*, 47 (1965), 217-41.

145   W.W. LEONTIEF, *Input-Output Economics* (OUP 1966).

146 W. LEONTIEF, 'An Alternative to Aggregation in Input-Output Analysis and National Accounts', *RE & S*, 49 (1967), 412-19.

147 W. LEONTIEF, 'Input-Output Analysis', in *International Encyclopaedia of the Social Sciences*, new ed., Vol. 7 (Macmillan and Free Press 1968), 345-53.

148 W. LEONTIEF, 'Environmental Repercussions and the Economic Structure: An Input-Output Approach', *RE & S*, 52 (1970), 262-71.

149 W. LEONTIEF and A. STROUT, 'Multiregional Input-Output Analysis', in T. Barna (ed.), *Structural Interdependence and Economic Development* (Macmillan, London 1963), 119-49.

150 C.L. LEVEN, 'A Theory of Regional Social Accounting', *PPRSA*, 4 (1958), 221-38.

151 C.L. LEVEN, 'Regional Income and Product Accounts: Construction and Application', in W. Hochwald (ed.), *Design of Regional Accounts* (RFF., Johns Hopkins 1961), 148-95.

152 C.L. LEVEN, J.B. LEGLER and P. SHAPIRO, *An Analytical Framework for Regional Development Policy* (MIT Press 1970).

153 H.S. LEVINE, 'Input-Output Analysis and Soviet Planning', *AER*, 52 (1962), 127-37.

154 K. LEVITT, 'Inter-Industry Study of the Economy of the Atlantic Provinces', in S. Ostry and T.K. Rymes (ed.), *Papers in Regional Statistical Studies*, (Toronto 1966).

155 C.H. LITTLE and G.A. DOEKSEN, 'Measurement of Leakage by the Use of an Input-Output Model', *JFE*, 50 (1968), 921-34.

156 E.M. LOFTING and P.H. McGAUHY, *Economic Evaluation of Water: Part IV, An Input-Output and Linear Programming Analysis of California Water Requirements*, No. 116, Water Resources Centre, UCLA, (Berkeley 1968).

157 H.S. LUFT, 'Computational Procedure for the Multiregional Model', Reprint 16, (*HERP*, September 1969).

158 D.I. MACKAY, 'Industrial Structure and Regional Growth', *SJPE*, 15 (1968), 129-43.

159   E. MALINVAUD, 'Aggregation Problems in Input-Output Models', in T. Barna (ed.) *The Structural Interdependence of the Economy* (1954), 189-202.

160   W.E. MARTIN, *The Use and Value of Input-Output Models in the Analysis of Water Pollution Abatement*, Harvard Water Program Discussion Paper No. 68-5 (Harvard University 1968).

161   P.N. MATHUR, 'Economic Implications of Cost Minimisation in a Dynamic Input-Output Framework', Fifth International Conference on Input-Output Techniques, (1971).

162   T. MATUSZEWSKI, P.R. PITTS and J.A. SAWYER, 'Linear Programming Estimates of Changes in Input Coefficients', *Canadian Journal of Economics and Political Science,* 30 (1964), 103-10.

163   J. McGILVRAY and D. SIMPSON, 'Some Tests of Stability in Inter-industry Coefficients', *Em,* 37 (1969), 204-22.

164   L.A. METZLER, 'A Multiple Region Theory of Income and Trade', *Em,* 18 (1950), 329-54.

165   W.H. MIERNYK, *Elements of Input-Output Economics* (Random House 1965).

166   W.H. MIERNYK, E.R. BONNER, J.H. CHAPMAN, Jr., and K. SHELLHAMMER, *The Impact of Space and Space Related Activities on a Local Community, Part I, The Input-Output Analysis* (NASA 1965).

167   W.H. MIERNYK, 'Sampling Techniques in Making Regional Industry Forecasts', in A.P. Carter and A. Brody (eds.), *Contributions to Input-Output Analysis* (North-Holland, Amsterdam 1970), pp. 305-21.

168   W.H. MIERNYK *et al., Impact of the Space Program on a Local Economy* (West Virginia University Press 1967).

169   W.H. MIERNYK, 'Long Range Forecasting with a Regional Input-Output Model', *WEJ,* 6 (1968), 165-76.

170   W.H. MIERNYK and K.L. SHELLHAMMER, *Simulating Regional Economic Development with an Input-Output Model* (Regional Research Institute, West Virginia, July 1968).

171   W.H. MIERNYK *et al., Simulating Regional Economic Development: an Interindustry Analysis of the West Virginian Economy* (Heath Lexington, Lexington 1970).

172   W.H. MIERNYK, 'An Interindustry Forecasting Model with Water Quantity and Quality Constraints', *Systems Analysis for Great Lakes Water Resources, Proceedings of the fourth Symposium on Water Resources of the Ohio State University, Water Resources Center* (October 1969).

173   W.H. MIERNYK, 'The West Virginia Dynamic Model and its Implications', *G & C*, 1 (1970), 27-32.

174   R.E. MILLER, 'The Impact of the Aluminium Industry on the Pacific Northwest: A Regional Input-Output Analysis', *RE & S*, 39 (1957), 200-9.

175   R.E. MILLER, 'Interregional Feedback Effects in Input-Output Models: Some Preliminary Results', *PPRSA*, 17 (1966), 105-25.

176   R.E. MILLER, 'Interregional Feedbacks in Input-Output Models: Some Empirical Results', *WEJ*, 7 (1969), 41-50.

177   J.R. MINASIAN, 'Elasticities of Substitution and Constant Output Demand Curves for Labour', *JPE*, 69 (1961), 261-70.

178   K. MIYAZAWA, 'Input-Output Analysis and Interrelational Income Multiplier as a Matrix', *HJE*, 8 (1968), 39-58.

179   K. MIYAZAWA, 'Internal and External Matrix Multipliers in the Input-Output Model', *HJE*, 7 (1966), 3-55.

180   F.T. MOORE, 'Regional Economic Reaction Paths', *AER*, 45 (1955), 133-45. Discussion by L. Moses, 149-55.

181   F.T. MOORE and J.W. PETERSEN, 'Regional Analysis: An Interindustry Model of Utah', *RE & S*, 37 (1955), 363-83.

182   O. MORGENSTERN (ed.), *Economic Activity Analysis* (Wiley, New York 1954), 3-78.

183   Y. MORIMOTO, 'On Aggregation Problems in Input-Output Analysis', *RES*, 37 (1970), 19-26.

184   M. MORISHIMA, 'Prices, Interests and Profits in a Dynamic Leontief System', *Em*, 3 (1958), 358-80.

185   L. MOSES, 'The Stability of Interregional Trading Patterns and Input-Output Analysis', *AER*, 45 (1955), 803-32.

186   L. MOSES, 'A General Equilibrium Model of Production, Interregional Trade, and Location of Industry, *RE & S*, 42 (1960), 373-97.

187   L. MOSES, 'General Equilibrium Theory of Location', in *Encyclopaedia of the Social Sciences* (Macmillan and Free Press 1968).

188   NBER, *Input-Output Analysis: An Appraisal*, Studies in Income and Wealth, Vol. 18 (Princeton University Press 1955).

189   National Planning Association, *Community Readjustment to Reduced Defense Spending*, (Washington DC, Centre for Economic Projections 1965).

190   National Planning Association, *Capacity Expansion Planning Factors, Manufacturing Industries* (Washington, April 1966).

191   L. NEEDLEMAN (ed.), *Regional Analysis* (Penguin, 1968).

192   P. O'SULLIVAN, 'Forecasting Interregional Freight Flows in Great Britain', Colston Symposium on Regional Forecasting (Bristol, April 1970).

193   P. O'SULLIVAN, 'Linear Programming as a Forecasting Device for Interregional Freight Flows in GB', *RUE*, 1 (1972), 383-96.

194   J.D. PARIS, 'Regional/Structural Analysis of Population Change', *RS*, 4 (1970), 425-43.

195   A.T. PEACOCK and D.G.M. DOSSER, 'Regional Input-Output Analysis and Government Spending', *SJPE*, 6 (1959), 229-36.

196   H.S. PERLOFF, 'Relative Regional Economic Growth: An Approach to Regional Accounts', in W. Hochwald (ed.) *Development of Regional Accounts* (RFF; Johns Hopkins, 1961), 38-66.

197   H.S. PERLOFF and C.L. LEVEN, 'Toward an Integrated System of Regional Accounts: Stocks, Flows and the Analysis of the Public Sector', in W.Z.

Hirsch (ed.) *Elements of Regional Accounts* (RFF, Johns Hopkins, 1964) 175-210.

198   R.S. PETERSON and C.M. TIEBOUT, 'Measuring the Impact of Regional Defense-Space Expenditures', *RE & S*, 46 (1964), 421-8.

199   R.S. PETERSON and R.A. WYKSTRA, 'A Provisional Input-Output Study of Idaho's Economy', *WBR*, 27 (1968), 11-27.

200   A. PHILLIPS, 'The Tableau Economique as a Simple Leontief Model', *QJE*, 69 (1955), 136-44.

201   K.R. POLENSKE, 'A Case Study of Transportation Models used in Multiregional Analysis' (Ph.D. thesis, Harvard 1966).

202   K.R. POLENSKE, 'A Multiregional Input-Output Model – Concept and Results' (*HERP*, July 1969).

203   K.R. POLENSKE, 'A Commentary on Both Models and Their Uses', *G & C*, 1 (1970), 39-40.

204   K.R. POLENSKE, 'An Empirical Test of Interregional Input-Output Models: Estimation of 1963 Japanese Production', *AER* Papers, 60 (1970), 76-82.

205   K.R. POLENSKE, *A Multiregional Input-Output Model for the United States* (HERP, Report No. 21, December 1970).

206   K.R. POLENSKE, 'Empirical Implementation of a Multiregional Input-Output Gravity Trade Model', in A.P. Carter and A. Brody (ed.) *Contributions to Input-Output Analysis* (North Holland 1970) Vol. I, pp. 143-63.

207   K.R. POLENSKE, 'The Implementation of a Multiregional Input-Output Model for the United States' Fifth International Conference on Input-Output Techniques (January 1971).

208   G. REY and C.B. TILANUS, 'Input-Output Forecasts for the Netherlands, 1949-58', *Em*, 31 (1963), 454-63.

209   H.W. RICHARDSON, *Regional Economics: Location Theory, Urban Structure and Regional Change* (Weidenfeld and Nicolson 1969).

210   H.W. RICHARDSON, *Elements of Regional Economics* (Penguin 1969).

211 R. RIEFLER and C.M. TIEBOUT, 'Interregional Input-Output: An Empirical California-Washington Model', *JRS*, 10 (1970), 135-52.

212 G. ROSENBLUTH, 'Input-Output Analysis', paper read at the AUTE Conference (York 1968).

213 K.W. ROSKAMP, 'Fiscal Policy and the Effects of Government Purchases: An Input-Output Analysis', *PF*, 24 (1969), 33-43.

214 J.I. ROUND, 'A Further Statement on the Construction of a Regional Input-Output Model for the Welsh Economy', Discussion Paper (May 1969).

215 P.A. SAMUELSON, 'Abstract of a Theorem concerning Substitutability in Open Leontief Models', in T.C. Koopmans (ed.), *Activity Analysis in Production and Allocation* (Wiley, 1951), 142-6.

216 P.A. SAMUELSON, 'Spatial Price Equilibrium and Linear Programming', *AER*, 42 (1952), 283-303.

217 A.D. SANDOVAL, 'Constant Relation Between Input-Output Income Multipliers', *RE & S,* 49 (1967), 599-600.

218 J.D. SARGAN, 'The Instability of the Leontief Dynamic Model', *Em*, 26 (1958), 381-92.

219 W.A. SCHAFFER, 'Estimating Regional Input-Output Coefficients', Georgia Institute of Technology, Discussion Paper 16 (March 1970).

220 W.A. SCHAFFER and K. CHU, 'Nonsurvey Techniques for Constructing Regional Interindustry Models', *PPRSA*, 23 (1969), 83-101.

221 W.A. SCHAFFER and K. CHU, 'Simulating Regional Interindustry Models for Western States', Georgia Institute of Technology, Discussion Paper 14 (1969).

222 P. SEVALDSON, 'Changes in Input-Output Coefficients', in T. Barna (ed.), *Structural Interdependence and Economic Development* (Macmillan 1963), 303-28.

223 T.Y. SHEN, 'An Input-Output Table with Regional Weights', *PPRSA*, 6 (1960), 113-19.

224 A.L. SILVERS, 'The Structure of Community Income Circulation in an Incidence Multiplier for Developmental Planning', *JRS*, 10 (1970), 175-89.

225 B. SLOME, 'The Interregional Input-Output Model and Interregional Public Finance', *PF*, 24 (1969), 618-21.

226 V.L. SMITH, 'Minimisation of Economic Rent in Spatial Price Equilibrium', *RES*, 30 (1963), 24-31.

227 S. SPEIGELGLAS, 'Some Aspects of State to State Commodity Flows in the US', *JRS*, 2 (1960), 71-80.

228 G.P.F. STEED, 'Commodity Flows and Interindustry Linkages of Northern Ireland's Manufacturing Industries', *Tijdschrift Voor Econ. en Soc. Geografie*, 59 (1968), 245-59.

229 D.B. STEELE, 'A Numbers Game (or the Return of Regional Multipliers)', *RS*, 6 (1972), 115-30.

230 B. STEVENS, 'An Interregional Linear Programming Model', *JRS*, 1 (1958), 60-98.

231 B.H. STEVENS, 'A Review of the Literature on Linear Methods for Spatial Analysis', *JAIP*, 26 (1960), 253-9.

232 F.J.B. STILWELL, 'Regional Growth and Structural Adaptation', *US*, 6 (1969), 162-78.

233 F.J.B. STILWELL, 'Further Thoughts on the Shift and Share Approach', *RS*, 4 (1970), 451-8.

234 F.J.B. STILWELL and B.D. BOATWRIGHT, 'A Method of Estimating Interregional Trade Flows', *RUE*, 1 (1971), 77-87.

235 R. STONE, *Input-Output and National Accounts* (OEEC 1961).

236 T.T. SU, 'A Note on Regional Input-Output Models', *SEJ*, 37 (1970), 325-7.

237 D.B. SUITS, *Survey of Economic Models for Analysis of Disarmament Impacts* (University of Michigan, 1965: Report submitted to the US Arms Control and Disarmament Agency).

238 K. SUZUKI, 'Observations on the Stability of the Structure of the Interregional Flow of Goods', *JRS*, 11 (1971), 187-209.

239 A. SZALAI, 'Cohesion Indices for Regional Determination', *PPRS*, 4 (1966), 1-6.

240 T. TAKAYAMA and G.C. JUDGE, 'Equilibrium among Spatially Separated Markets', *Em*, 32 (1964), 510-24.

241   C.E. TASKIER, *Input-Output Bibliography, 1955-60* (UN, New York 1961).

242   C.E. TASKIER, *Input-Output Bibliography, 1960-63* (UN, New York 1964).

243   H. THEIL, 'Linear Aggregation in Input-Output Analysis', *Em*, 25, (1957), 111-22.

244   H. THEIL, *Economics and Information Theory* (North Holland 1967).

245   H. THEIL and P. URIBE, 'The Information Approach to the Aggregation of Input-Output Tables', *RE & S*, 49 (1967), 451-62.

246   E.M.F. THORNE, 'Regional Input-Output Analysis', in S.C. Orr and J.B. Cullingworth (eds.), *Regional and Urban Studies*, (1969), 97-120.

247   C.M. TIEBOUT, 'Input-Output and Foreign Trade Multiplier Models in Urban Research', *JAIP*, 23 (1957).

248   C.M. TIEBOUT, 'Regional and Interregional Input-Output Models: An Appraisal', *SEJ*, 24 (1957), 140-7.

249   C.M. TIEBOUT *et al.*, 'Symposium: The Regional Impact of Defense Expenditures', *WEJ*, 3 (1965).

250   C.M. TIEBOUT, 'Input-Output and the Firm: A Technique for Using National and Regional Tables', *RE & S*, 49 (1967), 260-2.

251   C.M. TIEBOUT, 'An Empirical Regional Input-Output Projection Model: The State of Washington 1980', *RE & S*, 51 (1969), 334-40.

252   C.B. TILANUS, *Input-Output Experiments, The Netherlands, 1948-61* (Rotterdam University Press 1966).

253   C.B. TILANUS, 'Marginal v Average Input Coefficients in Input-Output Forecasting', *QJE*, 81 (1967), 140-5.

254   Ministry of Transport, *Road Goods Survey, 1962* (HMSO 1967).

255   B. UDIS, 'Regional Input-Output Analysis and Water Quality Management', *Journal of the Rocky Mountain Social Science Association,* October 1965.

256   US Department of Commerce, *Input-Output Structure of the US Economy: 1963,* 3 vols. (US Government Printing Office 1969).

257 P.J. VERDOORN, 'Complementarity and Long Range Projections', *Em*, 24 (1956), 429-50.

258 P.A. VICTOR, 'Input-Output Analysis and The Study of Economic and Environmental Interaction', Ph.D. Thesis, (University of British Columbia, April 1971).

259 R. VINING, 'Determination of Economic Areas: Statistical Conceptions on the Study of the Spatial Structure in an Economic System', *Journal of the American Statistical Association,* 48 (1953), 44-64.

260 H.A. WADSWORTH and J.M. CONRAD, 'Leakage Reducing Employment and Income Multipliers in Labour-Surplus Rural Areas', *JFE*, 47 (1965), 1197-1202.

261 A.A. WALTERS, 'Production and Cost Functions: An Econometric Survey', *Em*, 31 (1963), 1-66.

262 G. WASSERMAN, 'The French Regional Accounting Framework: An Alternative to the Keynesian Approach', *Oxford University Economic and Statistics Bulletin,* 29 (1967), 311-51.

263 F.W. WAUGH, 'Inversion of the Leontief Matrix by Power Series', *Em*, 17 (1950), 142-54.

264 M.L. WEIDENBAUM, 'Shifting the Composition of Government Spending: Implications for the Regional Distribution of Income', *PPRSA*, 17 (1966), 163-7.

265 R.B. WILLIAMSON, 'Simple Input-Output Models for Area Economic Analysis', *LE*, 46 (1970), 333-8.

266 R.B. WILLIAMSON, 'What the Literature Holds for the Practising Regional Analyst', *G & C*, 2 (1971), 3-4.

267 A.G. WILSON, 'Interregional Commodity Flows: Entropy Maximising Approaches', *Centre for Environmental Studies,* Working Paper 19, (1968).

268 M.K. WOOD, 'Design for an Interregional Economic Programming System', Paper read at Fourth UN International Conference on Input-Output Techniques, (Geneva, January 1968).

269 P. ZUSMAN and I. HOCK, *Resource and Capital Requirements Matrices for the California Economy* Giannini Foundation Research, Report No. 284, (Berkeley, August 1965).

270   B. BERGMANN, 'The Urban Economy and the "Urban Crisis"', *AER*, 59 (1969), 639-45.

271   W.Z. HIRSCH, 'Input-Output Techniques for Urban Government Decisions', *AER*, 58 (1968), 162-70.

272   W.Z. HIRSCH, S. SONENBLUM and J. ST DENNIS, 'Application of Input-Output Techniques to Quality of Urban Life Indicators', *K*, 24 (1971), 511-32.

273   J.I. ROUND, 'Regional Input-Output Models in the UK: a Reappraisal of Some Techniques', *RS*, 6 (1972), 1-9.

274   E.T. NEVIN, A.R. ROE and J.I. ROUND, *The Structure of the Welsh Economy* (University of Wales Press 1966).

275   D.B. HOUSTON, 'Input-Output Analysis and Regional Forecasting: Some Problems and Possible Solutions' (Mimeograph 1967).

276   M. PESTON, *Elementary Matrices for Economics* (Routledge and Kegan Paul 1969).

277   C. ALMON, Jr., *Matrix Methods in Economics* (Addison-Wesley, Reading, Mass., 1967).

278   J.H. CUMBERLAND, 'Application of Input-Output Technique to the Analysis of Environmental Problems', prepared for Fifth International Conference on Input-Output Techniques, Geneva, January 1971.

279   O.C. HERFINDAHL and A.V. KNEESE, 'Measuring Social and Economic Change: Benefits and Costs of Environmental Pollution', paper prepared for NBER Conference on the Measurement of Economic and Social Performance, Princeton, New Jersey, November 1971.

280   R. LECOMBER, 'A Critique of Methods of Adjusting, Updating and Projecting Matrices, together with Some New Proposals', Cambridge Growth Project, Discussion Paper in Economics, No. 40, August 1971.

281   D. BRADWELL, L. KUNIN and E. LOFTING, 'An Interindustry Analysis of the San Francisco Bay Region with Emphasis on Environmental Impact', *1971 Proceedings of the Business and Economic*

Statistics Section of the American Statistical Association (Washington, 1972), 90-8.

282 B. UDIS (ed.), *Adjustments of the US Economy to Reductions in Military Spending* (US Arms Control and Disarmament Agency, ACDA/E-156, December, 1970).

283 A.J. WALDERHAUG, 'State Input-Output Tables Derived from National Data', *1971 Proceedings of the Business and Economic Statistics Section of the American Statistical Association* (Washington, 1972), 77-86.

284 D.B. STEELE, 'A Numbers Game (or the Return of Regional Multipliers),' *RS*, 6 (1972), 115-30.

Name Index

Subject Index